The Good Supervisor

Palgrave Study Guides

Authoring a PhD
Career Skills
e-Learning Skills
Effective Communication for
 Arts and Humanities Students
Effective Communication for
 Science and Technology
The Foundations of Research
The Good Supervisor
How to Manage your Arts, Humanities and
 Social Science Degree
How to Manage your Distance and
 Open Learning Course
How to Manage your Postgraduate Course
How to Manage your Science and
 Technology Degree
How to Study Foreign Languages
How to Write Better Essays
Making Sense of Statistics
The Mature Student's Guide to Writing

The Postgraduate Research Handbook
Presentation Skills for Students
The Principles of Writing in Psychology
Professional Writing
Research Using IT
Skills for Success
The Student's Guide to Writing
The Study Skills Handbook (2nd edition)
Study Skills for Speakers of English as
 a Second Language
Studying the Built Environment
Studying Economics
Studying History (2nd edition)
Studying Mathematics and its Applications
Studying Modern Drama (2nd edition)
Studying Physics
Studying Psychology
Teaching Study Skills and Supporting Learning
Work Placements – a Survival Guide for Students
Writing for Engineers

Palgrave Study Guides: Literature
General Editors: John Peck and Martin Coyle

How to Begin Studying English Literature
 (3rd edition)
How to Study a Jane Austen Novel (2nd edition)
How to Study a Charles Dickens Novel
How to Study Chaucer (2nd edition)
How to Study an E. M. Forster Novel
How to Study James Joyce
How to Study Linguistics (2nd edition)

How to Study Modern Poetry
How to Study a Novel (2nd edition)
How to Study a Poet (2nd edition)
How to Study a Renaissance Play
How to Study Romantic Poetry (2nd edition)
How to Study a Shakespeare Play (2nd edition)
How to Study Television
Practical Criticism

The Good Supervisor

Supervising Postgraduate and Undergraduate Research for Doctoral Theses and Dissertations

Gina Wisker

First published 2005 by
PALGRAVE MACMILLAN
Houndmills, Basingstoke, Hampshire RG21 6XS and
175 Fifth Avenue, New York, N.Y. 10010
Companies and representatives throughout the world

PALGRAVE MACMILLAN is the global academic imprint of the Palgrave
Macmillan division of St. Martin's Press, LLC and of Palgrave Macmillan Ltd.
Macmillan® is a registered trademark in the United States, United Kingdom
and other countries. Palgrave is a registered trademark in the European
Union and other countries.

ISBN 1–4039–0395–6

This book is printed on paper suitable for recycling and made from fully
managed and sustained forest sources.

A catalogue record for this book is available from the British Library.

Library of Congress Cataloging-in-Publication Data
Wisker, Gina, 1951–
   The good supervisor : supervising postgraduate and undergraduate
research for doctoral theses and dissertations / Gina Wisker.
      p. cm. — (Palgrave study guides)
   Includes bibliographical references and index.
   ISBN 1–4039–0395–6
      1. Graduate students — supervision of. 2. Faculty advisors.
   3. Dissertations, Academic. 4. Doctor of philosophy degree. I. Title. II. Series.

LB2371.W57 2004
378.1'94046—dc22   2004051234

10   9   8   7   6   5   4   3   2   1
14 13 12 11 10 09 08 07 06 05

Printed and bound in China

Contents

Acknowledgements

This book has only been possible because of all the generous support, tolerance and sharing of my family, friends and colleagues. Thanks to Alistair, Liam and Kitt for putting up with the work schedule, Yehuda Ben-Simon, Shosh Leshem, Gill Robinson, Miri Shacham, Dan Shenkar, Avishai Tal, Vernon Trafford, all our PhD candidates in the School of Education International programme, and the English PhD students. Thanks also to generous and thoughtful UK, Australian, New Zealand and University of West Indies colleagues with whom I have worked in conferences, supervisory development workshops and joint writing exercises. In particular, I would like to thank Angela Brew, Margaret Cahill, Linda Conrad, Margaret Kiley, Eric Meyer and Margot Pearson.

Thanks also to Emma Creighton, Jaki Lilly and Mark Warnes for analysing much of the underpinning research. Christine Beck, Michelle Bernard, Lorraine Silk, Emma Warnes and Tess Youngs have helped me turn it into a presentable shape while all my PhD, EdD, Masters and undergraduate students have been the guinea-pigs and a great source of elements of practice.

Many thanks go to Maggi Savin Baden and anonymous reviewers for reading and commenting on the text before final revisions.

Thanks finally to Suzannah Burywood and Anita Sethi at Palgrave Macmillan for investing their critical patience in the project.

1 Introduction

Rewarding, essential, potentially taken for granted and relatively under-theorised, research supervision plays a key role in higher education in empowering students to become researchers. As both undergraduate and postgraduate student numbers grow in universities, we are increasingly being invited to supervise students' research projects, encouraging, supporting and enabling them to develop skills, values and practices essential to learning the roles and rules of research. Research is defined here as *the* crucial element of learning – a fascination with questioning the world, ways of enquiring, solving problems, creating and innovating and developing discourse, strategies and interpretations. In this dynamic context, there is a clear need for sound, supportive and empowering supervision practices for students' research study, whether for dissertation, project or thesis. This book builds on shared experiences of good practice in research supervision at all levels (see Delamont *et al.*, 1998; Wisker and Sutcliffe, 1999; Wisker, Robinson and Trafford, 2000, 2001, 2003), and on research (e.g. Pearson, 1999; Brew, 2001) into what makes for effective supervisory practices.

The Good Supervisor intends to engage supervisors and students in a learning dialogue. It provides supervisors with research-informed suggestions about the dimensions of supervisory practice, that is systems and practices of working with conceptual frameworks, methods, processes of students' research, issues and practices of personal effectiveness in this long-term, interpersonal interaction between supervisor and student. In its conception, and through my own extensive personal and workshop interactions with supervisors and those supporting the development of students and supervisors alike, it has been absolutely crucial that the book should provide opportunities to engage readers in dialogue between research and experience, supervisor and supervisor, supervisor and student. This intends to be a useful, non-patronising book. It could not succeed if it tried to talk down to or 'train' supervisors. Instead, this book encourages reflection, dialogue and an exchange of good practice. Development suggestions are built *upon* and out of these practices. You are invited to engage with research evidence-based practice and reflective and evaluative stories from supervisors, students and educational developers, in a dialogue with your own experience. In each chapter, discussions, suggestions and activities or tasks to encourage reflection and good practice are integrated with experience and research.

Focusing on the role and support demanded of supervisors working with students, the book follows the shape of students' work. It considers how supervisors can support and enable students in their research towards, writing up and defence of dissertations, projects and theses at undergraduate and postgraduate levels. Although primarily intended for supervisors, it provides insights and task-oriented developmental suggestions that students could use on their own or in groups, with or without supervision.

The book takes novice, intermediate and experienced supervisors alike through the working life of supervisory relationships with research students. It invites the reader to consider the academic and administrative elements of enrolment and the development of a proposal. It deals with the development of a clear conceptual framework; the choice of appropriate research methodologies; information searches and dialogues with authors and theorists in the field; and the acquisition, management and analysis of information and ideas. The book also considers organisation and how to maintain momentum; as well as ways to ensure successful supervision and support for students through to the later stages of writing up, submission and, where appropriate, taking part in a viva. The final chapter looks at what may lie beyond completion of the research.

Issues of equal opportunities, including gender, sexuality, ethnicity, culture, power and authority, class, origin, learning style, language and tertiary literacy inform the discussion throughout, in terms of choice of learning approaches, access, study methods and supervisor–student interactions. Also considered are the needs of international students, those studying at a distance or 'offshore', and candidates studying part-time and/or in professional contexts. The supervision of one's colleagues, students undertaking creative research and the PhD by publication are also covered. Research and supervision involve human interaction and, in this respect, the book invites you to work with your student, considering both research ethics and interpersonal skills.

While those who are relatively new to supervision might find more of use in Stages 1, 2 and 4 of the book, established supervisors might find stage 3 extends their thoughts and practices. There is something here for all of us, throughout our supervising careers.

The Good Supervisor is unusual in that it is designed to support supervisors of a variety of research students on a variety of research projects. However, what the students all have in common is the research project. The book intends to be:

- accessible for supervisors *and* for students; there are exercises and discussions of good practice;
- underpinned by research and by the scholarship of learning and teaching, much of my own work and work from the UK, USA and Australia;
- pitched at undergraduate as well as postgraduate supervision. The scope is different, the authority/equality relationships are different, the length and depth of both the work produced and the time it takes to produce it are different, but otherwise many of the interactions and good practices have much in common.

The primary focus is supervising research projects in the social sciences, humanities, performing arts, health and related areas, but there is also much of relevance to colleagues supervising scientific research.

The idea for this book came about originally through reflecting on my own practice as a student and as a supervisor, both at postgraduate and undergraduate level, and finding there was a dearth of literature and of guidance for me in the supervisory role. This is not unusual in educational development, especially when a role, somewhat taken for granted and assumed to be an everyday activity, suddenly takes centre stage. Postgraduate students have been proportionally the greatest growth area in higher education in the UK, USA, Europe and Australasia over the last ten years, and recent learning and teaching agendas increasingly focus on the student as researcher. Research into and support for the learning of undergraduate students in greater numbers is well established (see Gibbs, 1991). Now the growth in the numbers of postgraduates brings with it similar issues of student diversity. Suddenly, during the 1990s, there were noticeably more women, more international and more distance postgraduates. Additionally, while postgraduate full-time study was common among younger students in the sciences, where they were often joining a research group, an increase was taking place amongst more mature students, and in the social sciences, the arts and humanities. The rise of the Educational and Professional Doctorates (EdD, PrD) began to take account of differing needs, as did the gradual development of a Masters in Research (MRes) and research elements in masters and undergraduate programmes, albeit often only single sessions on dissertation planning prior to supervisions. After the publication of the Dearing Report (1997), ongoing debates about the importance of research as an essential learning activity have helped us to concentrate on developing research methods and skills in all our students. In the light of diversity, change and demand, supervisors and institutions need to focus on supervisory developmental needs and practices.

The role has become visible, and it needs to be clarified and developed, recognising differences from one subject to another, one institution to another, one supervisor to another. Initially, like other educational developers, I ran some supervisory development sessions in my own university to bring together supervisors, to consider and share our own experiences of good practice. I found that many who attended were already supervising undergraduate projects and dissertations, and were hoping to supervise postgraduates. Although many of us perform this role, there have been few opportunities to reflect on, develop, or share good practice with others. Supervisor development workshops 'took off'. I found that, nationally and internationally, I was being asked to run sessions on supervising generally, although specific topics were becoming more specialised: the supervision of international, offshore and distance students; supervision in the creative and performing arts; supervision in professional contexts and issues relating to gender and diversity. Supervision is a demanding and rewarding learning and teaching experience that takes place within an international community of academic practice. Reflecting on and sharing experience of evidence-based good practice strategies can benefit all of us – supervisors and students, both postgraduate and undergraduate, at home and abroad.

In Australia and New Zealand, postgraduates now only attract funding if they complete a directive. The supervisor has an important role to play here (see Chapter 2). As our students increasingly push the boundaries of research topics, practices and outcomes, we are invited to explore creative, supportive modes of developing supervision to guide and empower them. This book does not pretend to dictate how to carry out the diverse and demanding supervisory role, instead it builds on successful development sessions I have been part of or have facilitated. Latterly, in researching and studying the role further, particularly in relation to my work with colleagues on a successful APU Israeli PhD programme, I have been made aware of the differing stories we all have to tell of our supervisory experiences and journeys. Indeed, the journeying model is one Australian colleagues have used extensively in supervisor development programmes (see Chapter 2). Some have developed online support, and Geof Hill, Tania Aspland, Coralie McCormack and Barbara Pamphilon, among others, use storytelling and journeying. This for me accords with the feminist and action research paradigms from which much of my own work springs. I am grateful to them, and to others, particularly Delamont, Atkinson and Parry (1997), whose use of individual case studies were the first I read dealing with supervisory role exploration. All of these examples are at postgraduate level. A focus on postgraduate supervision, and the current emphasis on students as researchers (Alan Jenkins and colleagues), enables us to share and explore the role and build communities of good practice. This transfers into all our research supervision, whether it be with postgraduates or undergraduates.

In order to develop students as researchers, we need to help them focus on asking research questions and exploring fields of study in critical, problem-solving, creative ways, matching this with a dedication to organisation and planning and achieving coherence and clarity of expression. Apart from discipline differences, a number of generic issues impact on all students undertaking research and success in these areas leads to a variety of postgraduate and undergraduate skills including, among others:

- time management
- problem-solving
- conceptualisation
- critical thinking
- conceiving and actualising projects through to successful conclusions
- writing for different audiences

If we consider the development needs of undergraduates and postgraduates, we can begin to imagine some of the requirements of supervisors who work with them, and so begin to devise supportive, developmental activities and programmes. However, there are no fixed behaviours which need to be trained – instead the relationship between supervisor and student is more like a dance, matching the steps of one to the other, and working together to produce a research artwork of quality, creativity and substance.

▶ Why are learning and research important?

Learning is essential for human growth. Research is *the* fundamental human learning activity, involving enquiry, problem solving, diversity, flexibility and decision-making. It encourages and enables the development of creative thinking, problem-solving strategies and abilities which in turn help others to approach everyday life as well as professional, political, local, national and international questions and issues.

'Lifelong learning' (Reeve, Cartwright and Edwards, 2002), 'learning organisations', 'learning societies', 'learning communities', 'communities of practice', even 'learning cities' are all current buzz words which suggest that communities recognise and wish to promote continual learning, reflection, awareness, problem-solving and improvement, and intelligent, creative responses to the complexities of life and of knowledge generation.

Research as a form of learning is crucial in societies for energy, motivation, creativity, linking theory and practice, establishing informed habits and skills for continuing to ask questions and seek information and answers, in context. One anonymous reviewer shared a definition developed with other Australian colleagues:

> Research describes any critical and creative activity undertaken on a systematic, disciplined basis and dedicated to increasing knowledge. The results of research therefore take many forms. Research can contribute to knowledge directly through discoveries, or otherwise through innovative ideas and techniques, conceptual refinements, or constructive critiques and syntheses which extend existing knowledge or its applications.
>
> The defining characteristics of research include (i) a dependence on formal, disciplined modes of inquiry, (ii) technical, conceptual or episte-mological innovation, (iii) an open, rigorous approach to the testing of results, and (iv) a commitment to publication in some form. Publication in a general sense is the goal of a research enterprise, but the results of research activity can be 'published' in many ways, from a printed book or article, an architectural design, a patent or a computer program, to a creative composition or artefact in the visual or performing arts which adds to the body or range of knowledge or creativity.   (Reviewer's comments)

Carrying out an important research project can provide us with an intellectual quality of life and an opportunity for emotional growth and satisfaction.

▶ **Learning steps**

A first piece of research is a major personal and learning achievement and for many the dissertation is *the* key moment when they begin to appreciate the stages, problems and potentially successful practices of research: from interest, to enquiring, question-forming, design of a study project, activating a piece of research through the use of a conceptual framework, underpinning theories, methodologies and methods, handling and analysing data, identifying findings, managing and discussing their significance at factual and conceptual levels and finishing a sound piece of research. Alongside these, students learn, we hope, the human interaction skills of making the most of their supervisor, of other institutional support, and that of family and friends. An undergraduate dissertation is a relatively small and time-bounded process and product when compared with a PhD, but in essence it involves many of the same skills, cast of mind and hard work. When it is undertaken, usually the final year of a student's degree, it is also usually the longest and possibly, therefore, the most daunting piece of work so far. In this it resembles a master's dissertation and a PhD, with changes in research complexity and depth. Each is a learning step, a challenge, a development moment. Completion will involve a student immersing themselves in and making progress with the discourse and concepts of the subject and with the discourse of research. It will enable them to begin to develop a dialogue in their academic community. In addition to subject-specific skills, generic, transferable research method skills should be developed at both undergraduate and postgraduate stages. Many undergraduates may already have begun to develop research for essays and projects, engaging with the academic community through having new (enough) ideas and arguments. Many will find they need supervisory guidance to identify subject-specific and research skills and then to develop them. Students must be encouraged to reflect on these skills, to recognise them, adapt and utilise them in the future.

As undergraduate dissertations are one of the first formal steps in research, supervisors will probably need to structure and guide undergraduates rather more than postgraduates. For many academics, supervising an undergraduate dissertation is the first experience of supervising student research. Some may develop their own supervisory skills purely through dissertation supervision, while others, may develop these skills in the capacity of management, mentoring or similar roles. For some, the guiding of research and the kind of interaction necessary could be a developmental issue.

In discussing and sharing developmental ideas and practices in this book, we will be drawing on supervisory expertise and research into supervisory good practices at *all* levels of the students' and our own careers. In the main, the focus is on postgraduate supervision because of the length of the supervisory relationship, the complex, conceptual level of the work involved and because it is a developmental opportunity. Those undertaking undergraduate supervision might well be thinking ahead to postgraduate supervision. Differences which relate to the undergraduate and postgraduate levels – in scope, time, autonomy, structure and guidance – will be indicated and debated throughout, and if there are special issues related to undergraduate supervision that arise in the focus of a particular chapter then they will be highlighted.

▶ The PhD as a learning step

The PhD is a major academic, professional and personal achievement. Upon undertaking and then completing a PhD, a student will have made an original and valuable contribution to knowledge. Their work will be read by, built on and used by others – to build theory, to fuel change and encourage good practice. The achievement of a PhD is also a beginning – the student has made a major entrance into the academic community. By carrying out research through the full cycle of planning, actioning, drawing conclusions and communicating, they will have developed a range of valuable skills.

Nor is the PhD an end in itself. The learning never stops. It is essential to share work with others in the academic community and beyond. Here I am talking about several kinds of sharing. First, we have shares in others' work – sharing and working with others as a learning community as they develop their research pre- and post-doctorate. Following the achievement of a doctorate, students are involved in sharing and communicating, supporting and enabling, building on each other's research and learning in learning communities (Barnett, 2002), and contributing towards enlightened learning societies (Eagleton, 2000; Gibbons, Limoges and Nowotny et al., 1994; Halpin, 2003), which make enlightened, creative decisions about fundamental human issues and practices (Squires, 1994; Rudd, 1985). This is essential work. It is partly enabled through continuing to move forward in learning. It is also enabled by transferring learning into professional and practical work through disseminating and sharing with others in:

- conferences and symposia
- publications
- consultancies.

▶ Continuing to research and continuing to develop research skills

It is important for students to build on the research they have carried out, continuing to ask new questions, extending both old and new boundaries – looking at those earlier designated areas 'for future research . . .' or considering where in their own thesis they imagine others taking their work further, indicating 'other researchers might . . .'. For many, practical outcomes are a main research aim so, following the achievement of their PhD, they need to put research work and its outcomes into practice, researching the effects. Carrying out new research and developing further research skills are also important next moves.

Reflecting on and identifying the wealth of skills developed during research is an important activity both during and after the research. This identification contributes to performance development, personal self-esteem, confidence-building and effectiveness. Encouraging and supporting our students in these developmental activities are also part of being a supervisor.

▶ Content and sources of the book

This introduction establishes the importance of research as a knowledge-building, creating and sharing activity, identifying the key role the supervisor plays in empowering and enabling students to engage successfully in research. It introduces readers to the similarities and differences between undergraduate and postgraduate research supervision, and to different educational and staff development paradigms underlying the book as a whole. *The Good Supervisor* utilises three kinds of sources and paradigms. It draws from solid research-based evidence, as appropriate for a book dealing with supervising research practices; and from a narrative paradigm, where stories and interviews enact theories in practice for sharing and consideration to fuel development. And it uses the logically oriented 'good practice' paradigm.

The book is structured to explore supervisory roles and practices in relation to the development of the student's research project, from identification of a possible research area and question through to completion, submission and, in the case of PhD students, the viva and beyond. Each chapter combines systematically identified explorations and suggestions of good practice arising from research and experience with the self-reflective 'community of practice' mode of sharing and developing your own, owned response to ideas and issues arising. Some researchers or supervisors might be more comfortable with one mode of expression, others with another. The idea is not to dictate but to engage in a dialogue, exploring suggestions that have arisen from sharing experience, undertaking research, and through face-to-face sessions with practitioners worldwide. From experiences of supervision related to me by students, participants in postgraduate supervisory workshops, colleagues working with undergraduates and postgraduates across a wide range of subject areas, and from my own experience as supervisor, educational developer and researcher, I have compiled extracts of narratives, interviews and case studies of supervision in action. These represent some 'typical' or exemplary cases of supervisor and student experience to illustrate issues and particular points. A number of issues are raised in each chapter concerning challenges faced by students and supervisors alike and how we as supervisors can enable and support students in making choices which suit their research, empowering them to be successful researchers.

As a reader, you are invited to consider ways that might inform supervisory practice. This active and reflective element is prompted throughout, but particularly in a number of boxed tasks and activities. Some tasks and activities are less reflective and are intended to be used or adapted in your interactions with students. Such involvement is designed to lead to owned self-development as a supervisor.

▶ Structure of the book

The book is divided into four parts. Its focus is on the work of the supervisor, and development suggestions for that work are mapped onto stages of students' research, completion and beyond.

Stage 1:   First Stages of Research Supervision – Getting Started

This stage takes you, as supervisor, through the early stages of working with students, contexts and subjects and of establishing and maintaining effective working relationships. It considers programmes designed to support supervisors in their development of good practice.

Stage 2:   Establishing Research Processes and Practices

The second stage concentrates on the construction of the research, helping students to develop workable research questions, conceptual frameworks, literature reviews or theoretical perspectives. It discusses methodology and methods and the design of the study and proposals as well as considering research ethics.

Stage 3:   Working with Students – Issues for Supervisors

The next stage turns to issues of interpersonal relations; overtime; considering roles and supervisory dialogue interactions; helping students to set up support groups; dealing with differences, difficulties and practices related to gender, etc.; international students; and distance learning. It looks at the variety of research, including relatively new forms – using creativity, research degrees by publication, and professional practice-based research. It also looks at how, as supervisors, we can support students to get on with their work and overcome difficulties, so maintaining momentum.

Stage 4:   Managing the Research Process to Completion and Beyond

The fourth stage looks at writing up; preparing for the examination and assumptions underlying examining; supporting your student's viva preparation; carrying out any necessary post-viva work, and supporting them as they head off into their academic lives – conference presentations; publications; research; and recognising the skills they have developed.

▶ Structure of the chapters

Each chapter begins with a summary of areas to be covered, raises issues and questions in task boxes, and pulls together good practice suggestions from research, scholarship and experience for your consideration. The initial focus in each chapter is on postgraduate research, although it is assumed that the necessary stages of developing research are very similar in kind if not in scope to those needed by undergraduates. Where they present as very different from postgraduate supervisions, specific sections will look at masters and at undergraduate supervision.

Several chapters contain practical or reflective activities/tasks for students to undertake as part of the process of being supervised and of carrying out effective research. Each chapter ends with a summary of the main points and, where appropriate, further reading.

The primary readership for this book is anyone who supervises undergraduate or postgraduate research projects and dissertations and theses, although students will also find its ideas useful to them in their research. Based both on research and experience, this book provides an essential, accessible, yet scholarly guide for both new and experienced supervisors.

Stage 1

First Stages of Research Supervision – Getting Started

2 Supervision Differences

In addition to research evidence-based information, this book uses the learning journeys and interviews of a range of students and supervisors. It is only fair then that I should start with myself and my research as a learning journey to begin debates about the different experiences of being supervised, the postgraduate project, undergraduate study, and learning communities – that is, fitting supervision into a broader context of support.

The chapter considers disciplinary differences, different supervision models for different stages and current trends and tensions in research for the PhD in particular.

This chapter considers:

- *being supervised and studying*
- *postgraduate and undergraduate supervision*
- *different forms of supervision for different learners in different disciplines*

▶ My experience as a research student

Undertaking an MA and then a PhD were two of the most important decisions I ever made. Achieving them both was amazing, giving me a real sense of progressing in my own learning and boosting my confidence. In addition, although that is not why I undertook either of them, they have proved enormously useful professionally. My MA was part-time, Monday evenings, while I taught at a local school and then at an FE college. It enabled my brain to get into gear. Mine was an English MA; we looked closely at poetry, Shakespeare and modern fiction. There were only a few of us, so we all discussed furiously. The tutor was one of the group. We made friends. When the teaching stopped, we carried on learning, supported each other, met regularly, socialised, passed on references, looked at work-in-progress and discussed critical issues touched on in seminars. Most of us were local, but one person commuted for two hours each way.

Then I undertook a PhD. This was a six-and-a-half-year venture, although I certainly had not planned it to be. To begin with, I experienced loneliness and isolation. I had just a vague idea of an area I wanted to look at, no question. That emerged later on. I was in an individual learning relationship with my supervisor, who was happy to talk about my work (sent in advance); on one occasion for seven hours non-stop until the penny dropped – a fundamental theoretical and conceptual issue engaged in my mind with the actual work I was doing – and I made a learning leap out of the fog of incomprehension. After that I would send chapters, drive the 120 miles to reach him, talk for an hour about the work, and get on with it. There was no email and I rarely phoned. The meetings were special and immensely supportive. When I first started, my supervisor showed me a whole filing cabinet drawer of students who had never completed. However, apart from archery, long distance running was the only sport I ever even thought of doing reasonably well and this was certainly a long haul. Thank you, Brian Lee (Nottingham University), for sticking the course!

Another thing my supervisor did was to suggest that I was part of an academic community, so I went to conferences and contacted experts. One of these experts lent me books and introduced me to his research group. Then I had friends to talk with about our writers. We punted, ate at each others' houses, passed journal articles between us and eventually, after job moves and life changes, I finished (this is still a surprise!). My external examiner was internationally renowned. He told me, via my supervisor, that I had 'passed' in advance of the viva. This was so liberating. It was the equivalent to being told, prior to my A levels, and as part of my interview, that I only needed an 'E' to get into university. Something critical that I've learned from this is that taking the pressure off produces the best results with some tense candidates. Thank you, Tony Tanner (King's College, Cambridge), my external examiner. We had a collegial, but nonetheless rigorous, hour and a half of viva, which I actually enjoyed. However, one reviewer of this book commented that this revelation is expressly forbidden in some universities and can be seen to encourage an 'old boys' club' attitude – inviting some students in but making others undergo the strains of not knowing. Recent experience as an examiner has suggested to me that while 'you've passed!' reduces anxiety, it can also lead to unstructured, incoherent discussion and some silences (e.g. candidate *and* examiner).

My own MA students are mostly local and have developed support groups. My PhD students are a mixture, some locally based, one in Africa and several in Israel. Some are studying English, some women's studies, some learning – and teaching – related areas.

Undertaking research means students are entering a dialogue with academic communities in their subject, eventually contributing in the shape of dissertations, theses and conference papers. Setting up academic communities of learning, locally or at a distance, via email, supports learning and reduces isolation. Likeminded colleagues can act as a research group, discussing issues and work-in-progress, contributing ideas, and enthusiasm for reading and writing opportunities during and after the long slog that is data collection, analysis and writing up (see Chapter 13). Academics in the same field might also be happy to discuss ideas, so putting students in touch with them can help nurture dialogues and careers.

▶ The postgraduate project

Postgraduate work needs to be original in some respect, although it does not have to be world shattering. Often postgraduates imagine their MA, MPhil or PhD is a huge and unmanageable piece of work. Well, it might seem so at the start, but the main point is to see it as a 'doable' project, recognise not only those gaps in their knowledge (to be addressed) but also boundaries to the work. There will be variables the student will not address, sub-questions others can ask, and, depending on the subject area, action resulting from findings and evaluation that could lie beyond the frame of the research. In the sciences, and some social and health sciences, it is not unusual to have an experimental model where a problem, question or hypothesis leads to experimentation, the design and testing of models, producing results that feed into further work beyond the scope of the thesis or dissertation. In the arts and humanities, and again some social science and health projects, there is exploration, problematising and questioning areas of knowledge in writing, music, art, history, etc., to answer specific or broader questions about values, representations and cultural contexts. Models for change would usually lie elsewhere, beyond the research itself, although in some research designs, models for change are the subjects of the study.

Boundaries are important. Your student cannot research the whole field, everything about the subject, or all the questions that interest them, but rigidity is also a problem. Planning a piece of work which has a rigid design, with questions to which the student already knows the answers, will probably not result in a masters dissertation of real quality and certainly will not produce a PhD. Research should be planned, but should also throw up some surprises, extending thoughts in the field in critical ways. All research, and particularly postgraduate research, needs to engage with previous work in a dialogue, so that while it might start with a literature review, this should not be a dead list of summarised reading, but should comprise a dialogue between experts' and the candidate's own research. Undergraduate research also needs to be original in its contribution, insofar as students make their own synthesis of existing research and carry out their own fieldwork, experiment and analysis. The best undergraduate research is very original, and creates a good basis for further research. With increases in student numbers, the length and frequency of undergraduate written work throughout the course has tended to be reduced, making the research project or dissertation into a daunting learning and writing task. However, there are other opportunities for students to develop research skills in, for example, independent learning modules if these focus on research skills. Indeed, students should be encouraged to start developing sound research skills for their early essays as these will stand them in good stead when a long and deep project or dissertation must be tackled.

▶ Developing and enabling supervisory relationships

Students need to be able to engage with and work with their supervisors (often very busy people, who nevertheless benefit from development, experience and the sharing of good supervisory practices). Working in a research dialogue with a student focusing on areas of mutual interest, is a most rewarding interchange, but it is also a job which, like a concertina, seems to expand. Supervisors can worry that they have not been in touch with students enough, or that they are doing too much of the work – translating ideas into research activities, suggesting reading and clarifying. Students in research methods development sessions often laugh at the idea that supervisors could do too much, but it is necessary to guide students into autonomy and away from dependence. The supervisory relationship varies with subjects, cultural expectations, learning differences, gender, distance and whether the student is part-time or full-time. Full-time students engaging in scientific research alongside their research group and supervisor might meet regularly for small amounts of supervisor input, a masterclass, monitoring and directive, but then they could find that they are not sure which parts are their *own* work, which decisions they have made and what is more properly the work of the group and supervisor. These are issues of ownership that must be sorted out early on, so students can identify their own research progress and achieve *their* outcomes.

Many research students work in relative isolation, especially in the arts and humanities. Perhaps this avoids the group ownership problem, but there are benefits to be gained from developmental dialogue with an academic community of practice which both supports research *and* helps the development and clarification of complex conceptual ideas through the opportunities it offers for articulation and debate.

My distance students tend to send me 40–50 pages of revised chapters and expect immediate responses. Sometimes their English creates a stumbling block to understanding their argument. Students can phone at awkward moments with serious concerns, then 'disappear' for months on end, unresponsive to promptings by mail or email. Students working at a distance, studying part-time and those whose learning culture background differs from that of their supervisor or whose English does not allow them to express all their thoughts clearly are in a very different position to those whom we meet regularly. My Master's students and I enjoy a study weekend away at the seaside. Apart from sharing each other's work and getting to know each other, there is ample opportunity to ask questions about their research and share research developments. None of this is on offer to students studying overseas. Clarity of mutual expectations, ground rules about regularity, the type and focus of supervisions and agenda setting are all essential in a good supervisor/student relationship. So, too, is the involvement of the student in a supportive academic community. This is true of *all* disciplines, all levels, all geographical areas.

▶ **Quality time**

Students require specifically focused moments to concentrate on the development of their individual projects. Casual regular meetings or group activities are not focused enough on the individual. For those studying part-time and/or at a distance, regular contact times should be arranged. Supervisors could ask students to send email drafts of work and comment on these in a regular online office hour, sending back annotations and following this up if necessary with phone calls when tricky conceptual moments or learning leaps arise. For supervisors with postgraduates from different cultures, it is important that both halves of this relationship work in the context of some understanding of each other's cultures, expectations and learning backgrounds (see Chapter 12).

Supervising at a distance is a difficult skill to learn. It is preferable to meet: (1) at the beginning to clarify working arrangements and directions of the research; (2) in the middle to maintain momentum; and (3) at the end of a large research piece such as a masters or PhD. As they complete, students need support in expressing the coherence of their work; ensuring the conceptual framework is clear and that theorising underpins their work; and that theories, arguments and findings weave throughout the research as a whole and are finally pulled together in conceptual findings and a conclusion. Students often need guidance to ensure there are clear links between chapters and good signposting throughout so that the completed dissertation or thesis emerges as a cohesive, well-focused contribution to debates in the field.

▶ Undergraduate study and supervision

For some reason that I no longer remember, I did not do a dissertation as an undergraduate, so the shock of planning, undertaking and writing a long study at masters level was considerable. Some academics would like to remove the dissertation from undergraduate courses, arguing that it carries too much weight in a degree. As someone who was not required to produce one, I disagree totally. A dissertation offers students the chance to undertake a piece of research in an area of interest to them and to pursue it through to completion. Undergraduates present with broad areas of interest just like PhD students. Our work together is to define a research question, provide a workable title, be exploratory and problematising, but also specific, enabling them to avoid trying to cover too much ground, too many texts, too many questions. Undergraduates are not expected to carry out quite the original, creative, problem-solving work that is expected of a PhD candidate, or at least not to the same extent. Their project is much shorter – in effect, much more like the kind of research project you meet in a job, during your professional life, something manageable of approximately 7000 words, with the right kind of scholarly apparatus (abstract, references, etc.) and research approach. However, now that many students are on modular courses writing only 1500–2000-word essays, a dissertation feels like a large task. It is so much more than the sum of its parts, which themselves *could* be described as four or five short essays (to let it seem manageable in terms of length). Actually, the dissertation is a conceptualised, well-argued, holistic product with theories, references and themes running from the opening pages through to the final and conceptual conclusions. An undergraduate dissertation is a first step in research, demanding the development of research skills. A postgraduate dissertation or thesis is a similar product and process, but is much longer, deeper, more original and more conceptually complex.

► Making it real

Students need regular supervision to define their research project and under-graduates might need a much tighter rein than a PhD student. It is a shorter project in terms of *time* as well as length, with none of the potential elasticity of completion time accorded to postgraduate study (although this is increasingly less true as completion becomes an institutionalised objective). Undergraduate dissertations have to be carried out in less than a year, which means they must be well-planned, achievable and capable of being completed quickly.

Undergraduates learn to define a realisable project for their research, to plan the timeline and to select and defend methodology and methods. They select samples and develop a research design, and learn the art of data analysis and of keeping good referencing records. They also learn presentation skills, if presenting to peers, and writing skills, such as good expression and coherence between abstract, introduction, chapters and conclusion. All of this will contribute towards ensuring an organised piece of work and establish good working practices for longer projects later. Many will produce work which is *not* staggeringly original, but it:

- should contain originality, whether this is a combination of arguments against which is set the student's own argument and discussions; a new combination of areas; or a focus which is explored in depth;
- will avoid plagiarism, using the work of theorists and critics in a dialogue with the student's *own* arguments and findings;
- must contain:
    (1) an argument, not just a survey
    (2) good referencing
    (3) development of methods in action
    (4) evidence of working at a conceptual level – making meaning
    (5) recognition of significance, and argument and ideas.

Supervising students carrying out research for postgraduate and undergraduate dissertations or theses is probably the most rewarding teaching we can do. At least I have found it so and have met colleagues who agree, both locally and internationally, in everyday practice, at educational development sessions, and especially in relation to the large cohort-based international PhD programme on which I have worked since its inception in 1997. My colleagues, the programme director Dr Gillian Robinson, co-tutor Prof. Vernon Trafford and latterly three of 'our' post-doctoral colleagues, Dr Shosh Leshem, Dr Miri Shacham and Dr Yehuda Ben Simon, have all contributed to the learning conversations about supervisory practices, and the learning conversations that form supervisions for us. It is colleagues at workshops and students at PhD, PrD, EDD, Master's and undergraduate levels who have produced some of the suggestions about supervisory practices that form the bulk of this book. It is a truism, of course, that we learn from our students, but nonetheless true for all that! And how, we might ask, can undergraduate and postgraduate supervisors be rolled together in this way? One of the distinct differences is that of the scale of supervision or the scope of the project.

▶ The role

The supervision role is much more clearly defined as a professional relationship than that of tutor, friend or colleague and it relies on more than goodwill and spare time. It needs to be, and in many cases is, the focus for development and 'training', although I don't like the mechanistic overtones of that term. Students at all levels need guidance, modelling and managing so that they can start to develop as independent researchers. This seems to require a mixture of the specialised, developed skills discussed above – developing reliable research questions, conceptual frameworks, methods and analytical skills and tools to enable the research to come to organised fruition – and people skills. We will consider here generic research supervision at undergraduate and postgraduate levels, using postgraduate practices and perspectives as fundamental underpinning models as well as interpersonal skills. Colleagues I have discussed supervision with confirm my own sense that we are always expected to 'tuck' supervision in, lacking focus on the very systems and practices of teaching and guidance it requires. Currently, increasingly driven by government objectives and quality assurance demands, the role needs to be clarified and supported by explicit development, recognition and reward. This is particularly so in Australasia where postgraduate supervisory practice development is now increasingly compulsory, possibly because funding is attached to postgraduate completion (students are funded from the outset, but their completion feeds into funding a formula for future students, each completion being worth approximately 50 per cent for a new student). Supervisory development enables us to discuss and adopt good practices we share and develop in such contexts (and the horror stories from which we have learned). These feed into all our supervisory work, at every level. We can also now benefit from a growing research base. The next sections look at research into supervisory practices, models, and at supervisor development programmes.

▶ Tensions and developments in postgraduate research and its supervision

At the start of a doctoral supervision I make a point of underlining the possibility of failure. It has to be crystal-clear that enrolling, even as a well-qualified student with a good Master's degree, as a doctoral candidate has no implications for success either with the thesis or on the job market. Hard facts, but honest ones. By definition, there can be no guarantees that a project will produce an original contribution to knowledge. Society needs a contingent of people who have understood that ideas cannot be bought, and who resist the creeping managerialism besetting intellectual inquiry. Putting 'pure research' (the quest for knowledge) first is not the product of an ivory tower; it is deeply political. If we are to be defined only in terms of the needs of one profession, how can change occur? How will old injustices and prejudices be overcome? Great research is original, challenging, and the product of minds able to see beyond narrow, pre-set goals. The current trend towards managing research (in theory, only its infrastructure and resources) has already led to a preference in the funding bodies for neat, well-planned projects, commercially contracted in advance, as opposed to 'blue skies' research. (Newman, 2001, p. 16)

Newman's comments on the dangers, tensions and social context for research students in English spell out issues for all disciplines. A manageable piece of research might be produced at the expense of real creativity and contribution to knowledge. Students can fail. Debates about supervisory practices and their development are located right at the centre of such tensions.

Key issues when we consider research supervision are the nature of the research process, the aims and scope of the research itself, and the student's own self-development. Here a major tension emerges between the managed and manageable piece of research and the creativity, arguing and space to make mistakes and learning leaps that the research experience offers.

Leonard (2001, p. 39) acknowledges the tensions between the usefulness of postgraduate training courses, ICT to aid doctoral learning and supervision, and the current over-bureaucratisation of the supervision process – a possible problem for developing a creative atmosphere. Of importance here is the argument that the culture of emphasising completion could lose us the exploration, creativity, problem-solving and sheer originality of research, especially at PhD level.

In the UK, the ESRC's pressures to complete match those in Australia and New Zealand to link funding to completion: 'a powerful mechanism for research steerage' (Ozga, 1998). This could lead to a different kind of thesis at PhD level, one which could be more time-managed, feasible, boundaried, planned and achieved – but *alternatively* could be less creative, less involved in risk-taking or originality.

> The PhD thesis used to be conceived as a major piece of work on which authors could draw for their first monograph and several important articles. Increasingly, however, even in the humanities (where the AHRB has still not made a requirement for taught courses) all doctorates are becoming 'Kentucky fast research'. That is to say, they 'should' all now be pitched at a 'manageable level', with the capacity to succeed under pressure, and time management, of paramount importance – rather than a PhD at least tackling an issue of importance to the discipline and the individual student, however long it takes. In the natural sciences, more original work has always waited till postdoctoral level, but research here has been steered towards 'more boring but patentable paths'. (Power, 1997, p. 100)

The conveyer belt version could threaten creativity. Students are now being more explicitly encouraged to see even the PhD as an opportunity to develop a wide variety of research skills for future use in researching and other areas of professional practice. Vital elements are:

> learning to exercise disciplinary judgement, that is to say acquiring the academic equivalent of 'good taste': knowing when an experiment has 'worked', how best to gain access to a research site, how to evaluate sources, how best to choose theories and critical cases, what there is to be seen in the data, when a reading is plausible and an analysis correct, how to construct an argument, and how to write and present a good paper. (Leonard, 2001, p. 41)

Supervisors play a key role here – modelling, advising and supervision are part of our own development process:

> Newcomers need neither to be left to reinvent the wheel nor to have didactic teaching. Rather they need a practicum, with supervisors who can demonstrate, advise, observe performance, detect errors of application and point out correct responses. This is the induction which students find exciting and the reason why they submit to many years of (often unpaid) work. It is also why it is essential for academics to combine teaching and research – not to acquire a knowledge base, but to have a feel for the process of construction of disciplinary knowledge. (Leonard, 2001, p. 42)

Cramming the PhD into only two or three years of work could result in the loss of a creative element. Leonard and others suggest that important postgraduate research skills could be learned either in a period as a postdoctoral student, as in the sciences, or in an initial period of employment before 'tenure' is granted, as in the American system. Alternatively, the widespread development of the Master's in research could enable students to learn skills before embarking on a PhD. Some supervisors of research argue that instead of enhancing research, the focus on skills could result in a decline in research standards.

People undertake research for a variety of reasons. For many undergraduates it is a compulsory part of their degrees; for some postgraduates it is an opportunity to engage in work that informs their professional practice. For many, this is not mutually exclusive – it is a chance for personal growth and intellectual development.

So why is research worth the effort? Undertaking research in any subject consists of problematising whatever is given, putting enquiry into action and learning how to develop an evidence base for knowledge claims and contributions. Research is *the essential learning process*, cast of mind and set of skills.

▶ Different sorts of supervision for different disciplines and learners

Supervising research demands that we too, as supervisors, develop a range of research related and interpersonal skills: we·must align our practices and learning behaviours with those of our students, nurture, prod, push, support, encourage, insist and guide them, and then encourage independence. It's a tough job, but endlessly rewarding.

Delamont *et al.* (1997) note that all supervision is a self-conscious rather than intuitive activity: 'good, pleasurable supervision is based on self-consciousness, not intuition or flying by the seat of your pants' (p. 1). Supervising is partly a set of skills that can be learned and improved with practice. Like other studies suggesting good supervisory practice, the Delamont *et al.* study arises from research, the earliest example of which was the Spencer Foundation's 1987 three-year research programme in five countries (Clark, 1993). In taking into account the effects of mass higher education, the labour market demand for advanced education, knowledge expansion and an increased government role in the patronage and supervision of research, Clark (1993) discovered greater similarities within than between disciplines in terms of supervisors' needs, despite national differences, In effect, Japanese historians had more in common with the ways other historians went about their research than they did with Japanese biologists, for instance.

Clark argued 'the future of British academic science is quite problematic' (1993, p. 369), because the 'tension between university and state is great' (p. 369). Becher *et al.* (1994), contributing to a book on global aspects of research in graduate education (Clark, 1993), went on to publish the British chapter as a separate monograph. Following concern about poor completion rates (Blume, 1986, pp. 217–22), the British ESRC launched a research initiative on the social science PhD (Burgess, 1994). Two ESRC-funded projects on science PhD students and their supervisors followed, so that by 1995, the UK had developed a substantial body of data on doctoral study.

International comparisons reveal differences in postgraduate education:

> France has the CNRS system, as well as the 1984 reform of the doctoral degrees, which led to the single doctorate followed by the *habilitation*. The USA has the largest and most diverse system. (Delamont *et al.*, 1997, pp. 8–9)

However, the overwhelming effects of supervisory cultures and provision for research are more significant than national differences.

> The supervisory cultures and the existence or absence of a laboratory setting for research are more important for the life of the individual student than the particular nation state, despite Traweek's findings on physics. (Traweek 1988, in Delamont *et al.*, 1997, p. 9)

Different disciplines might demand different kinds of research paradigms and behaviours (Conrad, 1999). Parry *et al.* (1992) note that anthropology students require immersion in the field, while Gumport (1993) and Becher (1993) indicate that historians are expected to be independent practitioners, in contrast with students in the physical sciences. Acker, Hills and Black (1994) use interviews with supervisors and students to define strategies and styles of supervision contributing towards students' successful research practices and completion in relation to disciplinary differences, considering different stages of supervisions and matching different stages of the students' work. Acker *et al.* (1994) comment on the social sciences alone, considering two subjects, education and psychology, in three different universities, which conceptualise knowledge and ways of undertaking research in their fields in rather different ways. They also suggest two modes of supervision: 'The *technical rationality* model gives priority to issues of procedure or technique, while the *negotiated order* model conceptualizes supervision as a process open to negotiation and change' (Acker *et al.*, 1994, p. 483). These are based on contrasting beliefs about learning and the student/supervisor relationship. Of the 'technical rationality' model they say:

> The PhD can be either a training exercise or an original contribution to scholarship; the student an apprentice to a faculty member or an independent scholar; the goal scholarly creativity or speedy completion. The discussion to follow considers another such tension.   (Acker *et al.*, 1994, p. 484)

In contrast to the 'technical rationality' model:

> The *negotiated order* model, alternatively, derives from the interpretive or interactionist approach to organizational cultures and the student career in higher, usually professional, education (Becker, 1970; Oleson and Whittaker, 1968; Strauss and Corbin, 1985; Woods, 1990). Actions of students and supervisors are based on perspectives derived from their past and present experiences, interactions with others, and interpretations of situations. Situations are characterized by uncertainty, uniqueness and value conflict (Schön, 1987, p. 6) making the application of technical rational solutions unrealistic. Mutual expectations between supervisors and students are subject to negotiation and change over time. The student, like the supervisor, participates fully in negotiating and interpreting meanings.   (Acker *et al.*, 1994, p. 485)

Built on emotional intelligence, differing from more didactic, scientific, established methods, the model is more natural to and possibly best suited to professional interactions possible with students who are career professionals themselves or likely to move into professional roles.

Acker *et al.* (1994) scrutinised 67 students' transcripts, 56 supervisors and 14 other related persons such as administrators, tutors in charge of research, heads of departments and secretaries. They found differences of opinion and experiences with regards to stock elements of supervision ranging from: (1) tutorials where agendas were seen as set by students or supervisors *or* as negotiated; and (2) work consisting of reporting or guiding or nurturing. Several students found it difficult to take responsibility in tutorials. There was enough agreement as to the conduct of a good tutorial to provide academic guidance on running one.

Different supervisors had style preferences. Some were directive and task-oriented; some seemed too busy to give the time to the students. Supervisors saw students as differing in the amount and kind of direction and supervision they needed, some modifying practices after the ESRC's directive on completion.

Dimensions of the relationships between supervisor and learner were also discussed. Some supervisors preferred to be close, inviting their student to dinner, having international students to stay for Christmas, for instance; while others retained a distance. Students responded to differences in supervisors by adapting their own styles (although some could not):

> Several students indicated that infrequent supervision had taught them how to be assertive, perhaps seeking help elsewhere, or to be better organised. Some thought that their supervisor had intended this outcome. (Acker *et al.*, 1994, p. 494)

One major problematic issue indicated in the study is that supervisors who are pressed for completion rates move towards the 'technical rationality' and directive models while most have been seen to prefer to work in the 'negotiated order' model, and indeed this latter model seems to better fit the demands of a broad range of supervisors and students.

Kiely (1982) and Bargar and Duncan (1982) argue that supervision should be devoted to the fostering of student creativity. Doctoral research should be a 'lived, integrated experience of creative problem-solving' (Kiely, 1982, p. 5). The supervisor's task becomes one of facilitating rather than directing. Blanton (1983) terms this 'midwifing the dissertation'.

Burgess *et al.* (1993) suggest that the business studies supervisor was likely to start out as 'project manager' and end up as a 'critical friend'. Some researchers indicate that more 'direct' supervisions get good results, while others prefer negotiation. Culture, discipline, study stage and personality probably play equal parts in this. Wright and Lodwick (1989) use factor analysis for interviews with 43 supervisors to identify six styles of supervision, finding that supervisors who were 'outstanding' in terms of completion rates used 'intellectually nurturing' and 'flexible' styles – negotiated, flexible styles moving between the directive and the nurturing at different times have more likelihood of enabling students to work towards completion. Certainly this claim fits in with the supervision paradigms which I and colleagues (Wisker, Robinson and Trafford, 2003) have discovered in our own work with cohorts of Israeli PhD students. Whether supervisors are acting as midwives, critical and creative friends, managers or directors will affect the differing work responses of students, but so too will the students' kinds of research. Recent studies (Brew and Peseta, 2004) identify a range of styles accompanying different stages in the student's work as much as differences in disciplines.

Delamont *et al.* (1997) highlight clashes:

1   students needing more carefully organised direction when a supervisor has a more casual approach
2   supervisors feeling that students need their hands holding while they should be encouraging independent thought.

Apprenticeship models, more common in the sciences, probably encourage less initial autonomy or authority questioning in the student. It could be argued that some international students, for instance, expecting the apprenticeship model and finding a 'negotiated order' model would need careful induction into the very different kinds of expectations and interactions it encourages.

Along this continuum there are many potentially successful matches and an equally large potential for mismatch. It is the mismatches that result in unhappy students and non-completed work.

We will return later (in Chapter 8) to consider supervisory roles and supervisory dialogues. Both research and supervision are becoming more professionalised in practice. As students are increasingly expected to undertake research training and development (see Chapter 3), it is not surprising that universities expect supervisors to engage with support and development programmes, and to become more reflective and professional in their roles. Increased research student numbers and national pressure to improve completion rates have all contributed towards the innovation and enhancement of supervisor development programmes. The next chapter explores and discusses some of these programmes with a specific emphasis on programmes in Australia and the UK, and on my own supervisor development workshops.

▶ Further Reading

Acker, S., Hills, T. and Black, E. (1994) 'Thesis supervision in the social sciences: managed or negotiated?', *Higher Education*, 28, 483–98.
Delamont, S., Atkinson, P. and Parry, O. (1997) *Supervising the PhD: A Guide to Success* (Buckingham: Open University Press).
Leonard, D. (2001) *A Women's Guide to Doctoral Studies* (Buckingham: Open University Press).
Newman, J. (2001) 'The shape of graduate studies in English'. *Issues in English: Doctor! Doctor! Doctoral Studies in English in Twenty-first Century Britain,* 1 pp. 15–24.

3 Supervisors Studying: Development Programmes

The policy in Australasia is for postgraduates to be funded upon completion rather than registration of their studies. In the UK, recent publications (e.g. the Metcalfe report, Metcalfe *et al.*, 2002), have shifted attention to the need for development programmes or opportunities for supervisors to support them in focusing on improving research supervision so that research students can benefit and, hopefully, complete in greater numbers.

> *This chapter considers:*
>
> • *supervisor development programmes – workshops and online*

Metcalfe *et al.* (2002) identify the proportion of UK universities training and developing supervisors, insisting on the improvement of the extent of provision, while recognising institutional differences:

> Training should be specified by the institution and compulsory for [new] supervisors. All supervisors, whatever their level of experience should have regular training.

> 57% require training of new supervisors
> 24% require training for all supervisors

> Specify the means by which a supervisor can seek independent advice on supervisory issues, especially if they have concerns about a student's ability or application to the study programme.   (Metcalfe *et al.*, 2002, p. 46)

As professionals, supervisors can benefit from development models enabling the sharing of good practice. Workshops, accredited programmes, online support and opportunities to enhance practice using narratives are the models favoured by UK, Australasian and other colleagues. We will explore examples of each.

I have run a number of traditional workshops on postgraduate supervision (see the boxed example of a three-day programme, held at the University of the West Indies in 2003 and 2004). At such workshops, colleagues from a variety of disciplines, some very experienced, some relatively new to supervision, work together to explore case studies, exchange good practice, and consider ways to enhance their own supervisory practice. I wish to thank-them and workshop colleagues from other universities for insights.

Programme Example

PhD Supervision: A Supervisor Development Workshop
Professor Gina Wisker PhD

Day 1
Establishing good supervisory practices for a successful PhD

Welcome and introductions

Outcomes for the workshop

1. Deciding who to supervise; what to supervise; and being supported in your supervisory development
2. Establishing and maintaining good supervisory practices
3. Starting to supervise – defining titles, developing proposals, the importance of the conceptual framework
4. Concepts of research: an introduction to choosing research methodologies and methods
5. Supervisory roles and dialogues – empowerment? challenge?

Day 2
Maintaining momentum and successful learning/supervisory practices

1. Dealing with difference; working with different learners and learning styles

---

2. Developing critical thinking and good writing habits
3. Gender and other differences in the supervisory relationship
4. Supervising cross culturally, at a distance and offshore
5. Helping students to help themselves and each other
6. Writing transfer and progress documents

Day 3
Completing and achieving the PhD

1. Dealing with difficulties: (1) in the research and development of the dissertation, project or thesis
2. Dealing with difficulties: (2) in the supervisory relationship
3. Writing up and submitting
4. Getting ready for the viva, mock vivas, the viva process
5. During and afterwards

Review and close

Models of supervisory development programmes range from training and instructional to narrative storytelling and sharing (McCormack and Pamphilon, 2004). Some programmes are workshop-orientated, some online, and some are mixed mode (Wisker, Robinson and Trafford, 2003). Those using reflective practice and online case studies exist at both Queensland University of Technology (Aspland *et al.*, 2002) and the University of Sydney, where, in the light of the new research training agenda in Australia, Angela Brew and Tai Peseta (2004) run a research supervision development programme, the 'Recognition Module', inviting research supervisors to produce an online case study of their own supervisory practice for supervisory development.

Since 1993, approximately 400 supervisors have had some relationship to the University of Sydney Recognition Module, which provides an opportunity for colleagues involved in research supervision to draw together their work, building on workshops, and utilising scholarly reading on research supervision. The development of an informed case study moves supervisors on from their own established practice, often modelled on how they were supervised, encouraging awareness of this and how they incorporate research information on good practice. Case studies show reflection and development. The tutor team provide feedback and the case goes online as a resource.

Participants are invited to focus on the stages of research development, differences in learning, culture, distance, gender and subject area, and different research paradigms within which students are working, whether they are undertaking research related to professional practice or more thematically based disciplinary or interdisciplinary research.

Case studies depict incidents of teaching and learning and raise pedagogical issues and prompt discussion of them (Hutchings, 1991, p. 1).

Reflective practice is enhanced if a case study contains four dimensions.

1   *Authentic* – the issue must be anchored in real-life experience.
2   *Concrete detail* – sufficiently rich in context so readers can make decisions about how to proceed.
3   Cases are most effective when written in *narrative form* – so the reader identifies with the issues and characters, and has some emotional investment in how the action unfolds.
4   *Open-ended* – 'open to various interpretations and not suggestive of a particular or correct course of action'.   (Brew and Peseta, 2004, p. 9)

Brew and Peseta (2004), McCormack and Pamphilon (2002), Aspland *et al.* (2002) and Delamont *et al.* (1997) all use case studies. Examples include extracts from narratives, interviews and *short* real life case studies for consideration. These help to develop and share ideas on good practice in supervision.

> Writing case studies as a form of scholarly and professional development within the context we have outlined is our attempt to engage with what Boud, Cohen and Walker (1993, p. 9) call 'moving colleagues beyond their experience and what they observe around them into new worlds of practice'. Ottewill *et al.* (2002) point to seven ways in which case studies can inform educational development in this way:
>
> 1.   By arousing curiosity thus preparing the way for experimentation.
> 2.   By disseminating good practice.
> 3.   By moving the emphasis from how to do something to how it has been done by others.
> 4.   By stimulating ideas and discussion and reflective practice.
> 5.   By helping to develop learning communities.
> 6.   By providing legitimacy for variety in educational practice.
> 7.   By providing a basis for generalisation on the basis of collective experience.
>
> (Brew and Peseta, 2004, p. 10)

The intention of larger case studies is to encourage reflection, rich practice descriptions, and to identify recurring themes, motifs and metaphors.

▶ Stories and narrative-based supervisory development

McCormack and Pamphilon (2002, 2004) use narratives in workshops as well as self-study for supervisors. They comment:

> Bruner (1986) has argued that narrative is one of only two primary knowledge forms, the other being the paradigmatic form typified by scientific logic. To narrate a life experience is to tell a story and to create a story, in a way that is coherent to both the narrator and the audience. By appropriating, interpreting and retelling the past from the perspective of the present, the self constructs itself (Kerby, 1991). Further, this personal sense making must be acknowledged as a dialectic engaging the person within her/his cultural location. As people interact with the popular and marginal narratives of their culture, they learn how to regard themselves and how to make themselves intelligible to others.   (McCormack and Pamphilon, 2004, p. 25)

McCormack and Pamphilon's workshop manual (2002) provides a well-researched argument for the use of narratives and storytelling for personal and professional development purposes. In their workshops with postgraduate supervisors, they base group work and individual reflection around typical scenarios or stories of postgraduate supervision and postgraduate research, constructed from discussions and interviews with others, individually or in groups. It is important to involve those seeking development in the construction of their own stories, their own versions of supervisory activities arising from reflection upon examples. Reflection and deliberation enable supervisors to interpret, question, develop and own values and good practice for postgraduate supervision. The articulation of ideas and practice formation arise from storytelling and sharing.

Inviting people to share their stories as a way of understanding experience is a well-established procedure in group work. Naming experience (Linden, 1999) and the extensive analysis of stories over several sessions in collective memory-work (Haug, 1987; Lee and Williams, 1999; McCormack, 1998) are examples of this. Storytelling, as McCormack and Pamphilon tell us, is 'a strategy used by therapists' (White, 1997; White and Epston, 1990). It has parallels with the feminist consciousness-raising groups of the 1970s and 1980s.

> her/his story may be appropriate or problematic, functional or dysfunctional. However at the centre of most approaches is the belief that the

individual must learn how to change her/his story to a better one. By locating the problem within the individual no account is taken of the discursive locations of that person and the impact of contradictory and competing discourses on the individual. A post-modern understanding of the issue allows a more complex awareness of the individual to emerge. (McCormack and Pamphilon, 2002, p. 26)

This is suitable in group work that addresses the needs of a variety of individual supervisors. Postmodern use of storytelling does not aim to help find 'the Truth' and any single 'right' way to carry out supervision. Instead, using storytelling as a basis for identifying varieties of the role and good practice enables acknowledgement that supervision takes place in a cultural, historical, economic context related to the subject area and mode of supervisory relationships.

▶ Using stories and narratives built from experience

Stories open an individual (and group participants) to the possibility of re-storying their life because such narratives have the potential to reveal both the individual and the collective nature of experience (McCormack and Pamphilon, 1998; Richardson, 1990, 1997). Stories act as a mirror – we learn about ourselves – but also as a window – a way of looking into the past, present and future experiences of others (Jalongo, Isenberg and Gerbracht, 1995). Searching for the individual and the collective aspects in stories encourages readers to examine and question their own experiences.   (McCormack and Pamphilon, 2004, pp. 3–4)

Boud, Keogh and Walker (1985) suggest that a three-part process of describing the experience, attending to feelings and interrogating the story enables readers or participants in group processes to turn experience into learning. Questioning and reinterpreting enables consideration of 'new perspectives on an experience' leading to 'changes in behaviour' (p. 34). I hope you could use a similar structured questioning process to take you through the chapters and onto suggestions for good practice that have arisen from workshops on good supervisory practice in a variety of contexts. In the process you could uncover your own assumptions and constructs (myths) about what you do as a supervisor, what you feel is successful, what might work in other contexts, what is less successful, what needs some development, and where you might move to next in your practice. Following a reflective questioning process is helpful (see the box on p. 36).

Levels of reflective questioning

Describe the experience
- What, in your words, is the story being told here?
- What is the point of the story?
- To what extent is this also your story?
- In what ways is it different from your story?

Attend to feelings
- What feelings did the story trigger?
- What do those feelings reveal about your experience of the story-teller?
- What do those feelings reveal about your experience?
- What positive responses are in the story?
- How do you feel about these responses?
- Are some responses not present? Which ones?
- Why might they be absent?
- How do you feel about their absence?

Interrogate the story
- Are there words or concepts that suggest a particular world view?
- Which cultural values are elevated in this story?
- What ways of being have been elevated in this story?
- What might be the history of these ways of thinking?
- What other ways of being and thinking are made invisible by this way of thinking?

Source: McCormack and Pamphilon (2004) using Boud *et al.* (1993) pp. 7–8

Brew and Peseta's (2004) have drawn up a list of criteria for good supervisory practice, developed from online work and accompanying research (see the box on p. 37).

At Anglia Polytechnic University (APU) a workshop programme is now augmented by online 'blended' support in line with Australian examples. Colleagues can visit the site and/or undertake a newly validated MA module in postgraduate supervision, based on working through the online programme.

Our sense at APU was that, because of the likely academic track record and position of supervisors, as well as their varied but often extensive expe-

Criteria for good supervisory practice

1 Interest in and enthusiasm for the supervision of postgraduate research students.

2 Appreciation of a range of good practice approaches to supervision and an understanding of what constitutes a productive research learning environment.

3 Establishment, for and with students, of clear goals and expectations in the light of up-to-date knowledge of the University's requirements.

4 Productive and regular meetings held with students, which provide them with sympathetic, responsive and effective academic, professional and personal support and guidance.

5 Careful management of the supervisory process to achieve timely and successful completion of the thesis.

6 Development of a partnership with students that takes account of the need to assist them to develop a range of generic attributes and to introduce them to the research community.

7 Open communications established with students with timely feedback, which is both supportive and challenging, given on progress.

8 Utilisation of a repertoire of supervisory strategies to take account of the differing and diverse needs of individual students, including assisting students from equity groups and those off-campus to achieve success in their study.

9 Evidence of systematic evaluation of competency in supervisory skills and of critical reflection and engagement with salient and emergent issues in their own field of research, to improve supervisory practice.

10 Use, by the supervisor, of the literature on the scholarship of supervision pedagogy, and of relevant policy issues in research education to enhance the postgraduate research experience of their students.

Source: Brew and Peseta (2004)

rience, a developmental forum that enabled reflection, aided identification and the sharing of good practice, making the implicit explicit, would be most appropriate, beneficial and likely to encourage supervisor 'buy-in', while a more structured and didactic programme would not. There is a precedent in terms of resources and provocative thoughts online in the UK: Pat Cryer's website: http://www.cryer.freeserve.co.uk/supervisors.htm. This is a 'one stop' web resource for information and advice on research supervision; a resource rather than a course. In Australia, the FIRST programme is a developed online site maintained by Jo MacKenzie at the University of Technology in Sydney (UTS), which pulls together specifically rewritten materials for supervisory development online.

Peter Kandlbinder and Tai Peseta (2000a) have launched an online and workshop support model so that:

> supervisors could choose to complete the programme as flexibly as their schedules permitted. Some supervisors completed just the web-based modules, some only attended the workshop programme, while others elected for a combination of both. (Kandlbinder and Peseta, 2000a, p. 1)

They built a flexible learning programme of three interrelated elements: web-based resources, workshops and supervisor case studies. Self-study enabled supervisors to work through the programme in a variety of ways, or to access just the elements they felt they needed when they wanted to. A key element is an online discussion forum aimed at encouraging reflection.

Similarly, Geoff Hill and colleagues at the Queensland University of Technology (QUT) use 'journeying postgraduate supervision', tapping into the narratives of postgraduates and supervisors, developing their practice, identifying with journeys, experiences and the case studies of others and reflecting on implications for their own practice.

In the UK, the Open University (OU) EdD supervisory forum uses First Class to promote online discussion of supervisory issues and practice, part of the OU's support for postgraduates, undergraduates and supervisors ('First Class' is an online messaging and discussion environment which is password-protected). Supervisors have a staff room on a virtual campus with bulletin boards, chat rooms and a supervisor development forum. I e-moderated a six-week long discussion in 2002. The OU have the infrastructure to support a complex development; at APU, they do not. The activity there was necessarily going to be smaller.

The idea of an online supervisors' development forum for APU supervisors came about from my experience of supervising Israeli, Arab, Chinese and African postgraduates at a distance. As a supervisor and 'guardian supervisor' of the Israeli PhD programme, I felt I needed to discover and share examples of good practice between myself and other colleagues in a similar situation. Distance supervision is a rather lonely, sometimes troubling role, although as students begin to develop their clarity of thought and writing skills, it is also a very rewarding cultural experience. I was convinced that supervisors needed some support for their own role development. Since January 2003 I have been interviewing students, post docs and supervisors about their supervision experiences. They all have stories to tell – mostly very positive – about their relationship with their students and supervisors at a distance. However it can be difficult to get in touch with supervisor colleagues living far away, but establishing an online supervisory development forum can go some way towards facilitating the sharing of practice and support.

The programme had to be designed to augment face-to-face provision; specifically to address the needs of distance supervising affected by cultural difference; bring together groups of supervisors spread widely around the country; provide a discussion forum and means of keeping in touch with supervisors; and provide a staff room in which to exchange and develop good practice. This dovetailed with an opportunity to produce an accredited MA Learning and Teaching module for supervisors. Our intentions were to produce an online supervisory development provision that could provide developmental support and the option of an accredited programme for both new and well-established supervisors.

Our development was fed by our different experiences and by ongoing discussions with both students and supervisors on the programme. Some of these we felt were rather more analytical and specific to the programme itself and others generic to supervision. Supervisor/student interactions, working with international students, learning styles, supervising at a distance (see Chapter 13) have all formed discussion and development topics. Strategies developed to address these include ensuring that distance supervision encourages the appropriate critical, reflective, developmental and research-as-learning practices.

▶ Why an online support and development programme?

We wished to build a community of practice and so an online and face-to-face (blended) mode suited us best.

It is assumed that supervisors would find a variety of online provision differently suited to their needs and interests at different times. To this end, a team of six put together a WEB CT-, then ANET-based online supervisory support and development programme comprising:

- bulletin or notice board containing important dates, times, announcements and points of interest
- resource area to post up links, presentations, essays, useful items
- discussion forum, which involves supervisors and programme team in developing, leading and nurturing asynchronous discussions set up by different supervisors or team members and e-moderated over time
- supervisor development programme containing information, ideas, questions, tasks and a 30-credit MA Learning and Teaching module.

Benefits and potential

This format of online development is appropriate for

- busy people
- distance usage
- sharing practice rather than following on a programme
- ongoing debate and dialogue
- 'exchanging' information and keeping in touch.

Action research accompanying the programme will enable us to monitor and develop it further.

Palgrave Macmillan has launched an informative site including a variety of study skills and activities – see the 'Postgraduate Skill Zone' available at: www.Palgravestudyguides.com in 'Skills4study'.

▶ Further reading

Brew, A. and Peseta, T. (2002) *Improving Research Higher Degree Supervision through Recognising and Rewarding Supervision Development* (Australia: University of Sydney).

Delamont, S., Atkinson, P. and Parry, O. (1997) *Supervising the PhD: A Guide to Success* (Buckingham: Open University Press).

Kandlbinder, P. and Peseta, T. (2000) http://cea.curtin.edu.au/tlf2000/kandlbinder2.html Teaching and Learning Forum, accessed 16 December.

McCormack, C. and Pamphilon, B. (2004) 'More than a confessional: post-modern groupwork to support postgraduate supervisors' professional development', *Innovations in Education and Teaching International*, **41**:1 (Birmingham: Routledge, January–February).

Metcalfe, J., Thompson, Q. and Green, H. (2002) *Improving Standards in Postgraduate Research Degree Programmes* (HEFCE, October).

4 Establishing and Maintaining Good Supervisory Practices

The relationship between student and supervisor(s) is a very important one and it is essential that you can get on with each other professionally and personally, without necessarily being the best of friends. You need to respect each other in terms of scholarship, academic credibility and practices. For all students and particularly those working at a distance, the supervisor is the link with the university, and an essential guide, teacher, colleague and mentor in the research process.

This chapter considers:

- *supervisory relationships – management and organisation*
- *potential problems and pitfalls – how to avoid or overcome them*
- *clear communications and ground rules*
- *what research students can and cannot expect of supervisors*
- *stages of supervision*
- *first supervision*
- *learning contracts*
- *thoughts and ideas on supervising*

Research students have embarked on what is perceived as a large-scale project (the PhD, MA, the undergraduate dissertation), but, building on previous experiences of supervision, teaching or work practices, they might have unrealistic beliefs about the amount of contact and the amount and kind of guidance *you* can be expected to provide. This could range from expecting to get on with their research project now with only minimal contact with you as supervisor, to believing they need to ask your advice about every single thing they do. Cultural, gender and age differences, the level of award sought, as well as differences in everyday practices and learning styles could affect expectations and relationships.

▶ Experiences and practices, supervising and being supervised

Reflecting on previous experience of supervision is a good way to start defining good practice, and ways of establishing sound ground rules, building on your own experiences of supervising and being supervised.

Activity

Draw up a list of six characteristics you think a good supervisor should possess.

▶ Negotiating procedures and regulations

When undertaking the supervision of research students, you will need to ensure you are familiar with all the university procedures and regulations involved. These will deal with areas such as acquiring research and post-graduate students and formally agreeing to supervise their research. You must formulate at the outset realistic expectations for yourself as supervisor, and for the student, detailing aspects such as frequency of meetings and how to report on them, involvement in research development programmes, the length and format of progress reports required, dates for submission, length of work, etc. Working through the following questions will help to focus you on how you intend to practise.

- How can and do prospective research students find you?

- What is (are) your specialism(s) and would you be willing to supervise beyond this range? If so, why? What are the implications of stretching your expertise a little too far, or refusing to take 'your share' of the growing number of students who need supervision?

- Are students genuinely working in an area close to your own? Can you supervise them in relation to methodology and methods rather than subject?

- How can you know if students are suitably qualified? What are the procedures? If they are not adequately qualified, what does the university offer to help bridge any gaps?

- Is their English language of sufficient standard? How do you decide? What are the university regulations for international student language standards, and are there courses or support available for your student?

- To whom do you refer unanswered issues? Do you have a referral sheet with phone numbers?

- Do you have time to supervise students? What is this likely to be and how is it accounted for? Are there guidelines about supervising, the time allotted per student at undergraduate, masters, PhD level?

- Who can be the second supervisor? And how do you decide this? (usually only PhD and EdD level). Would one of you be more concerned with the subject and the other with methodology?

- Do you/how can you work effectively in supervisory teams? Will you set up meetings? What could you do to avoid students having to juggle conflicting advice? Or is this actually a useful experience for them?

- When do students have to register and how? Is it before or after they develop a proposal?

- What are the various documents which students need to complete at your university in order to:
  (a) register?
  (b) complete a research proposal?

- How much time are you allotted to help students with their development of the research proposal?

- At what point does the proposal go before a Research Degrees Committee (or similar) and what is your role in supporting it at this stage? Who else advises on the proposal before acceptance?

- Can you help with revisions?

These questions are designed to help you consider experiences and raise issues. Several of these issues can lead to further considerations of:

- tensions
- regulations
- expectations
- resolutions

Colleagues and the published literature suggest there are tensions between autonomy and dependence and fundamental issues about what a doctorate is now. How far is it research training for future academic or research work? How far is the thesis a unique large-scale product as an end in itself? How far is it conceived as a manageable project at a sufficient level, achievable in the time available?

▶ Supervisory relationships: expectations

Aim to establish a clear relationship between student and supervisor, with defined parameters right from the start.

Task 1

In the following section, there are twelve situations where students may or may not reasonably expect help from a supervisor. Consider and reflect whether the students are being:

- realistic
- too demanding
- problematic

What issues are raised in these stuations? What should you do to set up good practice from the start?

Students' expectations of supervisors

1   Students expect to be supervised – guided to clarify research questions; develop a conceptual framework; address gaps in their knowledge and establish research sufficient for a PhD, Master's or undergraduate award; identify boundaries; develop structure and a design for the study; and decide on methodology and methods. They can expect to be told if their work goes off-course, seems misguided or is likely to be too adventurous and large-scale. You cannot give this kind of guidance without seeing and discussing the work in progress, of course, so setting up ground rules, frequency of meetings and agendas help to focus guidance and production of work.

2   Supervisors should read students' work thoroughly, and in advance. This

is aided by agreeing agendas and the timing of dispatch of parts or chapters ready for comment. It is important that students identify areas and issues which in their view need discussing and shaping, and for you to indicate areas to discuss, in advance of each regular supervision meeting.

3 Students expect supervisors to be available when needed. Although you can together plan regular supervisions, students need to know you are approachable in between more formal sessions, if necessary, to ask key questions, through a 'surgery' or other system. However, do be clear about your work demands, informing students of periods when you are not available, or pressurised, and decide whether or not you *do* want to be contacted at home on a Sunday evening in the event of a crisis. For international students in particular, such clarification can help avoid embarrassment, excess intrusion or – the opposite – disappearing, over-polite students.

4 Students expect supervisors to be friendly, open and supportive with academic issues and establish a consultative, supportive relationship.

5 Supervisors need to be constructively critical, giving praise where relevant and informative, not harsh, criticism, so students can develop their work further. Without helpful information and feedback, students might become discouraged. If they do not fully understand the feedback, they could carry out unnecessary, misguided work. This is probably more of an issue with students from other cultural backgrounds, or when working at a distance. In both cases, very careful wording of constructive criticism, examples and models can help. Gradually, students should need less explicit guidance and criticism as they develop autonomy and their own sound judgement.

6 Students expect their supervisors to have a good knowledge of the research area, and/or some expertise in both the supervision process and the methodology and methods being used. Where you are not a subject expert, provided the student has both formal and informal access to others who are, and the division of responsibilities between first and second supervisor is clearly made, you can still effectively supervise.

7 Supervisors need to know how to ask open questions, how to draw out ideas and clarify or define problems, and how to elicit information, even if students find communication difficult. This can be facilitated by working for some time with more than one student present, to aid discussion, or by identifying areas to discuss, in writing in advance. Your

student will need to interact with other students you supervise, those researching similar topics, students supervised by other supervisors, and the broader, academic community (see Chapter 10), encouraging sharing and autonomy.

8 Supervisors need to put students in touch with information, reading, resources, contacts and internet sites.

9 Supervisors should encourage students to enter the academic community by helping them attend appropriate conferences and introducing them to others in their field. Students should also be encouraged to publish appropriately and given support with writing and editing. It is important to define the amount of work to be published, since too much published from a thesis before submission might endanger the originality of the thesis itself, and too many publications on tangential topics could take a student's mind off the main focus. However, publishing does develop credibility in the field, providing students with practice in developing elements of their work through to completion, ensuring clear arguments and structure, like a mini thesis. A balance needs to be kept between publishing and saving the work for the thesis or dissertation.

10 Supervisors are expected to be sufficiently involved in students' success to help them after graduation with publication, jobs or promotion. It is a good idea to encourage students to be realistic, to make and follow up academic contacts, using the supervisor for advice and references.

These situations highlight issues such as how supervisors can enable students to enter research culture and gain from opportunities, with support. Supervisors also need to consider how to tease out complex conceptualising and research questions, encourage good design, plan fieldwork, analyse findings and determine their contribution to knowledge. Supervisors are also involved in editing parts of the written thesis or dissertation. Science students working in research labs, or social science students in project groups tend to work alongside their supervisor, maybe seeing them daily, but 'quality time' supervisions are also needed for students to focus on their work. For all candidates, close or at a distance, it is important to arrange specific times for supervisions with agreed agendas, taking into consideration expectations, stages of their work, individual personalities and relationships, and other pressing demands on your time and energy as a supervisor. Distance supervisions (see Chapter 13) require very careful management because it is even easier to lose contact with the development of the research, and to mistake the meaning of exchanges.

Now consider two further aspects of student and supervisor expectations.

11 Students should not expect you to do the research for them. They might find this a ludicrous suggestion but there should be limits to *your* time spent on copying journal articles, looking up references, etc., if *they* are to learn the strategies of research.

12 Supervisors must not steam-roller students into something totally irrelevant to their project but topical for the supervisor. In science or funded research there is a greater danger of this happening. While a larger research endeavour is important, a specific, contained, manageable, sufficiently complex research project needs defining if students are to progress with their research, own it and develop skills to allow them to be part of the research community. They need to produce a finished piece of work from scratch, not just be part of a larger project.

▶ Planning Work and Supervisions: The first supervisions

Activity

Consider:

- What do you really want to achieve in supervising students' research?
- How can you, as supervisor, help students to achieve research goals?
- Are the suggestions of supervisory activity at each stage of the student's work realistic? manageable? problematic? How can you organise your work with students to support and enable them at each stage?
- Early agenda-planning
- Can you develop a learning contract?
- What outcomes do you seek and which problems do you want to avoid?

Considering some of these issues and practices list in the above Activity should help you to plan and managing your supervisory relationship with your research student. Ultimately, it is up to the students to manage the project and their time and to have a clear idea of their goals and how they are to achieve them. However, it is also a learning experience for even the most confident and well-prepared student throughout the research process and project, so you will need to encourage your students to be realistic abouthow they plan and work, and show them how to change direction, refocus and tackle problems when things are going wrong or well, ensuring they produce a conceptually complex, well-researched, well-expressed and argued, well-presented research project, which genuinely contributes to research in the field. This can and should be a very satisfying process and experience.

One useful early activity with students is to conduct *a skills audit.* This enables students to see what skills they need to develop further in order to be more successful in their research project. Such skills are both generic and subject-specific at the level of research method and subject area (see Williams, 2003).

First supervision: some activities

- setting the ground rules for supervision and student activity
- developing learning contracts
- undertaking a skills audit, and planning how to address skills needs
- developing a title from a general topic area
- scope of research
- considering stages of the research overall and working with students to begin to plan/see ahead
- developing research questions
- developing the conceptual framework
- starting to put the proposal together

Defining the research area, choosing the title and asking the main research questions are essential points of entrance into the research process.

Title, question and scope of the research project

At these first meetings you need to discuss the overall research project with your student. Ask them to clarify the research title, research questions and how they intend to get started in terms of reading and contacts. Remind them how important the title and question are, since they will underpin and drive the whole research project, its arguments and conceptual level. You need to clarify and offer support where it is useful – but not force a title or an area on a student just because it is your 'pet' area. Students need to be enthusiastic and involved in a project of their own. If they are going to be working in a research group with you and others, or if they have responded to an advertisement for a research student to complete funded research with a PhD as part of the process, they still need to feel they have negotiated elements of the area on which they will work, and that they can 'own' the process. In the case of groups of lab scientists, project work and contract work, this could lead to some conflicts of interest unless handled sensitively. If a student does not 'own' or share the project he or she might:

- become disassociated from the research as a whole and concentrate only on localised tasks;
- not work at a sufficiently conceptual level because they are carrying out tasks and seeing only a fragmented process;
- be unaware of developing research skills that are transferable and are actually expected learning outcomes at this level to enable them to become professional researchers in their future employment (whether as academics, project researchers, or other professionals carrying out practice-based research in a variety of job contexts);
- lose motivation and direction.

Are there any tensions here for you in terms of your own subject or research work? How might they be resolved? Some supervisors have said there is a tension between the need to get a funded project finished and the carving out of a sufficiently appropriately designed and achievable research project for a student. Overcoming such a tension is important for both of you, so sitting down early on to explore how a manageable research project articulates with a longer piece of funded research is important.

In early supervision meetings

- defining the topic area
- what do they want to research
- deciding on a title that gives sufficient scope to ask research questions but does not attempt too much
- considering gaps in their knowledge and how their work might address these
- considering boundaries to their research – everything related to the area cannot br researched. What will your boundaries be? why?
- developing a hypothesis or research question
- setting up a plan of activities and starting to identify resources and information
- planning the time – and the critical path
- deciding how they will seek any necessary funding and support

- seeking a support group or suitable person
- beginning work on the literature search, the reading, initial plans, writing the first and subsequent drafts of the proposal for university agreement
- what questions and concerns they have about developing good research practices in their context
- how they can work to overcome any problems
- what future needs they foresee?

> The research student should ensure that they are engaged on a promising topic that might fairly be expected to produce sound results and within the agreed time frame. Students should work with their supervisors to develop standards of achievement that will result in a good quality thesis.
>
> (*University of Queensland Calendar*, 1984, www.uq.edu.au)

Ask your students if their research really *is* promising or rich enough and likely to produce sound results. Will it be completed within the time allotted?

It is important that supervisors work with students to look closely at the stages of development of the research project proposal. It is also important you both agree that this is a promising, manageable project that *should* achieve a good quality thesis/dissertation. Learning contracts and ground rules can help with this process.

▶ Managing supervisions and setting agendas

Before each supervision, you and your student could usefully prepare an agenda considering:

- What questions you need to look at, arising from the stage in the work, identified by either of you.
- What problems either of you feel might emerge.
- What outcomes they have in mind – for example, what they would like to achieve from this particular supervision at this point in their research. It might be assurance that their direction is right, their data is interesting and valid, or a chance to test out a hypothesis, consult on a problem, or check out parts of what they have written to see if they feel that they make sense, are fluent, and are written for the right audience.
- What the next stages are in their research.

Drawing up an agenda beforehand for each face-to-face, online/email exchange, however informal, can help you both focus on important current and longer term issues. Ask your student to send you work well in advance so you have time both to read and to think about it before a supervision. After reading it, you could email the issues you would like to raise and/or a commentary and feedback on the piece ready for discussion. If there is nothing to read you could send them some questions to consider ready to discuss.

▶ Clear communication and ground rules

These need to be established at the outset and altered when necessary. Student dissatisfaction with the development of their work (Cryer, 1996; Moses, 1984), and with relations with supervisors, can be avoided if there is clear and open communication on all aspects of the project. Identifying appropriate supportive structures and negotiating effective, regular, not too intrusive, open, enabling communication strategies will allow students to have a good experience of being supervised, even in cases where there might be personality clashes with supervisors.

Learning contracts can help you to negotiate workable expectations and relationships together and act as an objective vehicle to discuss any breakdowns. Setting agendas and keeping formal notes also scaffold the supervision process and relationship.

▶ Learning contracts

It is important for the sake of clarity and equality that learning contracts are drawn up, clearly defining how much time and what kind of support the supervisor(s) can offer, and the expected behaviours of both student and supervisor. Learning contracts (see Anderson *et al.*, 1996; Boud, 1995) can be drawn up making each party's expectations explicit. These can help everyone involved in supervision to manage their work, and to point out problems fairly and *objectively*. Contracts focus on terms of work, communication and responsibility. As you discuss your roles and draw up an informal contract, it helps make explicit your expectations, frequency and kind of supervision, and what to avoid.

Contracts have stages:

1 Identifying needs and stakeholders
2 Identifying learning outcomes
3 Resources, strategies needed, planning and agreeing rules, work, roles

4   Assessment – how can the agreed work be seen to be accomplished?
5   Review of success (or not) and evaluation

Learning contracts are a learner-centred way of encouraging learners to identify and be involved in their own programme-planning, recognise their learning outcomes and objectives, and become fully involved in their own learning – developing their learning approaches and styles, making the most of their learning opportunities and monitoring their own learning needs and achievements.

A sample learning contract for research degree supervisions appears in Wisker (2001). A shorter version is shown in the box below, but there are many alternatives. You will need to decide what suits your situation and that of your students and develop your own.

Learning Contract

Research student:
Supervisor:
Title/research topic:
Date of registration:
Approximate proposed date of completion:
Agreed frequency of supervisions:

Research student: I agree to:
Negotiate supervision agendas, send work in advance
Communicate about questions, blocks, problems (usually in short emails)
Produce work at agreed intervals and work steadily

Supervisor: I agree to:
Negotiate supervision agendas
Respond to short questions immediately (email)
Read work sent in, comment, advise, determine agenda, action points
Advise on accessing the research community

Signed...

Addresses and contact points:...

A draft learning contract
What might this involve?

Draft Learning Contract

Name:...

Supervisor:..

- Goals, aims and outcomes
- Appropriate learning tasks
- Time plan for activities
- Ways of identifying achievement
- Contacting

Agreement between ....
and ....

Date: ....

Addresses and contacts..

▶ Research skills audit

Is your student ready for independent research? A sample skills audit is given below and and could be used with students, pehaps forming the *objective* basis for several supervisions.

Students, particularly postgraduates, may already have developed research skills from previous research projects and more generally in life. However, moving into postgraduate or undergraduate research is taking a learning leap – more is expected of students and more complex and diverse research skills will be needed to maintain momentum on a manageable and achievable research project. It is useful to consider what research skills they might need to (further) develop in order to improve their chances of success. In consultation with your student, it could be a useful practice in early on (probably too daunting at the *first* supervision) to audit the studemt's skills together. Most are generic. You might want to add subject-specific skills, and to delete some as irrelevant. The audit can be carried out by students alone, in discussion with you, or, if there is a research group, with peers. The process aids reflection, helping to develop a learning plan. You will need to find out what you, your student, peers and the university can offer students to bridge gaps in the skills they need to undertake this research project and to develop as good researchers more generally. You might direct them to research development programmes, books on specific methodologies or methods, a course at the university or at the Open University, online or locally, or you could work to help them bridge the skills gap yourself. Supervisors who have used the audit have found it a useful objective vehicle for reflection, discussion and planning future work with their student. It is also useful as a developmental vehicle because students can measure distance travelled. Skills developed later in the year, during the thesis/dissertation process or in future years can be mapped against the audit tool. Finally, it helps to build and articulate an awareness of transferable research skills, useful for employability and self-esteem.

To the student
The box lists some of the research skills you might need. Audit them now. Mark the extent of your current skills and your skills needs.

Then ask yourself, and discuss with your supervisor, how you might address needs that you have in relation to *your* research, noting where and when you can work to develop those skills.

Skills Audit

Topics	Scoring	Notes about kind of version of your skill	Notes about need for a place to find and develop help
1 Turning a research topic into a research question, which addresses a gap in knowledge	1 2 3 4 5		
2 Project planning	1 2 3 4 5		
3 Time management	1 2 3 4 5		
4 Knowledge and retrieval	1 2 3 4 5		
5 Knowledge management	1 2 3 4 5		
6 Bench skills	1 2 3 4 5		

7	Fieldwork skills	1	2	3	4	5
8	Analytical skills	1	2	3	4	5
9	Critical skills	1	2	3	4	5
10	Calculation skills	1	2	3	4	5
11	Interpretation skills	1	2	3	4	5
12	Evaluative thinking	1	2	3	4	5
13	Problem-solving in different contexts	1	2	3	4	5
14	Creative thinking	1	2	3	4	5
15	Networking with others to share and develop ideas and work	1	2	3	4	5
16	Reading for different purposes	1	2	3	4	5
17	Reviewing the literature critically and in a dialogue	1	2	3	4	5
18	Managing and interpreting data	1	2	3	4	5
19	Drawing conclusions, both conceptual and factual, and backing up with data	1	2	3	4	5
20	Using appropriate computer packages and programmes e.g. SPSS and NUDIST Nvivo	1	2	3	4	5
21	Writing for different audiences	1	2	3	4	5
22	Writing at different levels e.g. for theses and articles	1	2	3	4	5
23	Structuring and presenting papers	1	2	3	4	5
24	Managing discussions about your work in context and with a variety of colleagues and experts	1	2	3	4	5
25	Finishing off pieces of work	1	2	3	4	5

[1 = new to develop, 2 = some skills, 3 = quite confident, 4 = confident, 5 = a strength of mine.]

Students might find it useful to complete this skills audit again when they have nearly finished their research project, to measure how far they have developed and to identify skills to transfer into future study and employment.

▶ What students might expect at different stages: a summary

At different stages of the supervision process, supervisors support students' work and advise in different ways, while maintaining close contact without over intruding. You might like to map your own work with your student against the following stages (adapted from Wisker, *The Postgraduate Research Handbook,* 2001).

---

(1) The beginning of the supervisory process

Supervisors should be expected to help students to:

- define and clarify a title and research topic
- refine research questions
- refine and define the field, scope and nature of the research, defining gaps in knowledge and boundaries
- develop realistic approaches and outcomes
- develop a conceptual framework
- evaluate and decide on methodologies and methods
- carry out any necessary preliminary and ongoing research skill development, for example, developing further research methods, statistics training
- shape initial plans and design outlines
- develop an acceptable and doable research proposal of an appropriate standard
- gain some entry into the meta-language of research to understand and use terms such as 'conceptual frameworks', 'boundaries', 'inductive and deductive'
- access subject and methods contacts and reading
- develop good time management
- agree a pattern of supervisions early on
- get in touch with other research students
- identify and contribute to the design of useful learning situations and take advantage of activities and experiences that could help them develop
- start to write early, developing good habits of articulation, refinement, editing

---

Question
How can you set up an appropriate pattern of effective supervisions? What can you do to help students develop and action their proposal? How can you help them enter the research community?

---

(2) Ongoing supervision – in the middle stages of the student's work

Supervisors should be expected to:

- stay in touch, but not to over intrude (unless necessary)
- care about the development of the research and work on this with the student
- encourage supervisory learning conversations, enabling students to conceptualise and deal with difficult underpinning ideas, theories and constructions of knowledge
- establish a role model of modes of research, ethical decision-making, commitment and perseverance, being realistic, etc. (this might involve students shadowing you or others in research practices)
- teach the craft of research, that is, ensure that students are aware of the importance of setting up well-defined ethical experiments, managing data appropriately and fairly, producing sound reports and a well-argued, well-documented, well-evidenced thesis/dissertation (this might involve explaining examples of others' work and identifying learning points)
- read students' work thoroughly and in a reasonable, agreed time-frame
- consider students' questions, prompting questions they should be asking
- help to tease out difficult issues and problems
- give constructive criticism and sensitive, developmental feedback, challenging where necessary
- continue to wean students away from dependency into autonomy, gently and gradually
- encourage students to maintain momentum in their work and to revisit proposals, refocus and recast work where necessary as surprises and problems emerge

- encourage academic role development, that is taking part in the academic community, maintaining ethical and organised research practices, sharing (without giving away) their work and supporting others
- encourage students to make good use of peer and academic support groups and networks locally, nationally and internationally to try out and discuss their own and others' work, exchange advice and provide more personal support
- encourage students to keep very good notes, maintain learning journals, catalogue and manage data and to keep references carefully
- support students realistically through crises in their work
- encourage students to keep writing as they go along, and to edit and refine their work

Question

How can you support rather than intrude, help your student deal with frustrating results and conceptual work, and help him or her to get over that threshold or learning leap that makes their work meaningful, coherent and new? What is your role in helping with expression in early drafts?

(3) Towards the final stages of the student's research

The supervisor should be expected to:

- encourage students to complete a first draft as soon as they can, and alter it as necessary (but don't leave it too late)
- encourage students to edit, edit, edit until the work is well organised and clearly articulates an argument throughout
- encourage students to disseminate at conferences and through publications as soon as they and their data are ready, helping them with this without taking over or stealing their work
- encourage students to produce a well-presented final thesis/dissertation through exploring models, working together over practices of coherence, expression and presentation
- encourage students to prepare thoroughly and fully for the viva (if there is one at PhD, EdD), believe in themselves and have confidence; practice responses to general, possible and likely questions and to consider potentially problematic questions

- encourage students to move on further as appropriate in the field when they have achieved their postgraduate or undergraduate qualification

Question

How far are *you* their editor? How do you work with them to ensure they show they really understand, can interpret and argue about the data they present? How do you ensure they write up a sufficiently conceptually complex, accessibly written, lively, owned dissertation or thesis?

The relationship between supervisor(s) and student is a long-term one, designed to help students become sound and successful researchers. Students should neither depend too much on supervisors nor take too much for granted. It is essential to be open and frank about mutual expectations and needs. Ingrid Moses comments:

> Becoming a supervisor is a two-way process. Openness in the initial discussions may prevent years of frustration for you and the student if your personality and learning–teaching styles are mismatched and no common style or ground is found. Openness about your own and the student's competence may prevent the student from withdrawing or failing.   (Moses, 1985, p. 10)

▶ Other support systems

The supervisor is not the only supportive person in the student's research life. Increasingly, research development programmes help underpin and augment the supervisor's work because they provide a structured opportunity for students to develop research skills, to consider issues that arise in their ongoing work, and to build a community of practice with other research students, leading to peer support. *Peer support systems* using *co-counselling* have developed alongside or as part of such research development programmes. Programmes and peer systems are particularly useful if a supervisor has a large number of students; if the skills gap the student has to bridge is too great for the support of a single supervisor; if students are studying at a distance and/or part time, and to encourage the development of autonomy, rather than dependence on the supervisor for all aspects of the research development process (see Chapter 13).

Students, when interviewed, talk of finding a critical friend with whom to discuss and share work; others use family members.

► Undergraduates

For undergraduates, the issue of autonomy is different. This is probably their first large-scale piece of relatively independent work, but it is completed in under a year and its length is strictly defined (approximately 5000–8000 words). The need for a simple, mutually acceptable set of ground rules is paramount, as students can so easily let their other work (and life) take over from the necessary, staged development of a dissertation. They are also more likely to be on-site, but this does not mean that regular meetings will just happen. Many undergraduates avoid supervisors through guilt because their work is not developing. The power relationship is also different and potentially difficult; the collegial exchange perhaps longer in developing. Supervisors need to draw very clear boundaries and ground rules, specify the frequency of meetings, agenda-setting, timescales, due dates and note-keeping. Unused to developing autonomy, students might become mired in data collection, work excessively off the topic or fail to write and rewrite as they go along. Scaffolding undergraduates' research work with them will help them develop good research and working habits for the future. Such a scaffold should be enabling, managed and linked with previous creative and critical thought, risk-taking and lateral thinking. This is a boundaried exercise, but it is also one that helps grow an enthusiastic, skilled, fledgling researcher.

► Potential problem areas

Research (Moses, 1985; Delamont *et al.*, 1997; Metcalfe *et al.*, 2002; Wisker *et al.*, 2003) indicates that there are problems between students and supervisors that could hamper the development of a successful research project. The supervision process involves:

- learning
- personal interaction
- institutional regulations, context, interface – all of which supervisors help to manage smoothly

Might any of the following problems arise in your own supervision of research and, if so, how might you ensure that you identify, avoid or overcome these problems as experienced by students?

Personality factors
Problematic personality areas include:

- neglect by supervisor
- lack of contact
- clash of personalities
- barriers to communication arising from difference, including age, class, race, gender
- differences in approach to work

Neglect can be avoided with regular, scheduled contacts established early on with ground rules so *both* of you stay in touch. Supervisors need to be able to get on with their student, but it is a professional relationship, so personality clashes should be handled carefully. See Chapters 11 and 12 on working with students from different cultures and backgrounds.

Professional factors

Problems of a professional nature include:

- a misinformed supervisor or a supervisor without sufficient knowledge in the area supervised
- a supervisor with few genuine research interests, or ones which differ fundamentally from those of the student (both of these can be avoided by making your experience, willingness and personal boundaries clear)
- excessive and/or unrealistic expectations of supervisor guidance and involvement from the student
- the student ignoring the supervisor's guidance
- the student having difficulties with the research process – such as finding information and sources, samples, access, and so on

Organisational factors

Organisational problems include:

- a supervisor having too many students to supervise (does your university have a limit? Ensuring that *all* your students are not starting or finishing at the same time helps to balance the load)
- a supervisor too busy with administration or other work/life demands
- departmental facilities and arrangements isolating the student
- inadequate support services and equipment (are students' expectations realistic? Can you act as an advocate to improve provision?)
- various hitches in the research process

adapted from Moses (1985)

▶ Autonomy *or* dictatorship?

One of the main tensions supervisors identify in workshops is knowing when to guide, or change work, and when to allow the student to get on with it and own the project. Research students need to develop autonomy. Autonomy, negotiation and the development of shared responsibilities should result from the establishment of sound research practices and good, clear relationships, putting supervisors in the position of facilitator, while students are:

- well informed
- sure of what to expect in the nature of supervision
- well aware of rules and formats, dates, and what they can ask of their supervisor
- aware of where their peer groups can help them to share ideas and develop
- clear about their research question, theories, methods, rules of the university and able to ask if unclear
- confident enough to get on with the research and writing but secure enough about the supervisory relationship to ask the necessary questions and check out interpretations, problems, etc.

Some students set up their own peer groups; others can be facilitated by departmental or university-wide processes. Still others can be initially launched and, where appropriate, supported by supervisors themselves. For example, in the UK there are Open University self-help groups who run their own sessions and develop their own agendas but *can* invite tutors/supervisors in to contribute and provide information and advice. As useful additions to formal, time-tabled supervision sessions, peer- and group-based sessions and systems can make life easier and more productive, encouraging lower drop-out rates and better quality of work (see Chapter 10).

▶ Getting on well with your student

Research students have commented on problems, for example, with a recalcitrant supervisor who seems never to respond, or an interfering supervisor who can't let them get on with anything and checks their every move. It is hard for them to maintain a steady rate of work in these instances. You need to ensure that you have a clear working relation with your student, do not let them intrude on your personal life, keep the balance between friendship and professional working relationships so neither of you relax too much and forget that the supervision of a research project is to be completed in a realistic timeframe at an appropriate level. A friendly and professional relationship should result. However, if you do *not* get along with your student, it is important to remain cordial at least because social impasses will affect work adversely. Interpersonal relations need handling with sensitivity as the supervision process moves on. They are likely to be influenced by gender, culture, learning styles etc. (see Chapters 11, 12 and 14).

Case Studies

Please consider the following short scenarios of potential problems with research students and reflect on how you could overcome them.

1   Although you have a mutual interest in the subject being researched, you and your research student do not seem to be getting along well. The student misses meetings and does not provide sound reasons. He tends to ring at awkward moments and make unrealistic demands on your time – requests for books, articles, extra supervision, etc, – and seems to be totally unable to accept the advice you give on what he or she writes. What should you do?

2   A new student presents with a rather mechanistic research question which she is convinced can be answered swiftly through research. The student is not keen to get involved with research methods development programmes and views the audit with scepticism. The student argues that she knows exactly what methods to use, has the skills, and will get the work done rapidly and successfully. What issues should be taken into consideration here? And what should you do?

3   You have been invited to a fellowship in the USA for six months but have a number of research students working closely with you, one of whom is about to complete, another in the early stages of the work. What should you do? What could you offer to put in place to support them?

4   Your research student seems to be avoiding you, crossing the car park at a distance, not answering emails – and you suspect that

something has gone badly wrong in the research but he does not seem to want to meet to discuss this, and gave a rather feeble excuse for missing the last supervision – what should you do?

5 An international PhD student has very noble, grand, change aims for her proposed thesis but, in your view, the research methods are accumulation-based, entirely quantitative and there seems to be some dissonance between the methods and the outcomes. However, blank looks appear when you try and discuss this and you are told that the methods were fine at home for the MA/MSc, so they should be fine here now. What do you do?

▶ Managing supervisions – keeping notes of meetings

Many universities now expect supervisors to keep a journal, log or reports of their meetings with students. This aids the management of the research supervision process, allowing both looking back to consider previous advice and discussions should problems arise, and planning ahead to keep track of the ways the research is progressing.

Some universities (e.g. the London School of Hygiene and Tropical Medicine, and Warwick) have pro formas for research supervision notes. A sample is given in the box below.

The following two extracts offer examples of the sort of notes the supervisor and student would make:

Supervisor Refine the research proposal – ensure Jon has a clear question and has identified the theories and theorists that will underpin his work. Suggest journals and books – 'Over here', and *City of Words* (Tanner). Also suggest contacting iafa@ct.edu.au for discussions to build up early literature search; sign and agree learning contract to enable us to proceed with supervisions

Student Refine research proposal.
Gain access to Cambridge University library for more sources to underpin literature search/theoretical perspectives part of the research proposal. Is there an email group to discuss my interests with? Determine frequency of meetings and mutual expectations

Supervision log

Date, time and length of supervision with ....

Agenda and agreed discussion areas ....

Work agreed for supervision....................................

Questions ....

Issues discussed ....

Progress made
-
-
-
-

Conclusions and agreed work towards next supervision ....

Student ....

Supervisor ....

Supervisor and student

- Defined appropriate research question from topic area
- Discussed and agreed learning contract (*attached*)
- Refined proposal – addressed question of appropriate theories and theorists, interpretation of appropriate methodology and methods
- Jon agrees to read texts suggested and bring notes about the texts in a dialogue with each other and own ideas to next supervision
- I agreed to ensure Jon has access to Cambridge University library – provided an introductory letter
- I agreed to find out details of the conference on the American Gothic – send to Jon via email

Next meeting:

Finish off working on the proposal (November 6 for research degrees committee)
Jon will enrol on first research methods programme session

Signed: .... (*Supervisor*)

.... (*Student*)

Activity

Please consider:

- Could you use such agendas and notes?
- How, when and where?
- Are you already keeping such agendas and notes?
- How have they been useful?
- How might you adapt this system for yourself?
- What are the benefits what might note-keeping avoid and enable?

▶ Further Reading

Anderson, G., Boud, D. and Sampson, J. (1996) *Learning Contracts: A Practical Guide* (London: Kogan Page).

Delamont, S., Atkinson, P. and Parry, O. (1997) *Supervising the PhD: A Guide to Success* (Buckingham: Open University Press).

Metcalfe, J., Thompson, Q. and Green, H. (2002) *Improving Standards in Postgraduate Research Degree Programmes* (Bristol: HEFCE).

Moses, I. (1985) 'Supervising Postgraduates', *HERDSA Green Guide No. 3* (Kensington: Higher Education Research and Development Society of Australasia); revised 2002.

University of Queensland Calendar, 1984, www.uq.edu,au,

Williams, S. (2003) 'Postgraduate Training in Research Methods: Current Practice and Future Needs in English', *English Subject Centre Report*, no. 3 (Lancaster University).

Wisker, G. (2001) *The Postgraduate Research Handbook: Succeed with your MA, MPhil, EdD and PhD* (Basingstoke: Palgrave Macmillan).

Wisker, G., Robinson, G., Trafford, V., Creighton, K. and Warnes M. (2003) 'Recognising and overcoming dissonance in postgraduate student research', *Studies in Higher Education*, **28**(1), pp. 91–105.

Stage 2
Establishing Research Processes and Practices

5 Defining Titles, Research Questions, Conceptual Frameworks and Developing Proposals

This chapter looks at the first stages of our work with students, supporting them to turn research ideas and interests into research questions and proposals, underpinned by sound conceptual frameworks.

> *This chapter considers:*
>
> - *turning a fascination or a professional directive into a research area*
> - *turning a research area into a question*
> - *gaps and boundaries*
> - *defining possible research approaches*
> - *moving from topic to title*
> - *starting to define the research design*
> - *developing conceptual frameworks*
> - *writing the proposal.*

Students choose to undertake dissertations or theses for many different reasons. The dissertation is a compulsory part of most honours degrees and MAs. However, *what* the student decides to research and *why* can be governed by a host of reasons, including work demands, personal choice, what is available, and what has been successful to date. Students might consider a topic that a manager or a scientific team leader feels will fit in with developments and needs at work, or with the overall research project being undertaken by the team, or they might choose an area which personally fascinates them. Different contexts and drives to undertake the research project affect the research question asked. For students undertaking research related to their profession, a limited focus may be expected, or a focus that could result in the development and evaluation of a change, with recommendations – all of which would be more suited to a report based on a project and might actually *not* have the theorising and problematising necessary for a thesis or dissertation. Students undertaking research related to a science group project might find their focus limited to a straightforward and specific experiment with limited generalisablity. Some students choose research topics that will enable them to pursue cultural, intellectual, emotional and personal fascinations. Some choose research projects they know they can manage, some to deliberately stretch themselves into new skills, new topics, new areas and perhaps into creativity.

▶ Developing research questions for research proposals and the research

Early supervision sessions with students involve activities of definition and clarification, the identification of appropriate, focused research questions to drive and underpin the research throughout, and the development of conceptual frameworks to the research.

The next stage is the development of a research proposal so that the research itself can be launched. For the PhD, and increasingly for a master's dissertation, the research proposal development stage is quite a lengthy one, with students repeatedly refining proposals with the aid of supervisors and peer groups where possible, until it becomes workable, manageable, not too grand, well-designed in terms of how it can be actioned, and genuinely practicable. In short, if it were a piece of sewing, they would have the exact dress pattern to work from – and any deviations would be the result of deliberate changes, happy accidents or creativity. This is where the 'conceptual framework' becomes so important, because it frequently appears as a lead question in vivas for PhD. For undergraduates, we might not need to use this term itself – but will certainly need to ask the same kind of question of the student and his or her research.

The supervisor's role is asking prompt questions, providing suggestions and models, and helping, enabling and empowering students to:

- **Problematise** – question and unpick what is given or taken for granted as 'natural'.

- **Conceptualise** – move beyond the descriptive to identifying concepts or ideas that underlie the representation of experience.
  Moving from, for example, a group of boys hanging about kicking

things, slightly threatening, bored, to 'disaffected youth' – so that you can ask Why? What? How? What could this lead to? What could be done?

Or, taking another example, moving from colleges on the outskirts of towns with students from rural areas who have less money and educational background than those in the inner-city colleges but who succeed in study through the way the college works with them, to the issue of 'access and regional college provision'.

- **Plan** – organise ways of asking research questions or testing hypotheses that are realistic, achievable, timed.

- **Action** – translate a plan into a series of actions, processes and linked activities.

- **Manage** – pull together data, activities, and ideas.

- **Analyse** – ask questions of data, theories and theorists, drawing them together into categories and themes that emerge or have been identified, helping the student to make sense of and sum up the meaning and contribution of what they have found.

- **Reflect and evaluate** – What happened? What was found? What does this mean? Does this make any significant contribution, challenges, change?

- **Make it all coherent** – find the right format, language, shape, expression, connections between arguments, sense of the impact, and meaning of it all – so it is coherent:
  1 at the level of argument;
  2 at the level of expression and presentation;
  3 conceptually – the piece of research finally expands and clarifies ideas or concepts *because* the questions were asked using those concepts, theories and methods and were analysed and reflected on.

First let us consider the demands of a research proposal in order to contextualise the research question.

Most universities expect students to construct a research proposal for a dissertation or thesis, since the design of a workable proposal suggests students are engaged, organised and articulate enough to undertake research. While a good proposal is no guarantee of good research, as so much could go wrong or deviate from a proposal and plan, it does lay down a useful map of the research. Its construction makes students match conceptualisations, theory and passion to what is achievable, and how to put it into practice. A common format for a research proposal at PhD level is a very good blueprint for constructing one at MA, Msc or undergraduate levels.

Format for a research proposal

Shape of proposal	Prompt questions

Indicative title (should be a statement rather than a question)

Aim and focus

• Research question or hypothesis – problematising the statement, identifying underlying concepts so that the area under study can be interrogated not just described. There can be sub-questions in a hierarchy helping ask the question. Science research usually has a hypothesis, basically an assumption to be challenged and explored.	• What is your research question? • Are there any sub-questions? • What is your hypothesis?

Context

• Establishes students' own context, that of the research, topicality, timing, key issues, the gap in knowledge this work will fit. • What are the concepts (ideas) that the research will deal with?	• What is *your* context in relation to your research? What is the brief history of the field? • Why undertake this study now? • What is *unusual* about it? Now? • What concepts or ideas underlie it?

Theoretical perspectives

• Theories and interpretations/ arguments in the field into which their work fits. Includes the key theories and theorists	• Which theoretical areas, theories and theorists underpin your research; help you ask your question?

Shape of proposal	Prompt questions
in a dialogue with the student's own ideas and plans.	• Who are the key figures and theorists? What are the debates? • How does *your* work engage with the debates?

Methodology and methods

• Choices of research approach based on beliefs about how the question can be asked – theory-building (inductive) or theory testing (deductive). • Interventionist (causing change) or non-interventionist. • The active vehicle or vehicles that enable the student to question the area or field and to ask, observe, explore, experiment and take part using interviews, focus groups, experiments, tracked processes, observation schedules and questionnaires, etc.	• Is your work inductive or deductive/theory-building or theory-testing or both and if so *why?*, Where? Does it make an intervention or not? • Which methods could you use to ask your question/vehicle your enquiry? Why? Why not others? • What are the limits of each method?

Design of the study

• How you are going to undertake the research? • Why, in what roles, using which sample or experiment? • Where, when, how many and why? Boundaries – what's *not* studied and why. This helps plan ahead.	• What will you do and in what order? • What's your field, sample, population and why? Do you have access to them? How? • What will you *not* be looking at in your work and why?

Ethics

• Considerations about risk, harm, confidentiality, invasiveness, participant consent, full information, withdrawal and the use to	• How will you gain informed consent from human participants? • Can you ensure they will come to no harm?

Shape of proposal	Prompt questions
which research is put.	• Can you ensure there's no risk to you? • Can you ensure the information will be kept confidential and not used for other means?
Outline plan	
• Essentially, a plan of what each chapter could focus on – suggests themes, developments and differentiation.	• What do you think the shape of your dissertation or thesis will look like? Which chapters and why? • Do you intend to separate results from discussion (scientific) or move between extracts of results and discussion along the links of themes and developing argument? • How will this dissertation/ thesis shape help you to develop an *argument*?
Justification for the level of the award	
• Some of this will have appeared in the aim and focus but here students make statements about contribution to knowledge and understanding, why it is important and meaningful and how it could lead to further work and insights.	• How and why is this making a contribution to knowledge? • Why is it important? • Why bother doing it? • Who could use it or do further work with it?

Research questions

How do you work to help students turn an area of interest, a problem, a desired development or an area of inquiry into a research question?

Students' research focus and question

Students need to be really *interested* in what they will be researching. Probably because it is their first piece of research, even an undergraduate dissertation seems to be a very long project and interest is needed to maintain focus and motivation. Whether it is a new or a long standing interest, it needs to be shaped and focused into a research question. Both enthusiasm and organisation will help students to sustain their interest, maintaining momentum even in the darker days of too much or too little data and of writing up.

Students need to determine what form their research will take: experimental, exploratory, explanatory, action research, evidence-based, etc. It is perfectly acceptable to carry out a *theoretical* research project rather than one dealing with the real world and empirical data.

A dissertation/thesis expanding and arguing about the different ideological constructions underlying our perceptions of, for instance, something as serious as 'homelessness' would produce several different angles and so different theoretical perspectives, for example: it is a social construct; due to psychological defects; a selfish choice; sustained by weak social policies; a symptom, of an uncaring society; or due to anomie. Students can choose questions as theoretical and philosophical as contested views about the existence of God. Each of these can be approached using different theoretical perspectives and so utilise different methodologies and methods.

Any topic can be approached in a variety of ways, and so can lead to particular kinds of research. Sometimes getting students to share their fields

---

Research approaches: which are yours?

Ask your students to consider various approaches to research:
- Theoretical exploration
- Reflection on experience
- Empirical research
- Experimental
- Descriptive
- Exploratory
- Predictive
- Explanatory
- Action

(See Wisker, 2001, for full explanations of these approaches.)

of enquiry and questions with each other early on helps them identify whether their research is theoretical or experimental (trying, setting out and measuring results), or based on their own experience, etc. If they approach their field, area or question from as many of these paradigms as possible, they will see how they might theorise differently, open up their area of questioning, and use a variety of methodologies and methods to ask their question. It helps them to expand the boundaries of their work before choosing the exact area they want to research and to be able to defend exactly why they have chosen a theoretical study using documentary research, or an empirical study using interviews and questions.

▶ Boundaries and gaps

Gaps

Students can be helped to define the gap in existing knowledge that their work fills by completing a mind map identifying: (i) the whole possible field of study; (ii) the area on which their work will focus.

On the subject of 'international postgraduate student learning', such a map could look like the illustration in Figure 5.1.

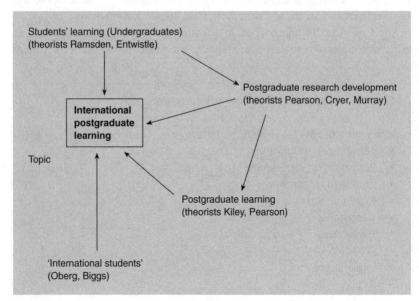

FIGURE 5.1   MIND MAP FOR 'INTERNATIONAL POSTGRADUATE STUDENT LEARNING'

My student wants to explore 'International postgraduate student learning', and then some of the strategies for supporting this learning. He or she finds research in:

- undergraduate learning
- postgraduate learning
- international students
- postgraduate research development programmes

The student then *uses* these areas and the theorists (in parentheses above) to focus on the gap in knowledge in this work.

From topic to title

- Keep it tight and properly boundaried – your 'slice of the cake' – others can ask other questions and explore other areas and issues
- Do not set up a purely descriptive dissertation/thesis
- Set yourself a problem or a set of critical questions and/or a set of contrasts – contrasting arguments about or approaches to ...
- You are contributing to ongoing debates and entering a dialogue in the academic community

---

Boundaries

Whatever a student's research area, there are other questions he or she could ask, other data, other experiments and other approaches. If students don't define their boundaries, they will lack focus and, possibly, as they pull together a vast amount of data they will find they cannot say anything coherent. So, the research question is important because it will start to help define *exactly* what the research hopes to ask, and answer – the gap in the knowledge – and also the limitations or boundaries to the area in which they will work. Candidates can explore other questions and areas of information later taking their work further post BA, MA or PhD. An analogy can be drawn with a slice of cake (Figure 5.2).

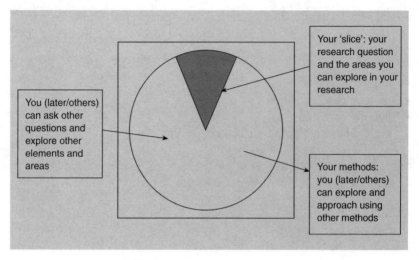

FIGURE 5.2   RESEARCH AREA AND BOUNDARIES

Activity

Consider:

- Could you use these questions and analogies about areas of work with your student?
- What example of research areas and questions might you work on with them?
- What sorts of issues about approach and interpretation arise depending on the kind of research question and paradigm, research methods and methodologies chosen to explore it?

▶ Conceptual frameworks

- How do you work with students to clarify what is meant by a conceptual framework, or underpinning concepts and theories that will help to scaffold, underpin and structure their work?
- Consider strategies you have used, conceptual frameworks that have been formed from specific questions, and cases of students who find this difficult.
- What would you define as good practice?

Anecdote

One of my own research areas is women's vampire writing. The Gothic in literature is a very popular area in the late twentieth and early twenty-first centuries. There are several students who want to do undergraduate dissertations in the field of the Gothic and of horror, with vampires being favourite examples. One day, after the undergraduate dissertation titles have been agreed, one of my second year students comes into my office, about to start out her research, with what I would hope to call the conceptual framework, to begin to guide her reading over the summer.

She is dressed in black. Her dissertation is on nineteenth and twentieth century writing about vampires. 'Why do you want to research vampires in writing?' I ask. Her reply is interesting: 'I really love vampires! My boyfriend thinks I might be a vampire.'

Aha – enthusiasm! Always a good start.

'What do you feel the vampire is being used for? What does it represent? How is it being used as a metaphor or an argument?' I ask. Blank. Oh dear. No, she is not working at a conceptual level but at a level of enthusiasm. What has she read? Is she familiar with any of the theorists who clearly explore how the figure of the vampire has been used in different ages and places to carry certain arguments about outsiders, contagion, gender and power?

No – the idea of theorising something so entertaining is far from her thoughts.

We had several meetings, of course, as the dissertation developed, but I never managed to ignite that small conceptual spark, and the dissertation (which actually failed), never really engaged with any theory or argument, it merely detailed examples of vampires in literature. What had happened was that her enthusiasm had not been coupled with intellectual enquiry, with the kind of theorising and analytical approach that problematises what we see before us and asks why? Why not? How could it have happened? What if it had not? How could it have been? How could it be otherwise? What's the point in all this? Why does it matter? And so on.

Conceptual frameworks are essential for students to establish a theoretical underpinning to their work at whatever level, be it a first-year undergraduate essay or a research thesis for a PhD – although of course they are operating at very different levels. Recording and detailing are only *part of* the research process – and are really only useful in the service of argument and investigation, and problematising and speculation, all of which are driven, informed and underpinned by theories and by ideas, or, more complexly, concepts.

The conceptual level is crucial for research projects. The conceptual framework that will run throughout the student's work and throughout their thesis or dissertation is the scaffolding of the work, the informing backbone. Work which is under-theorised tends to be reducible to a collection of facts and data, and the description of the predictable, unproblematised, unquestioned and merely stated. It is important for students to get into good habits in their research towards a dissertation, or a thesis. In this the conceptual framework is of central importance. Students need to consider:

- planning the conceptual framework carefully from the beginning of their work;
- using time fruitfully in a planned way;
- keeping a log of research to note key moments, decisions and choices for or against processes in the work; and moments where ideas, concepts and meaning become clarified and extended
- getting into good habits of writing up drafts as they proceed and ensuring they engage with concepts or ideas and meaning throughout their drafting.

Planning provides students with a route through the journey of their research, but it does not have to be a blueprint for rigidity, closing out new ideas. All research contains some surprises, some unpredictable developments; that is part of its contribution to the field, to knowledge and to originality. Being open to surprises and needing to incorporate changes as a result of findings, is not the same as having no real plan in the first place.

The student's conceptual framework is the framework of ideas, questions, and theories and methodologies that help them ask develop the ideas underpinning their research and thesis/dissertation. It keeps them focused and, having a conceptual framework means that what they discover from their reading, fieldwork, experiments and explorations can be seen to be underpinned by their initial questions and theories, to arise from them and go some way to answering or addressing them. Students need to identify those key concepts and theories that inform and drive the asking of their research questions.

For PhD students who experience a viva in which they literally defend their research and their thesis, there is usually a question directly about what this conceptual framework, skeleton or scaffold *is* in their work. For MA and undergraduate students, the readers of the dissertation will be looking for evidence of this framework, because it shows how, naturally and logically:

- *concepts* or underlying ideas have been questioned, problematised, explored
- ideas, aims and questions were underpinned by and enabled by particular *theories and theorists*
- *research methodologies and methods* actually served as the vehicle by which the student asked these theoretically underpinned questions

The framework also allows readers to *analyse and interpret what they find* – be it themes in an author, responses from a focus group, documentary evidence from archives or statistical responses to a questionnaire in relation to underpinning ideas, concepts and themes. Readers can *draw conclusions* and perhaps make recommendations (depending on the dissertation or thesis) based on these questions and aims, theories and methods and findings. Conclusions should be both factual and *conceptual* – understanding and ideas should be clarified and actioned meaning added to and enhanced.

An activity follows that you might like to carry out with your students to help them clarify their conceptual framework at the beginning of their work.

Activity

Briefly consider your developing conceptual framework, filling in the spaces below:

1   How clear are the **ideas and aims and questions** underlying your research and work for the dissertation/thesis?
2   How are your ideas and questions underpinned or enabled by particular **theories and theorists**? Which theories and theorists will you be using? And why? And why not others?
3   How can your **research methodologies and methods** act as the vehicle by which you ask these theoretically underpinned questions? Which methodologies and methods will you use and why? And why not others?
4   How can you **analyse and interpret what you find** – be it themes in an author, responses from a focus group, documentary evidence from archives or statistical responses to a questionnaire, so that you can **draw conclusions** and perhaps make recommendations (depending on the dissertation or thesis) based on these questions and aims, theories, methods and findings. In what way?

Some examples of areas of research

How could you support and help the student develop research questions and conceptual frameworks for the following areas and intended outcomes?

- 'I am interested in researching how first world countries help third world countries to develop and to adopt the successful practices of the first world countries.'
- 'I want to find out why hospital nurses, who know about safe practices, still do not take appropriate precautions in their work.'
- 'I would like to look at writers who are interested in writing about representing the self, modern ones, a bit like Virginia Woolf.'
- 'I want to find out how effective my programme is to help stroke victims overcome physical and psychological problems and get back to health and work.'

An example of finding a conceptual framework

Let us take an example of a research interest or area and turn it into a question with the beginnings of a conceptual framework.

- This student wishes to look at 'airline terrorism'.

One of my first questions as supervisor is:

- Why is this interesting, and interesting *now*?

Then I want to know:

- What is it about airline terrorism that interests you?
- What angle are you taking? And what kind of research is this?
- Is this a theoretical exploration into the range of airline terrorism, its effects, its prevention, spectacular examples?
- Or is it a practical, experimental, experiential study using fieldwork, experiments, empirical evidence?
- Will you be looking at examples using documentary evidence, e.g. newspapers or perhaps you have had first hand experience? Or you know someone who has?

The exact question will dictate the kinds of theories and concepts used to underpin the research, the methodologies and the methods used to ask the research question, the design of the study itself, and the ethics. If this student intends, for instance, to find out first hand how airline terrorism operates, he might be involved in contacting hijackers! This could be unethical and problematic. How could he have access to the hijackers? In addition, how could he deal with what they tell him? Should he keep their identity and sources secret? Alternatively, he could interview survivors, but confidentiality emerges again. The nature of the question affects the theories and concepts.

This student might need to read in the following areas to find current and established work and theories:

- Piracy (probably the first form of travel terrorism)
- Political groups and their ways of making their views heard
- The airline industry, its growth and development in relation to needs and difficulties
- Bravery and heroism
- Developments in terrorism, particularly airline terrorism
- Responses to airline terrorism, especially within the airline industry

Narrowing the question and introducing key questions about topicality, gaps in knowledge, boundaries and 'doctorateness' will help to focus the question. This helps the student to frame a question that is more likely to be asked and to some extent, answered by the conceptual framework in action, articulated through the methods and approaches taken.

After applying this process to the idea of 'airline terrorism', the research begins to narrow down to: 'the effects of the increase in airline terrorism on precautions taken by airlines'. This is much more manageable, although it is important to ask: which airlines? Is this a general survey or an in-depth study?

How can the student gain access to this information? If he does gain access, there will be problems of confidentiality, since airlines would not necessarily want readers to know about their security precautions. There are many ethical issues and problems of access to the sample or population.

The student will need to address these questions in order to not only narrow down but also access and action his question. Working on an area and turning it into a question with a conceptual framework when addressing this kind of study is a time-consuming activity and can become obsessional. If we force students into our own interpretation of what needs asking and how it can be asked, they might lose interest and ownership. They also need to know that asking research questions is a finely tuned management of issues in practice to do with context, access, theories and concepts in action, appropriateness of methodologies and methods, and, often, human interactions.

If he asked this question in a *deductive* manner, for instance, he would use hypothesis testing, checking out in his research, perhaps, whether airlines have responded to a provable increase in airline terrorism or the felt threat of it, based on interpreting the threat in a number of ways. The deductive piece of research would probably involve him in circulating a questionnaire to airline management and staff, for instance, or to passengers experiencing increased security arrangements, or obtaining some documentary analysis of management and policy documents detailing new procedures and so on. If the research is *inductive*, he is more likely to be asking questions, interviewing, observing and conducting focus groups to discover whether there is an increase in security and an increased sense of the potential of airline terrorism, and how people are responding to it. He can then build a model of perception and response from the inductive, largely qualitative research he has carried out.

Moving from a topic to a framework

Different approaches and conceptualisations of the problem might be equally valid while others may not. As a supervisor, it is your job to work with the student to develop a research question, conceptual framework and design of the study that can be actioned, yielding interesting, useful, achievable results, and to ensure that the student is engaged with the development process, owns it and can be empowered to take it forward. Otherwise it might turn out to be more your project than theirs.

Figure 5.3 illustrates the process of identifying, conceptually underpinning, planning and actioning a research project, that is asking a research question in action.

Students could find it useful to talk through ideas and links between questions, information and data with a colleague as they work and after their initial attempts at writing. This should help them organise and clarify their work. 'Work in progress' seminars help with this ongoing process. Peers can ask each other questions about the conceptual framework in action, how and why the student has used the theories, methodologies and methods used, what boundaries were drawn (what was left out, what they chose and why) and how they have had to make decisions, change direction, etc. because of the way the research has proceeded. If seminars are not possible, then students are advised to work with a friend, family member, mentor or colleague to ask and answer the same questions of each other's work.

In the USA and University of the West Indies models, students have structured work-in-progress seminars where they share their ideas, conceptual frameworks and work to date. In some instances this is formalised and assessed, while in others, for example the PhD group in APU studying English or the MA Women's Studies group on the 'Knowing Women'

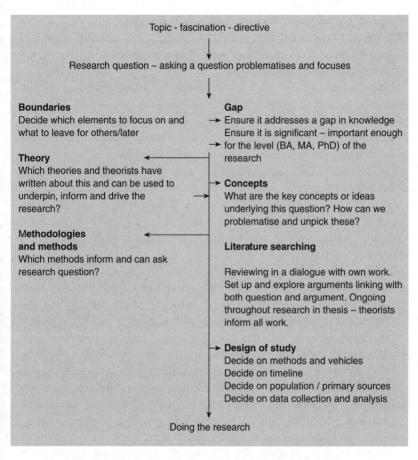

FIGURE 5.3 DIAGRAM ASKING THE RESEARCH QUESTION

research methods module, it forms part of the session, encouraging formative feedback and support.

▶ Developing the framework of different chapters

Areas your students will have considered when writing their proposal provide a key to the main elements of the developing dissertation or thesis. For your students you could use this as a document to provoke discussion about production of elements of the proposal.

Shape of the dissertation or thesis as it develops

When your students consider the actual shape of the dissertation or thesis they can bear several models in mind. There is both the *story or narrative focus* and the *argument* to consider.

A dissertation or thesis often has a narrative or storyline running through it and some secondary storylines. These are the trains of thought or argument in which investigations, readings and findings fit. Suggest to your student that they start by thinking what case or major argument they want to make, then consider the questions they may need to ask, where and how they might ask them, the research methods and vehicles enabling them to ask questions and start to answer them, the main reading and theories informing their work, and how this all fits together. Then they can explain and tell the story of how the elements of their research design put the research question into action, asking and even answering it. Broadly speaking they consider:

- The research area and how they have defined the topic and questions
- Thoughts and arguments exploring why they are asking certain questions and using certain methods in particular ways to help explore the research question
- Discussion, analyses and reports on work they have done, discoveries and arguments, and the way some information leads to other thoughts, links to other information and ideas and helps develop arguments further. This involves looking at data that they are producing, analysing it, asking it further questions, speculating, making creative leaps of ideas, and pulling ideas and findings together.
- Some of the solutions, conclusions and thoughts on future work – recommendations for others' developments, actions and explorations beyond the scope of the dissertation or thesis.

The narrative focus explores problems and surprises, changes in approach and unexpected hitches, looking at how and why the research proceeded or proceeds as it does. When they have finished, the dissertation or thesis will read like a story or journey. Keeping a log or journal helps inform awareness of the stages, and for those undertaking a viva, the journey could be a theme or section of the argument running through the developing dissertation or thesis so that each element articulates with, links together, draws from and is connected to each other element and a reader is able to follow the argument from questions or hypotheses through what can be asked of and interpreted from the data, and turned into findings. The argument coheres throughout, and new ideas, theories, data and interpretation contribute to it, not for their own sake. The student's written argument is the spine, the central point around which all the dialogue, evidence, statements and findings circle. Apart from commenting on the journeying research processes, they do not need to write about all the other details and information met while going about their research, except and only when it relates and contributes to the argument.

▶ Discipline differences

There are differences between dissertations and theses in different fields of study. Humanities dissertations and theses tend to concentrate on exploration of arguments in a storyline throughout, rather than having extensive sections on methods and findings. Often conclusions are used as a way of conceptualising the contribution and worth of what the student has found and shown overall, proven and well-founded in the reading.

Social science and health-related dissertations and theses tend to have more complex defences of methodologies and methods, more explicit chapters detailing both factual findings (data from fieldwork) and conceptual findings (how this contributes to debates in the field, to knowledge, and the overall meaning of what they have developed and discovered).

Science dissertations tend to set up a hypothesis, establish the theoretical underpinning and list the methods. Less defence is needed with typical experimental methods and processes, so students present data, analyse and draw findings and conclusions from these. Chapters in science dissertations and theses are more likely to be concerned with looking at, analysing and interpreting information and data and moving conclusions forward to new stages of investigation than coming to some proven contributions and suggesting further work.

Models

It will certainly benefit your student to look at other people's dissertations and theses in similar areas. These will probably be lodged in the university library. Suggest they do not get too embroiled in the arguments, but to look at them for shape: the abstract; the way the arguments are introduced and maintained between chapters; how the introduction sets the scene and conceptualises the work; how the conclusion contains both factual and conceptual conclusions; and how the scholarly apparatus of references, appendices, etc. operates.

Activity

Look at a number of dissertations or theses in areas similar to their own and to think carefully about the following aspects:

- the shape
- the introduction
- how to produce an abstract for this field of study
- the conclusions
- how they deal with conceptual findings and contribution to knowledge
- how links in terms of underpinning theories informing the work, and emerging themes can be traced through the dissertation or thesis.
- look backwards and forwards between the beginnings and ends of chapters to see how arguments are introduced, linked, changed and developed in the text.

It is advisable to read a couple of introductions to see how context, ideas, questions, arguments and contribution to knowledge are established, and to consider conclusions to see how both factual and conceptual conclusions are developed. Finally, students can look back to the research question and the thesis / dissertation as a whole, focusing on its overall, internal coherence.

▶ A basic plan for a dissertation or thesis

A typical plan for a dissertation or thesis would look something like this:

- title
- abstract
- preface/acknowledgements
- introduction
- theoretical perspectives (containing the literature review – in dialogue with your arguments)
- methodology and methods (including the design of the study, sample, timings, choices made)
- presentation of results, findings, data
  - separate chapters in science
  - intermixed in a dialogue for social sciences and humanities

- discussion of results, findings, data
- conclusion, containing a summary, factual and conceptual conclusions and possibly recommendations
- appendices/statistical tables and illustrations
- references and bibliography

Advice to student

Running through a dissertation or thesis is an argument and a narrative or storyline that develops by linking the underpinning reading, themes, theories, ideas, methods, findings and arguments together. Students should get into the habit of going back and forth through the dissertation or thesis as they write it up and edit carefully to ensure that this coherence develops – taking a reader clearly and logically through the work.

Activity

Ask your students to consider the following questions:

- Look back over the research questions formulated and the brief outline of what the dissertation or thesis will be about, at your developed proposal, especially the theoretical perspectives element
- How clear is this?
- How logical is it?
- What is the gap in knowledge that the research addresses?
- What are the boundaries?
- What methods are being used and why, or not being used and why?
- What is the scope of the work and what other or further work is there for others to do?
- What shape should the dissertation or thesis take and why?
- Will any appendices be needed; what sort and why?

In the period before the viva (if the student is undertaking a PhD thesis), the conceptual framework may need some revision and clarifying so the student is ready to articulate it when asked (see Chapter 20). For *all* students the framework must clearly underpin their work so that even in the conclusion it is evident that conceptual conclusions (adding to understanding, meaning and theorising) can be drawn *as well as* factual conclusions.

6 Enabling Students to Carry Out a Successful Literature Review and a Theoretical Perspectives Chapter

The process of the literature review involves the researcher in exploring the literature to establish the status quo, formulate a problem or research enquiry, define the value of pursuing the line of enquiry established, and compare the findings and ideas with his or her own. The product involves the synthesis of the work of others in a form which demonstrates the accomplishment of the exploratory process.   (Andresen, 1997)

A successful literature review engages students in a dialogue with writing and arguments in their field and helps to set the pattern of critical thinking and good writing. It is the vehicle for identifying reading, and beginning to make use of others' arguments, and the work of key theorists whose theories and interpretations will guide the focus and analysis of the student's own research and arguments.

This chapter considers:

- *what constitutes a literature review and how it differs from a theoretical perspectives chapter*
- *how we might encourage students to undertake a successful literature review*
- *literature searching*
- *the ongoing literature review throughout the dissertation or thesis*
- *engaging students' own work with the literature – summarising, analysing*
- *critical evaluation, contributing and engaging in* dialogue

Students frequently mistake a literature review for a semi-annotated list of books that they summarise and write about, so showing they have read in the field. When we ask them to go off and read certain texts or find out and forage for literature that is both absolutely fundamental and topical in their area, we are actually asking them to engage in the academic community, to enter into a dialogue with work in the field, rather than undertaking a note-taking exercise. However, since much reading takes place early on in their work, by way of an introduction to the field, students can tend to feel that a rather sterile record of literature is required. Students might not be fully aware of the debates at this stage, and may feel that, as they are starting out in their research, they have little to contribute to an established field or ongoing arguments. However, becoming involved in debates is essential if their work is to make a contribution to knowledge in the field. They need to enter discussion about the topic and question they have chosen, knowing their work will engage in dialogue with established, ongoing literature. An old habit of accumulation-oriented note-taking will not provide the basis for this informed dialogue. Students need to determine a series of themes, arguments, paradoxes, dilemmas and key issues. To do this they must read critically. The supervisor's role is to engender interest in critical reading and engagement to feed into their developing work, encouraging a critical, problematising, analytical, reflective attitude.

There are several reasons for literature reviews. Students need to read themselves into the field of study in order to gauge where their own ideas fit, what can inform them, what others think and have discovered, and in what ways their area of questioning and research could contribute to existing knowledge. This might seem a tall order, because they cannot possibly read everything that has been written in their field of study, and probably, unless it is very specialised, not everything about their particular area. By searching out the literature to which their own work will contribute, they are not trying to cover and summarise everything. This would be an endless, daunting and ultimately pointless task. They need to read the background literature to contextualise and underpin their own work rather than substitute for it. This indicates to readers and examiners that they know the field and have something to contribute to it.

You might like to focus your student on the importance of the literature review as a way into managing reading, entering critical debates, keeping good notes, and writing critically. Some universities produce guidelines for students; the box illustrates one from the London University Institute of Education.

Activity

This exercise will guage the skills students have to conduct a literature review.

What skills do you have already and what do you need to develop?

- literature searching
- finding and using subject indexes and abstracting databases
- selective, analytical use of the academic online service provided by the library to access journal articles
- searching via the internet more broadly
- quick and effective reading
- summarising
- reference-keeping
- interweaving reading and notes into arguments and discussions

---

Review of relevant literature

Candidates should demonstrate that they have detailed knowledge of original sources, have a thorough knowledge of the field, and understand the main theoretical and methodological issues. There should not be undue dependence on secondary sources.

The literature review should be more than a catalogue of the literature. It should contain a critical, analytic approach, with an understanding of sources of error and differences of opinion. The literature review should not be over-inclusive. It should not cover non-essential literature nor contain irrelevant digressions. Studies recognised as key or seminal in the field of enquiry should not be ignored. However, a student should not be penalised for omitting to review research published immediately before the thesis was submitted.

A good literature review will be succinct, penetrating and challenging to read.

Source: http://www.ioe.ac.uk/doctoralschool/info-viva.htm)

Literature reviews or theoretical perspectives chapters differ to some extent in different fields of study or subject areas. The sciences and social sciences require extensive literature searching and review before the research question is posed. The literature tends to be written up in a separate chapter at the beginning of the thesis, known as the theoretical perspectives chapter, to establish key theories against which the argument and research are developed. In the humanities, extensive reading is also required, but will be filtered into the introduction, establishing the theoretical background, underpinning theories and critical approaches. Key theorists informing the thesis will appear both in the introduction – setting the scene for research questions and major arguments of the research and thesis – and then throughout the work itself, taking different elements of the thesis argument on in different places and providing a coherent thread of reference for key arguments and ideas. For all dissertations and theses, theories and theorists, the literature of the field is referred to throughout in a coherent fashion.

Students must not stop reading early on as if it were only a stage in the research, but should be encouraged to keep reading throughout. It is perfectly possible that new discoveries or key texts will appear close to the end of their work, and students will need to acknowledge these, if only to say that they could not be incorporated into the research design because of when they were produced. This shows they have an awareness of the field, of the learning conversations taking place within it, and can see where their own work contributes.

▶ The literature review in the arts and humanities

A literature review or theoretical perspectives chapter in English and other Arts or Humanities fields would be likely to involve discussion of the methods of critical approaches derived from, for example, postcolonial theorists, or feminist theorists, structuralists, deconstructionists, etc., whose work is being used to ask questions. For example, a literature thesis looking at the ways elements of texts engage with their context might well be using key theorists such as Foucault, Bakhtin and Said, and establishing, for instance, Marxist historicist or postcolonial ways of reading, and critical analysis. The ways the texts (the subject of the study) will be read and debated, are, then, informed and indicated by the theorists themselves throughout. Arguments would be established in an introduction incorporating the theoretical perspectives, and interacting throughout the whole thesis. A methodology chapter as such would not be needed, unless different research methods were used, for example by using interviews as well as textual or artefact analysis.

Literature reviews establish background and context, involving reflection and analysis. This is the place to indicate where the student's enquiry and research will be located, and what underpins it, rather than to discuss any findings. A literature review: 'seeks to describe, summarise, evaluate, clarify and/or integrate the content of primary reports' (Cooper, 1985, p. 8).

According to Andresen the purposes of a literature review are:

- becoming familiar with the 'conversation'; in the subject area of interest
- identifying an appropriate research question
- ascertaining the nature of previous research and issues surrounding the research question
- finding evidence in the academic discourse to establish a need for the proposed research
- keeping abreast of ongoing work in the area of interest

(Andresen, 1997, p. 48)

An essential part of planning a student's research, the literature review helps them develop their own line of thought, keep abreast of progress in their subject and field, and make contact with others working in the same field. Examiners looking for how far a thesis or dissertation contributes to knowledge in the field will concentrate on the literature review or theoretical perspectives chapter in the first instance, then seek to find theories and arguments woven throughout, finally tied up with the conceptual conclusions. Being able to develop a critical hierarchy of works read and used, of key theories and themes, and more peripheral theories, themes and arguments is an important task for students, whose work needs to be focused and coherent.

▶ Literature searching – the library and internet

There are several activities associated with handling a literature review or theoretical perspectives chapter. Literature searching is one activity.

Students need to explore their university library and associated libraries, using a computer to help search in online journals, and academic online catalogues, although this never substitutes completely for investigating shelves close to a useful book. Supervisors could advise students to look in the reference sections of key books and articles they are using, and of others' theses on similar topics. Here they might find something that could be a minor reference for others' work but could possibly be a key background reference for their own, due to differing lines of argument. Put students in touch with specialist librarians to run a literature searching session for them, or advise them yourself, showing them how to use the academic online journals, going through the library using Athens or other passwords so they can access whole essays and abstracts rather than just odd postings to the web. Using email and the web to keep in touch with other researchers and their supervisors is also important (see Chapter 13).

There is often too much information on the web, it is not quality-controlled and it is unlikely to be organised so students can use it – so they need to be careful with managing, organising and sifting it. Students who merely download topical material are plagiarising.

Activity

Ask your students:

- whether they used libraries, CD ROMs and the internet for research before
- which libraries they might need to join and whether they need a letter of reference, signed by you, to gain access to another local university library, for example in their home town
- what experience they have of accessing subject indexes and abstracting databases; for example, having an Athens password to access journals, etc., online
- whether they need to gain, develop or update their skills in using internet online archives, online subject indexes?

Online literature searching
In your own library

Although the software will differ, libraries carry online public access catalogues (OPAC) to help students search the library using, for example, author, keyword, subject or book title. COPAC (for UK students) enables students to search a number of university library holdings, and your university might also have an agreement with specific other libraries for such searches and exchanges. If students want to order books or journals they can do so through the library interloan service, which collects items from libraries with copyright collections, for example the Brtitish Library at Boston Spa (UK). There is often a charge, and a heavy fine for the late return of books, although journal articles (copies) can usually be kept.

Ask the library about online journals and information databases. The former is a cheap way for publishers to enable readers to access writing in their field. Tantalisingly, often only extracts or abstracts appear, but you can usually identify suitable essays and can either order them through interloan or find them in their entirety by going through the various information gateways. Information databases are exclusive and are bought by libraries. They can be searched using keywords.

Via the internet
Your students will need some familiarity with and access to a computer and browser (e.g. Netscape Navigator www.netscape.com/download or Microsoft Internet Explorer www.microsoft.com/windows/ie/default/htm). If they are working from home they will need to be signed up to an Internet Service Provider (ISP). They will also need to find which search engine they feel comfortable with: for example Alta Vista (www.altavista.com) or Google (www.google.com).

Accurate searching requires a little know-how and plenty of practice. Using exact keywords, quote marks or a + sign will help to limit what could be a huge list of hits. On a search for 'werewolves', I found a great deal of unnecessary items about wolves generally, and some rather nasty pornography (you will, it seems, *always* find pornography whatever search item you put in, even if university computers have filters). Ninety per cent of what I found was totally irrelevant for my work: sifting is crucial.

As a student's research becomes more focused and specialised, it is possible to look at academic databases straightaway. BUBL can be accessed at: www.bubl.ac.uk/link and there are many more specialised websites and databases for the sciences, social sciences, medicine and art, for example the social science information database: www.sosig.ac.uk.

Library online portals or gateways usually list many of these online websites of databases for students to access. In the UK, the various subject centres and funding agencies have websites that can be searched for articles and recently published reports, or discussion documents. For learning and teaching, for example, try the Institute for Learning and Teaching in Higher Education (ILTHE) website: www.ilthe.ac.uk.

Students will also need to consider how to handle the information they gain in their literature searching throughout the research. One model suggests they acquire a great deal of information, summarise the key points, keep careful references, and write the introductory literature review from this. Another view is that, as the literature review process is ongoing throughout their work, they will need to keep returning to the field and reviewing and re-reading, certainly catching up on new texts, and new areas of study that become more obviously relevant as their work proceeds. A reflective approach to literature searching is the most useful, that is. one

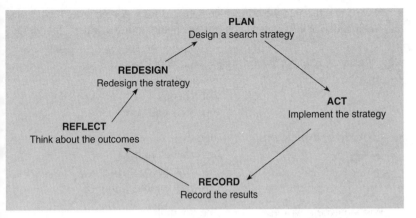

FIGURE 6.1 REFLECTIVE LITERATURE SEARCHING MODEL
SOURCE: ANDRESEN, 1997, P. 16, INFLUENCED BY KOLB (1984).

that enables them to develop a cyclical approach: searching, paradigm processing and researching as new sources or new ideas become clear (Figure 6.1).

Literature searching leads to the incorporation of ideas, quotations, arguments and references into student'sown work. They will need to establish a sound set of study and working strategies to make full use of this.

Some examples of searching and reading

After you have assessed what literature searching and analysing skills your students have, perhaps using the two activities earlier in this chapter, you could ask them to look at the examples below and identify books, articles, chapters, etc. that they have found in each of the following places for their theoretical perspectives chapter.

- the university library and other specialist libraries (perhaps via online catalogues)
- their own bookshelves
- academic elements of the internet
- catalogues of holdings
- bookshops, including Amazon online

Starting with a broad area, work out which aspects, theories, theorists and writers come to mind immediately to start researching. We will consider an example:

My research is into ways in which South African women writers expressed their sense of identity and cultural belonging during and post-apartheid."

Map of areas of reading: subject, concepts, authors

- Apartheid writers:　　　　　　Bessie Head
　　　　　　　　　　　　　　　Zoe Wicomb
　　　　　　　　　　　　　　　Ingrid de Kok

- Looking for expressions of:　　identity
　　　　　　　　　　　　　　　cultural belonging
　　　　　　　　　　　　　　　　– what prevents this
　　　　　　　　　　　　　　　　– what enables this

- Post-apartheid writers:　　　　Zoe Wicomb
　　　　　　　　　　　　　　　Ingrid de Kok
　　　　　　　　　　　　　　　Farida Karodia
　　　　　　　　　　　　　　　'Like a House on Fire' collection
　　　　　　　　　　　　　　　What else?

These are just some writers and a few ideas about texts. More can hopefully be found, and some might only be available by contacting South African bookshops (e.g. Clarke's in Capetown, who have an online catalogue).

Another question can be posed: are there any specific forms of their writing, such as:

- life-writing, semi-fictional, autobiographical
- political treatise.

Now it will be necessary to discover some reference to life-writing, etc., in other writers, some critical work (for example *Autographs* by Gillian Whitlock), or some examples on the web.

Theoretical issues and theorists

In this example, it will also be necessary to consider how to underpin the thesis writing using theoretical perspectives and theorists. These are a few which come to mind:

- Postcolonial theory　　　　　Childs, Williams, Said, Tiffin, Fanon, Kristeva
- Postcolonial feminist theory　Suleri, Spivak, Smith, Trinh Minh-Ha
- Identity theory　　　　　　　?
- Cultural belonging theory　　?

Some interesting information has been found while searching the post-colonial and feminist areas and some of the books will have been found or their position identified, but it still remains to trawl the library and the web to find key theorists in the other two areas, which in this case intersect with the original interests and question.

The next move is to consider narrowing and focusing the search on the specific examples needed, and broadening it to fill in the context.

- **Narrow search**: theorists and background reading in relation to the forms of their writing, i.e. life writing, semi-fictionalised, autobiography, political treatise, etc.
- **Broaden search** for background, e.g. culture, history, politics, other Black women writers dealing with identity, cultural belonging and or using life writing or other forms.

Note that once some of the reading has been completed, it will be necessary to sift out and extract the aspects relevant to the research project, but he student will have a broader underlying knowledge enhancing what he or she is able to write and argue.

Activity

You might find it useful to consider your *own* research area, brainstorm it and identify where you would find theories and coherent information. Next, work with your students in their topic area or another quite different area to practise searching.

▶ Searching, using and referencing

Figure 6.2 illustrates in diagrammatic form the brainstorming and searching process.

Note taking activity
Students can usually take one photocopy of a journal article under copyright law. They will need, however, to take notes from and 'process' journal articles, books, chapters and other sources. You might think of working with individuals or a group to enable them to try the 'SQ3R' note-taking and processing method:

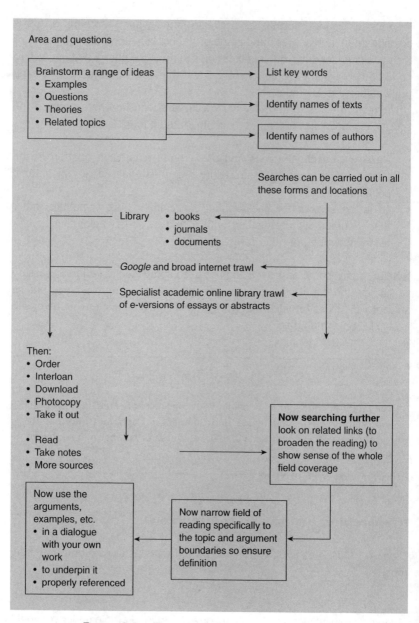

FIGURE 6.2 BRAINSTORMING A LITERATURE SEARCH

- **Survey** – quick read through
- **Question** – what was that about?
- **Re-read** – look through it all, reading it carefully; re-read only if necessary.
- **Record**
  Take notes under main key headings (having identified these main points in the survey); take full quotations and full citations of other references to be followed up.
  – Summarise major arguments and quote to refer – always indicate with references where the ideas and the quotations come from.
- – Make some sub-notes and discussion points alongside these notes. Underline or highlight in colour the main ideas and arguments.
- – Start to structure the notes and process the arguments – under keywords, headings, linked elements of an argument.
- **Review** – a quick look back at the piece to check that the most important points and the main arguments have been caught; has everything required been noted? have the references been recorded appropriately? are the quotations correct? has anything been missed? (Sometimes a holistic sense of the discussions or continuation of the piece emerges at this stage.)

Critical evaluation

Guided note taking of the main points of an article or book chapter is only the first part of a student's work, followed by making summarised notes and their selective use. Critical evaluation of the article or chapter for use in a dialogue with other work in the field and with the student's own research is also essential.

Filing

Students need to keep full informative notes, either a card index file (rather old fashioned but good for those less comfortable with a computer), or on their computer, noting all the sources they consult, their contacts and correspondences.

Keeping notes from reading up to date and carefully referenced on a regular basis will help students to remain engaged with the literature in a dialogue with their own work. Management of reading on a computer is one good way to both compile and reference reading; suitable software programs include Procit, Notebook, Reference manager and Scholars Aid.

Cataloguing reading

Students should establish a list of headings that fit their research – subjects, questions, theories, methodology and methods, etc. It is also important that

---

Good research habits

Students need to ask themselves regularly, have I:

- updated my literature search and review?
- returned to key sources to investigate further what have emerged as important issues?
- fully and accurately recorded the references I have found?
- been writing up and using what I have found, using the ideas and spurring on more of my own ideas?
- been leaving my reading to stockpile (and possibly go stale!)

(Wisker, 2001)

---

they read papers and parts of books as soon as they get them and assign headings to the material so that they can record it and later access it via these appropriate headings, for example:

- author
- title
- methods
- keywords and areas
- date of publication
- contribution to arguments in the field (e.g. 'discourse with Lacan over self-image').

Activity

Carrying out the beginnings of a review of a piece of literature:

- Trawl through (i) library, (ii) internet, (iii) online academic journals
- Select a journal article relating to the area of research
- Process it using the SQ3R methods (see above)
- Write down the key points, and the full citation details – the author, subject, etc. *on an index card*
- Decide where and under which headings (author, keywords, area of argument, methods, etc.) to store the information so that it can be retrieved when writing chapters
- Summarise the main argument as it relates to the current research interest. Note briefly any other areas of argument it touches on (you ight need to return to this to use it for something else).

Students need to link these headings and areas to their file management system so that when the system is interrogated it indicates work collected under the appropriate heading as required.

This is obviously more sophisticated than a card index file, which tends to force the keeping of information under author in alphabetical order, making it difficult to go straight to information on a particular subject area. Card index files, however, are portable, cheap, and can be marvellously idiosyncratic. Students will need to find the system that suits them and that they can manage. The most important element of any storage system is that the students have the information they will later want to retrieve – so ensure that they are aware of the need to acquire and keep information.

▶ Ensuring the use of literature engages in a dialogue with the student's own work

Select two essays in the student's own subject area that relate to the student's topic. Ask them to carry out the following activity, which encourages them to discriminate between two different kinds of use of literature in their own research work. One published example should be a rather dead set of notes or little more than a linked run through references on different essays or books, that is which does not engage in any kind of dialogue with the argument and so would be difficult to engage with the student's own work. The other should interweave references to different texts, building on the different points of view and the developing themes they represent. The researcher's own work should be seen as possibly contributing to this dialogue. This second example should act as a model for the students' own use of literature in their theoretical perspectives chapter or section of their thesis or dissertation.

If students can do this activity in a group then they can discuss their responses to the different texts, collect these together on a flip chart and review the pros and cons of each piece of text, and compare suggestions of good practice in a literature survey, review or theoretical perspectives chapter or section.

A good theoretical perspective or literature survey chapter should:

- not be a dead list of annotated comments about texts but an ongoing dialogue with the experts, theorists and theories underpinning *the student's* research
- indicate that the student has read widely (more than is needed) for context and debates

- shows that the library and internet have been utilised selectively but thoroughly for sources
- be firmly based on careful notes and recorded sources
- summarise only in order to engage in critical debate – showing how arguments arise from, relate to, and are underpinned by the experts in terms of subject, themes and methods.

Activity

Ask your students to read the examples you have chosen of essays that use a wide variety of literature and then consider the following questions:

- How do they use the literature?
- Is it a dead list, organised, only summarised?
- Is it vague? Too broad? Too narrow? Disorganised? Reading too widely?
- Do they summarise to add to debate or not?
- Do the texts read and presented within these essays engage with the arguments developed by the author? Or do they only look like a book list?

Further Reading

Andreson, L. W. (1997) *Highways to Postgraduate Supervision* (Sydney: University of Western Sydney).

Basch, R. and Bates, M. E. (2000) *Researching Online for Dummies* (Foster City, CA: IDG Books).

Cooke, A. (1999) *A Guide to Finding Quality Information on the Internet: Selection of Evaluation Strategies* (London: Library Association Publishing).

Greenfield, T. (ed.) (2002) *Research Methods for Postgraduates* (London: Edward Arnold).

London University Institute of Education: www.ioe.ac.uk/doctoralschool/info-viva.htm

7 Methodology, Methods and Ethics

Helping students to select appropriate methodologies and methods for their research is one of the key roles of the supervisor, supported by expert others, and research development programmes. The supervisory role alsoinvolves advising students on how to research in an ethical manner.

> *This chapter considers:*
>
> * *how to help students to choose appropriate methodologies and methods for their research*
> * *how to take ethics into consideration.*

There is insufficient space in a book of this nature to cover the enormous range of methodologies and methods that students might could conceivably use to address their research questions. Similarly, it would be impossible to do justice to the complexity of issues, needs and problems that could arise in your own practice with students. However, you will have expertise in a range of methodologies and methods that will be discussed here in an introductory manner and could be worked on developmentally, should the need arise, by taking part in supervisory development programmes, and consulting appropriate books. A self-reflective audit could be a first step, and you could subsequently repeat the audit with your student.

▶ Terminology

It can also be useful to work with students to help them clarify some of the key terms that are used, often rather confusingly, in research, especially those fundamental terms that relate to one's philosophical view of the world,

---

Task: Methodology and methods exercise

Consider:

1 Which of the following methodologies and methods do you use and feel confident about in your own research?
2 On which methodologies and methods could you offer some advice and support to others?
3 Which would you like to know more about, in terms of being made aware of further reading or courses?
4 Which ones provide problems or concerns for you?

List (please feel free to add to this list)
- Experimental research methods
- Ethnography
- Action research
- Phenomenography
- Inductive research
- Deductive research
- Quantitative research
- Qualitative research
- Combining across methodologies and across methods
- Grounded theory
- Interviews
- Questionnaires
- Focus groups
- Case studies
- Observation
- Participant observation
- Documentary analysis
- Textual analysis and criticism
- Synectics
- Others . . .

---

which tend to underlie personal research approaches, constructions, interpretations of the world, evidence and research findings.

Broadly speaking, there is a continuum from our sense of reality or 'being in the world' (ontology), through our versions of what constitutes knowledge in the world (epistemology), to the methodology that might be used (positivist, post-positivist, inductive, deductive and so on) to enquire about the world and then on to the methods used to action an enquiry (interview, questionnaire, experiments, documentary textual analysis, etc.).

One end of the continuum is philosophical, the other is immensely practical; that is, it streches from theory and thought to action and interpretation. Having a conversation with students about world views, beliefs about reading and evidence, and beliefs about how and what you can ask or can prove from research is not an academic indulgence but is an essential activity. Fundamentally, a researcher might, for instance, hold a view of the world that everything is describable, real, fixable and yet be asking research questions about shifting perceptions that need to be interpreted according to individual perspectives and differing contexts. For example, a *positivist* world view based on realism is one that would lead a student to believe their knowledge consists of discrete facts which can be pinned down, measured and quantified, and so phenomena can be understood. If students are then engaged in researching a political, social, psychological, philosophical, personally related, ultimately contextualised issue, they are quite likely to find they cannot fix a shared reading and measure evidence that proves a version of the world.

Let us take an example. Student J wants ultimately to contribute towards an improvement in Arab–Israeli relations, with research based on values, beliefs, perceptions and feelings, combined with cultural context. But, as a realist in a positivist research tradition, he seeks out a provable, fixable version of reality, of the world. He believes that he can find data that absolutely and accurately provide information – so he uses a questionnaire, but he is looking at values (which shift and are ill-expressed). He is destined to find he cannot capture the reality he seeks, only data about people's stated behaviours and actions. He is likely to *miss* what he seeks – values and a change in these values. His world view (ontology) has directed his sense of how and what constitutes knowledge (epistemology) into a version of methodology (positivist) and methods (questionnaires), which miss their aims and outcomes.

However, let us consider another example. Student F wishes to find out about sexual harassment in the kindergarten playground. Her assumptions are that it exists and that it is tolerated by the staff either because they do not recognise it or because they do not believe it to be a problem in this age group. She is therefore investigating the existence of a phenomenon, attitudes towards it and the behaviour of staff and children, both male and female. She knows she is studying something nebulous, contextual, to do with perception, so she *cannot* fix this reality with a questionnaire (nor would some of her subjects, children, be able to respond). Instead, she tries a mixture of quantitative and qualitative research methods – triangulation, to try and represent the phenomena. Observation enables her to see the harassment in process, and the categories she develops to analyse her observations allow her to fix certain kinds and levels of harassment, and of response in this (quite quantitative) method. Beyond that, she relies on looking at perceptions, attitudes, values, labels, interactions (very much post-positivist and phenomenographical) so she interviews using semi-structured (there are definite answers she wants to find out), open ended (but the interviews could yield some fascinating information she cannot predict) interviews with staff, with some focus group discussions with the children, where they explore their experiences and feelings about their experiences (values, perceptions, attitudes, rules, etc.).

Supervisors might find it useful to work with students to consider:

- **ontology** (position, being in the world) – do you feel secure in your identity, believe that reality is shared, or feel identity and 'reality' are contested constructions and representations we do or do not invest in?
- **epistemology** (knowledge construction) – how do you think knowledge is constructed and captured? How does this happen in your subject? In your view of the world and in context?
- **methodology** – will positivist, post-positivist, post-modernist, inductive or deductive methodology suit your research question?
- **methods** – what methods can help you ask this question?

Following this line of discussion and enquiry should help your student to determine the appropriate methodology and methods for their research. Various terms are explained further in Wisker (2001) and the bibliography of specialist texts to aid the use of particular methodologies, research strategies and vehicles.

▶ Questioning and defending methodology and methods

When your students reach the end of their research, they will be questioned about methodologies and methods.

Some of the questions that *could* appear in the viva, focusing on methodologies and methods, are considered below, accompanied by some hints and tips on how to approach your answers, and some comments giving the examiner's point of view. These questions can act as a useful checklist for students to ensure they reflect on why they have chosen which methodologies and methods to answer their research question. Additionally, the questions below give an indication of what an examiner reading a dissertation or thesis could be looking for. Finally, they can be adapted for use in a mock viva (see Hartley and Wisker, 2004, CD Rom).

(1) What methodologies and methods did you select and why?
Hints and tips

- Did you explain why you selected the methodologies and how they helped you to ask your research question?
- Did you explore how the methodologies were used in operation?
- Did you explain why you selected certain methods, what they enabled you to ask and answer, how you were able to combine methods to ask your question?
- Did you say why they were particularly appropriate for the kind of data you were seeking?

The Examiner's view
I want to discover why you selected the methodologies and the methods in order to ask your research question and conduct your research. I expect to hear a defence of the choices and an explanation as to why these methodologies and methods enabled you to approach their research area, to ask questions and to interpret the kinds of information and ideas which resulted from your research. It is important that you can defend your choices.

(2) Why did you not select other methodologies/methods?

(3) How did you gain access to your sample(s)?
Hints and tips

- Did you explain how you selected your sample?
- Did you explain how you persuaded your sample and/or those related to them (whether people or objects or animals) to take part in the research?
- Did you explain how you gained any necessary ethical clearance for your research?
- Did you explain actual details of physical access – timing, regularity, numbers and frequencies, etc?

The Examiner's view
This question seeks to find out how you gained access to your sample, whether people, animal, vegetables or objects, etc. I want to find out about the ways in which you gained ethical and other clearance for your work, which enabled you to gain access to your sample. I would like to know what

strategies you used to persuade others to take part or to allow them to use their materials, their animals, etc., and what kinds of permission you were involved in seeking.

▶ Ethical issues and practices in research

In the 21st century, most universities expect anyone undertaking research to do more than nod in the direction of ethics. In some respects, it could be argued that the procedures for ethical clearance could be so onerous and the bureaucracy so labyrinthine that students are put off carrying out research involving human subjects, however harmless and benign it might be. As a supervisor, you are very likely to be involved in supporting your students through ethical clearance.

Typical procedures and their history

Historically, students undertaking research involving human subjects in medical or health procedures would, as they still do, be expected to seek formal ethical approval. The aim of this is clear: to ensure that no research processes impinge on or infringe human rights, cause any kind of harm or reveal the confidential nature of the individual's involvement. Many health researchers comply with the Helsinki agreement that protects human subjects. Other researchers also now need to comply with similarly strict regulations.

Students undertaking action research are made aware of the need to involve their research subjects (not *objects*) as fully-aware participants who collaborate in and jointly own the results of the research and any interpretation or use of it. In much feminist research the same processes of agreement, openness and shared ownership are also commonplace. Many students carrying out experimental research using animal subjects have traditionally complied with complex scientific ethical procedures. Students engaging in research into text analysis are less likely to find they need any ethical clearance before carrying out their work. However, more students are involved now in multidisciplinary research, or research using a variety of methods. Text analysis accompanied by interviews of the authors would be a case in point. This latter method, using human subjects (in interview) would need ethical clearance, and a commitment that details are kept confidential, *or* are approved for release by the participant(s) by informed consent.

Universities have codes of practice and, often, ethics committees overseeing approval. You will need to guide your students on whether their work needs full ethical approval or not, and if it does, how to complete what could be a very lengthy application. Students are also strongly advised to do this in advance of the data collection because data *cannot* be collected until approval, if it is needed, is given. Applications could wait months for the next sitting of the ethics committee and any subsequent referral for clarification would hold up the entire research enterprise.

Supervisors should not only support students, but also help them with their timelines so that they are usefully carrying out literature reviews and other research, writing up methods chapters and so on, while awaiting approval (not idly waiting anxiously). There are apocryphal tales of students on Master's dissertations (6 months) who gained their ethical clearance at the point of submission. For PhDs there is, at least, a longer lead time.

Given in the box is an example of an ethics checklist from my own university for those research projects which are:

1   *not* merely library or literature based;
2   *not* being carried out in schools as part of a Higher Education course (when the project is approved by the appropriate school/college authorities);
3   using human subjects.

Ethics checklist

1   Does the study involve participants who are unable to give informed consent? (e.g. children, people with learning disabilities, unconscious patients)
2   Are drugs, placebos or other substances (e.g. food substances, vitamins) to be administered to the study participants?
3   Will the procedures use human tissue or include the penetration of a participant's skin or body orifices by any substance or device?
4   Will participants be presented with painful stimuli or high intensities of auditory, visual, electrical or other stimuli?
5   Could participants be required to undergo long periods of sleeplessness, confinement, sensory deprivation or any other form of stress?
6   Is there any foreseeable risk of physical, social or psychological harm to a participant arising from the procedure?
7   Will deception of participants be necessary during the study?
8   Will the study involve more than a minimal invasion of privacy or the accessing of confidential information about people without their permission?
9   Will the study involve NHS patients or staff?

(www.apu.ac.uk/research/gradsch/gshome.shtml)

Even if 'no' is the answer to all the questions on the checklist, when using human subjects postgraduates and staff send copies to the committee and complete a full ethics clearance form, in addition to producing participant information and participant consent forms. Undergraduates and taught postgraduates (those not doing dissertations) need not do this, but *all* staff and students must abide by the university's ethics rules: causing no harm, ensuring confidentiality, seeking participant compliance, and observing data protection regulations.

Typical questions on a request for ethics approval form

Completing an ethics approval form as part of a supervisory discussion helps students to focus on their research, and some sections can often be more or less filled in by copying and pasting in parts of the proposal. It is ultimately a useful metalearning activity because it foregrounds rationales of research and research design. In answering the questions on the form, students often realise flaws in their research design. Additionally, students are expected to develop: a participant information sheet; a contact letter; and a participant agreement/consent form. Human subject data must always be kept confidential – under lock and key or on a password-protected computer.

The checklist for ethical approval given in the box, could be used in a face-to-face discussion with students or expanded with space for answers for them to complete.

Request for ethics approval

- Briefly describe the rationale for and state the value of the research you wish to undertake
- Outline the sitability/qualifications of the researchers who will undertake the research
- What are the aims of the research?
- Briefly describe the overall design of the project
- Briefly describe the methods of data collection and analysis
- Describe the subjects: give the age range, gender and any particular characteristics pertinent to the research project. *For experimental studies indicate the inclusion and exclusion criteria*
- How will the subjects be selected and recruited?
- How many subjects will be involved? For experimental studies, specify how the sample size was determined. In clinical trials, a Power calculation must be included
- What procedures will be carried out on the subjects (if applicable)?

- What potential risks to the subjects do you foresee?
- How do you propose to ameliorate/deal with potential risks to subjects?
- What potential risks to the interests of the researchers do you foresee?
- How will you ameliorate/deal with potential risks to the interests of researchers?
- How will you brief and debrief participants? (*Attach copy of information to be given to participants*)
- Will informed consent be sought from subjects? **Yes** (Please attach a copy of the consent form) / **No**
- If there are doubts about subjects' abilities to give informed consent, what steps have you taken to ensure that they are willing to participate?
- If subjects are aged 18 years or under please describe how you will seek informed consent
- How will consent be recorded?
- Will subjects be informed of the right to withdraw without penalty? Yes / No
- How do you propose to ensure subjects' confidentiality and anonymity?
- How and where will data be stored?
- Will payments be made to subjects? **Yes/No**
- Modification of proposal
- Has the funding body been informed of and agreed to abide by APU Ethics Procedures and Standards? **Yes/No**
- Has the funder placed any restrictions on (a) the conduct of the research; (b) publication of results? **Yes/No**
- Are there any further points you wish to make in justification of the proposed research?

(www.apu.ac.uk/research/gradsch/gshome.shtml)

Students also need to think about whether they have ever had to 'do things' to research subjects as part of a research project organised by someone else. What is their role when it is not their research project?

Informed consent
Participants in research need to know the:

- purpose of the research
- exact procedures involved
- qualifications of the researchers
- funders of the research
- way in which the findings will be used
- consequences of not taking part in the research
- amount of time involved for participants
- effects on participants who do take part – will there be loss of dignity, side effects?

> To consent to something just means that you *agree* to it. But to give *informed* consent implies that you have sufficient information to make a valid judgement. (*Nursing Times*, 1992, p. iii)

Those who *cannot* give 'informed consent' include:

- people who do not speak fluent English and who do not have access to an interpreter
- children under the age of consent
- people who are either mentally handicapped or mentally ill
- people who are acutely ill, terminally ill or dying, and those who are very old, frail and infirm
- embryos, foetuses and the deceased.

> Not all these categories are clear-cut, and people vary a good deal in their capacity to make decisions. In many such cases, consent to participate in research would be obtained from guardians or next-of-kin. However, they might not be the best people to decide what is in the best interests of the client concerned. And nurses may find that they are asked to advise on whether their clients are able to give informed consent or not. (Robinson, *Nursing Times,* 1992, p. iv)

Ethics are broader than obvious harm, however:

> Eroding dignity and confidentiality are real issues in health research. Although the researcher is obliged to respect confidentiality, they are also obliged to disseminate results, including an account of what happened.
> This tends to be more of a problem if specific features of the research make the subjects easily identifiable. For example, the research might be about a new therapy available only in a few centres, or it might concern a

problem which affects only a very small group of people. Just as the researcher needs to take steps to ensure the people in the study cannot be identified as individuals, it is important for any practitioner involved in the research to make sure that the policy is maintained.   (Robinson, 1992, p. v)

Codes and committees

Because ethical issues can and do arise so frequently in research of any kind which involves human (or indeed any living) subjects, a number of general and specific codes of practice now exist.

> The production of ethical codes began after the Second World War when the horrific results of uncontrolled experimentation on human subjects carried out during the war was revealed. The Nuremburg Code of 1947 spelt out the principle of informed consent.   (Robinson, 1992, p. v)

The Declaration of Helsinki stipulates:

- clinical research should be based on adequate scientific principles and research design;
- the individual conducting research should be scientifically qualified;
- the inherent risk to subjects should be in proportion to the importance of the research objective.

Therapeutic research (benefits the research subject) and non-therapeutic research (has no obvious benefit to the subject) are distinguished, and stringent constraints are placed on researchers undertaking the latter.

  Ethics issues also include access and truth so, in some instances, students might find they either cannot get access to the people or information they need, or they meet a whitewashed situation, missing the real issues they set out to research. Considering access to pensions, Bulmer notes:

> Organizations as settings for research have a number of special features. They are bounded institutions to which one must seek, negotiate and gain access. Once admitted, the researcher must establish a workable and convincing role in which to gather data.   (Bulmer, 1988, p. 151, in Horn, 1996, p. 551)

Suspicion can result. Researchers in applied settings describe being seen as 'spies' (Hunt, 1984; Johnson, 1986; Warren, 1988). Initially, those being researched might be suspicious of a researcher in their midst. Lorraine Gelsthorpe (1990) recalls that the officers in the prison in which she was researching:

thought it was particularly devious of the government to employ 'women as spies' (p. 96), and she found it difficult to convince some officers that the researchers were not working for the government. Bryman (1988, p. 16) sees one of the chief difficulties of researching in organizations being that researchers are 'often seen as instruments of management who are there to evaluate or spy on their subjects and will report their findings back to senior officials'. The presence of a researcher is feared, writes Lee (1993) in his book on researching sensitive topics, because of the possibility that they will reveal deviant activities, and the researcher is seen as explicitly seeking such information.   (Horn, 1996, p. 551)

Power is as much an issue as access. Dingwall (1980) comments 'in a highly structured organization, such as the police, a "hierarchy of consent" can result in researchers obtaining official permission to conduct a study, but receiving only token co-operation from those lower down the hierarchy'. (Horn, 1996, p. 552).

Respondents should understand the aim of the study and feel that the researcher will listen to them and be trustworthy (Buchanan, Boddy and McCalman, 1988, p. 59). *Who* the student is might also help or hinder them, and they certainly must be honest about the role. Researchers have to establish themselves in an acceptable role and might have to undergo loyalty tests: 'Ethical issues arise from clashes between personal and professional interests' (Easterby-Smith *et al.*, 1991, p. 64).

Ethical problems may be greater, therefore, when researching a group whose values and world views are very different to one's own. In order to be accepted by the group, one must, to some extent, deceive them, in that one must appear to sympathize with their beliefs and the way they view the world.   (Horn, 1996, p. 552)

Role play can lead to compromise especially with groups at odds with the researcher's values. Alan Bryman notes that researchers 'brought up on a diet of text books and sanitized research reports sometimes report their feelings of something being wrong with themselves when things do not go according to plan. It may be far more responsible to make prospective researchers aware of such facts in advance than to imbue them with self-doubt as their plans go awry' (Bryman, 1988, p. 9). Ultimately, reflection and self-awareness result, enabling researchers to understand the processes of research and produce more credible results.

Organising appropriate methodologies and methods, as well as ensuring ethical clearance, consent and confidentiality are sensitive issues crucial to the researcher's own sense of involvement in and responsibility with the research, the field, sample, group and data. Sensitive negotiation of ethical issues is necessary to enable students to carry out useful (and safe) research.

▶ Further reading

Bryman, A. (ed.) (1988) *Doing Research in Organisations* (London: Routledge).

Buchanan, D., Boddy, D. and McCalman, J. (1988) 'Getting In, Getting On, Getting Out and Getting Back', in A. Bryman (ed.), *Doing Research in Organisations* (London: Routledge).

Gelsthorpe, L. (1990) 'Feminist methodologies in criminology: a new approach or old wine in new bottles?', in Gelsthorpe, L. and Morris, A. (eds), *Feminist Perspectives in Criminology* (Buckingham: Open University Press).

Horn, R. (1996) 'Negotiating research access to organisations', *The Psychologist*, December.

Lee, R. M. (1993) *Doing Research on Sensitive Topics* (London: Sage).

Robinson, K. (1992) 'R4: the real world of research', *Nursing Times*, 88.

8 Supervisory Dialogues

This chapter discusses the function of dialogues in supervision. Supervisory dialogues, whether face-to-face or through electronic/postal/textual means, are the main way in which we work with our students to encourage, direct, support and to empower them to get on with and complete their research and writing. In Chapter 2, we considered some of the roles and interactions between supervisor and students.

> *This chapter looks closely at supervisory dialogues of all kinds, and in particular at:*
>
> - *the importance of supervisory dialogues*
> - *the varieties of dialogue in relation to roles, stages of a student's work, personality, other factors and the kind of research the student is involved in*

Supervisory guidance for postgraduate and undergraduate students has become an important research area in the last few years, as the numbers of international and home-based postgraduates increase. The supervisory relationship is the primary one for ensuring a wealth of personal and cultural issues and experience are addressed, as much as for ensuring that students are guided and empowered to be autonomous learners engaged in a topic sufficient to gain an MPhil, EdD, PhD, Master's or first degree. For previous work in these areas see, Aspland and O'Donoghue (1994), Brown and Atkins (1988), Delamont and Eggleston (1983), Lowenthal and Wason (1977), Philips and Pugh (1994), Wason (1974), and Wisker (1998, 1999, 2000). For international students, in particular, different levels of dependency and need are also significant factors. Ballard and Clanchy (1984), and Ginsberg (1992) indicate that some Asian students, more used to the Confucian study model (particularly Chinese learners), are more likely to adopt learning approaches involving deference to authorities, accumulation of knowledge and a relatively uncritical approach, somewhat at odds with the problem-solving dialogue-with-experts mode of European and western research. These students might expect direction where a western student expects debate.

Other mismatches between students' expectations, preconceptions and the learning and research culture into which they are entering arise for both international and home-based students. Each could cause difficulties for student–supervisor relationships and the successful development of the research project. Potential difficulties arise as students move into different learning cultures and meet different learning expectations. This is probably particularly the case for postgraduates, whose study requires a learning leap and sustained focus on research, over time.

▶ Undergraduates and postgraduates

There is a variety of roles and interactions required for supervising undergraduate and postgraduate researchers. Research development and autonomy vary between levels, culturally and individually. Undergraduates are making first, significant steps into research methods, the management and planning of time and research processes, and writing up a substantial, significant piece of work. While we might assume postgraduates have already made their first steps, undergraduates will probably require more explicit guidance, more regular supervisions with more direction, and they have *very* limited time. However, they will also need to learn independence, research skills, time management and writing skills to produce coherent work. As we look at supervisory dialogues, it could be useful to consider what kinds of dialogues and roles, at which stages, suit your undergraduates and postgraduates.

The leap between undergraduate and Master's level work is matched by that between master's and postgraduate PhD/EdD/PrD, where greater autonomy and originality are required over a greater length of time for a longer, more significant project making a contribution to knowledge, justifying the award of a doctorate.

For students from professional practice, this can be a leap into *academic* work. Time is also an issue. Some students are given time to research, while others juggle full-time work with part-time research. Some work at a distance from their supervisors. Some expect the work they do will 'change the world' because of the scale of the project. This could lead to excessively grand aims and outcomes, and projects which are unmanageable in the time available (see Chapter 11). Such expectations can be so daunting that starting and maintaining work momentum seems almost impossible, and writing up, looks like a life's work.

All research is a dialogue with other experts. All research needs boundaries, to be realistic in its aims and outcomes and manageable in its scope. It does indeed feel like a life's work for many students, but for others it is a stage in their development as researchers, or a stage in their professional development – a vehicle for change and professional advancement. It is a time of all-consuming activity. As supervisors we need to be aware of various different motivational tensions, backgrounds and perceptions, as well as research practices, which our students bring to the research process. We need to engage in dialogue with students, encouraging them, in turn, to engage in dialogue with published work in the field. This is a tall order for the new supervisor, but if the student is to be successful, the supervisory relationship is to work, and the research outcomes are to be at the appropriate level, making a real contribution to knowledge, then negotiating practices, interaction and learning conversations based on both insights and good use of training, development and experience are essential.

Students' research is relatively autonomous. They need to be gradually weaned away from reliance upon supervisors once the project has been well-established and approved. Students also need development opportunities and guidance in research methods throughout their research process, with increased guidance and support as they complete, write up final drafts and submit their work.

Research students are engaged in dialogues not only with their supervisors but with other experts in their field, involving themselves in the contribution to knowledge. The development of high-level dialogue skills, both verbal and written, is essential for students and supervisors, or the outcomes and research product might only be a work of deference and synthesis. Students need to contribute to the knowledge and research culture in their fields, and to do this they need to develop dialogue skills. Many of these will begin in interactions with their supervisors, who draw out questions, engage in debates, set off trails of thought, help focus work and thought, and enable students both to conform to the needs of the research degree requirement and to conceptualise, plan, act and complete their work using the appropriate problem-solving, risk-taking, creative, original strategies.

▶ Supervision as a learning conversation

In many ways, supervision should be seen as a form of teaching, and research as a form of learning. However, supervision is far from the didactic teaching mode found in the Oxbridge tutorial model. Learning conversations between students and supervisor are dynamic and engaged.

In discussing varieties of supervisory relationships, Ingrid Moses cites Hartnett and Katz (1977) who suggest that staff should give more time to supervision and so 'assess the students' intellectual development'. That is not enough in itself. Supervisors should, say Hartnett and Katz, become more 'nurturing to postgraduates in both attitude and practice.' This means being aware and responding to 'the developmental and situational ambiguities in the lives of many graduate students' (Hartnett and Katz, 1977, p. 652).

Anthony Love and Annette Street see supervision as collaborative problem-solving. An integrative approach to postgraduate research education (1998, p. 149) better prepares students for the forthcoming world of work, where skills of collaborative working are more likely to be welcomed and useful to prospective employers than the isolated individualism of lone academics of the past. Their argument for the nurturing of collaborative skills relates largely to employability and lifelong learning.

> The problem-solving approach requires that both sides be able to take the perspective of the other reason and see the questions from his or her wisdom or viewpoint. This also wants the supervisor to be supportive and show real care for the learners while at the same time being as tough as possible on the problems they encounter. It is growth-oriented, and the unique perspective of the supervisor allows him or her to set goals that are designed to challenge the student, without being overwhelming or threatening. (Love and Street, 1998, p. 154)

My own arguments concur with these, but I would also stress the necessity of collaboration and interaction as collegial equals in order to empower students to undertake and maintain momentum with their own research, while ensuring that the responsibility and self-awareness this involves encourages them to own both process and outcomes. This process is begun when working with undergraduates engaged in research, although at this stage in their research learning careers and with a short project and time span, undergraduates usually need *more direction* and guidance than many postgraduates. Nonetheless, they also need to begin to enter the problem-solving experience, including development which 'ensures that the supervision is responsibility-focused, with the student moving from an almost entirely dependent situation in relation to the supervisor, to one of matter interdependency' (Stollenberg, McNeill, and Crethar, 1994). Love and Street (1998) see the interaction as matching that of organisation in life, avoiding individualism and seeking collaboration. Additionally, they recognise the difficulty of maintaining such a relationship when giving bad news which needs to lead to developmental responses:

there are times when the supervisors have to be very tough and let the candidate know when things are not going right. The ability to offer criticism and feedback, while still maintaining a developmental focus, is probably the most challenging task for a supervisor to accomplish. A balance has to be struck between being supportive and caring, yet tough on the problem.   (Love and Street, 1998, p. 155)

Learning contracts are indicated as a sound basis for proceeding to developmental and problem-solving interaction (see Chapter 4). They provide a way of objectifying and agreeing working relationships which, when things go wrong, can help both student and supervisor to agree ways forward.

In relation to student learning and project diversity, we need to consider ways we can develop 'productive learning conversations' at all stages of the student's research.

Supervisor colleagues from outside the UK have commented on the different tones that different cultures might find acceptable in supervisory dialogues and supervisory interactions. Research into supervisory dialogues (1998–2004), with international and UK students in dialogue with supervisors in a number of discipline areas (Wisker, Robinson, Trafford and Warnes, 2003) has led to the identification of interaction categories.

At different stages in a student's work, the supervisor needs to engage in a variety of modes of interaction: to guide, prescribe and inform, confront, elicit, clarify, support, summarise and move the student on. It is a dynamic, long-term human relationship between students, supervisors and a body of work. There are bound to be both learning leaps and blockages: there will be disagreements and times when students have to recognise that they have to fulfil certain requirements or recognise that progress is dependent on them and their ability to problem-solve, make choices, take risks, be original, and pull together ideas and information into a synthesis, and to engage what they have read in a dialogue with literature and theoretical underpinning. Following our thematic analysis of dialogues (Wisker, *et al.*, 2003), supervisory questioning themes were divided into 11 intervention categories, developing and drawing on John Heron's (1975) 'six-category intervention analysis':

- didactic
- prescriptive
- informative
- confronting
- tension-relieving/social
- encouraging and facilitating analysis and a critical approach

- eliciting
- supporting
- summarising
- clarifying
- collegial exchange.

Directing students too much removes autonomy. This is the students' own work and the aim is for them to learn the necessary skills to conduct research in the future. Explicit direction also removes ownership. A student who is very tightly directed, particularly at the stage of shaping the initial research proposal and design, might neither fully understand what you are telling them to do nor how to do it and might feel the research they are going to spend so much time on sounds more like yours than theirs. Dialogues need to match cognitive processes so each partner understands the other. The language of the dialogue must also be appropriate anf three forms are required: (i) *communicative language* in which the supervisor and student can discuss the developing work; (ii) *subject language* in which they can discuss specific subjects, approaches, issues, epistemology, knowledge construction and expression; (iii) *meta-language of research* – words such as 'conceptual framework' and 'doctorateness'. These need to be fully understood by students and used in their work so that, as it develops and when it is presented and defended, they can stand back, define and describe what they have been doing in a shared meta-language. It is in early stages of supervisory dialogues in particular that supervisor and student start to learn to respond to each other and to get inside each other's way of expressing, conceptualising, structuring and thinking – using these kinds of language. For students from countries different from the supervisor's, some language or tertiary literacy elements could complicate the process.

It is possible that the supervisor might take the process over, leaving students with a list of directives, a lot of writing on the text – with things to fix in some instances – and some confusion over exactly what is wanted. This could happen unless they have both matched language and cognitive processes and come to an agreement about what is to be done or changed, articulated, and written down by the student in their words and understanding. Some supervisors might be too eliciting and, as international colleagues have phrased it, too polite to indicate to students that there are questions to answer, problems to deal with and actual work to do here. In trying to encourage students to express their ideas and develop their thinking, supervisors might use only supportive and eliciting prompts but, by not being clear, directive, informative and prescriptive at key moments, leave the students still confused about what is to be done next, and how their work is *progressing*. Looking through the range of dialogues presented below, and thinking about how you could improve on the interactions, using your own words, could be a first step in developing that range of discourse useful to manage the most important work we do as supervisors.

Study of developmental supervisory dialogues (Wisker *et al.*, 2003) reveals that different kinds of interaction are necessary at different stages in a student's project, and at different stages in a single dialogue. Viewed holistically, dialogues often run through a variety of interactions, some informing, some eliciting. A variety of interactions is necessary for the development of the project discussion. It is very important that students are clearly aware of requirements, dates and rules, but it is also essential as that, largely independent learners, they are fully involved, creative partners in the inception, clarification, development and progression of the research, then of the interpretation of data and the drawing of conclusions. For ownership, responsibility and for the project to be the student's own, it could be preferable to have a high initial number of eliciting interactions, gradually evolving into the student taking control. However, sometimes it is necessary to challenge students in order to help them overcome sticky points, and to take learning leaps in their work.

Within single supervisions, supervisors and students can move through a variety of interaction categories and this could be seen as a repertoire.

Early conversations between supervisors and students

Early supervisions have three aims:

- establishing supervisory relationships and learning conversations to better enable future interactions
- focusing on students' development of the research proposal and conceptual frameworks to enable the development of an appropriate research design and scaffolding for their research;
- identifying skills and skills gaps in order to address these in future work on research methods and practices.

With the author's international cohorts of PhD students, there is a range of strategies that enable students to engage more fully with their own research, including research developmental programmes and supervisory dialogues. Individual dialogues are clearly focused initially on research questions, identifying a conceptual framework, choosing and defending methodologies and methods and second on developing aspects of the proposal to be effective, cohesive and realistic. The dialogues encourage students to describe their question, concepts, theories and methods.

At the beginning of research, dialogues seek clarity in planning and processes while later supervisory dialogues pinpoint and ask for logical connections to be made and argued through, asking students to 'tell the story' of the research, to develop and argue a visualisation of the research journey. Logic helps some students, for others metaphors help. In practice, some of the phrases we tend to use in different dialogue categories might sound like the following, but you will need to identify your *own* voice and expressions when deciding how and when to interact in which categories:

Didactic (teaches)	'The abstract should be only 500 words and you must ensure it is concise, clear, accessible to your examiners. Look at these models and try to produce a draft version following one of them.'
Prescriptive (prescribes a solution)	'No, don't cut the results part away from the discussion and interpretation. They need to be woven together.'
Informative (provides straight forward information about, e.g., dates)	'It needs to be referenced – using the Harvard system.' 'Ramsden & Entwistle would be good researchers to follow up here.'
Confronting (used if thereis a problem orissue which the student has not tackled after several suggestionsfrom the supervisor)	'Really, how do you think you are going to access this sample?' 'You have not yet made a realistic suggestion – there could be problems – how will you tackle them?' 'The statistics so far just don't answer your question. You must re-design the research for the next phase'.
Tension-relieving (often after a difficult exchange, at the start and finish of a supervision)	'Oh no! Not more of those bar charts!' 'How are you fitting all these interviews into your busy holiday schedule?!' 'Is your daughter well?!'
Encouraging and facilitating (developmental	'I see you have written about how Virginia Woolf engages with inner thoughts. Is this just a formal experiment in your view? or is she saying

comments to move the student on)	something about self, experience, and the ways we perceive and express it?' 'You have shown how widening participation agendas appear in government documents and in university mission statements. Do you perceive any contradictions, paradoxes or problems with the equally popular comments about fee payments?'
Eliciting (this draws out further comments)	'If you wanted to observe the children, how might you do this without affecting their behaviour?' 'Could you just explore what these different interview categories suggest in terms of your argument about disclosure?' 'What could happen next?!'
Supporting (these comments support a good idea by positive responses and help nurture a growing argument)	'This is an impressive participation rate.' 'The work is going well, you have responded critically and evaluatively to the results of your interviews and fed these into changes in your proposal. Good!'
Summarising (these comments help to mark a stage in the development and ownership of the research. They pull together and agree on work so far)	'It seems you have found a range of themes here and have analysed and discussed them according to the categories you have developed.' 'So, as you argue, Lacan's mirror phase is challenged from a feminist perspective by Kristeva's essays as quoted in your second chapter.....'
Clarifying (these comments support the student in clarifying terms, arguments, elements of the design or expression, etc.	'Are you arguing from your results in the two class-rooms you observed, that it seems girls are more likely to tidy up than boys? If so you probably need to . . .' 'I'm not sure what you are saying here about the effectiveness of that procedure on re-growing coral – could you revisit the data and then explicitly link it to your argument?' 'What do you mean here by the term

postcolonialism? Is it (a) in opposition to the colonial or (b) *after* the colonial?'

Collegial exchange 'This is a fascinating argument – have you looked
(as colleagues and at the work of Lave and Wenger on communities
equals, students and of practice? because it's absolutely central to what
supervisor discuss you are saying here.' 'There's a conference on the
reading, ideas, Gothic coming up in Liverpool in the summer –
research, differences, had you thought of giving a paper?' 'Yes, this is
agreements about the same kind of result I came up with after
interpretations) running the experiment 12 times – what did you
do to get over that problem about the water filter?'

These are examples of the various interactions, in practice, but they are in words that practising supervisors might use. You would need to find your own words to engage with each kind of interaction.

Activity 1

Look back at the 11 interaction categories on p. 000 and consider:
- Do you feel comfortable using all of these?
- Which ones do you use more frequently? Where? How? Why? to what ends?
- Which ones are you less likely to use? Why? Could you use them? Where and why?

Task

Look back at the research categories and then at examples of excerpts from supervisory dialogues:
- What is going on in these exchanges?
- Are students empowered?
- Are the dialogues clear? What else could be done or said?

Example of an early supervisory dialogue
Given below is an example of a dialogue between a supervisor and student

A, who is researching bullying in the playground among small children. She is a kindergarten teacher but her participants are not *her* classes. It is a first stage, second dialogue:

Supervisor: Yes, OK, because you're trying to fix something which will be quite hard to fix. I don't think you're a participant observer though. (*clarifying*)

A: No?

Supervisor: No, you're not a child – are you? (*confronting*)

A: No.

Supervisor: To be a participant observer you're meant to be the same as your group. You're an observer. (*informative, clarifying*)

A: Only an observer?

Supervisor: Yes. You're participating in the group of therapists or teachers, but you're not participating in the children's group as a child are you? (*clarifying*)

A: No but I can [??] (*too faint*)

Supervisor: Yes. But that means that you're not – I don't know what the term is, and I don't know what they're doing with it, but I think to be a participant observer you've got to be the same as your group. (*clarifying, informative*)

A: (*Too faint*) (*sounds of pages turning*). No, I wrote 'would be both an observer and a participant', OK . . .

Supervisor: Yes! But you're not a participant observer of the group of children, because you're not a member of the group of children. If you were a participant observer and a motorbike rider, you'd have to ride the motorbike. (*clarifying, informative*)

As this dialogue proceeds, the student becomes aware of the research methods and methodologies that might aid her in her research, and which of these to avoid. It is a clarifying and informative exchange.

There might well be more informative, didactic, prescriptive interactions with undergraduates who are working in a very tight timeframe and are starting out in research. However, with students producing first research work, dialogues also involve collegial interactions at the outset.

Supervisory dialogues towards completion
Learning conversations and supervisory dialogues towards the end of a postgraduate research project include dialogues clarifying the conceptual framework, contribution to knowledge and argument of the work, and mock vivas.

(see Chapter 21). Students indicate crucial change moments in the course of their research. In so doing, dialogue should enable them to reflect on the importance of development, on the significant changes they have made and how their learning and research fit into the overall critical framework of the research as a whole. Facing up to and identifying the effects of critical incidents moves learners on in their ownership of learning.

One way is approach dialogues towards completion is to ask the students to concentrate on 'telling the story' 'mapping the journey', and ensuring a clear conceptual framework running throughout. Students are encouraged to answer questions about their research question and aims; show how their conceptual framework springs from this; explain how their research methods have enabled them to action and direct their research, and demonstrate how their analyses, findings, and results grow from the question and methods. They describe the stages as a journey, with pitfalls and creative leaps, moments when the research fell into place. They indicate any problems experienced (most often these turn out to be related to methods). They could include observation that did not enable them to pinpoint specific change moments, and questionnaires which asked the wrong questions and generated heaps of relatively useless information. They discuss moments when they learned to jettison much of the information, focus in tightly down onto what mattered, adding further methods and vehicles if necessary.

Task

Look at the following dialogue. How is the supervisor working with student K? What kinds of interactions provide what kind of response? How successful do you think this could be in encouraging a critical attitude and enabling or empowering the student to move on in their work towards completion?

Student K

K: An exploration and they are very profound in many of her books. So, here I believe I should take quite an important look at the development.

Supervisor: Well, that's a chapter. (*clarifying and supporting*)

K: It's a chapter.

Supervisor:	What you've done so far with the construction of the thesis is chapters on books really. You've talked about . . . (*clarifying and supporting*)
K:	Chapters on book, yes.
Supervisor:	That's fine for starters, then you need to take the threads that run through these chapters on books and make the theme of the thread. (*prescribing*)
K:	Assembly.
Supervisor:	Yeah, the theme of the thread becomes the chapter and the books become examples within that chapter. So building the framework back in of course, think about the conceptual framework, if you're asking about dual identity and about her writing from a woman's point of view, you need to bring in theorists that are related to . . . (*prescribing and clarifying*)
Supervisor:	Well, there's still a way to go, but once you've got your theory in place I bet your re-writing won't be that . . . can I have your theory chapter when I see you in the Summer? (*supporting*)
K:	I hope so, I hope so.
Supervisor:	You might be coming for . . .
K:	I'd love to have my theory chapter by then.
Supervisor:	Yes, that would be a real step forward (*supporting*)
K:	How long should it be?
Supervisor:	6,000 words? (*informative*)
K:	That's about 10 pages, something like that, or more?
Supervisor:	12. ? (*informative*)
K:	12, doesn't matter.

This dialogue begins to focus the student on organising the writing, explores how the conceptual framework and argument can be expressed through construction of the thesis itself and finally ends up with a practical discussion of page numbers. The dialogue clarifies and moves the student on.

Students are also involved in peer support dialogues with their colleagues, family and critical friends. They can work supportively together shaping each other's research and providing peer feedback and support. These peer support opportunities can point to invaluable learning conversations (see Chapter 10 on peer support).

Supervisory dialogues are the major way supervisors work with students to support their development. The process seems to resemble a dance, building different dialogues at different stages in the student's work, getting inside how their question, conceptual framework and methods accumulate together in order to work *with* them to plan, action, reflect, evaluate, achieve and write up their research. If the supervisor 'takes over', students might not *own* or understand the research; if supervisors elicit excessively they might feel confused, unclear and not directed. In our research at APU with PhD students (Wisker *et al.*, 2003), three of us have noticed our styles becoming more flexible to match specific development, individual learning, and needs. It might be useful to consider the kinds of dialogues and interactions which suit *you* in your role as a supervisor with *your* student.

▶ **Further reading**

Heron, J. (1975) *Six Category Intervention Analysis* (London: Tavistock Institute).

Love, A. and Street, A., in Kiley, M. and Mullins, G. (eds) (1998), *Quality in Postgraduate Research: Managing the New Agenda* (University of Adelaide: Advisory Centre for University Education).

Wisker, G. (1999) 'Learning conceptions and strategies of postgraduate students (Israeli PhD students) and some steps towards encouraging and enabling their learning', Paper presented to the 2nd Postgraduate Experience Conference: Developing Research Capacity in the New South Africa, conference proceedings, Cape Town, South Africa.

9 Encouraging Good Writing

Learning how to develop an argument throughout a dissertation or thesis, and how to ensure an argument is organised, well expressed, informed by theory and backed up by appropriate evidence is crucial for a student. Let us look at ways in which we might support students in developing their writing skills through encouraging critical thinking, argument, writing strategies, clear expression, the development of their own voice, and engagement with and in the discourses of their subject(s).

> *This chapter considers:*
>
> - *the importance of critical thinking in writing*
> - *what constitutes good writing?*
> - *getting on and keeping going – supporting student writing*
> - *writing exercises*

Some people 'write like a dream', seemingly effortlessly structuring sound arguments, leading the reader from a carefully posed question through the exploration of debates in theories with experts in the field and developing a dialogue with them. They move on through clarification and argument of why specific theorists and arguments relate to their own developing work, frame it and drive it. They present contrasting arguments, linking these with their own original contribution, moving on into clearly explained and defended methodology and methods, through to a discussion of the data, drawing findings from it. They develop totally appropriate thematic comments arising from theory underpinning the questions they asked and the data produced, weaving argument and analysis in with the information, using data selectively, whether tabulated or in quotation from poets or interviewees. Their writing moves fluidly onto clear, logical, elegantly expressed discussion and expression of both factual and conceptual findings. Their factual findings both evidence and explain what has been discovered. The themes are present, the arguments exist. Their conceptual findings lead on from the research, contributing meaning, enhancing understanding, clarifying concepts and theories and taking them further. So, this suggests that, this contradicts and poses these further questions; we need to rethink our focus on this and that. And, elegantly again, the abstract indicates the area of research and its questions, why they matter, the theories involved, the ways in which the absolutely appropriate use of theory articulated in action through the right methodology and methods have shown this, argued this, contributed that.

Not everyone, however, is effortlessly perfect in their writing! Writing well or well enough is often very hard work, the result of drafting, re-drafting, editing and re-editing to finally make the words clearly express the arguments and ideas.

▶ Further encouraging students to write

Students often feel they have nothing to write about until they have finished their reading or research. This is dangerous nonsense! They might not be contributing stunningly original ideas yet, but the sooner they begin to write the more they will be able to reflect, alter, develop, jettison, add and hone what they have. Getting their ideas and arguments on paper helps *form* those ideas and arguments. All the literature on thesis or dissertation writing indicates that students need to be encouraged to start writing early and to learn the conventions of their disciplines in terms of how they write, what they write, the language they use and even the shape of the thesis or dissertation (Dunleavy, 2003; Murray, 2002). In the EdD or PrD and in some MAs, development is structured naturally and incrementally around a number of writing tasks building up into the final thesis or report. In PhDs, students are often expected to produce confirmation of candidature or other such work in progress that encourages them to write a well-structured and clearly organised and expressed piece. They are also expected to produce draft chapters for their supervisor.

Some researchers take a naturalistic approach, indicating that students construct themselves within the discipline. Murray (2002, p. 12) concurs, adding that each subject area represents a distinct 'discourse community'. Each thesis or dissertation sits not just within the distinct discourse community of the discipline but, also, within a smaller, no less complex, sub-set of that disciplinary discourse, their specialist area. Many students undertaking Master's and PhDs are combining across discipline discourses. Often postgraduate study is multidisciplinary or interdisciplinary and in that resides some of the originality. Students need to learn their way into the epistemology and discourse of their version of the discipline(s), in which their work sits. They also need to learn the meta-discourse of research and thesis writing itself; discourse foregrounding the journey of the research, the structural principles upon which it and the final thesis are based: conceptual frameworks; mapping; 'design of the study'; theoretical perspectives; and choices and defences of decisions made during the research, with explanations of the writer's own context and that of the topic. These areas of writing explain choices and directions. They also explain decisions on methods and structure.

In educational and social science research, students weave their way round a variety of established terms by which they can identify their methodology and methods. These include: inductive and deductive, triangulation, validity and reliability. Specific terms frame and focus the work, yet they are unlikely to be words used by either a scientist or a literature researcher, whereas, for the latter the actual process of research, the critical practice and the framing of questions, methods and decisions made about the approach are quite likely to be taken for granted, and are certainly not foregrounded in a metalanguage. Of course, in literary studies and performance arts, students might claim they have no need to be as 'jargon ridden' as their social science colleagues, but in fact they too ask research questions, develop theoretical perspectives, research designs, methods and conceptual frameworks, and need to make these evident to a reader to situate research arguments, ensuring that they focus and clarify the critical approaches taken. Perhaps the skeleton supporting the research, the methods, will be less of a topic, but some revelation of choices, approaches and conceptual frameworks actually helps to establish the direction, shape and significance of the research and its expression in all dissertations or theses and so should be encouraged.

Working with an English PhD group, I have found both an initial resistance to generic research development training because of this focus on metalanguage, and an eventual acceptance that a discipline-specific interpretation and utilisation of what it seeks to structure, discover and express can be developed. Sessions on defining research questions, on conceptual frameworks and on working towards the defence in a viva have worked well with this subject-specific group because they *can* interpret these terms as stages in their own work. For social scientists, it is rather like the Pompidou Centre in Paris: the pipes and workings are on the outside, visibly expressed from the start. Literature, performance and some humanities students need to make the implicit somewhat explicit, and to be encouraged to identify their conceptual and theoretical underpinning and the appropriateness of the methods they have chosen. Otherwise, they might be neither conscious of these aspects of their work and how they could use them again, nor able to articulate this in a viva.

▶ The well-written dissertation or thesis

The really elegant, well-structured thesis or dissertation argues a well-substantiated case throughout, and gives a sense of the coherence of the whole conceptual framework in action, as explored, with each paragraph and chapter indicating where the argument is going and where it has been. It interweaves the themes and underpinning concepts, theories and questions throughout, so that in the end there is a beautifully crafted, elegant piece, its arguments and themes running throughout like threads in a piece of weaving, motifs in a poem, or a piece of music. Additionally, it feels engaged and somewhat personal. It takes the reader on a journey of discovery. This might be a coherent and well-woven piece, but on reading it you also have the sense that there were decisions made, problems met and addressed if not overcome. Some things worked better than others, some things could not be discovered, while new revelations appeared as a result of the research itself. The research might have set out like a bit of a route map, a planned set of trips with dates, times and a journey foreseen, but in reading it and, if there is a viva, hearing it, we can see that actually it was vibrant, alive to discovery and danger. The finished piece reflects the corners turned, the journey, the explored nooks and crannies and whole vistas revealed (see Chapter 18).

This is an exuberant celebration of an ideal thesis or dissertation. But not all of our students and not all of us (I would dare to say) do write 'like a dream' and indeed, like good craftsfolk, even those who produce such fine work have actually had to craft, shape, mould and edit, edit, edit until the finished product emerges. For many, it is actually quite a difficult task to turn the gradually clearing ideas into questions, to engage in a dialogue with those experts whose work seems to have said it all, when it would appear more deferential to that work to summarise it and move on. It is a challenging task to identify the arguments between experts and theorists, to analyse, contrast, debate and *add* to what they say in terms of your own work.

▶ Notes, logs and journals

Keeping good notes is an important step in good writing. Referencing them well saves time searching at the end (see Chapter 6). Good notes should be focused on the subject, the topic, field notes from experiments and research activities, and notes on texts. These need to be augmented by notes about methods and methodology, and contextual underpinning. Students will then be able to explore and explain why and how they went about their research. If they have not kept notes of the 'nuts and bolts' of research, their reflection and evaluation will be more difficult. The twistings and turnings of the research need to be recorded in a log or journal. These feed into the parts of chapters exploring why and how research decisions are made. The activity of taking and reflecting on them can also prove useful if students lose their way, or have a writing block. Writing notes about thoughts, problems and decisions can generate writing energy contributing to the writing of the thesis itself. It is actually such a long slog doing a dissertation or thesis that the accumulation of information, quoting and detailing of what has been found can take over from putting it into perspective and extracting from it to illustrate a point. This set of ideas and evaluations could be used as a blue-print for action – something to head towards as well as, later, to reflect back on and see where the research, the dissertation or thesis developed.

▶ Activities with students

Even the eloquent and intellectually lively, rigorous, alert students can benefit from looking at a well-organised dissertation or a particularly well-argued paragraph as a model. To this effect, on the research development programme for the OU EdD, students and supervisors alike explore the construction and expression of literature 'reviews' (see Chapter 7). The session begins by analysing journal articles and moves on to define good practice, providing examples in action of carrying out work on literature reviews. On the postgraduate programme for International PhDs at APU, we conduct a similar exercise, additionally asking students to look closely at paragraphs in journal articles, considering where the links and arguments are, so they identify *when* a question moves clearly to an exploration and critical examination of experts and data, leading to conceptual as well as factual findings, in an argument. We look at published papers at the level of the sentence and paragraph as well as at the level of the paper as a whole. Analysis of published writing forms points for group discussion and individual reflection, and then feeds into individual writing tasks.

On APU's MA in women's studies, in the fourth, research-orientated module, students are encouraged to carry out three assessed writing tasks building on generic research strategies. On two Saturdays, all MA students work together on generic strategies such as turning topics into questions and developing conceptual frameworks. Taught sessions follow focusing on research strategies – interpreting the generic in a discipline-specific way. In this case, it means feminist research practices, which tend to be collaborative, non-invasive, often personalised in terms of language as well as focus, and ideologically driven and structured. Arguments underpinned by feminist criticism and critical apparatus are translated into the inter- or multidisciplinary focus of the research and students must learn a variety of discourses in which to express their research. Students learn to continue the variety of research methods, discourses and the metalanguage of research itself.

Specific sessions focus on research in progress. Everyone defines questions, clarifies conceptual frameworks, and explores which theorists to use and how, which methodologies will enable them to ask their questions, what kind of data analysis they need to use, and how to categorise, analyse and express arguments. Explaining to others gets the thoughts out into language. Writing it down *before* and altering *afterwards* helps the writing process.

The first piece of work is an annotated bibliography requiring students to select ten key texts they will be using and to explore them in a dialogue both with other specialists in the field(s) and, importantly, with their own intended work so they can see and show how and where they will engage with these writers. Of course, others will emerge, but this begins the practice of getting into a dialogue with experts, in relation to their own work. The second piece is a critical analysis or evaluative commentary on a key text, exploring the establishment of a question, an argument, theories and methods. Students go on to explain and explore how their *own* work will engage with this in dialogue. This gives them the opportunity to explore and express the shape of a piece of research and argument, see it from the inside, turn it inside out, and judge its coherence so it can become a model (if it is a good piece). Additionally, they can critique, engaging thoroughly in an argument with the work. The final assessment hurdle is the research proposal. Each session and assessment involves work in progress. As supervisors, we can scrutinise their writing and they can share ideas and writing with others. They have to write what is actually going to be part of the dissertation in the end. This is a useful way to break writer's block and a good starting point for writing some early sections.

Another writing task on this PhD programme asks students to briefly attempt a first stab at an abstract. Of course, it is too early to do this even in the third stage of the programme because they haven't finished the work, but trying out the specific language of an abstract by examining several abstracts and analysing models is good practice. It is particularly useful for those who find it difficult answering questions about the point and aim of the work, the conceptual as well as the factual areas under question, the design and reason for it, and the conceptual as well as factual findings. The abstract enables them to start working in that metalanguage, and to stand back and look at their work at a time when they might be overwhelmed with the size and enormity of the task. They answer relatively straightforward questions, getting it in perspective, then writing down what they have said aloud and working on it. Often, the exercise involves them changing what they write into the third person passive rather than the first person and helps them avoid providing a chapter summary (which some students might think is the function of the abstract).

▶ Two main issues about good writing

There are two main issues students need to consider about good writing: taking a critical stance and arguing; and expressing themselves in a coherent and interesting manner. The first is about the level of thinking and conceptualising – being able to imagine, stand back, see the whole picture and ask questions of it all the time, develop arguments about it, then show how what has been discovered engages with, relates to, and puts these arguments into action. This level of work can be informed by research into student learning. The work of Erik Meyer *et al.* (Morris and Meyer, 2003) concentrates on exploring threshold concepts – key conceptual ways of looking at a subject that mark a transition in student learning from what could be descriptive to what gets hold of the central problems and ways of looking at the world. Without moments where thresholds are crossed into conceptualising, students might well be stuck at the level of description, however elegantly expressed. Asking critical questions that engage students in identifying concepts, of which detail and data are evidence in action, can help them to work at a higher level than the merely detailed and descriptive. Students need to be encouraged to work at high conceptual and critical levels. This we can help them do with exercises and questions prompting thought translated into writing.

Another major issue is that of expression – the right words in the right place, linked into a coherent whole. This involves being aware of how to develop links between the parts of work as a whole, and between chapters, paragraphs and sentences. It involves being able to use linking phrases, to ensure themes are interwoven, that theorists and arguments are picked up and used throughout, referring backwards and forwards to make it a coherent whole, using phrases such as 'in this respect', 'additionally', 'while it has been argued that this evidence/work, suggests . . .', etc.

Supervisors need to ensure students have developed and can use both of

Task: Critical writing activities

Select two articles in your own field/the student's field. One should be well-written in terms of both conceptualisation, critical thinking, and at the level of sentence structure, grammar and eloquence of expression. The other should be less satisfactory in both respects. This could be an individual, or a small group exercise, as students can work well together to identify good and problematic elements without feeling the supervisor is judging their critical faculties.

Ask the student(s):

- How well is the research question expressed? Is it clear? Or is the writer only *stating or describing* an area of work or a situation, rather than problematising and exploring the area and developing a question?

- Has the author summarised background and contextual work, and work by experts and theorists? Have they referred to it at all? Are they showing contrasts in work and arguments developed by others? Are they analysing the work and drawing out some main points of difference, not just in terms of facts that differ but conceptualisation and interpretation? Or do they just seem to have noted a list of other experts and produced a summary of the experts' work?

- Is it clear what kinds of methods and methodologies they have used in their work? Do they explore how these help them ask their question? Do they mention them in passing, then move onto what has been found, all in a bit of a muddle in the middle of the paragraphs? Do they defend why they chose their methods, or do they not really mention using any at all?

- When the data are presented, is it a mass of quotations or tables with little commentary? Or are there themes and arguments being drawn out of the data and explored through selective extracts? In quotations from books or interviews, do we see themes and excerpts developing, making a contribution to arguments? Do any comments really grow from the data? Or is there a mismatch?

- In the conclusion, is the whole piece just summed up with a list of what happens in each chapter? Or does the writer draw themes and questions together, explaining how some facts have been discovered, and how the work has contributed to conceptual development – areas of thinking, meaning and argument about the subject?

these kinds of writing – the conceptual and critically engaged, and the coherently expressed. It is particularly difficult if students come from a different language culture and might be able to express themselves elegantly in their own language but less so, they feel, in English. It is particularly difficult if we are working with drafts sent through the post or email – because we are tempted, perhaps, to fall into the trap of correcting all the errors of expression and syntax (important because they enable or prevent the argument to be expressed) at the expense of encouraging critical thinking and a critical, conceptual, analytical approach.

It could be useful for you to work with your student and identify problems with others' writing, as well identifying successful strategies for writing conceptually, critically, eloquently and, coherently. This can be done through close analysis and critique of any journal article, book, chapter or thesis/dissertation.

Choosing or writing some examples from your own subject to work on with your students will enable a focus on what constitutes good writing or good enough writing at the conceptual/critical level and the level of expression. Negotiating agreed responses to extracts helps pave the way for feedback on students' writing.

▶ Reading, thinking and asking questions

One way of encouraging critical and conceptual work that is analytical rather than descriptive and factual, is to set up good reading practices and supervisor—student interactions that draw on these to develop thinking and writing. Delamont *et al.* (1997) mention three kinds of reading needed for carrying out research. We can develop their suggestions, indicating the levels of response and conceptualisation that students employ in their work. 'For arts and social science students there are three types of reading to be done: reading on the topic, contrastive reading and analytical reading' (1997, p. 57). They offer worked examples of three kinds of reading. Student *thinking* also need to be at three levels, the descriptive which sets the scene, identifies evidence; the conceptual and critical which engages with theories and critiques argument; and the analytical which explores and clarifies, unpicks arguments, relates evidence to claims, builds a well-argued case backed up by careful analysis of findings. Giving selective feedback should better enable engagement at the more than descriptive but also conceptual, critical and analytical levels. Consider some of the stages of students' writing and kinds of writing needed. You might take students through the examples given below or other pieces from your own discipline – asking critical, prompt questions – helping students to develop conceptually, critically and expressively. Developmental feedback could ask students to turn topics into questions, to be critical, analytical and to theorise.

We will look at an example of how (i) a topic area is developed into a question, which in turn prompts (ii) thoughts about reading to be undertaken, and then (iii) the beginning of conceptualising rather than describing and detailing.

Example
Topic area: skateboarding and youth
Title: A study of skateboarding as a radical youth activity in New York

Research question
- In what ways does skateboarding operate as a radical activity and expression for youth in New York?
- What are the instances of skateboarding in New York, and internationally?
- In what ways is it a radical youth activity?
- How does it enable youth to express freedom, individuality and energy?
- How does it reconfigure and re-express the cityscape?

Theory
To ask this question and sub-questions in terms of my reading and theorists, I will need to use and explore a variety of areas including:

- Youth movements – a range of activities including clubbing, drug use, *specifically* sports and radical sporting activities (e.g. windsurfing, surfing, BMX bike riding, snowboarding).
- Geographies of urban environments and interpretations of these geographies – town planners' views, alternative other views, e.g. 'take back the night' women's marches, and views on the safety of urban spaces and their meanings.

A descriptive piece
Working at a merely descriptive and factual level, a student might produce the following:

> Skateboarding has grown as an activity in our cities and skateboarders can be found in most major cites including London and New York. It is estimated that there are 100,000 skateboarders internationally. They are noticeable because of their seemingly dangerous active use of the various

parts of the city which other people are working or living in. Skateboarding is a sport which involves young people in the main although some of the great boarders such as Tony Hawkes are well over 30.

A conceptual piece
Working at a more conceptual, analytical, critical level, a student might produce the following:

> Many of us have nearly been knocked over by a self-absorbed individual on a skateboard thoughtlessly crashing down the steps at the library or swimming pool, racing along pavements and mindlessly leaping benches, steps, railings. However, Skateboarding is more than merely an irritating intrusion on the daily lives of ordinary people working in and using a city. It represents both an example of a radical youth activity and one which re interprets city spaces to reclaim them for young people. Skateboarding has grown as an activity in our cities and skateboarders can be found in most major cities including London and New York. It is estimated that there are 100,000 skateboarders internationally. Skateboarding as a sport involves young people in the main, although some of the great boarders such as Tony Hawkes are well over 30, and the popularity of skateboarding has turned it into something of a youth cult movement with all the trappings of its own language (ollie, kick flip), own international communities which others can enter upon indicating their status as boarders, videos and marketable wares. Skateboarding represents an element of a youth counter culture. . .'

Giving feedback to encourage the improvement of critical thinking to underpin good writing
Comments on the first short piece might include:

> Skateboarding has grown as an activity in our cities and skateboarders can be found in most major cities including London and New York. It is estimated that there are 100,000 skateboarders internationally.

This is an interesting and informative piece about the worldwide urban existence of skateboarding. What might its popularity suggest about this as a youth movement or cult activity?

> They are noticeable because of their seemingly dangerous active use of the various parts of the city which other people are working or living in.

Yes indeed, we see and try and avoid them daily! Is this dangerous active use of the city just selfishness or does it suggest any other interpretation or ownership of the city? Does it 'stand for' or 'represent' anything?

> Skateboarding is a sport which involves young people in the main although some of the great boarders such as Tony Hawkes (on whom computer games have been based) are well over 30.

This is seen as very popular – more than just a youth activity then? What might the implications of the involvement of older boarders be? What might the production of computer games indicate not only about the popularity but cultural significance and impact of skateboarding?

The reason for this kind of questioning feedback is to encourage critical, conceptual and analytical thinking. Giving students an example of such feedback should help them to problematise and conceptualise. Asking them to work together or individually on 'marking' journal or local newspaper articles on a related topic might encourage critical and conceptual thinking in their own work. Students might be asked to provide feedback to improve the *second* piece on skateboarding.

The next part of the exercise involves students auditing and editing a piece of their *own* work, marking it up and giving themselves such feedback as above, then improving on the work accordingly.

There are many books on academic writing that can aid students in expressing their ideas succinctly and elegantly. They should be advised to consult these when producing early drafts and particularly when writing up final drafts and editing. For international students, the issue of tertiary literacy is explored further in Chapter 12, but contributes considerably to their experience of translating into acceptable subject and research discourse the critical arguments they wish to make. Their language facility might hamper these arguments. See Chapter 18 for a discussion of coherence on the finally submitted dissertation or thesis.

▶ Encouraging critical and creative thinking to improve writing

It is important to set up working situations in which creative thinking and expression are released, in which students can approach issues and ideas in a number of ways – some imaginative, some more systematic, planned and finished – and then work to incorporate them into an organised, analytical answer, whether written or spoken. Harnessing a diversity of thoughts, experiences and responses and helping to shape them are enabling processes.

Feedback on drafts

Feedback to encourage writing that is critically informed, well-argued and well-expressed is essential for the development of a good thesis or dissertation. When students are given feedback on drafts of their work, any miscommunication could result, for them, in confusion about direction, leading to extra unnecessary work or writer's block. Students have commented on confusion at what seem to be cryptic or shorthand comments, for example:

- 'Please clarify'
- 'This might not add up';

comments that suggest further work or reading, but don't indicate how much:

- 'More was needed here'
- 'Have you looked at Deleuze and Foucault?';

which seem to contain veiled threats of failure:

- 'Conceptually weak'
- 'No!'
- 'You will need to really pull this together before sending it to me'
- 'Too many errors of expression here';

and even those that generally suggest a satisfied response:

- 'Lots of interesting work here'
- 'Yes!'

If any of these rather vague 'phatic' comments are used, they need to be backed up with clarification and specific advice, including examples of good expression. For all students, and perhaps most specifically for those from culturally different backgrounds, clarity of guidance is essential both in the very early stages and as the student writes up first and final drafts.

Colleagues with whom I have worked have indicated their strategies supporting good writing. Some encourage students to write early drafts so they can share discussions about critical and conceptual levels, involving reading and theorists in a dialogue with the students' own work rather than merely summarising. This helps students develop a style of their own, suitable for the level of the work. Some activities encourage the use of the meta-language of the subject, and others of their own voice.

Rowena Murray (2002), concerned about explicit guidelines from the student's point of view, asks about feedback:

> Are the comments global or detailed or both? For supervisors, there is a decision to make about what type of feedback to give. Do they want to make you focus on the 'big picture' of your whole argument, or a section of it? Or do they want you to tidy up the style? Is clarification of terms paramount? Given that these are all quite different questions, requiring different focus and action, the supervisors may recognize that one is more important, at this stage, than the others. For example, they may decide that the priority is to get you to define and use key terms with more clarity. There may be other aspects related to clarity that they want you to work on and this would make for an effective theme in their feedback. You may have been expecting more feedback on what you think of as the 'content', but they see the use of terms – and assessing whether or not you can use them properly – as a priority. You can regard this as a tension between what you expect and what you get. Or you can accept that you have work to do – and who would not have – in clarifying what you have written. (Murray 2002, p. 78)

Selective feedback and hierarchies of feedback enable students to focus on some issues at a time. Often it is a good idea to write specific suggestions in margins, providing models of argument or expression that you feel are necessary, or as extracts for students to analyse and consider, alone or as part of a supervision. Both students and supervisors indicate the real usefulness of seeing *models* of writing required. This can be provided at the level of paragraph or abstract, extract, or the whole thesis or dissertation. Preferably, at least two examples for comparison should be provided so students don't rigidly follow one model. When they have produced short examples of writing, you could work very closely on providing feedback on a single paragraph of their work in terms of expression, grammar and punctuation, and asking them to take the changes in the text through the whole chapter then return it to you for further assessment. This means you have indicated and exemplified the kind of changes needed to improve the writing, but have avoided doing all the writing for them.

Writing blocks

You could encourage students to break writing blocks by asking them to continue writing in their log or journal, or employing a series of other tricks to liberste their thinking and initiate writing. Some suggestions for students include:

- Start writing in the middle of something, a chapter, an argument or a dialogue with an expert. Just begin where you feel comfortable to write. Step back and produce a brief diagram of where this could fit in your chapter so you can jigsaw it in when you have written other parts.
- Remember it is only a draft! – write fast as it comes to you and then return to edit for:
  (i)   Conceptual level – ideas, theories, themes as well as concepts,
  (ii) Expression – does it say what you want it to? Clarify expression, deal with grammar and punctuation, and inexplicit words and expressions.

Practise 'free-writing' to loosen up the thought process and creativity. In my own work I call it 'splurge' and write fast (and inaccurately). Then I go back over it and form it, find the right words, and turn the sentences the right way round.

> The most effective way I know to improve your writing is to do free-writing exercises regularly. At least three times a week ... simply write for ten minutes (later on, perhaps fifteen or twenty). Don't stop for anything. Go quickly without rushing. Never stop to look back, to cross something out... If you get stuck it's fine to write, 'I can't think what to say, I can't think what to say' as many times as you want ... The only requirement is that you never stop.   (Elbow, 1973, p. 3)

Murray comments 'This is the opposite of knowing what you want to say first, and writing about it second' (2003, p. 78).

The potential danger here is that it could just produce bad writing. If your students cannot change it into something coherent and eloquent, then they should avoid the exercise of 'splurge' or 'free-writing', but for many 'getting it down' then dealing with the appropriate expression is paramount.

Freewriting is not just a therapeutic way to release the thinking and expression process. It might take a lot of practice to produce something and then work it into a well-expressed piece, but it can be a first step in the production of more written work and can also help those who find themselves hampered by the expectations of academic writing:

> Free-writing isn't just therapeutic garbage. It's also a way to produce bits

of writing that are genuinely *better* than usual: less random, more coherent, more highly organized.   (Elbow, 1973, p. 8)

Students should be encouraged to try to:

* brainstorm initial ideas without having to express them perfectly
* get out of a writer's block by doing some writing – physically
* work through psychological, intellectual or emotional responses
* open up ideas by writing them down a little
* get the ideas and expressions circulating in their heads down on paper so they can move on
* gain confidence by writing – producing an *amount* to be edited later by articulating ideas and arguments in their head, however (initially) poorly
* help avoid using halting, formalised phrases and getting tied up in them, and therefore *saying* nothing.

Visualisation

Using diagrams and visualisation is another way of starting to write freely. Students could try:

* expressing contradictions through writing about both or more sides of an issue, separating, then linking them.

Example 1

Figure 9.1 illustrates a visualisation of a topical UK issue.

Expressing different strategies and paradoxes and indicating contradictions can help clarify a student's argument, making the problems more explicit. Suggest prompt questions and how and where they can add information, activities, references, quotations, other reading and data to the different bubbles or boxes of the arguments, starting to express the contradiction clearly and build a case.

Example 2

A student needs to explore the contradictions and tensions in postmodernism as they relate to postcolonial women's writing – and she is 'stuck'. Perhaps she could try expressing this as a visual image and then put it into words (Figure 9.2).

On the one hand, postmodernist theory argues that there is no coherent sense of 'I', self or subject and it argues 'the subject' is a contextualised construction. But on the other hand it argues that because *everything* is a contextualised construction, there are no canonical texts or hierarchies with

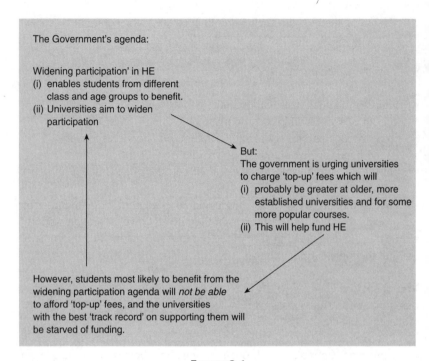

The Government's agenda:

Widening participation' in HE
(i) enables students from different class and age groups to benefit.
(ii) Universities aim to widen participation

But:
The government is urging universities to charge 'top-up' fees which will
(i) probably be greater at older, more established universities and for some more popular courses.
(ii) This will help fund HE

However, students most likely to benefit from the widening participation agenda will *not be able* to afford 'top-up' fees, and the universities with the best 'track record' on supporting them will be starved of funding.

FIGURE 9.1

one culture's privileged over another. It allows readers to recognise the importance and value of writing from a whole variety of cultures previously silenced, but notes that writers from 'silenced' cultures often work to assert identity, I and self, so they speak out *against* the silencing, claiming the empowering elements of postmodernism (but refusing those disempowering elements which reject the culturally constructed self, I, subject).

Visualising complex or contradictory ideas can help to build up elements of an argument, then underpinned and informed by theorists, critics and primary sources. Like free writing, visualisation helps express the kinds of complications and paradoxes inherent in research. Elbow has some points about further work that suit visualisation also:

> After the exercise take a few moments or more to rest and think about what you wrote. Think, too, about the digressions you started and perhaps continued. Notice when they occurred and where they took you. Think about their connections. Consider them as paths you should explore. (Elbow, 1973, p. 10)

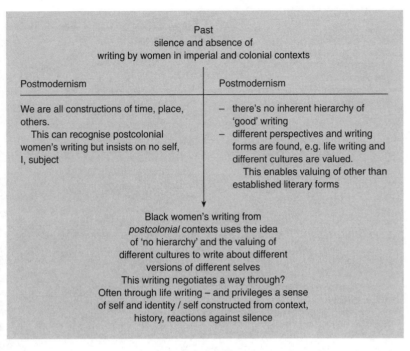

Past
silence and absence of
writing by women in imperial and colonial contexts

Postmodernism

Postmodernism

We are all constructions of time, place, others.
   This can recognise postcolonial women's writing but insists on no self, I, subject

- there's no inherent hierarchy of 'good' writing
- different perspectives and writing forms are found, e.g. life writing and different cultures are valued.
   This enables valuing of other than established literary forms

Black women's writing from
postcolonial contexts uses the idea
of 'no hierarchy' and the valuing of
different cultures to write about different
versions of different selves
This writing negotiates a way through?
Often through life writing – and privileges a sense
of self and identity / self constructed from context,
history, reactions against silence

FIGURE 9.2

Example 3

Other diagrams that can release thoughts might express an argument as a continuum rather than a polarity, such as the exploration of colonial and postcolonial expression illustrated in Figure 9.3.

The advice given by Elbow and Murray is useful for free-writing. Diagrams or visualisation can also help by opening up writing, and what Boice (1990) calls 'generative writing' is also useful. Generative writing involves fast writing (which can be shaped later):

- write for five minutes
- write without stopping
- then go back and re-shape it

Students can reflect back on their writing, using it as a prompt for discussion and future writing. Suggest they take a different coloured pen and annotate or correct it, perhaps cutting it into bullet points – writing more for each key point – cutting out elements that now seem irrelevant, clarifying the hazy ones, adding new ideas, expanding or enhancing contradictory arguments,

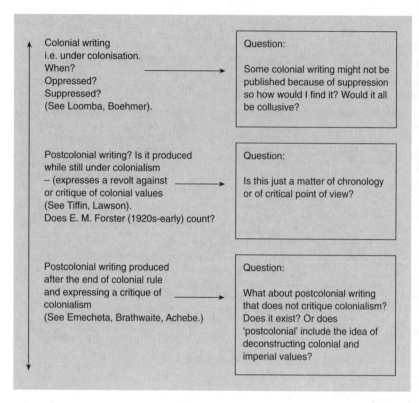

Colonial writing
i.e. under colonisation.
When?
Oppressed?
Suppressed?
(See Loomba, Boehmer).

Question:

Some colonial writing might not be published because of suppression so how would I find it? Would it all be collusive?

Postcolonial writing? Is it produced while still under colonialism
– (expresses a revolt against or critique of colonial values (See Tiffin, Lawson).
Does E. M. Forster (1920s-early) count?

Question:

Is this just a matter of chronology or of critical point of view?

Postcolonial writing produced after the end of colonial rule and expressing a critique of colonialism
(See Emecheta, Brathwaite, Achebe.)

Question:

What about postcolonial writing that does not critique colonialism? Does it exist? Or does 'postcolonial' include the idea of deconstructing colonial and imperial values?

FIGURE 9.3

and seeking exactly the right expression. They could do this alone, or with another student, critical friend or family member with writing skills. They can also do it as part of a supervision with you, their supervisor.

On his creative writing course at Ruskin College, Oxford, Alistair Wisker asks students to share portfolios of developing writing, critique, comment and then reflect on how this peer exchange informs *their* writing.

> [...] students emphasized that although the critiquing process was power-ful and useful, it was also highly emotional and at times frustrating. The findings suggest that ... instructors should be very clear about the purposes and benefits of a strong and sustained critiquing process, and assist students in learning how to both receive and give useful feedback. (Caffarella and Barnett, 2000, p. 39)

Providing constructive and developmental feedback?

Students can be silenced by over-critical feedback or confused by too much feedback (see above). When annotating email attachments from students it is useful to use the 'Track Changes' mode in 'Tools', and to alter text in a colour, making other marginal notes in another colour (not red! This signals *bad* errors and looks patronising). Murray (2002) has developed a useful list of the intentions of critical comments for students' work. Murray's (2002) typology recognises comments at both the conceptual and critical level, and addresses presentation:

- argument
- clarity
- 'develop'
- 'discuss'
- 'distinguish'
- 'expand'
- the mechanics, i.e. punctuation etc., praise, probe, prompt, role switch, style.

Murray proceeds to suggest how students can translate and act on supervisors' comments. Discussions with students also produce some helpful ideas on feedback. Supervisors need to use explicit comments to model examples, to encourage clarification by providing detailed ideas – and/or examples of parts of this clarification in detail – and to differentiate between social and critical comments.

I have developed comments that attempt to encourage critical thinking and are derived from counselling. Look at Chapter 8 on supervisory dialogues for examples of wording that suits interaction categories and, slightly altered, could be used to comment on written scripts.

Examples of kinds of comments
- You need to ensure apostrophes are in the right place: it's = 'it is', 'belonging to it'; instead of 'people I worked with' try 'people with whom I worked' (*punctuation, grammar, spelling, style*)
- Please comment on your table; discuss how the quotation exemplifies your theme (*argument, specific relevance*)
- What do you understand 'ontological insecurity' to mean in Plath's poetry? (*asks for conceptualisation and further discussion*)
- Tell me more about the link between the specific act and general trends (*expand, important point*)

- You say 'it was an age of great change'. For whom? When? In what ways? (*clarity needed*)
- Why do you think Heads expressed role conflict? (*probing and prompting*)
- Another person might argue that (*changing perspectives to expand thinking*).

Issues of clarity (specifically, expansion, discussion, inclusion of data in a discussion to ensure it acts as evidence for claims), encouraging argument, conceptualisation, critical thinking *and* suggesting accurate, referred detail and appropriate expression are all important in feedback. You might find it useful to signal different kinds of concerns. These could range from the conceptual/critical to issues of clarity of argument, to use of data.

- You have obviously covered a great deal of reading here ...? (*comment on momentum*)
- Add a short paragraph about Bloom's main points here (*expanding the information in your points*)
- Do Bloom and Dewey really disagree about curriculum models? List them, expand where they agree and where they differ (*developing the complexity of student arguments with differentiation*)
- You have repeated various phrases here – can you find another word for 'focus' or 'refocus'? (*Tidying up writing style*)
- Be more specific. This is a little generalised (*focus, expression*)
- How many exactly argued that the curriculum was too packed? (*accuracy*)
- What did they mean and do you mean by 'packed'? (*asking the student to be more specific, detailed, accurate, refined and discriminatory*)
- Were there any more differentiated points about the 'packed' curriculum made by the respondent? (*expand, open up*)
- Read more of Entwistle's (1998) points here (*Guiding reading by being more specific*) See pp. 34–8, 120–2. What does he argue about the changing purpose of the HE curriculum?

One supervisor comments on the use of feedback to aid student writing quality:

> I see a development of critical thinking, of rigorous examination of information, rigorous questioning of information in order to establish its validity, its relevance and so on and I think that process develops in practice.

They go on to say:

You ask questions. You say, 'Why do you say that? What has it come from? What's the connection between this statement and anything that you have stated before, as the material from which this statement, this conclusion apparently derived?' and if there's a good answer to your question then there's a secondary question, 'Well, why doesn't it say that in your writing?' and if there isn't a good answer then it's an indication that the student needs to go away and think more carefully and not to present conclusions – even low-level conclusions in the form of statements or assumptions – that don't arise from that evidence. As I say, I think that most students are quite receptive to that because they have begun their doctoral work with a higher than average acuity for critical examination of information – much higher than the general population.

You will probably find it useful to look over some of your own examples of feedback to ensure you are being absolutely clear in the guidance of student writing. Developing writing exercises using extracts and activities related to *your* subject and *your* students' needs will also help encourage good writing. A key point for all students, no matter their level or subject, is to *start writing early* and get the ideas and argument out there so together we can help shape them into the best possible form for communication.

▶ Further reading

Boice, R. (1990) *Professors as Writers: A Self-Help Guide to Productive Writing* (Stillwater, OK: New Forums).

Dunleavy, P. (2003) *Authoring a PhD* (Basingstoke: Palgrave Macmillan).

Elbow, P. (1973) *Writing without Teachers* (Oxford: Oxford University Press).

Gower, E. (1986) *The Complete Plain Words,* rev. edn S. Greenbaum and J. Whitcut (London: HMSO).

Morris, J. and Meyer, J. H. F. (2003) 'Variation in the conceptions of learning of physiotherapy students in England and Wales: a longitudinal multicentre study', in C. Rust (ed.), *Improving Student Learning Theory and Practice – 10 Years On* (Oxford: OSCLD).

Murray, R. (2002) *How to Write a Thesis* (Buckingham: Open University Press).

Stage 3
Working with Students – Issues for Supervisors

10 Helping Students to Help Themselves and Each Other

Supervisors cannot provide all the support students need to carry out successful planned research through to completion. Students can greatly benefit from entering, and contributing to, a supportive academic community – this can be a very fruitful way of working towards creative solutions to problems. Indeed, Margot Pearson and Angela Brew (2002, p. 142) advise expanding the 'dydadic' relationship to include a broader academic community.

> *This chapter considers:*
>
> - *setting up peer groups and academic community support*
> - *staff and student seminars*
> - *online support*
> - *research development programmes – including specific workshops and models.*

Research at all levels is an individualistic endeavour in which students become involved in developing their own ideas, carrying out their own research, and completing and writing up their work. For the PhD or EdD,students also have to defend their work on an individualistic basis in the viva. However, experience and current research into student retention suggests that friendship groups, peer groups and social networks are essential for the maintenance of momentum and continuation of a student's commitment to study; in short for success. To some extent, some of this support comes from the supervisor – one person certainly interested in the development of their students' work. But the supervisor is not alone in providing support, development and contact for students. Instead, increasingly, institutions are recognising that formal, institutional support, in the shape of research development programmes, days or sessions (depending on the level of study) as well as peer group support can ensure students do not become overly dependent on their supervisor. This also prevents supervisors being swamped by their students' various needs (some of which are better addressed outside the supervisor–student role). In some instances, the supervisor can play a key role in establishing and helping to maintain peer groups or student research groups. In others, the momentum is the students' own.

> Discussion of coaching and mentoring may seem to indicate an implicit assumption of dyadic relationships. Yet, research students can and do depend on a range of people to provide various forms of assistance in learning research expertise and how to be a professional researcher. These significant others can be those in a department, a laboratory, a disciplinary network, or a university and its resources. (Pearson and Brew, 2002, p. 141)

► Reading groups and sharing work in progress

Reading groups are one form of student self-help. They are essentially groups of students exploring ideas together and sharing various problems, whether of motivation, methods, fieldwork, expression or completion. Such support minimises the need to contact supervisors for relatively minor technical questions, ensuring several students can approach the supervisor with key, well-thought out issues. Our English PhD reading group provides work-in-progress seminars, inviting staff to contribute, for example, to mock viva development. This leads to joint publications and co-presenting at conferences. English has hosted a number of postgraduate/staff and postgraduate conferences either specific to APU or in conjunction with, in our case, Cambridge University. These serve developmental, confidence-building ends and help to build a wider academic community. Students mock viva each other, lobby for facilities, and nurture the growth of each other's academic success. The MA Women's Studies dissertation students stay in touch less formally – by email, by joining in a weekend away and having working lunches.

► Online chat-rooms and discussion forums – Examples

Not all students are available, mobile or close enough to get involved in reading and work-in-progress groups. For many, replicating such a community in an online environment provides opportunities for sharing, debate, support and development. Online chat-rooms and discussion forums related to research can enable the exchange and development of ideas and support over difficulties.

In our MA Learning and Teaching, students talk with each other and with the staff or supervisors in the web environment. In the discussion area, staff and students post up questions and answers, engaging in debate around texts read and work requested. In the chat-room, the 'MALT café', students discuss their progress and queries.

In some instances, staff may or may not have access to a chat-room or they may have their own chat- or staff-room for development and discussion purposes. This creation of an online community only works if everyone can be logged on and into the Web CT, First Class, or other environment, and if they feel comfortable participating. Initially, establishing such comfort involves staff and students undertaking diagnostic activities to determine their levels of usage of IT facilities, and the virtual learning environment (VLE), with the whole group playing with the environment, posting comments and generating discussion. Tasks requiring discussion and then the printing out of assessable materials, which are relevant, staged, timed and compulsory, encourage regular usage. Once regular, learning-oriented usage is established, the habit of entering the environment encourages discussions and chat. This in turn reduces isolation, helping students (and staff) articulate their success, and the queries they have about research development. If students share amongst each other, they might feel more able to explore problems and solutions with peers. If staff join in, a single helpful idea or piece of information often saves a great deal of time and anxiety. Alternatively, mixed discussions can promote ongoing debate about complex conceptual issues.

An international Master's course based at the Cambridge Programme for Industry developed some of these strategies, involving students grouping over great distances, posting questions and discussion to each other and copying this off for assessment purposes in a portfolio indicating reflection, activity, engagement, support and development. One group leader for each group moderated discussions, ensuring everyone felt engaged. 'Lurking' (reading others' comments without participating) might be fine in an online discussion, but when generating work towards assessment, it is parasitic of others' ideas. Involving work-related activities is essential.

▶ Seminars, peer group exchanges and conferences

Building on US models, at the University of the West Indies, students are encouraged and expected to disseminate and share their work-in-progress with their peers, supervisor and other colleagues at staged seminars throughout their research. Here they deliver on the questions, conceptual framework, design of the study, problems faced, surprises, analyses, findings and changes in their work. They compile seminar presentations marking stages in their progress. The contribution of others present as critical friends greatly helps the continued development of students' work, helps build confidence and reduces isolation, giving students a sense that they can share problems which may be specific to their work but, more often than not, are quite common and generalised and in relation to research stages. Students practise discussing their research and defending it in preparation for a viva. Students can, effectively, join and maintain a 'community of practice'.

Delamont *et al.* (1997) build on an apprenticeship approach developed by Lave and Wenger (1991), situating learning in communities of practice involving a range of participants, each with differing histories of membership – apprentices, established acsdemics, relatively new masters, 'journeyfolk'. Learning occurs through participation in the social practice of the community. The apprentice has a special status as 'legitimate peripheral participant' (LPP), invited and enabled by a master or sponsor to participate as a potential member, accessing the practice without being fully expert. Commenting on research-oriented apprenticeship and LPP models, Pearson and Brew note:

> Under these circumstances, it seems typical that apprentices learn mostly in relation with other apprentices. Further conceptualisation of 'communities of practice' by Wenger provides additional understandings of the complexity of how people learn 'on the job', and the relationship of more structured training where the learner learns 'about what to do', with the learning that occurs in practice where participants 'do things together, negotiate new meaning, and learn from each other' (Wenger, 1998, p. 102). The value of this approach to apprenticeship according to Guile and Young (1998) is that it offers a conceptualisation of learning that avoids the separation of learning from knowledge production, a concern raised by student groups (Smith, 2000). Lave and Wenger are careful to insist that communities are not static nor necessarily peaceful. (Pearson and Brew, 2002, p. 142)

▶ Research development programmes

Increasingly, students undertaking a Master's, MRes, EdD, PrD and PhD are involved in research development programmes to enable their construction of workable proposals and appropriate, manageable, significant research. Often, with input over time, programmes enable students to develop their skills, research methods, question framing, literature reviewing and the integration of theoretical perspectives to drive the research. Programme inputs and exercises model and encourage good practice in the analysis and interpretation of data, turning these into findings and drawing conclusions, both conceptual and factual. Such programmes also focus on developing the skills of writing a good dissertation or thesis and, in the UK and European traditions, viva defence preparation.

Professionalisation of the PhD development process is paralleled by smaller scale development activities, commonly undertaken by Master's and undergraduate students. All of these complement the supervisor's work with students throughout their research, and their thesis or dissertation writing. Research training might be only an hour-long talk or a couple of Saturday workshops. These kinds of events serve many purposes: development, and academic community building. However, research development programmes are contested, forming part of the 'training' model of postgraduate learning and support. On the one hand, they offer development activities, clarification and a community that an individual supervisor alone could not. On the other hand, in their professionalized approach to developing research skills, they are enabling, but homogenising.

Cullen, Pearson, Saha and Spear (1994) argue for a structural response in research encompassing more than individual supervisory arrangements. Pearson (1999) suggests that a 'training' model is too limited. Instead, PhD students should be positioned as learners of the professional practice of research and scholarship in a form of professional education. Following Holdaway (1996), Pearson suggests a:

> conceptual framework of activities and foci distinguished. In this framework the emphasis is on the interrelationships of the components of a graduate programme. The intent is to show that although the production of the thesis is the primary focus and outcome, other learning is important. Primary activities are given as: research; required coursework; reading; reflecting; discussing; and writing. Secondary activities are: optional coursework; teaching; publishing; preparing conference papers; and preparing research proposals. Holdaway sees the secondary activities as 'an integral part of the graduate education experience'. (Pearson, 1999, p. 277)

In many universities worldwide, a Master's in Research is now required before undertaking a PhD, EdD or PrD. This staged activity recognises the need to equip students with appropriate research skills and building blocks, not only for their intended award but for future research. The award of a Master's is an incentive for many. For UK Open University students embarking on the EdD, a Master's in Education is essential. More recently, even those with a Master's have taken E835 'Educational Research in Action' *because* it focuses on stages of developing a research proposal *and* on research skills building blocks. The course is assessed by three assignments focusing on developing an effective research purpose, one other assignment and an exam on distinguishing between research methodologies and methods. Additionally, in the exam, students critically evaluate the match between research claims made, and research-based evidence provided. With EdD and PrDs, students move through a series of staged progress reports, building up to a final thesis. Programme support enables this development.

Research development programmes commonly follow the stages of a student's research. We will consider one model, an RDP developed for the cohorts of International- and UK-origin PhD students at APU. This RDP is accompanied at each stage by action research – encouraging reflection on their own learning to establish students as collaborators and reflective learners. The first stage of the programme focuses on the development of a research question, the conceptual framework, introducing research methods and the writing of a research proposal. It helps students articulate, share, develop and – if necessary – change their research design and research methods. It also helps to build peer support through group work. Additionally, involvement in reflective and evaluative activities during and after workshops helps further develop metalearning – an essential prerequisite for the aware learning development necessary to undertake and learn from research activities (see Biggs, 1991; Flavell, 1977). Elsewhere, we have written about the specific workshop, supervisory dialogue and action research elements of the three stage RDP that encourage metalearning (see the EARLI 2003 Conference – *IETI* 2004 special edition).

Action research set within the framework of the RDP enables students to focus on key stages in their work. They work on the proposal (stage 1), the progress report 'confirmation of candidature' (stage 2) and writing up/ preparing for the viva (stage 3) (see figure 10.1). At each stage, a major consideration is exactly how their research methods genuinely enable them to achieve research outcomes. Results of action research feed directly into workshops, supervisory dialogues, and students' and staff reflections, combining both quantitative and qualitative methods. The quantitative methods (RoLI, 'Reflections on Learning Inventory', in Meyer and Boulton-Lewis, 1997; the Research-as-learning questionnaire in Wisker, 1998) enable us to identify patterns of learning approaches and conceptions of research-

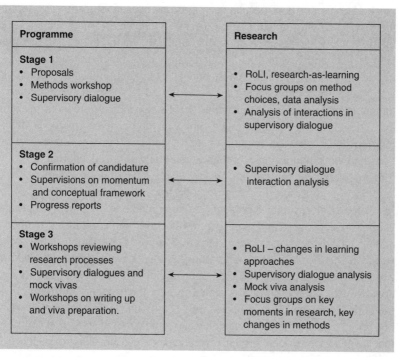

Programme		Research
Stage 1 • Proposals • Methods workshop • Supervisory dialogue	←→	• RoLI, research-as-learning • Focus groups on method choices, data analysis • Analysis of interactions in supervisory dialogue
Stage 2 • Confirmation of candidature • Supervisions on momentum and conceptual framework • Progress reports	←→	• Supervisory dialogue interaction analysis
Stage 3 • Workshops reviewing research processes • Supervisory dialogues and mock vivas • Workshops on writing up and viva preparation.	←→	• RoLI – changes in learning approaches • Supervisory dialogue analysis • Mock viva analysis • Focus groups on key moments in research, key changes in methods

FIGURE 10.1   ACTION RESEARCH AND 3-STAGE RESEARCH DEVELOPMENT
PROGRAMME

as-learning for individuals, across and between cohorts. The qualitative methods (focus groups, supervisory dialogues) enable us to see how students grapple with, carry out and interpret their research aims and progress, using methodologies and research methods within conceptual frameworks. Each runs alongside, making direct use of intervention processes of research development workshops and supervisory dialogues.

Workshops addressing research methods and conceptual frameworks

Workshops in stages 1 and 3 of the RDP focus on the development (stage 1) and then the final coherent clarification (stage 3) of the students' conceptual frameworks.

In an early 'Methods workshop' (stage 1), following some input on methods, a number of activities aim to engage students in developing sound conceptual frameworks and appropriate research methods. The session is held in small groups and collective responses to workshop activities are taped, after completion. Results from sessions indicate student reflection on methods, showing a correlation between choice of methodology and methods, students' research questions, which the methodology and methods help to ask, and research-as-learning approaches taken by students. They expose ways students might realise difficulties inherent in using research-as-learning approaches producing large masses of data somewhat removed from their object or outcomes, for example. Results also indicate students' growing awareness in some instances that a variety of approaches or methods, differing from those planned, might be better suited to their own research questions and aims than a single, probably quantitatively based, approach.

Group work runs for an hour, then students reflect on the experience and feed back, one person reporting on both process and an individual case of his or her own or another person's research methods. In 2000, two groups chose to elect a spokesperson who fed back on someone else's methods, adding succinctness and clarity to the description. Observation of the group work on this occasion was fascinating. Students were clearly involved in explaining very precisely and then encouraging questions, suggestions and debates with others. All of this aimed to help them define and refine their methods (changing them if necessary). They found overlaps in methods – one group claimed they were all doing case studies – and some real contrasts that helped them to define their own choices. Co-counselling of supportive peers can enable students to clarify and focus on their methods. We hope such support will continue.

Methods clarification and sharing workshop

(1) **10 minutes**

- On your own: what methodology and methods are you using and why?
- How does this fit in with your conceptual framework?
- What changes (if any) have you made to your methodology and methods and why?

(2) **Get into groups of 5. Present to your colleagues (1 person feeds back)**

Rules
- 5 minutes each
- How did you decide on your methodology and methods?

- How do they spring from your conceptual framework and so help you *find out* what you are researching about?
- How have you *developed* or *changed* your methods? Why? To overcome what difficulties? Or to ask questions differently? Or?

(3) **Feedback**

- Sum up what your group members have said – chosen methods, changes, why?
- Select *one* as a case study to describe, defend methods, explain how they *really do* fit with the conceptual framework and help achieve research aims!

Remember:

A conceptual framework explains, either graphically or in narrative form, the main dimensions to be studied – the key factors, or variables – and the presumed relationships among them. Frameworks come in several shapes and sizes. They can be rudimentary or elaborate, theory-driven or commonsensical, descriptive or causal.   (Miles and Huberman, 1984)

(4) **Following the feedback, please reflect, discuss and share:**

How did being involved in . . .

- clarifying your methods . . .
- presenting to/discussing with the group . . .
- hearing about others' decisions . . .
- and overall summing up and giving feedback . . .

. . . help you in your research development at this stage?

Some responses from the group work on methods

Some students indicated cultural difference in their research approaches; others worked through their research methods to ensure they fit their aims and conceptual frameworks. One student, concentrating on interactions and power in a school, said that discussion with others in the group enabled her to consider how different people involved in her study might interact. She realised she needs to find a way to relate their responses and consider their interactions. Recognising the different people involved and interactions necessary enabled her to focus on ways she will build together the different elements of her research methods.

The sessions have proved to be enjoyable, building peer support culture, and also intellectually taxing. Note-taking, discussing and reporting accurately from a group process is a skill that helps students learn to present and engage in academic discussion about their own and others' work: all are transferable skills (and useful in a viva).

Students participating in the group work session reported a variety of responses. One was visibly seen to have an enlightening moment when, through relating her conceptual framework to her research methods, she could see how the whole fitted together. Both isolation and wastage could be counteracted by the sensitive development of support systems based on initial programmes of research methods training.

Data analysis Workshop Stage 1

A second workshop at stage 1, 'What do I do with all this data?', models problems of asking questions of data, when a great deal of data have been collected and students find they

- have collected too much and do not know how to manage it;
- have lost their sense of what questions they were asking and why;
- have become too immersed in the data to be able to work out how to problematise, question, organise, then analyse and present it.

This first stage workshop accompanies discussion on data handling and analysing findings, the managing of data through computer programmes such as SPSS and NVIVO, cataloguing, thematic identification, relating back to the research questions and moving towards drawing conclusions. Students are given data produced through analysing a questionnaire on their own learning (RoLI) undertaken earlier. In theory, they should be able to identify the research questions and, since we have discussed learning approaches, motivation, outcomes and so on, be able to go some way towards working out what kinds of questions can be asked of the data to make sense of the research questions. Ensuing discussions revealed several students to be at the stage Hodge (1995), calls 'negative postmodernism', that is they feel they are 'swimming in data'!

To run the workshop
Students need: A questionnaire, a data set, a pie chart and a bar chart, etc. drawn from the data, and some background information on the aims and outcomes of the questionnaire.

Data analysis exercise: What do I do with all this data?

In groups spend 30 minutes with the data discussing these questions. Select a chair to manage the discussion and a respondent to report back on your views:

- Look through the data produced from analysis of the Reflections on Learning inventory (YOUR cohort)
- What could you do with this data?
- How do you feel when presented with such amounts of data?
- What questions would you like to ask it?
- What do you need to know FIRST in order to ask any questions or interpret anything?
- Why might you want to use this particular data? What might you be seeking?
- Why use this *kind* of data?
- What else – what other information from other research vehicles and methods might you want to use to help back up (triangulate) your findings from this data? And why?
- Now look at the information about categories.
- Can you draw any tentative conclusions; make any suggestions about interpretation or meaning from any of this? How do the categories/does the further information help your analysis and interpretation?
- How could you represent this data, in what useful ways? Why? How might it be used to illustrate or argue? Defend your decisions.

Individual discussion and group report back

Now think individually, and then discuss in your group:

- What will you ensure you do in order to analyse and interpret your own data?
- What could go wrong?
- What kinds of precautions can you take to ensure little goes wrong in collection, analysis etc?

Now please present some good practice suggestions for managing, analysing and interpreting data.

Discussions about analysing and categorising data, producing and sharing findings, and drawing conclusions emerged from the workshop. For example, one student noted:

> Most of the people agree with it . . . links between movement. How can we show links? Sometimes the data that we got when collected can lead us to such assumptions that a lot of them . . . then we have to summarise them . . . select, decide which assumptions we want to research afterwards, and sometimes we have a previous assumption, and discover after we have collected data, we have a surprise – that nothing conforms to our thinking before, and we have to create absolutely new assumptions . . . so we need to research what's going on with our (prior) assumptions, then we collect the data . . . you have to check why it happens.   (Student F)

Students discuss links between their previous assumptions, the data and how they might develop findings and draw conclusions. Difficulties of showing links using qualitative methods emerged. The group felt more secure with quantitative methods.

Involvement in questionnaire completion, data analysis, discussions and focus group discussions as part of the initial development programme encourage a focus on any gaps and disjunctions between aims and methods, causing students to reflect on getting a 'best fit' between methods, data analysis, strategies and their own research. It is hoped that they are then more able to take a reflective approach, are likely to be more open to change and more able to accommodate and respond to 'surprises' and 'creative' elements of research as well as clashes in approach and aims (as they meet them) during their research work.

This is a PhD research development workshop, but could easily be used with students at any level. (Indeed, I have run a similar, shorter, easier version with OU Social Science Foundation preparatory course students). Other workshops, useable at all levels could:

1 Involve students working in groups to identify themes and categories from transcripts of taped interviews, deciding how to label, extract, then comment on these extracts in a dialogue.
2 Involve trialling dissertation schedules on each others' group participation actions then discussing
   • how you would categorise
   • how you would interpret and
   • how you would produce findings or conclusions from these in a meaningful way

   (See Wisker, 2001, for details.)

Postgraduate research development programmes – a summary

A good RDP provides support and development to augment supervisors' work and help students develop peer group support. Additionally, it contributes to metalearning, encouraging students to reflect on their learning, moving theories beyond the qualification, and developing transferable skills (some clearly related to research for example, methods; others more generic for example, time management).

Margot Pearson, considering generic programmes, suggests some common themes:

How does the programme:

- provide access to resources (and expertise) essential to conduct high-quality research?
- give students flexibility/choice of learning and research conditions within a negotiated structure?
- ensure adequate supervision for administrative matters and for intellectual leadership, and identify who is responsible for what?
- ensure students engage with practising researchers and are in conversation with a community of peers/experts/others?
- be responsive to students' career goals and the opportunities and demands of relevant employment markets?

These questions cannot be usefully or effectively addressed by generic institutional-level policy formulations, or by individual supervisors alone. They require an integrated approach to curriculum design for particular conditions and purposes.   (Pearson, 1999, p. 282)

Pearson and others consider the importance of workshops and programmes, supervisory guidance, peer support systems in a framework itself reflective of institutional commitment to good practice in support and development for research (corresponding to UK Metcalfe Report – see Metcalfe et al., 2002) and which helps build a community of practice, extending research capabilities:

The responsibility of the supervisor is to ensure that more than technique is learnt. To do this, the student needs to learn not only current practice but how to address the problematic and the unknown. Schön refers to this as 'an art of problem framing, an art of implementation, and an art of improvisation' (Schön, 1987, p. 13). In his approach, the student learns through doing and through critical reflection on that experience in conversation with experts, who can draw on their extended repertoire of skills and strategies. Similarly, in Collins et al.'s cognitive apprenticeship model, modelling, coaching and scaffolding are located within the context of students being encouraged to externalise their learning processes so that they can gain conscious access to and control of their own problem-solving strategies by articulating and reflecting on their knowledge, reasoning, or problem-solving processes and by exploring new avenues of interest to themselves.   (Pearson and Brew, 2002, p. 140)

▶ Conclusions

Completing research and PhDs successfully are long-term projects involving students, supervisors, institutions and the academic community in ongoing developmental work. Completing a Master's or undergraduate research dissertation might be less of an enormous project in terms of *time* and *length*, but coming, as they do, so much earlier in a student's research career, they appear equally daunting. In each research enterprise, students engage in a conceptualisation of the research, processes of research in action, strategies of research as a form of learning, and the tenacity, structuring and presentational capabilities that lead in the last analysis to a well-presented, well-articulated, well-conceptualised and structured piece of significant research making a contribution to knowledge and conceptualisation in the field, at the appropriate level. In this a great part is played by the supervisor. An equally large part is played by the academic community of which research development programmes constitute a formal part, and student peer support mechanisms including reading groups, etc., a less formal, perhaps more personal support and development mechanism.

▶ Further reading

Cullen, D., Pearson, M., Saha, L. and Spear, R. (1994) *Establishing Effective PhD Supervision* (Canberra: Australian Government Publishing Service).

Delamont, S., Atkinson, P. and Parry, O. (1997) *Supervising the PhD: A Guide to Success* (Buckingham: Open University Press).

IETEI (2004) Special edition.

Lave, J. and Wenger, E. (1991) *Situated Learning: Legitimate Peripheral Participation* (Cambridge: Cambridge University Press).

Metcalfe, J., Thompson, Q. and Green, H. (2002) *Improving Standards in Postgraduate Research Degree Programmes: A Report to the Higher Education Funding Councils of England, Scotland and Wales.* Accessed online at: www.grad.ac.uk/downloads/rdp_report/rdp_framework_report.pdf.

Pearson, M. (1999) 'The changing environment for doctoral education in Australia: implications for quality management, improvement and innovation?' *Higher Education Research and Developemnt*, **18**(3), p. 277.

Pearson, M. and Brew, A. (2002) 'Research training and supervision development', *Studies in Higher Education*, **27**(2), pp. 135–50.

Schön, D. A. (1987) *Educating the Reflective Practitioner* (San Francisco, CA: Jossey-Bass).

Wisker, G. (1998) *The Research as Learning Questionnaire* (Cambridge: Anglia Polytechnic University).

Wisker, G., Robinson, G., Trafford, V., Creighton, E. and Warnes, M. (2003) 'Recognising and overcoming dissonance in postgraduate student research', *Studies in Higher Education*, **28**(1).

11 Dealing with Difference: Working with Different Kinds of Learners and Learning Styles

In this chapter we consider working with research as a form of learning, and how we might recognise our students' learning approaches and better enable them to be successful in their research-as-learning.

This chapter considers:

- *how our postgraduate and undergraduate students approach their research as a form of learning and what do we know about their learning styles*
- *how they conceptualise their research*
- *the possible pitfalls that could arise from a mismatch between learning approaches and the demands of research*
- *using the research-as-learning questionnaire as a learning vehicle*
- *how to manage mismatches or dissonance between students' research-as-learning approaches and their research project.*

Autonomy, independence and originality are essential elements of successful postgraduate research outcomes, dissertations and theses. For undergraduate students, undertaking research is an opportunity for some first steps in the direction of independence and originality. Research at APU (Wisker *et al.*, 2003) indicates that there is much to be learned about how research students approach their research-as-learning. Insights of this nature allow supervisors to support them and enable them to match research-as-learning strategies and vehicles to research questions and intended outcomes. Equally, potential dissonance between learning styles, learning approaches and intended learning outcomes can be identified. If students can develop a diversity of research-as-learning approaches, closing gaps between their approaches and conceptions of research, and their intended outcomes, they should achieve greater success in their research.

When research students start their work, whether for a dissertation or for a PhD, they are making a great leap upwards into a more complex and demanding level of learning, just as they did when starting a degree, or the work that preceded that. It is, therefore, very useful to find out more about the learning demands of the research-as-learning, and about students' own preferred learning styles, strategies and approaches in relation to those demands. In this way, supervisors and students can recognise developmental learning and research needs together and supervisors will be less likely to expect students to learn in ways with which they are familiar. This is particularly important when working with students from other learning cultures.

Research into student learning deals with human subjects, their reflection and experience. It also deals with specific interactions. Students might well learn differently in different contexts or following different cues from staff and the curriculum.

▶ Potential difficulties in research-as-learning styles and approaches

Students must be encouraged to be reflective about their own learning styles, preconceptions and approaches so that they can develop metalearning, to acquire the research-as-learning practices needed by the research questions, methods and tasks in hand. You might ask your research students to consider:

- why they carry out learning and research, that is, what motivates them (parental examples, a sense of duty, a sense of fulfilment?)
- how they conceptualise their learning – seeing learning as accumulating more knowledge about the world or enabling them to fit new understanding into a conceptual framework and link to experience
- what kinds of learning and research approaches they take accumulating information and data, relating ideas and information holistically
- what sort of outcomes they seek – gaining status, seeing the world differently, bringing about creative change.

See Meyer and Boulton-Lewis (1997) in relation to postgraduate learning, and Meyer and Kiley (1998) and Wisker (1999) for further ideas.

It is interesting to clarify these issues and practices for several reasons. Learning as a postgraduate or as a research student rather than an undergraduate or a professional makes new and different demands upon students, and they therefore need to develop further learning strategies to succeed. For international students, culturally influenced learning expectations and behaviours might differ in their research university from those at home. An increased awareness of diverse learning approaches and the demands on learning development made by research studies can lead to the development of an appropriate diversity of learning approaches and behaviours suitable for any level of research. This could include a focus on reflection; integrating new learning with established learning; combining different learning practices from a range of subject areas to address interdisciplinary research; and learning how to rely on sound evidence for the learner's learning to ensure research questions, practices and conclusions are carefully founded in and underpinned by theory. Equally, students need to ensure that if they rely on activity and experience, it too is underpinned by theory. Research into student learning (Marton and Saljo, 1976; Ramsden, 1983) suggests that students broadly take one or more of *three* approaches to their learning (i.e., 'deep', 'surface' and 'strategic' learning).

▶ Learning styles: deep, surface and strategic learning

Established research into student learning initially identified two main learning styles: deep and surface learning (Marton and Saljo 1976, 1978, Ramsden 1979) to which was added latterly 'strategic' learning (Entwistle and Ramsden, 1983). It is suggested that 'traditional or didactic teaching' largely encourages *surface* learning and that this could be present in science subjects in particular, where there is a large information base, but that *deep* learning produces better results and longer lasting learning for the students, that is learning is likely to be internalised if it integrates theory and experience, and if new learning is linked to established learning. It is also more appropriate for research endeavours, particularly for postgraduates, because deep learning depends on asking critical questions, problematising given beliefs and interpretations, seeking new syntheses, as well as being creative and original based on understanding, questioning and expressing questions or solutions in new ways. Students tend to adopt a variety of approaches, partly dependent on experience and partly on the cues offered by staff or the learning situation.

The *surface* or *atomistic learner* tends to see knowledge as the acquisition of facts or information. Tasks and objectives are seen as discrete, as are the stages towards completion of a task. Time is very important, as is completion. A personal relationship or identification with the work is considered inappropriate and even misguided. This kind of approach relies a great deal on learning as 'memorising before understanding' (Meyer and Shanahan, 2002). Because students are not uniting ideas and facts, they find themselves unable to fit new information and ideas into already developed learning or concept 'maps', and into a relationship with their own experience. Such learning tends to be easily forgotten, little used. Researchers taking surface approaches will tend to accumulate vast amounts of information and data but are unlikely to marshal it towards addressing their research questions or contributing towards an ongoing argument.

The *deep* or *holistic learner* searches for meaning lying beyond or within specific tasks. They relate any discrete information to a general, already established learning or concept map, and relate new ideas and learning to prior experience and prior learning, and develop as new information and ideas are added. They tend to personalise learning tasks and integrate them. They see the whole problem, the general ideas, the main concept and fit the learning activity into these through using frames of understanding and personal experiential reference. They problematise what's offered up as given and so ask questions and make meaning. Such learning is more consistent with research insofar as it encourages problematising and problem-solving, creativity, the development of new ideas and concepts, and a concern with the longer term usefulness of the research findings.

Strategic learners focus on the end product – the marks – with the main aim being to pass or to achieve the completion of a dissertation or thesis. Students could 'grade chase' and only learn what appears necessary, thus lacking linking and retention.

Research students certainly need to have a clear vision of the end product – the dissertation or thesis. To achieve this, they need to accumulate data and information as evidence, but they also need to select and relate it to their research question, the gap of knowledge they seek to address and the boundaries to their research. They fit information into concept maps, and memorise it only after they have understood and sought meaning. They are strategic in the sense that they do not want to be overloaded with excessive, unnecessary detail and do need to direct their research and orient it towards completion in time. It could be argued that the successful research student combines a deep and a strategic approach, knowing how to acquire and manage data, information, evidence and arguments into a coherent, completed whole – the dissertation or thesis.

▶ How research-as-learning might differ in different disciplines

Different discipline areas and different parts of discipline areas might be taught in ways that encourage either surface or deep learning. Ramsden (1979) indicates that students can switch strategies to suit tasks. Biggs (1978) shows that while students might evidence tendencies for different sorts of learning, it is *both possible and desirable to encourage the development of deep learning approaches* because these are overall the most successful learning approaches to embed and use learning. The depth of processing learning implies meaningfulness in learning. This is particularly important in relation to research-as-learning since fundamental elements of the research process relate to enquiry, problematising, relating experience to theory and to practice and contributing new knowledge, none of which would easily be accomplished by the regurgitation of memorised, discrete items of information.

A deep learning strategy, based on wide reading, relating new knowledge in comparison to what is already known, results in better or deeper learning. This is defined as complexity of outcomes (Biggs, 1978; Marton and Saljo 1976), satisfaction with performance (Biggs, 1978, Ch. 6) and reflected and self-rated performance in comparison with peers or examination results (Schmeck, 1986; Svensson, 1978; Thomas and Bain, 1982, Watkins and Hattie, 1981).

Science students are usually more likely to adopt a surface approach and some subjects tend to call for surface or accumulated learning, at least as part of acquiring a knowledge base. However, the accumulation of data and evidence should be placed in a frame, in relation to research questions and arguments, leading to understanding. Research carried out by Svensson (1978) suggests, in relation to undergraduates, that those who learn to adopt a deep approach gain better exam results in the end and also become better learners. This would appear to be even more relevant at postgraduate level because of the need for reflection, creativity and ownership of the individual research project.

In all subjects there is an element that is information-heavy and requires some memorising so the students can, at will, use what they have encoded in their memory.

All subjects require data and evidence. The clue is mapping these against the research question, showing links, synthesising and adding to, rather than simply regurgitating knowledge.

Learners who contextualise their learning relate it to themselves and their own world. They become reflective, self-aware and more flexible. They concentrate on how they are learning as well as what they are learning (metalearning). They are likely to be higher achievers than those who are less aware of or consider irrelevant such consciousness and contextualisation. In terms of research undertakings, students who get stuck at the level of accumulating vast amounts of data might feel they are working hard but getting nowhere. It is the synthesising, organising, sifting and directing of information or asking questions and trying to answer them that makes it a research endeavour, and creates meaningful learning.

Students' approaches may differ at different times and in different learning situations. One influence may be a diversity of learning cues from supervisors. Learning relates closely to the way in which students see the world, to their reasons for undertaking research and the kinds of outcomes sought. It is useful to discuss with students why they are researching, how they conceptualise their research, how they go about it, what outcomes they seek and what skills they are developing. Some problems could be overcome by developing this kind of reflection and interaction. Our research into postgraduate learning, for example, shows a direct correlation between research students taking a largely accumulative approach and a lack of progress. Therefore, if students find they are largely taking a surface, accumulative approach, they could be left with large quantities of disparate data and little developed idea about how to fit it all together, or make meaning from it. This will lead to problems in both the progress and the quality of the research.

Consider the case of one researcher, Alan:

> When I took early retirement I knew exactly what piece of research I wanted to carry out. No-one to date had actually looked at a history of the company, and I think this is an important piece of work, to chart the company's history, looking at what it has achieved, the various setbacks and the successes. I have not had any problem gaining access to documents I need for my research, and I have looked back now over documents since the late nineteen forties when the company was first established. I work very systematically. I colour code the different issues and the different themes and ensure that they are all fully written up and labelled on my computer so that I can access any piece of data under whichever cross referenced headings I am using at the push of a button. I also work very systematically. I mean now I have retired this is the main task I am involved in, so I get up each day and do about five hours a day on the thesis

Alan is clearly an accumulative learner. He gathers facts and carefully stores them. Many of these strategies are admirable – he is well organised. But his work lacks any sense of problematising, questioning, wondering why? Why not? It is unlikely to be at PhD level, rather at MPhil *because* of this approach.

There are many theories that suggest tendencies towards learning styles (for example, Honey and Mumford, 1986; Kolb, 1984; Schön, 1983). For research students, spotting these in themselves can help them understand why they might find it difficult to learn from some situations and in some contexts and easier in others. A useful learning activity to encourage is the development of reflection and metalearning, that is students' awareness of how they are learning. This can partly be encouraged through involvement in reflective activities of completion, discussion of results from learning questionnaires and through keeping a reflective log. The growing interest in encouraging students to recognise the research skills they have acquired and developed, perhaps evidencing these in a personal development portfolio, and the encouragement to keep a learning journal or log act as activities to prompt deep learning.

▶ Reflection and metalearning

When students have such knowledge about their own learning, they can choose to play to their strengths and/or to work on their weaknesses and develop further the learning styles that are not the most obviously successful for them, especially in terms of learning demanded by different elements of the research, for example from brainstorming crucial, central ideas and problematising given interpretations through to data collection and the management and writing up of a high level, coherent, well-argued dissertation or thesis.

You could work with your research students to complete the Reflections on Learning Inventory (Meyer and Boulton-Lewis, 1997), or another learning styles inventory/questionnaire such as the Approaches to Study Inventory (Entwistle and Ramsden, 1983) or the Honey and Mumford (1986) learning styles questionnaire, and then discuss the results in terms of research-as-learning. Two activities follow to help supervisors and students to consider which of the four main styles describe their way of learning and then to reflect on the forms of learning demanded by their research processes.

Activity: for supervisors and students

Please consider Honey and Mumford's definitions of learning styles. If you want to complete their questionnaire and analyse your results for a more 'accurate' picture, it is readily available in their book *Using Your Manual of Learning Styles* (1986).

Learning styles
Each style has its own strengths and weaknesses. There are no 'good' or 'bad' styles. Your major styles will tell you what strengths you have as a learner, which situations and learning activities make it easier for you to learn and what you need to be wary of or to develop in your learning styles to benefit from different learning opportunities and situations. For example, studying tourism will tend to favour activists and English literature will tend to suit reflectors.

   The greatest variety of learning opportunities are available to those who can, to some extent, operate in all styles, but who are clear, when facing a problem or learning opportunity, which style is most effective for them, and which they need to develop.

Activists
Activists learn best from constant exposure to new experiences. They like to involve themselves in immediate experiences and are enthusiastic about anything new. They tend to act first and consider the consequences later. They enjoy new challenges, but are soon bored with implementation and consolidation. They learn least well from activities that require them to take a passive role. *As researchers*, they might be excited by experiences or interviews, but not so keen on reading the underpinning theorists or working solidly to write up their work to completion.

Reflectors
Reflectors learn best from activities that allow them space to ponder over experience and assimilate new information before making a considered judgement in their own time. They tend to be cautious and thoughtful, wishing to consider all the possible angles and implications before making a decision. They often spend a good deal of time listening and observing. They learn least well from activities that require rapid action with little time for planning. *As researchers*, they might need some support in 'doing', for example experimentation, performance of field tasks and data collection, but they should be good at considering the implications of research results, and what they are learning through conducting and writing up research.

Theorists
Theorists learn best from activities that allow them to integrate observations into logically sound theories. They like to think problems through in a step-by-step way, assimilating new information and experience into a tidy, rational scheme. They are good at analysis, and are comfortable using theories and models to explain things to themselves and others. They are less comfortable with subjective opinion or creative thinking. They learn least from situations that they are unable to *research* in depth. Theorists are usually very likely to involve themselves in the reading but might find they read themselves into stagnation. Conversely, they struggle to carry out experiments, interviews, observations or try to draw even factual conclusions. They might need prompting to conduct field work or experiments and to assimilate field work data, to start to put pen to paper, and actually commit themselves to arguments (rather than planning and theorising alone).

Pragmatists
Pragmatists learn best from activities that have a clear practical value and that allow ideas and approaches to be tested in practical settings. They tend to be down-to-earth people who like to get on with things. They also tend to be impatient with open-ended discussions. They learn least from situations where learning is not related to an immediate purpose. To some extent they can make really sound researchers, as they tend to both carry out the theoretical work – reading, in dialogue – and to engage with practical data collection and analysing. They might be better off producing *research reports* – that is 'useful' outcomes, rather than creating new knowledge or working at a deeply conceptual level, so for a PhD piece of research rather than a practical research project, they might need support in terms of learning to draw conceptual and factual conclusions instead of developing change programmes and recommendations, where change recommendations are actually *not* appropriate to the research design.

Activities to stretch and develop research-as-learning styles

With mutual agreement and planned development – if your students 'present' as a high *theorist* – you might suggest they: (1) carefully read one of the key essays related to their research; (2) critically evaluate how it makes an argued and well-evidenced case; (3) apply the theories or arguments *directly* to part of their own research sample, their field and their data.

Task

This activity is suitable for use with students in relation to their learning and by supervisors to assess their own learning.

Consider:

- Which description(s) of learning styles best fit you and your learning?
- Are there any situations or modes of research behaviour in which you find you are naturally happier? How do they relate to learning style? (for example, if you are a theorist and low pragmatist you might tend to read excessively before starting any fieldwork or beginning to draw conclusions from findings).
- Are there any learning styles, approaches or situations with which you are not happy or from which you learn easily?
- If you spot such an approach or research learning behaviour, for example, finding it difficult to learn from focusing deeply or reading and understanding complex theories, what might you do to strengthen your learning behaviour and approach to carry out this kind of research-as-learning more successfully?

If students present as high *reflectors*, the same kind of strategy is useful or any which encourages active engagement with research, building on reading and reflecting.

If students present as *pragmatists* or *activists*, ask them: (1) to gather three extracts dealing with theory and argument from other researchers and theorists related to their work; (2) to process these and then present them, showing directly how these ideas and theories underpin the work; and (3) to link questions, methods, data and findings directly to the theories. This analysis should help to act as a model for their own work, where they will need to engage *their* ideas and findings with the theories and previous work that underpin it.

If students present as *activists*, ask them to keep a reflective log of questions, problems, reading and achievements in their research processes and look at it with them, asking them to make links between the log, their actions and findings.

By definition, research students need to be self-directed learners for much of their time. A consideration of the adult learning-based learning theories of self-directed learning (Brookfield, 1986), experiential learning (Kolb, 1984) and reflective practice (Schön, 1987) can benefit students in their appreciation of their own learning styles and approaches, and the demands of the research process. As with the theories about research-as-learning (above), it could be useful to encourage students' metalearning and development of a repertoire of research-as-learning strategies. Suggest they read work by learning theorists, reflecting on it in relation to their current practice and the requirements of the research process.

These related theories and practices (as discussed above) feed into basic assumptions and guidelines underlying success in learning, in the setting up of learning experiences, the monitoring, evaluating and evidencing of learning (see Wisker, 2001, pp. 86–101).

It is possible to map learning approach theories onto the stages of students' research and the methodologists they might use. *Inductive research* is more likely to start Kolb's experiential cycle from experience and build up theory, explore and investigate it in practice, ask questions, then develop theory. *Deductive research* is more likely to begin with a hypothesis and some assumptions to be tested.

Considering their place on Kolb's (1984) learning cycle in relation to their specific piece of research could help students to identify whether their work is inductive, deductive or a mixture, and what their learning strategies are. This insight can lead them to develop clearer ideas about the necessary research methods to use in order to ask their research questions, test their hypotheses, if any, and approach their research problems. Beyond the research, students can continue to put findings into practice to cause change, reflect on the effects, research the effectiveness, try again – and so on.

▶ **Reflective practice**

Reflection helps to clarify and embed learning. Donald Schön (1983) in *The Reflective Practitioner* explores how professionals and practitioners learn from experience. He argues that professionals respond to and reflect on varied experience arising in their work, seeking development and change. Reflective practitioners use 'artistry' creatively to draw from a set of past examples and precedents to transfer from one situation to the next, continually. They create and learn anew in each situation, bringing previous learning to bear on new situations. This relates to research in several ways. Professional work and practice generate experience and knowledge naturally, but it is important to make this learning explicit in a learning situation, and to encourage learners to reflect on and articulate their learning from practice and from their work (see Winter, 1993). Students who are building on research for reflective practice will need to draw from professional work and practise the learning experiences that relate to the research they are undertaking. Reflective practice often inspires practitioners to carry out practice-based, professional or action research so it naturally informs and underpins some kinds of research questions, methodologies and methods. However, all students can benefit from using reflection to be aware of research skills and to develop their research decisions and discussions and findings based on reflection. Students should be encouraged to be reflective about their research practice and learn from this (use a log, a journal or discuss it with their supervisor).

Supervisors and students could Base the beginning and progress of the research around Kolb's (1984) experiential learning cycle, to see how and where they might enter the cycle and how their research progress can be changed by working out how they move through it. First let us consider the research topic and proposed methods. Could there be any moments of contradiction or potential clash? Could any particular research-as-learning approaches be less fruitful or suitable than others?

Clashes between approaches and the outcomes the student is seeking are likely to take place, for example, when students:

1. adopt a largely accumulation approach but seek a transformative outcome;
2. are overwhelmed with details and data and cannot easily order or map them.

Our research with PhD students at APU (1998–2003) has used questionnaires (Reflections on Learning Inventory, in Meyer and Boulton-Lewis, 1997), supervisory dialogues, interviews, workshops and focus groups to identify and then work with students to overcome these and other kinds of problems.

These are the two main problem areas revealed by study of the research project on which students are engaged, and their learning behaviours and approaches to the project as a piece of research. There could be many others. It is useful to consider potential clashes, limits and blockages, and talk through with your student about how they might more appropriately develop research proposals; temper their transformational aims to be more realistic within the size and scope of a PhD, MPhil, EdD, MA, BA, BSc etc.; match research methods to the intended outcomes, and avoid overload in terms of the amount of research to be undertaken.

▶ Research-as-learning questionnaire

The research-as-learning questionnaire asks students to identify and match their concepts of research to their concepts of self, understanding, beliefs, knowledge and the world. Their concepts, values and beliefs may include the following: knowledge and experience, personal subjectivity, a belief that all experience and evidence can be pinned down and proved, the importance of creativity and originality rather than recording, and the importance of research and contribution to the improvement of human life.

Beliefs and world views underpin research approaches:

- Positivistic researchers might record data and statistics and expect solutions to be provable and fact-based (validity)
- More predictive/descriptive researchers (often positivistic) believe everything is discoverable. They might take a more pragmatic approach to the 'right' questions to produce the 'right' answers
- Holistic, post-positivist researchers might look at living responses, variables and the whole context, and at interactions (*reliability* but not *validity,* i.e. can't *prove it*)
- Professional, practice-based, creative/morally-engaged researchers might seek some answers to effect change
- Some research is theory-building and some is theory-testing.

▶ Postgraduate research-as-learning questions

Complete the questionnaire for yourself first, then ask students to complete it and use it in discussions with them. Using the results consider what the implications are for the student's research-as-learning success, and what might be done to make the student aware of any misconceptions in the design of the study, any mismatches between research-as-learning approaches and the research itself.

The questions are designed to help to prompt reflection about the appropriateness of research-as-learning conceptions and approaches in relation to approaches and conceptions with which the supervisor and student might be most familiar, and in relation to the proposed research project. Some of the most familiar conceptions and approaches might differ between supervisor and student, or might not actually be suitable for the current research project, in which case discussion and development should follow and approaches and conceptions should be adjusted. Such discussions aid metalearning.

Ask your student:

- What are your main research questions?
- What are you hoping to find out?
- What is your research concerned with/about? What conceptions of research do you have?
- In carrying out your research, which of these descriptions describe your activities? Please score them from:
  - 1: 'this does not describe my approaches and activities', to
  - 5: 'this describes my approaches and activities clearly'.

Research-as-learning questionnaire

I believe my research is about/is concerned with:

1 Describing – finding out information about an event, a set of relations between variables or a situation and carefully describing it/them in detail.   1 2 3 4 5

2 Exploring – look for reasons why certain things have happened and what might have caused problems/ developments / situations.   1 2 3 4 5

3. Finding the right answers – if there is enough exploration and recording, there will be answers discoverable right to important questions that can then be recorded.   1 2 3 4 5

4. Experimenting – starting with a hypothesis and through trying out something and seeing what happens next, looking at the results and linking them back to the experiment.   1 2 3 4 5

5. Prediction – predicting the links from things, events and reactions in the past, similar to your area of research or setting up conditions and activities and speculating and predicting about what could happen in the future.   1 2 3 4 5

6. Weaving, interrelating – believing that aspects of areas are related both distantly or closely to others, even across discipline areas and finding out about these links and overlaps.   1 2 3 4 5

7. Metaphorical links/leaps – using metaphors/creative 1 2 3 4 5
comparisons between the imaginative and the real,
across disciplines in order to spot relations and
similarities. Making often imaginative or philosophical
mental leaps across areas that possibly seem logically
unrelated.

8. Being creative – trying out a new activity or change 1 2 3 4 5
mechanism, exploring 'what happens if . . .?' and
producing something original and creative/helping
others to produce something original and creative.
Pushing forward the boundaries of creativity and
making something new.

Students should be asked to consider how their conception of research fits their question and their chosen methodology and methods. Different conceptions of research will be more suitable for some kinds of research and questions than others – so the main *issue* here is matching the conceptions to the questions, subject area and the methodologies and methods rather than any suggestion that there's a final 'good way' and 'right conception'.

Scientific researchers who use experiments to test hypotheses might believe there are discoverable, provable 'right answers' (3 and 4). A discussion could follow about how they handle the likelihood of their experiments consistently failing and how they learn to persist, and sometimes to accept that experiments don't work or can't produce 'right answers'.

Social scientists, educationalists or health-related researchers might need to predict links (5) or describe relations at some point in their work (1), and explore reasons for actions (2), but these are unlikely to suit Arts and Humanities researchers who might make more metaphorical learning 'leaps' (7).

All researchers can probably see themselves as creative (8) at some point and a discussion about what this *means* in different subjects areas is most usefully prompted after completing the questionnaire. Students also need to realise that all research includes *taking risks* – they learn from them, push the boundaries of knowledge and their ways of seeing the world (and they might have to deal with resulting problems and surprises).

This research-as-learning questionnaire has been a useful aid in action research with groups of postgraduates at APU, and supervisors on development programmes.

Reflection on learning and research-as-learning should feed into insights and practice:

- when planning and carrying out research, analysing findings, etc.
- when reflecting on the programme of the research
- when diagnosing and coping with contradictions and problems – getting stuck in some parts of research where this relates to how a researcher goes about it as a learning activity
- when researching the learning of those the researcher works with or teaches.

▶ **Further reading**

Biggs, J. B. (1978) 'Individual and group differences in study processes and the quality of learning outcomes', *Higher Education*, **48**, pp. 266–79.

Brookfield, S. D. (1986) *Understanding and Facilitating Adult Learning Comprehensive Analysis of Principles and Effective Practises*. Milton Keynes: Open University Press.

Entwistle, N. J. and Ramsden, P. (1983) *Understanding Student Learning* (London: Croom Helm).

Gibbs, G. (1981) *Teaching Students to Learn* (Buckingham: Open University Press).

Honey, P. and Mumford, A. (1986) *Using Your Manual of Learning Styles* (Peter Honey Publications).

Kolb, David A. (1984) *Experimental Learning as the Source of Learning and Development* (Englewood Cliffs, NJ: Prentice-Hall).

Marton, F. and Saljo, R. (1976) 'On qualitative differences in learning – outcome and process', *British Journal of Educational Technology*, **46**, pp. 4–11.

Meyer, J. H. F. and Boulton-Lewis, G. M. (1997) 'Reflections on Learning Inventory (ROLI)', questionaire.

Meyer, J. H. F. and Shanahan, M. P. (2002), 'On variation in conceptions of "price" in economics', *Higher Education*, **43**, 203–25.

Schmeck, R. R. (1986) *Learning Styles and Learning Strategies* (New York: Plenum).

Schön, D. (1983) *The Reflective Practitioner* (New York: Basic Books).

Svensson, L. (1978) 'Some notes on a methodological problem in the study of the relationship between thought and language: Describing the thought content in terms of different conceptions of the same phenomenon', Report from the Institute of Education, no. 69, Gothenburg University, Department of Education and Educational Research.

Thomas, P. and Bain, J. D. (1982) 'Consistency in learning strategies', *Higher Education*, **11**, pp. 249–59.

Watkins, D. and Hattie, J. (1981) 'The learning processes of Australian university students: investigations of contextual and personological factors', *British Journal of Educational Psychology*, **15**, pp. 384–93.

Winter, R. (1993) 'Continuity and progression assessment vocabularies for higher education', unpublished research report data (Chelmsford: Anglia Polytechnic University Faculty of Health and Social Work).

Wisker, G., Robinson, G., Trafford, V., Creighton, E. and Warnes, M. (2003) 'Recognising and overcoming dissonance in postgraduate student research', *Studies in Higher Education*, **28**(1), pp. 91–105.

12 Supervising International Students

Increasing numbers of postgraduate and undergraduate students are studying at universities outside their own country in a variety of modes, either on site or at a distance. Students from, for example, the Near, Middle, Far Eastern or African countries are following courses at European, Australian and American universities. This chapter explores some of the issues making suggestions for good pedagogical and other practices.

This chapter considers

- *international students – cultural issues*
- *institutional contexts, practices and supervisory support*
- *internationalising the curriculum*
- *managing issues of cultural difference in terms of preconceptions, learning, interpretation, social and research issues*

▶ Cross-cultural Issues

We live in increasingly multicultural societies and a world where travel and communication enable us to move, mix, communicate with each other, live and work in each others' countries with what sometimes seems effortless ease. However, this ease of travel and technology mask continuing difficulties experienced within cultural contexts. If international students are to benefit fully from studying in cultural contexts other than their own, and if the universities that host and work with them are to gain some benefit from the presence of international postgraduates and undergraduates, we need to share good practice to facilitate real interaction as opposed to some form of travel and technology hype. It is crucial that all (and perhaps especially European, Australian and US) academic contexts enable students to achieve and negotiate carefully the cultural minefields of potential academic imperialism. This often accidental imperialism, where it exists, is reflected at one extreme in cultural arrogance, an assumption of cultural and academic superiority of ways of going about research, of who holds the knowledge and how one might access and work with it, and discourses of power in the supervisor–university–student relationship, all affected by cultural differences. At the other end of the continuum there can be a lack of attention to often basic needs – money, family, food, warmth, housing, access to communication, access to computers and libraries, work – which could be barriers to concentration and study for international students.

Embarking upon postgraduate and undergraduate research is an investment in terms of time, money and self-development. Students from different cultural contexts may view this enterprise in different ways to those from indigenous Western contexts. Their learning backgrounds and previous experience, as well as the conditions in which they are researching may be different. In addition, their approaches, the outcomes they seek, and their sense of the appropriateness of various research methods might all differ from those of the host university. If students have recently moved away from their home country to study, they might also encounter cultural differences that exacerbate difficulties in settling into another culture. At the potential difficulties need to be taken into account when we set up research and training programmes, and supervisory relationships.

Since the mid-1990s, there has been an increasing emphasis on the 'internationalisation' of higher education (Green, 1996), described in Australia as an 'export commodity' (Adam, 1995, cited in Green, 1996: p. 1). In Australia, culturally and linguistically diverse students are now thought to comprise 'up to one-quarter of the university population in some states' (Reid, 1996). In my own university, 20 per cent of the students are international in origin. One response to the increasing numbers of international students is to embrace internationalism in the university and in curricula. The presence of international students is not the only contributory factor to internationalising universities' curricula to reflect international contexts and concerns. 'Internationalising the curriculum' suggests introducing international perspectives on subjects rather than a UK, US or Australian view. It involves an expression of the cultural experiences and conceptualisation of knowledge for *all* students, since many will, in effect, end up working in international contexts (see Freckleton, Creighton and Wisker, 2003). Supervisors need to be aware that their international students bring with them both culturally-influenced ways of undertaking research and culturally-influenced constructions of knowledge. It is incumbent on supervisors not merely to tolerate these but to learn from them and where possible, share them with indigenous and Western students, who could benefit from skills in culturally influenced research. Free interchange of research processes and knowledge constructions could lead to a fruitful internationalising of all students' experiences.

▶ Australian and UK issues and practices: language, power and provision

Kisane Slaney reports on an Australian example of supporting international research students (Slaney, 1999). Curtin University of Technology attracts growing numbers of international postgraduates and undergraduates. Strategic planning initiatives prioritise the increase of numbers of postgraduates to a total of '15 per cent of the student body' (Parker, Kirkpatrick and Slaney, 1996, p. 1). Curtin is probably typical of a number of UK and Australasian universities that to maintain a high profile in the student 'market'. However, problems of seeing international students as a market frequently feature in the UK in *The Times Higher Educational Supplement*, which exposes universities seen to be selling their international students short, whether studying in the UK or at a distance, offer in their home country on Western university-franchised courses. Differing standards of tuition in the home country are one issue; another is the cultural inflection of what is studied, which might seem biased because of its Western, European focus. Yet another issue is support and provision, research skills and tertiary literacy support in particular. In spite of the identification of special supervisory requirements for international postgraduate students and their supervisors (Parker, Kirkpatrick and Slaney, 1996; Reeves and Robins, 1995), and policies and plans identifying the need for, amongst other priorities, development of cross-cultural understanding, recognition and support of cultural identity, there has been very little systematic response at institutional levels. At Curtin the 'Communication-in-Context' policy indicates the need to develop English language discipline-specific communication skills, particularly for those students for whom English has not hitherto been the language of study.

Issues of tertiary literacy are complex and fraught with potential cultural preconceptions. It is important that all students be enabled to articulate their ideas at the level at which they are working and thinking. Working in another language clearly hinders this. It is important to remember that literacy for any of us is evolving, developing and contextual. Tertiary literacy is not only about functional competence in complex texts (whether reading or writing them) but is also about being able to participate in appropriate ways in the discourse of one's chosen discipline – to enquire, interpret, hypothesise and challenge, in short, to negotiate meaning (Kirkpatrick and Mulligan 1996, p. 1).

Students studying in another country also need to consider issues of their cultural involvement, entrance into values, the study culture and discourses of study in their discipline. For some students, the level of language ability is crucial. At APU, in our 1999–2003 work with undergraduates and postgraduates, students have remarked in focus groups on the necessity to translate what they hear and read. They first translate, then slowly analyse, think complexly and approach problems, and move towards understanding, before translating back into English. Several international PhD students at APU use an image scanning, simultaneous translation device, but this works at the level of the word or phrase rather than holistically, slowing down comprehension. It hinders thinking and articulation, probably damaging the complexity of thought processes. Thi is particularly problematic at PhD level. It can also create an uneasy relationship between supervisor and student when the level of supervisory discussions does not match the level of the thought processes of either party. Ideas, developments and suggestions can be misinterpreted. Language support and development systems are needed for both students and supervisors.

Suggestions for institutional change frequently avoid issues of the cultural constructions of knowledge with which international students challenge us, albeit often unintentionally. A key issue is whether the approaches we have to learning and research and the suggested values and outcomes that underpin these are themselves culture- and value- free or are a product of a certain set of ideologies born of our own culture. A norm in higher education is to expect students from international contexts, who choose to study with us, to fit into the learning culture and practices of the host university, effectively becoming enculturated and assimilated into its beliefs and practices. We need to ensure that our commitment to certain kinds of learning and research behaviour is not merely a culturally inflected habit or approach per se.

There are concerns that some international students expect too much from supervisors by way of guidance, support and participation in the work. A related concern is that it is difficult to form relationships with some international students as colleagues and equals. The first step towards addressing these concerns is to understand the likely reasons behind them:

> Many international research students come from higher education systems where it is normal to venerate age and experience and where it would be impolite to treat academics as anything other than near infalli-

ble. Consequently, when removed to a Western culture the students find it inconceivable even to consider entering into debate with supervisors. It would be impossibly rude to imply that supervisors' judgement could be anything other than perfect, and it would be arrogant to assert their own ideas and opinions. Their role, as they see it, is to follow whatever instructions their academic superiors choose to give them.   (Okorocha, 1997, in Cryer, 1997)

The accessibility of language, the research matter and the supervisory and training discourses with which students must become familiar comprise power-inflected issues. High expectations and dependency are issues, as is the authority position of the supervisor, exacerbated in the case of international students by their working in another language.

Support can be provided by specialist subject-oriented language seminars. At APU, three learning and teaching fellowship projects accompanied by action research have focused on tertiary literacy for Master's students. For individual postgraduates and undergraduates, specialist help could be provided for writing needs. Additionally, students can be referred to courses in Academic English, and to individual EFL (English as a foreign language) tutors.

For 76 Indonesian students surveyed in the first year of Master's programmes at Australian universities, success was related not to language scores but to the kind and level of adjustments made by academic staff and departments to the students' needs (Phillips, 1998).

Different universities can share good practice. Some work effectively with postgraduate research students or undergraduates using adjunct or specialised courses and support. At Murdoch University an ESL [English as a Second Language] course is linked with a selected content course and provides integrated language instruction using the course content and materials. This approach is used with first-year undergraduates   (Beasley, 1990; Cargill, 1996). At APU, provision has now been successfully embedded for Master's students in Law, Business, Linguistics and Intercultural studies.

So how can our international research students ensure that *their* English is considered adequate? Some students find it useful to have their writing checked by an English friend or someone from their own culture whose English is better than theirs; others employ the services of translators. The concern of supervisors and universities is that the work is the student's own. Help with finding the right translation of a word, idea or expression does not constitute either cheating or plagiarism. English-speaking research students (like authors) are also well-advised to find a critical friend to help with editing and expression in a dissertation or thesis as it nears completion. The role of the supervisor is to start discussions about appropriate language, and to 'correct' or guide students with expression. It is not, I would argue, the role of supervisors to correct every language 'error' or inexactitude. To do so might entail substituting our own expression for that of the student.

Sometimes the language issue is oral, that is it concerns conventions, acceptable behaviours and expressions in supervisory interactions. International students might be unused to offering their points of view or of engaging in debate and argument. For some, to do so would seem to challenge the supervisor's authority and they are reluctant to do so. As supervisors, it is our responsibility to develop strategies for interaction with our students that enable them to learn and practise how to use the discourse of a subject, the metalanguage or discourse of research, and the kind of communicative language used in discussions (see Chapter 9). Various stereotypes now enter the debate. Some students, particularly Asian women, tend to be quiet and retiring in seminars and research groups. They need persistent enouragement to become involved, so that they can benefit from airing their ideas in exploratory talk. Okorocha (1997) offers some suggestions for intensive development:

> Once students find the courage and confidence to debate and express their own ideas and opinions, they may need help to do so. Supervisors can help by allowing the students time to express themselves and by making openings for them in group discussions. Since the students may lack experience of how to express disagreement or offer their own ideas and opinions in a socially acceptable manner, their comments and questions can come across as rude when they do manage to speak out. Supervisors can help by advising them tactfully on acceptable forms of words and body language. With some international students, such training in self-expression can be a lengthy process, but the earlier in their programmes it is started, the better   (quoted in Cryer, 1997)

Articulating and sharing first ideas and then work-in-progress helps to build students' confidence, contributing to the supportive research community of peers. Rather shy or linguistically-reserved international students need to be supported in their involvement in discussion. However, lack of such involvement is no indication that they are finding thinking and interpreting difficult. Language skills or tertiary literacy are not the only indications of a student's level of understanding:

> Most international students find 'receptive' language functions – reading and listening – easier than 'productive' ones – writing and speaking. However, the development of good oral communication is important if

international students are to become full members of the department, participating in debate, problem-solving and creative thinking. (Cryer, 1997)

There are widely-held assumptions that many international students rely on reproducing information and deference to, rather than argument with, authorities (Biggs and Collis, 1991). At postgraduate level, this would clearly pose a problem as engagement with research arguments and debates are essential. Liz Todd (1996) considers cultural differences, with regards to approaches to study and students, noting that:

> Students often come from an environment where they are not allowed to criticise teachers, raise questions that could embarrass them or even to correct them if they make a mistake. It is therefore not surprising that they find it hard to put forward their own ideas. However, in the UK postgraduate students are required to demonstrate that they appreciate that other findings are not to be simply accepted and reproduced, and to show that they understand how knowledge in a certain discipline is constructed. (Todd, 1996, p. 9)

Research and practice (Conrad, 1998; Phillips and Pugh, 1994; Zuber-Skerrit and Ryan, 1996) suggest that postgraduate students are supervised successfully when several support practices are in place, among which I would include cultural awareness and supervisor and student development focusing on avoiding unintentional cultural discrimination or disadvantaging.

When students are on site studying full-time for a three-year PhD or MPhil in reasonable numbers, universities and their staff are encouraged (or pressurised) to ensure mechanisms and enabling practices are put in place. What is more complicated and potentially much more fraught with difficulty are responses to international students based overseas, studying part-time and working full-time. There are a number of factors to be considered. Part-time study is a complication that makes supervision quite vexing, even with students who live round the corner, and this is exacerbated by distance and by cultural differences in approaches to research and learning.

▶ Context and shape of research into international postgraduate learning

Action research has been carried out from 1998 to 2004 with UK-based postgraduate students undertaking PhDs, MScs or MAs at APU (34 students, of which 30 were at PhD level, 2 at MSc level and 2 at MA level) and six cohorts of Israeli PhD students (approximately 250) working at a distance. The research has revealed certain discrepancies in the preconceptions of students and dissonance between their research-as-learning approaches and the expectations of UK postgraduate degrees as designated by the university's research degree committee in relation to international standards. Chinese students, one on an MSc and another studying for an MPhil, both reported being thrown in at the deep end, with little or no support to familiarise them with the computers and packages available, and little time allotted for one-to-one supervision. On the MA in Women's Studies, two female Chinese students – one from Taiwan, the other from Hong Kong – systematically underperformed, producing work that both reproduced authorities unquestioningly and failed to problematise key issues in the discipline, both during questioning within seminars and in dissertations. Individual support for their research development, tertiary literacy and expression has subsequently enabled each of these students to succeed.

The students in the international PhD cohorts have the experience of studying within a different context and learning paradigm to UK-based students. However, all are required to fulfil the requirements of European research paradigms. Cultural inflections in their study and in our research need to be fully identified and taken into account. Comments of international undergraduates about culturally-inflected learning differences and needs are equally true of postgraduates:

> There are many common sense reasons for arguing, and there is also emerging empirical evidence, that at least some aspects of students' conceptions of learning may be embedded in cultural (or even religious) beliefs and practices. (Meyer and Kiley, 1998, p. 8; see also Biggs, 1991; Hughes and Wisker, 1998; Samuelowicz, 1987)

Our work with international postgraduates indicates a need to recognise and develop supportive supervisory practices in relation to (culturally-inflected) learning styles and expectations without undermining students' aims and outcomes, or adopting an unintentionally culturally imperialist stance with regards to their work. We need to ensure that suggestions of development are not merely products of a different cultural context (the facilitators' or supervisor's) rather than necessary to effective research.

Our research with international postgraduates is informed by research into a broad range of international students' experiences of UK and Australian teaching and learning methods and expectations. Several studies (Bloor and Bloor, 1991; Landbeck and Mugler, 1994; Todd, 1996) suggest that while international students are aware of the different kinds of learning activities, and different learning demands in new learning environments, nonetheless, their lack of prior experience of tutor–student relationships and working in small groups, for example, could hamper their learning. Samuelowicz (1987) found that only 28 per cent of international undergraduates at the University of Queensland were familiar with any kind of tutorial and only 18 per cent with group discussion. Having no opportunity for exploratory talk in groups could lead to under-formed ideas and a lack of experience in debating and arguing points of view – both of which are critical for undertaking research. Harris (1995) noted of international students, particularly postgraduates that 'it is probably that the experience of being an overseas student itself encourages a cautious serialist approach to learning'. This approach could manifest itself in the desire for clear guidelines, and straightforward research questions and methods. Sometimes this can lead to accumulative approaches over meaning-oriented approaches, which, particularly at PhD level, could pose serious problems for analysis, critique, problematising and creativity.

Undergraduate and postgraduate international research students often have different expectations of the tutor–student relationship, and different views of knowledge construction. Ballard's (1991) continuum of student attitudes and learning behaviours ranges from conservation of knowledge (and reproduction) to extending, and encouraging questioning, problem-solving and creativity. This is a useful vehicle with which to consider students' work. 'The speculative approach; which is particularly characteristic of postgraduate students' (Todd, 1996, p. 4) is located at one extreme, and mechanical reproduction of given ideas and information at another. Students rewarded in a system encouraging reproduction of authorities without offering opportunities for debate and articulation of a variety of views might find it difficult to take a problematising approach in the first place. For researchers, this could cause particular problems which, it could be argued, are not actually products of a specific culture but of the level of creativity and argument required.

One result of our research with international students has been the discovery that those whose learning approach is more appropriately described as accumulative rather than meaning-oriented, and whose outcomes are transformational, are more likely to experience difficulties and 'dissonance' in the mismatch between approaches, methods and outcomes than students whose approaches are more meaning-oriented. Typically, this would take the form of a desire and plan to use large numbers of questionnaires and experimental methods, when more qualitative methods would better suit transformational aims (see Wisker, 2000). It has been important to work with students to enable them to identify this potential mismatch and own the ways of overcoming it at an early stage, by developing more appropriate research methods. However, it is essential to match understanding with the students rather than impose ideas and methods. Developments need to come from within the work itself, be owned and understood by the student, or they will not be successfully actioned. Developmental supervisory dialogues and involvement in the action research itself have facilitated students in this enterprise (see Chapter 8). Here, we have attempted to determine what kinds of interactions enable students rather than silence or direct them, and what kinds of questioning can draw out reasoned argument or intuitive leaps rather than merely factual statements, encouraging creative and analytical thinking and ensuring that as far as possible, language barriers are eased and complex interactions enabled.

In the case of many international postgraduates who are mid-career professionals, there is another issue. Their own status as professionals working for their doctorates part-time, but holding down important jobs as deans, head teachers and key staff members, means that there are difficulties of pride and hierarchy to be overcome in exchanges with supervisors, especially until working roles have been established.

All research students benefit from support and clarification in terms of what is expected of them. Research student seminars and methodology sessions can be offered as part of systematic training for *all* students.

Our research (1997–2004) has suggested that much developmental work with international students is carried out in facilitative and supervisory dialogues. In their comments on procedures, Aspland and O'Donoghue (1994), Brown and Atkins (1988), Delamont and Eggleston (1983), Lowenthal and Wason (1977), Philips and Pugh (1994), and Wason (1974) all note the importance of supervisory guidance. However, certain types of guidance might shut down thought processes and engagement, while others enable and empower (see Wisker and Sutcliffe, 1999; Wisker, 2000; Wisker *et al.*, 2003). Different levels of dependency and need are significant factors for international postgraduates. Research conducted in Australia (Ballard and Clanchy, 1984; Ginsberg, 1992) indicates that Asian and other international students are often dissatisfied with their postgraduate studies and that they need better study skills and an introduction to culturally-inflected learning behaviours in order to benefit more fully. It is the duty of the host institution to provide such developmental procedures, but also to provide training for supervisors who might themselves be culturally unaware of the issues their students present. Cultural difference might affect reasons for study, and expected outcomes. These need to be negotiated realistically, as do approaches to study at different stages in the research. Asking exploratory questions and problematising concepts is important throughout, while synthesis, analyses and debate with authorities also needs establishing. Access to important learning resources might be adversely affected by language abilities: perhaps universities could make some texts available in translation. Oversees students may need to be gently eased into the ways in which we tend to use libraries, journals and books and integrate them into original work. In supervision or discussion in seminars, students need time to translate the complex ideas presented, and contribute in necessary discipline-related discourses. Good learning practices or study skills need to be made explicit early on and reinforced

At APU, international PhD students receive a tight, coherent, bespoke programme, which, because it is compulsory, enables consistent and coherent, across-the-board engagement with the development of the whole 'story' or path of the PhD, that is ideas, titles, methods and the processes of research. In sessions, everyone is enabled to participate through the use of groupwork and pairs work around developmental questions. The particular moment for drawing out and developing ideas is, at research and PhD level, that of the supervisory dialogue.

However, supervisory dialogues and structured programmes only help maintain momentum to a certain extent. Many students at home and abroad have also found it useful to develop

student support groups amongst colleagues who work closely together (see Chapter 10), are working on similar projects, are using similar methodologies, or are at least geographically close so that there is someone to share developments, doubts and discoveries with. For some, just being in touch with the developmental trajectory of others is motivational enough. As with Open University, and other self-help peer groups (see Bochner, Gibbs and Wisker, 1995), students contact each other between elements of the programme or supervisory meetings and discuss progress, advise each other on methodological strategies, and maintain motivation. For part-time students with demands from work and home, this is essential, as it is when students are working at a distance from their supervisors, in another country and need support at home in terms of finance, space, libraries and other information acquisition opportunities and, in universities, an accessible, culturally-sympathetic supervisor (see Chapter 13).

It is dangerous to homogenise students, however. Responsiveness to individual differences in learning and need, for research and postgraduate study, should inform supervisory practices. There are differences that go beyond those of origin and include gender, class, status, religion and belief and all of this needs to be taken into account (see Chapter 14 on gender).

▶ Cultural issues and power relations

The relationship between supervisor and research student is always one that necessarily engages with and is affected by discourses of power and authority. The distance between one seeking acceptance for his or her voice and work, and one directing and advising, however supportively, is necessarily great, even if hidden, and potentially exacerbated where the supervisor might be younger or of lesser status than a mature student seeking a PhD, or of a lesser status within their home university than a professional seeking a PhD. Kisane Slaney's (1996) work with international postgraduate students at Curtin highlighted several strategies that both recognised and attempted to overcome the authority/discourse distance, enabling students to become empowered, and so develop their own voice.

Slaney's theoretical underpinning utilises notions of power structures and exchanges established within poststructuralist Foucauldian analysis, to which she brings her own position as a feminist. 'Poststructuralists acknowledge explicitly that meaning consists of more than signs operating and being operated in a context. Rather, there is a struggle over signifying practices. This struggle is eminently political and must include the relationship among discourse, power and difference' (Lankshear and McLaren, 1995, p. 13).

Foucauldian discourse recognises that relationships of power govern exchanges between people. Applied to the context of postgraduate–supervisor exchanges in a culturally mixed context, these discourses of power involve:

- the supervisor's position of authority within the university context – one who can support and agree and guide or prevent (to some extent) the students' acceptance and development
- the supervisor's position as one who 'owns' the discourse of postgraduate study by being part of the system and having already entered into and mastered the language related to the system of postgraduate study – everything from university regulations to the stages of research projects, to accepted norms about final degree quality
- in the case of international students, the supervisor's mastery of the discourse of the cultural context in which the research degree is being taken.   (Slaney, 1999, p. 72)

This last item is one affected by the kind and quality of the student's own command of English, and the supervisor's ability and sensitivity to engage in dialogues that enable entrance into this discourse rather than exclude the student from it, for example by not using too many obfuscating, jargon-ridden, words.

As members of what Malcolm (1996, p. 1) defines as 'discourse communities', supervisors in all contexts but particularly those working with international students need to be careful not to marginalise, 'otherise', or deny voice to the students. Slaney invited supervisors and students to work collaboratively on strategies to enhance students' English language skills at postgraduate level, setting up action research sets for supervisors and postgraduates to monitor and facilitate the development of these strategies and their usefulness. The action research involved collaborative developmental work with the supervisors; regular supervision and joint sessions to enable an exchange of ideas between supervisors and students; ongoing monitoring and final evaluative sessions in a collaborative mode 'to obtain a picture of the development/enhancement of the student and supervisors' communication skills, in the context of the supervisor relationship and the students' postgraduate studies' (Slaney, 1999, p. 73).

Slaney's summary of reflective questions for supervisors of students whose first language is not English provides a useful guide:

- Have I made my expectations explicit to my student?
- Have I seen the *totality* of my student, and taken into consideration the impact of her/his *life-world* upon her/his studies?
- Have I taken into consideration the possibility that my student will be going through a process of *transition*, as she/he negotiates cultural and disciplinary *border crossing*?
- Have I taken into consideration both my student's and my own need to work on *interpersonal communication*, addressing issues of *gender, race, ethnicity* etc?
- Do I have a process of *documentation* in place with my student, whereby we can record *actions, reflections* and *progress*?

Additionally, drawn from the author's work with international students, the following questions may be asked:

- Does my student need to develop a range of research and support skills because these have not been necessary in their previous university or workplace, perhaps because they are unavailable, or because others have carried out the tasks for them?
- Can I spend some time inducting my students into appropriately polite

behaviour to others in the university (including administrative staff,) when seeking their help. Lack of politeness might be due to shyness, or the acceptance of different behaviour at home.

- Have I made time demands and deadlines sufficiently clear? In some cultures meeting times and work deadlines are less clearly defined, more flexible than in the US, Australia or European context.
- Could I make contact with others in the student's culture or read up about it in order to be better aware of experiences, behaviours and norms? Could I call on these contacts if some difficulties in communication arise?   (adapted from from Slaney, 1999, p. 73, with additions)

Okorocha (1997) also has a series of suggestions, ranging from orientation about other cultures and cultural issues, examination of implicit assumptions, showing interest in students' welfare, and negotiating student–supervisor etiquette and meaning clarification.

International research students can benefit from our awareness of their culturally different learning and research strategies; our institutional lobbying and advocating for appropriate development and support provision for research skills and tertiary literacy; and our willingness to avoid cultural imperialism. The good supervisor will work towards a truly internationalised learning-as-research experience, and the mutual student and supervisor willingness to research and learn together will enable difference to be a reason for enrichment rather than confusion or power games.

▶ Further reading

McNamara, D. (ed.) (1997) *Overseas Students in Higher Education* (London: Routledge).

Bartlett, A., May, M. and Holznecht, S. (1994) 'Discipline-specific academic skills at postgraduate level: a model', in K. Chanock (ed.), *Courses in the Disciplines* (Melbourne: Language and Academic Skills Units of La Trobe Univesity, pp. 284–7).

Beasley, C. J. (1990) 'Content-based language instruction: helping ESL/ELF students with foreign language and study skills at tetiary level', *TESOL in Context*, 1, pp. 10–14.

Biggs, J. and Collis, K. (1991) 'Multimodal learning and the quality of intelligent behaviour', in H. Rowe (ed.), *Intelligence, Reconceptualization and Measurement* (New Jersey: Laurence Erlbaum).

Cargill, M. (1996) 'An integrated bridging program for international postgraduate students', *Higher Education Research and Development*, **15**(2), pp. 177–88.

Cryer, P. (1997) *Handling Common Dilemmas in Supervision: Issues in Postgraduate Supervision, Teaching and Management*, Guide no. 2 (London: Society for Research into Higher Education and the Times Higher Education Supplement).

Phillips, E. (1998) *Postgraduate Supervision, Teaching and Management* (London: SRHE).

Slaney, K. (1999) 'Models of supervision for enhancing the English language communication skills of postgraduate students', in M. Kiley and G. Mullins (eds), *Quality in Postgraduate Research: Making Ends Meet* (Adelaide: Advisory Centre for University Education, University of Adelaide).

Todd, L. (1996) 'Supervising postgraduate students: problem or opportunity?' in D. McNamara and R. Harris (eds), *Quality Teaching in Higher Education for Overseas Students* (London: Routledge).

Zuber-Skerritt, O. (2002) *Supervising Postgraduate Students from Non-English-Speaking Backgrounds* (Buckingham: Open University Press).

Zuber-Skerrit, O. and Ryan, Y. (1994) *Quality in Postgraduate Education* (London: Kogan Page).

13 Study and Support at a Distance

Increasingly, both undergraduates and postgraduates are seeking to study at a distance. Research students based abroad need systems by which to contact their university supervisor: fax, phone, letter, email and, if they are available, video conferencing links between individuals or groups of students and supervisors.

> This chapter considers:
>
> - issues in distance supervision including cultural differences
> - strategies for effective distance supervision including email, video conferencing, etc.
> - distance supervision with international students
> - institutional support.

Contact between supervisor and student is crucial with distance supervision, but it is not merely a matter of getting the communication medium or the technology right. Distance students might also be from a different culture to that of the supervisor, so finding out about, respecting and working with each other's culturally-inflected research and learning behaviours is very important (see Chapter 12). There could be a myriad of differences and potential difficulties in terms of communication rituals and methods that need to be dealt with early in agenda-setting and decisions about ground rules for distance supervisions. Getting into good habits about polite, social and supervisory communications will help the research and supervisory relationship to develop more smoothly. So will matching technology so that both student and supervisor can read, comment, question and return work with accuracy and ease.

▶ Using technology to keep in touch

Video conferencing is an interactive (if sometimes stilted) medium and not open to all students who would like to keep in contact and be supervised at a distance. However, it provides an excellent opportunity for supervisory discussions of a general kind, or work-in-progress joint tutorials to take place at regularly identified and organised intervals. For example, on one business and accountancy degree, audio tutorials are conducted between tutors at the University of the South Pacific. Dispersed students live and work on a variety of islands, including the Cook and Solomon Islands, some of whom are actually on a different day as well as a different time zone! The University of Helsinki piloted a WIRE project involving tutorial video conference link-ups from several different countries, enabling discussion among a wide variety of international students; sometimes managed by the tutor, sometimes independently. At APU, postgraduates on different, including remote sites, 'meet' regularly to share their work-in-progress and support each other. The tutor or manager of the supervisory group visits students' Friday morning video conferences to answer questions and stimulate the debates that develop within the group. International PhD students are sometimes able to discuss their work with supervisors via a web-cam.

Email is by far the most successful medium of contact between supervisors and students at a distance because students can type in queries at any time that suits them, time zones are no problem, and they can be readily answered at regular time slots by the supervisor. For particularly relevant questions, discussion groups between a number of students working on a research area can be established to share questions, discoveries and strategies, inviting the supervisor to join in and comment, add, query and dip in and out of the discussion group. Those of us involved in email discussion groups will know this provides a good sense of staying in touch with lively developments among peers. A colleague working on a distance MSc regularly exchanges emails with students (they are widely dispersed in Hong Kong and parts of South East Asia). Others phone her up at (sometimes) convenient times at home. The phone is probably a better medium at crucial moments when complex issues need discussing, when a pre-booked tutorial can enable real-time discussion.

With email, some attention needs to be paid to conventions of address and tone, bearing in mind cultural differences in particular. Email can be rather hasty. Sometimes the tone is inappropriate and 'flame mails' (originally keyed in haste) are unlikely to aid good supervisory practice. Supervisors need to develop skills in distance communication – the tone, language, regularity and variety of interactions to support learning. There are also issues in terms of accessibility of learning materials and ongoing communication between supervisor and student. Supervisors might need skills such as writing and uploading elearning materials and activities into an accessible place, whether it be the web or onto CD ROM. Not all supervisors need to be able to write materials, of course. However, those who have distance students need to communicate in a supervisory, developmental fashion, advising over the use of research development materials online, or any other format intended to support and guide the student. In a best case scenario, the student would be well-equipped with internet and email access, and any programme for taught Master's or research training would be written with full recognition of the pedagogical implications of distance and elearning.

Postgraduate work-based management diploma

Technology was harnessed to facilitate distance learning on a partly distance learning-based postgraduate diploma for students involved in management studies in the pharmaceutical industry based in Japan, the US, Europe, the UK and the Far East. The programme was carefully devised to comprise a variety of learning and teaching modes accessible to all. Intensive workshops involved group work. Materials were provided and individual tutorials and supervisions held to help develop project proposals and enable students to understand the learning approaches. In addition, there were interactive open and distance learning materials, that is workbooks and units that students worked on. Students, organised into small groups, were expected to read key trigger papers and discuss these with each other through a chat-room. Tutors could intervene in the chat-room with advice or to answer questions, but the discussion and support mostly took place amongst the students. In their final submission of research project and completed workbooks, students included the computer-mediated learning. It was evident that many students had made use of the chat-room and online work in progress discussions. Many had also fully utilised the email discussion and exchange facility, and formative comment available from tutors for work-in-progress. Developed drafts of work were included with final submissions as evidence of using the full set of distance learning processes.

Establishing a course that is internet-based or partially computer-mediated involving discussion and online support, is quite different from changing supervision to email mode. The change, in the case of one dissertation student Ming Lo, was student-led. Ming Lo returned home due to her grandmother becoming ill. Revisions to her failed essay and supervision on her developing dissertation were all carried out over email. This was only possible because her supervisor learned to work in this way, gradually discovered how to open email attachments and comment on them, and was willing to respond quickly to sent material. Even then, this was subject to a variety of blips to do with servers and materials lost in the ether. Staff learning curves and technology access can be an issue here. Additionally, pedagogically, supporting and tutoring or supervising students through distance media involves a different set of teaching and learning styles.

Pedagogically, email discussion enables both supervisor and student to interact as the work develops. Developmental thoughts and work-in-progress can be submitted, followed by an interweaving of questions and suggestions, changes suggested via 'track changes', attachments of texts for further reading, and rapid response to follow up questions (see Chapter 9). It can, however, be a rather exclusive activity, available only to some, and is dependent upon both the quality of the communication available to the students and staff and their combined skills in handling this kind of learning. In the case of Ming Lo's dissertation, email was more than a developmental chat; it took on the qualities of a supervision – interleaving comments and conducting a variety of supportive dialogues.

Demands on supervisors are great in distance mode, since students send work at different developmental stages and at times which suit them, expecting immediate responses because that is what the medium seems to offer. (Meanwhile, there is a struggling supervisor at the other end trying to keep pace with responding and carrying out all their other work tasks.) While it is satisfying to be able to keep closely in touch through the distance learning medium, it encourages a different kind of dependency among some students. It seems some need to check out each thought and piece of writing, both in progress and again when finished, which can lead to too much supervisory chasing and a great time commitment.

In some instances, postgraduate students could have a supervisor at the university, and one in their home country. In addition to ongoing contact between supervisors in the university and students abroad, there should be regular meetings with the home-based supervisor and support groups, so that conflicting advice is not given, and problems can be spotted and deliberated early on. Students studying part-time can easily be put off their research if problems develop alongside those caused by work and family, and they have no one to speak to quickly to share the problem with or to offer support and suggestions. Consequently, it is important for them to develop home-based peer group support, and for less formal, supportive supervisory interactions to be part of supervisors' repertoire with students.

Ideally, there could be consistent contacts and condensed research supervision periods either in the university or the home country. My own PhD was conducted part-time and at a distance (only 120 miles, but it often felt further!) and I valued those long sessions discussing the chapter I had sent in advance. Students closer to home can pop in with a query, but can also be too reliant on informal contact rather than a systematic discussion of work. Formal contact needs establishing and maintaining. Commitment is necessary on both sides, aided by both ground rules and learning contracts (see Chapter 4).

If supervisors can travel to students, they can become more aware of the cultural context in which students are working and so consider, for example library availability, supportive contexts and practices, blockages, communication problems and cultural differences. This is obviously very costly to the university. If students can commit to a condensed period of work in the university at fixed points (initially on registration, once a year thereafter), then the supervisory team, plus all those other useful on-site contacts, can be brought in to help them with queries and any needs they have at different stages in their research work. This certainly was most helpful for one of my individual students, and was also organised for the international cohorts of students for the 'Summer university' (first stage of the RDP. See Chapter 10).

Problems that can be exacerbated by distance include:

- misunderstandings over methodology – arising from different cultural practices in research, or from the level at which the students are used to working;
- students' own learning paradigms – some could be used to accumulate learning approaches and transmission modes of teaching and learning, leading to a rather positivistic approach to research methodology and a tendency to regurgitate rather than question authorities;
- mature students might be key figures in their own colleges, perhaps working alongside younger, more qualified colleagues in their institutions, and in the student groups. Receiving critical comment on their work might pose problems for them in terms of pride and status.

For those of us working with international students at a distance, a period of time in the university, either as individuals or as a cohort, allow face-to-face relationships to clarify explanations and interactions, enable modes of communication to be built, and ensure that cultural sensitivity is developed to avoid cross-cultural misunderstandings.

Potential distance research students need guidance and educational development-based induction into the scope of projects, demands, problems and strategies. They also need induction into agreed methods of distance communication and supervision. This can be provided in several ways. They:

- can be asked to read papers or specific books, to consider questions prior to defining their area and title;
- can attend a systematic and well-organised research programme held in their own country if there is a cohort of students or funds permit, and/or during an extended period in the university involving students from different parts of the world;
- need to ensure library and other information sources are readily available in their own country;
- must be committed to the appropriately defined and agreed frequency of contact with their university-based research supervisor(s) and, additionally, preferably, they need a home-based supervisor who can address daily needs and difficulties (preferably someone with subject expertise but who also has pastoral responsibilities and abilities);
- need to go very systematically (as with home-based students) through the processes of definition of title; methodology; outline of the project and timescale; they must have an awareness of stages of the project; make a commitment of time, space and resources; and set up of a scheme of work and establish contact with others who can inform, help and support ideas and development of research with support groups. This can be done both with any home-based adviser or supervisor, and with university-based advisers or supervisors;
- need contacts with a research culture, both at home and in the university. We can provide a version at a distance over time, condensed and organised when they are in the university; students studying abroad need to develop support groups to help progress (see Bochner, Gibbs and Wisker, 1995).
- need to put a system of reports, meetings, progress checks and responses to written work firmly in place; with distance, this cannot be casually left to chance and change.

▶ Coping with cultural difference and student research needs at a distance – some suggestions

There are several ways to alleviate the problems of distance learning for research students:

- Set up compulsory research development and support programmes involving induction into the culture and learning paradigms, inception and development of research questions, and development of methods and training in their use. If students come from a learning culture of accumulation learning and deference to authorities, a development programme and specific supervisory focus on research-as-learning strategies should help to shift paradigms from largely positivitic and accumulative learning modes to the more speculative, creative and original. If students cannot travel to programmes, can programmes be taken to students?

- Set up on-site and distance individual supervisory meetings that enable a gradual engagement with the underlying questions and issues of the thesis, dissertation or project and the natural development from this into appropriate research methods and plans.
- Methods training in staged programmes should be developed and available not only on-site but in distance learning formats to both help students establish their work, then discuss work-in-progress.
- Avoid the cultural imperialism of assuming knowledge from one culture is absolute, entering into debate, open minded discussion and exploration about this.
- Set up student support groups or encourage them to be set up in the student's own country or home location.
- Enable distance contact to be supportive in a variety of developmental ways – chat-rooms, email discussions, email tutoring, video conferencing, web-cams, interleaving or 'track changes' with attachments, distance learning materials.
- Encourage and provide opportunities for students and staff to be trained in the use of distance learning contacts and supervisory interactions.
- Put your distance learning students in contact with other academics in the broad international academic community – using email, discussion lists or contacts local to the student.

Many of these ideas are good practice per se, others are more useful when working with distance research students in their own context. With developmental programmes, institutionally supportive practices and sensitive supervisory arrangements in place, distance research students are more likely to feel able to get on with their research, and be successful in it.

▶ Further reading

Bochner, B., Gibbs, G. and Wisker, G. (1995) *Supporting More Students* (Oxford: Oxford Brookes University).

14 Gender and Research Studies

As we approach supervision, it might come as something of a surprise to consider that gender can play such a big part in the supervisor and student relationship, but there has been a wealth of work carried out now into ways in which culture and gender differences, as well as learning differences, affect the relationship, hence probably the success of the research.

> *This chapter considers:*
>
> - *gender in the supervisor–student relationship*
> - *the gender-inflected nature of knowledge*
> - *feminist research strategies*
> - *some problems that could produce gender clashes (and some ideas on avoiding or overcoming them).*

This chapter looks *in the main* at women's experiences, in line with published work (e.g. Leonard 2001; Moses 2002). A number of gender-inflected issues might arise in supervisor–student relationships, others arise in relation to feminist research methods, and still others are due to institutional practices or social pressures. If, for instance, the student wishes to carry out feminist research and the supervisor is not supportive or aware of this, there could be clashes between them. Some feminist researchers have been accused of being too personal and subjective when they deliberately place the reflective and the subject at the heart of their work. There is also much evidence that gender and power relations in the supervisor–student relationship can affect a woman's chance of succeeding in her research, particularly at doctoral level. It is probably the case that gender plays, or could play, a large part in the necessary matching of understanding and approaches, of values and behaviours, which enable supervisor and student relationships to proceed harmoniously, or otherwise. Gender and sexuality might affect success.

In supervisory contexts sexuality is relatively unwritten about, but clearly could affect the relationships and research. Homosexual, lesbian or hetero-sexual subject positions might affect research topics, theorising strategies and interpersonal behaviours. Whatever gender- or sexuality-influenced differences might be, professionalism is the key to successful working relationships. Supervisors should endeavour to understand the research questions of their students, work with them to produce a sound conceptual framework and achievable research, and support them in reaching their own research outcomes; in other words, empower, support, nurture, inform and enable the autonomous work that is necessary for research at any level. However, when gender or sexuality get in the way, supervisors must be aware of ways to avoid difficulties and handle any awkward conflicts.

Diana Leonard's *A Woman's Guide To Doctoral Studies* (2001), largely aimed at female readers, contains useful 'research-based information on how women are positioned inequitably within the supposedly liberal, cerebral world of postgraduate studies, and suggests how best to push back or move around problems and come out in front' (p. 2). Leonard considers the academic context in which women's research is conventionally masculine in itself. In the first instance, it was traditionally so – because students, historically, were also scholars and clerics, devoted to the church, leading ascetic lives, unhampered by families and domestic responsibilities, the very things which women must juggle as they study today. Leonard argues there is (in the early twenty-first century) a new kind of aggressive, business-like research context that also has little place for domestic balancing acts and for the feminist research paradigms within which many women might work. Feminist research practices *and* women's lives might be at odds perhaps with a 'new form of academic masculinity' (Leonard 2001, p. 43), deriving initially from professionalism and most recently from managerialism. This new, hard-nosed, positivist edge could fail to recognise the credibility of research that seeks collaboration, or works gradually, building upon questionnaire questions, to focus group comments and so on; does not impose research upon subjects, instead it grows from their needs and interests; and shares the findings and moves in an iterative fashion rather than either conducting a single 'hit' (i.e. pre-test/post-test) experiment or gathering data from people as if they were objects, not involved in the process. Even the shape and the language of research differ along the extremes of a continuum where one end is businesslike and positivistic, and the other is concerned more with action research and feminist-oriented research. There is often a gendered dimension to these differences, although the differences *need not* be gender-inflected.

It could be the case also that the culture of research training is somewhat at odds with the kind of creative, journeying approach to research that is possibly more common in much women's work. Leonard believes this to be the case, critiquing research 'training' and new definitions of the manageable, definable project or scope of the PhD:

> the applications of agreed skills to defined problems, bracketed off from issues of individual, social and public purpose and with disciplinary knowledge treated as a dangerous residue rather than an intrinsic feature of knowledge production.   (Leonard 2001, p. 45)

Leonard argues that there is a danger that development programmes and rigid timescales for the production of clearly defined PhDs arise from the application to the PhD process of forms and expectations deriving from rigid, limiting versions of masculinity and masculine world views. The results are reductions in the originality and quality of the PhD process and its products. So, although we might claim the PhD has moved on in terms of serving the needs of knowledge development and change, we nevertheless still produce 'the man of reason' and 'independent scholar' (Johnson *et al.*, 2000, p. 45). While Leonard's work, like that of Moses and others considering women's research, largely focuses on the PhD, my own work with MA women's studies students and undergraduates involved in research projects has thrown up remarkably similar experiences – some questioning of the seeming rigidity of forms of expressions, subject matter and modes of research more conventionally accepted within a largely masculinised (male-dominated in a rather intolerant form) research culture in university study (see Wisker, 1996).

It is this kind of recognition and exploration of the culture of postgraduate study in UK and international (European, US and Australasian) universities that contextualises and adds a philosophical element to our discussion of issues and practices involved in undertaking research more generally, and research in which gender plays a part in particular. It is possible that exploratory, creative, interactive, action research that follows the pace of those researched, involving the emotions and reflections of all involved, could have little place in the cut and thrust of turning out PhDs in three years, and producing theses or dissertations that rigidly conform to specific layouts and defendable shapes defined by Leonard as hard-nosed and masculine. However, if we revisit arguments from feminist critics such as Adrienne Rich and Jean Cocks (both in Culley and Portuges, 1985), we can argue against such rigid gender divides – 'reason and emotion are not antagonistic opposites' they insist, denying suggestions that women cannot be rigorous and critical in their work. Maybe some women (and men) might want to carry out post-positivist – feminist or action – research. This does not preclude them benefiting from research development programmes and the rigour that timescales, word limits and layout rules encourage. In a more rigorously monitored climate (QAA, HEFCE, Australasia completion funding), research cultures are better supported by developed, often qualified supervisors, recognised as professionals and rewarded as such, whose roles focus on and enable entry into academic cultures. Additionally, research students are or should be, supported by a sound infrastructure instead of, historically, being left to fend for themselves on the margins of academia. Professionalisation is far from being 'all bad' or an acceptance of a masculinist culture of rules and regulations. It can be used to support all students. It is particularly important, then, in a professional context, to ensure that everyone has adequate access to facilities, and a well-managed relationship with their supervisor based on mutual respect and commitment to mutual fulfilment of duty (as well as to the experience of research).

These aspects of professionalisation should improve the lot of marginalised, part-time women students (for instance) and should, equally, provide a professional and accountable context to which students could turn, should their gender be experienced as disadvantaging them. Disadvantage could include a range of things from the timing of research development programmes (family mealtimes; when no childcare cover can be found); demands of full-time research (when domestic responsibilities demand part-time research); fieldtrips; expected purchase, rather than loan, of costly computers; and so on (it is not that women are inherently financially worse off than men, but domestic responsibilities have been shown to inhibit flexibility and earnings).

Domestic pressures certainly affect women's studying and researching at all levels. During 1985, the author conducted a small-scale research project asking 45 students on two 'Return to Study' and one Open University Preparatory course to complete a questionnaire focusing on backgrounds, views and experiences of returning to learning. Twelve of these students were interviewed informally, in groups, about their learning experiences. Some expressed guilt. One said: 'I do feel pangs of guilt in that I am perhaps not contributing as much as I should to the running of the home, gardening and baking.' Another noted 'I have found guilt again for the self-indulgence of studying just for myself.' Others felt they shouldered an enormous burden of responsibilities which, not surprisingly, interfered with their study:

> The biggest problem that I foresee is that I am responsible for the house in general and if I don't do all the work I still have to arrange that it gets done by someone. This is the family woman's biggest disadvantage –

washing, cooking, shopping, cleaning, general management. (Wisker, 1996, pp. 7–8)

These are typical remarks from women returning to study at all levels. Many research students have similar experiences. Such comments about guilt and selfishness are examples of women's response to conditioning that leads them to view their study and research as stolen pleasures, self-indulgence and activities that should be sacrificed when other duties call. While some manage to balance both domestic and study responsibilities, for others it becomes a debilitating drain on their emotional and physical energies. Much has also been written about the effects of women's domestic responsibilities effacing study time, for example Rudd's (1985) work on higher education.

Women within either heterosexual or lesbian relations could find the contradictory demands of family and research enormously problematic. Whether supervisors themselves have children or not, they need to recognise the demands dependants present for women undertaking research.

The worth, value, status and volume of women's research has also been called in question. Women with domestic responsibilities have been seen variously as unlikely to produce such serious research in such large amounts fit for publication as their male counterparts, and *more* likely to do so – Margharita Rendel's work (see *Empowering Women*, 1996) suggests women with domestic responsibilities research and publish more than their counter-parts. One reason for this could be the absolutely essential developed skill of balancing work and home demands. It is certainly the case that such demands can cause domestic and time pressures. If we hope to support and enable women with domestic responsibilities to undertake learning and research, we need to have our voices heard on the committees that decide on childcare, part-time study, car parking, acceptable research discourse, access to on-line research materials, and research development programme presentation times.

Jane Thompson makes the following comments on adult learners and learning opportunities: 'The organization and provision of courses takes very little account of the social, economic, cultural and political conditions of being female in our society' (Thompson, 1983, p. 81). This short-sighted culpability is a result of an imbalance in gender and power between policy-makers, tutors and students. Just because students might have coped as undergraduates does not mean women postgraduates find the research culture any more welcoming. It should be. Thompson notes:

The career structure, the responsibility for organization and control, the arbiters of the curriculum, and the opinion leaders and policy makers who sit on bodies like the Russell committee are invariably men – men who operate firmly and squarely within the organizational structures, the cultural assumptions and the thinly disguised prejudices of patriarchal society. (Thompson, 1983, p. 81)

The present author has been in post sufficiently long to have seen 'Return-to-Study' students move through their undergraduate courses, postgraduate courses, doctoral and then postdoctoral study. The ones who survive have often had to be ruthless about childcare, social lives, children and conformity *because of* times of access to postgraduate research programmes. They have had to confront expectations that they will have a computer and a modem to allow online research; beliefs that paying for a postgraduate degree, over time, won't cause an immense domestic conflict of financial interests; and expectations that they can balance unpaid domestic work, childcare, and study, or paid work, childcare and study. One ex-'Return-to-Study' (then OU, PhD) students appeared last week, seeking a postdoctoral research post. How did she complete the 15 years in between? Tenacity is a skill she could be employed for, alongside her research powers! She was offered part-time work; she gained a full-time research post. Good!

The range of issues that can be affected by gender include all the practices and processes of undertaking a doctorate or other piece of research, and afterwards, facing up to informal structures and cultures in which research is undertaken. Current practices regarding the employment of teaching staff and the kind of apprenticeship expected of graduate teaching assistants could actually operate against some postgraduates, alienating and silencing them. This affects men as well as women. Leonard notes the low status and low pay of teaching jobs accompanying graduate studies, indicating that this affects women in particular. I have seen men and women doctoral students equally out of the loop of decision-making, or left newly graduated and underpaid.

▶ Culture

Some culture issues *are* of course gender-free, but others are gender-specific and still others are additionally inflected by issues of race), although racially- and culturally-inflected practices and views (where they exist) are just as likely to affect indigenous, black and Asian students as those from international locations.

Local, UK, black and Asian women are a case in point. Heidi Sofia Mirza (1995) and Diana Leonard (2001), argue that black women's success in higher education is not due to anti-racist, equal opportunities policies, but to the energies of the women. They have 'instrumental achievement strategies' (Mirza, 1995, p. 150). The motivation to 'go on' comes from the 'women themselves' says Leonard (2001). She points out, however, that identity politics deriving from beliefs in a kind of new colonialism, often actioned through such opportunities as access courses, can potentially prove harmful rather than helpful. Perhaps the recognition of black and Asian women students and researchers becomes less supportive and celebratory when their academic success deposits them in a competitive job market. Class and politics are important issues. Women's graduate and doctoral success is probably often class related. International black women students, for example from Africa, are or have been likely to be upper middle class and, during apartheid years, ANC-funded. It is likely that various strategies such as 'Australia in the Pacific' (since 1985) and increases in numbers of international students after the lifting of visa restrictions privilege middle class students, while providing the higher education system with substantial fee income. Poorer international students struggle to find funding to study abroad. This could also be exacerbated by gender. One MA Women's Studies student, 'Emily', left her child behind to study in the UK, found that she had to take low paid part-time jobs such as live-in caring (against Home Office rulings), and feared for her safety if she returned to Zimbabwe. She is caught in a poverty trap that students from richer countries or upper middle class backgrounds can avoid. The reasons for black and Asian women's postgraduate study might also differ from those of their *male* counterparts, as do their lifestyles and finances.

Diana Leonard quotes from her student, Akiko Nishio, studying Japanese postgraduates at London University. Nishio found that while men studied abroad to advance their careers and were probably sent by their companies, women's reasons for study were more varied, including escape from social restrictions at home, career development and making the most of their lives while abroad accompanying husbands. Most were young and single (Nishio 2001). Very similar patterns emerged from Jau Rong Chen's unpublished PhD (2000), which focused on largely Taiwanese postgraduates at the University of Warwick. Chen discovered that many women undertook study or research while accompanying their husbands, who were either working for companies or studying for doctorates. Still other women decided they needed to earn rather than study, so sacrificing their own development to help maintain husbands and families in a different cultural context. For several women students, cultural isolation is a real difficulty. Another student on a master's (MA Learning and Teaching) course left her son behind in China to study full-time. This is a sacrifice of her time as a mother. She has also found it impossible to gain paid work while studying because of visa restrictions, increasing the pressure on her to complete quickly and successfully, exacerbated whenever there are any difficulties in her study (such as the slow pace of the ethics committee).

It could be argued that coping with university research is useful training for future employment. However, this is rather ironic if it proves a financial and emotional burden. Hensel (1991) identifies how life outside work affects academic study and academic jobs, arguing that this can either help align dual home and work satisfaction (in the best cases) or lead to a conflict of interest problems for women in particular, in both spheres.

> In academic work there is a high correlation between career-and-life-satisfaction. The university, more than other places of employment, is highly influenced by life outside of work. In addition, universities are training grounds for future leaders and need to offer an effective model on how to balance family and career.   (Hensel, 1991, p. vi)

Hensel's study was an early comment on the 'work/life balance'. This plea for an effective model is rarely actualised in academic and research contexts. What women found was that tenure clocks ticked on while they raised families, falling behind in their research and publishing. To be effective, everyone needed 'a wife' to support an academic research career.

Leonard's study provides interesting generic information on issues such as employment after a doctorate. In the social sciences in particular, because academics are comparatively poorly paid, a doctorate might not always guarantee a higher paid job than that obtained by those without a doctorate (in non-academic careers). For women who have left their home countries and live in relative poverty to complete qualifications, as for any women who return to research, undertaking poorly paid part-time jobs to support it, the sacrifice might not be worth the reward (except in terms of self-development).

Gaps in knowledge (possible subjects for future doctorates) include information on jobs gained by those who start doctorates later, do them while undertaking an academic career, and what exactly happens to careers as a result of gaining a doctorate, that is whether women go back to their previous jobs or gain promotion. Leonard points out (2001, pp. 206–7), for example, that many women actually leave science once they have gained a PhD. This could be explained by the culture of working in science itself. Becher et al. (1994) found that women had a negative response to scientific experiment and research group cultures. Attitudes and accidental or deliberate exclusion are issues women might face, but they could also face an nhospitable research practice culture. Leonard identifies actual problematic scientific practices such as a culture of dangerous bravado with hazardous substances (p. 207), which, she argues, is less likely to appeal to women, but s seemingly expected in a largely male research group.

Motivation might also differ between the genders. Ingrid Moses (1990, 1993), conducting a national study, 'Barriers to Women's Participation as Postgraduate Students' in Australia in the 1980s found that, while women might be as equally dedicated scholars as men, they were more likely to have made a definitive decision about doing a PhD for its *own sake*, for their own development, and were less likely to be concerned with high salary and promotions, wishing to undertake the PhD as they had 'a need for a change', and to take charge of their lives (Leonard, 2001, p. 66).

Other gendered and generic issues include those of space management, paid work, and ensuring reasonable accommodation, income, grants and scholarships. There are well-established records about difficulties for women studying, ranging from their reception in the research context to sexism and harassment in supervisory interactions. For instance, Sandler's (1993) 'chilly climate', and sexual harassment, i.e. Diane Purkiss's (1994) recognition that 'pedagogy and seduction have been semiotically intertwined since Plato (at least)' (Purkiss, 1994, p. 224).

▶ Gendered knowledge

As I have noted in an earlier work:

> Definitions of knowledge and of the worth of varieties of knowledge are also produced by the same white, middle-class Western men. Within these relationships of power, what tends to be either excluded, marginalized or evaluated as second-rate are the experiences of women and whatever might be described as women-centred or women-produced versions of knowledge. Feminist debate about women in higher education has focused on the patriarchal production and dissemination of knowledge which defines what is considered both legitimate for academic study and how to receive and deal with this information, the ideas (Culley *et al.*, 1985; Ramazanoglu, 1987; Klein, 1987; Gray, 1994). One important issue centres on the notion of what it means to be an academic, what academic subjects comprise and whether women-centred curriculum choices or alternatives within a patriarchally defined academic curriculum are integrated within it.   (Wisker, 1996, p. 20)

For the supervisor–student relationship, definitions of what it means to be an academic, what subjects are suitable for research, and what methods are appropriate could well be subject to gendered inflections. Women likely to undertake feminist or women-centred research might meet a chilly reception from supervisors who discredit feminist, women-oriented, knowledge constructions and research practices. Stanley (1995, pp. 172–3) and Leonard comment on how women toe the difficult line of tolerance of jokes and putting down of women's research. Leonard comments specifically on difficulties for lesbians on field trips, and for feminists giving feminist papers and having their research paradigms undermined.

Many colleagues have found it difficult (in my own institution and in supervisor workshops I have run internationally) to know how to evaluate the likelihood of culture and gender-related research projects being at postgraduate level, being significant, and avoiding inflection of the personal. They have also found proposed methods (legitimate and well defined within feminist research practices) quite problematic. For example, research projects coming under question have been variously on: experiences of women in the Chinese take-away industry, using the researcher as a case study; female genital mutilation (clitoridectomy); and life-affirming journeys towards the achievement of identity of lesbians of a specific age group. These could be used as case studies to help supervisors explore *how* to deal with gender-inflected conceptualisation, knowledge construction and research practice. (One appears later in this chapter.)

Victoria Robinson focuses on ways in which gender and culture inflect perceptions, epistemology and academic perspectives:

> Gender, ethnicity and sexuality are still not established as ways of seeing the world in the way that class is within politics or history. More positively, though, if Women's Studies and feminist theory has only been in existence (in an institutionalized context) for twenty years, then even small shifts in mainstream thought can be seen as beginning to displace centuries of male academic bias and power. (Richardson and Robinson, 1993, p. 6)

The construction, knowledge, articulation and organization of knowledge from a feminist perspective are variously acknowledged by and affect the academy. The existence of Women's Studies can change traditional mainstream courses and also what is recognised as a suitable subject and method for research. However, radical change is distant as Robinson notes:

> But even in areas such as cultural studies and sociology for instance,

where feminist research is not only finding new answers but posing new questions about the invisibility and marginalization of women and their relationship to culture and the social world, a total intellectual revolution in the concepts, perspectives and methodologies of the subject area is far from being achieved.   (Richardson and Robinson, 1993, p. 6)

There are limited feminist interventions in the curriculum in the shape of specific women's studies accredited courses and modules at undergraduate and Master's levels where students are encouraged, supported and expected to undertake feminist research. More radical changes in theoretical perspectives and approaches, different constructions of knowledge and different discourses across whole subject areas, not just the women-labelled modules, can receive institutional and individual hostility. Rejection of feminist approaches is insidious and might well be seen to be personalised as an attack on the academic or student. Feminist researchers could be seen by those for whom feminist research is alien as encouraging students to conduct research and write in ways that are too personal and therefore irrelevant – you are not writing well enough; you are writing too polemically, too emotionally, and in a disorganised fashion, with too much personal baggage, to be published; what you seem to want included is marginal and trivial. This casts doubt on both the supervisor's and student's ability to use the discourse and analytical apparatus and research practices, and the rigour of the demands of the subject as interpreted through feminist perspectives and authenticated through feminist research practices.

Our feminist or women-oriented students undertaking research need to gain research skills and the appropriate discourse of their subject as well as to become fluent in feminist research methods. If they wish to study subjects, ask research questions and seize research opportunities that are inflected by feminist perspectives and practices, they need to be creditable, in terms of a variety of strategies, particularly those of feminist research.

A women-centred, student-oriented focus enables the validation, support and refinement of feminist theoretical perspectives, approaches and expressions. For academic supervisors still receiving rejection slips and the odd broadside at planning meetings or assessment boards, however, the argument that 'the battle is won' (for recognition of feminist or women-oriented perceptions and research practices) is laughable. Kitzinger (1990) explores her experiences in psychology.

When I write as a feminist, I am defined out of the category of 'psychologist'. When I speak of social structure, of power and politics, when I use language and concepts rooted in my own understanding of oppression, I am told what I say does not qualify as 'psychology'. (Kitzinger, 1990, p. 124)

Her writing, she says, seems unacceptable because she uses feminist research methods and feminist expression and has involved herself in her work, which is both personal and politicised:

> Central to these rejections, then, is the sense that my work is not 'balanced' or 'objective', that it is an attempt to 'persuade' the reader of a particular point of view, and that it is politically biased – 'polemical' or 'ideological'. Suggestions about my writing style are frequent: that it should be 'moderated' or 'toned down' – that it should be less 'journalistic' or 'emotion-laden' ... 'The text is replete with value-laden words' commented one anonymous reviewer, 'a more scientific presentation is needed', wrote another. (Kitzinger, 1990, p. 127)

Psychology is a science and, it is argued, a feminist approach to knowledge and its discourse is political, polemical, emotional – not science. However:

> An approach through a feminist perspective and expression which recognises oppression, context, the personal, is a legitimate one in all disciplines. Attempts to negate it as, for instance, 'not psychology' should be resisted. I could parallel this with dozens of examples from my own practice within literature and education and colleagues' reports from other subjects including geography, biology, medicine and history. Each of us carries around 'guilty secrets' of rejection and comments about inappropriateness and the 'wrong kind' of focus or discourse. We need to share positive experiences and build on the consolidation offered by women's studies. (Wisker, 1996, p. 26)

I would love to argue that times have changed. If women-centred approaches and expressions are constantly rejected in academic practice, it will be impossible to empower students engaged in gendered research (not all of them are of course) to recognize their validity, and the prejudice and bias of those who demote and reject them.

There are many feminist perspectives and research practices. One concern is recognising the multiplicity of views and versions, diversity of context, response and approach. This is essentially a *set* of approaches that refuses to just replace women-centredness or women-orientation for the established critical orientation. Instead, it opens up diverse responses. It recognizes the issues and effects of class, culture, ability, sexuality and age and other differences without losing sight of the affects of gender.

Feminist research practices, questions, knowledge and construction are likely to recognise:

- The importance of experience in constructing approaches and conceptualization
- How personal experience affects approach, reading, interests, arguments and expression
- Personal response, especially as it helps analysis and reflection
- A multiplicity of approaches and viewpoints critically arising out of different experiences and angles conditioned by class, context, race and gender.   (Wisker, 1996, pp. 24–7)

In terms of expression, women can learn to do formally what they do naturally: integrate both reason and emotion (Cocks, 1985, p. 44). Emotion, feelings and the self can be integrated with theory and exemplified in practice in feminist research.

It can be argued that not only feminists or women use feminist-influenced research strategies. Using the self as a case study, for example, has been popular with several PhD, OU and MA students in knowledge management or education contexts. The collaborative, sharing approach of action research itself springs from the same kind of egalitarian, empowering, reflective orientation towards research. Perhaps feminist research strategies *have* had a wide influence, or perhaps in situations where action research and more egalitarian, empowering, reflective practices of research exist, feminist researchers find their work recognised as perfectly acceptable. Either way, these changes are good news and could lead to:

- Treating others involved as subjects not objects of the research, hence involving them in the research aims, sharing the processes and the findings.
- Collaboration, sharing what is being questioned and discussed with those who help produce the information, not speaking for others. Feminist research builds research questions with the cooperation of the research subjects. Feminist researchers check out transcripts, analyse findings in conversation with subjects, and share the final report and conclusions.
- Recognising the experience and position of the researcher as a person. This could lend to using the self as a case, using 'I', acknowledging and recognising personal involvement.
- Challenging and reinterpreting what is considered knowledge. The epistemology of feminist research might well differ from established, that is,

white male (?) research, usually normalised (not necessarily deliberately so defined). Personal knowledge, a mix of the personal, of experience as well as systematic research constructions of differing views and expressions of findings might be in feminist research.

> Feminist theoretical approaches and expression in written or spoken assessed work and publications should not become a site for a wearing kind of battle: the slow drip of personalized disempowerment and humiliation.   (Wisker, 1996, p. 25)

► Women as supervisors

Supervision is likely to be a role chosen by and for many women because of its similarity to counselling and pastoral care and, yet, ironically in the higher echelons of HE, supervising research students is a sought-after role. When seeking job satisfaction, positions and academic recognition, we might well choose to supervise PhD students as part of that development. Some of us (as women) might also seek to supervise *women* students perhaps because of congruency of interests and perhaps because, once academically credible as a research supervisor, a female supervisor can support students taking more feminist, creative and alternative ways through a Master's, undergraduate dissertation or PhD thesis. If we do this, we need to ensure students are rigorous, perfectly prepared, and able to articulate a defence of their research.

► Gender conflicts and tensions

A rather darker side of gender influences of the supervisor–student working relationship can include bullying (Adams, 1986), sexually-oriented predatory behaviour and sexual harassment. Students need to know they are safe from such destructive and demeaning interactions that can lead to women leaving their research and/or their academic job (reported as a more frequent occurrence than male supervisors and students leaving, while male on female bullying and harassment is also more frequently reported than same sex or female on male – which is *not* to say these don't occur).

Some of the gender-inflected case studies, given in the activity below, can help us explore not only how to avoid gendered problems in supervising research students, but also to work out what to do should they arise.

Gender and culture related case studies

Activity

Please consider and discuss these situations in relation to issues that have arisen over gender and culture – what should you do/what should be done?

1   A student wishes to undertake feminist research and proposes to interview women about their lives using open ended, semi-structured interviews. She intends to ask rather sensitive questions, but is working within a tight-knit lesbian community and is very clear that she will seek the permission of the respondents, check out the research questions with them, tape and transcribe the interviews herself and check them out with the respondents again before encoding them then extracting in order to illustrate her exploration of life journeys among this particular community. Finally, she wishes to archive the material (names anonymised) for further researchers to use as there is so little available on the gay or lesbian community. One or two colleagues on the research degrees committee have problems with the use of life histories and the seemingly rather unstructured flow of the work. The ethics committee is worried about allowing others access to the material.

Thoughts
The committee has problems both with the subject and the research strategies.

2   One colleague, more senior and male, is supervising a younger female colleague as director of studies. During the course of their supervisions it emerges he is beginning to suggest they meet in pubs and in his house in the evenings. *He* has just broken up with his wife and is clearly rather distressed, but *she* is worried about the changing nature of their relationship and insists that they meet as ever in the office for their supervisions. His next communication to her is to belittle her work and suggest that she is 'not up to this kind of research', that the work is ill-conceived, poorly researched and going nowhere. She is now in a state of embarrassment and confusion.

Thoughts

Even as a younger female colleague, she must be in a position to explain to him that the relationship was going in the wrong direction. She has obviously not responded as he wanted. They are colleagues and this produces *one* problem. The only way to handle it is institutionally but very carefully – they could close ranks. This is happening within the institutional framework so that is how it has to be tackled. Ask for a change in supervisor – but the problem with this is professional and personal, so it could have wide-ranging effects on both department and student. It needs some counselling, too.

3   Upon taking early retirement, Peter was commissioned to undertake historical research by his ex company into the history of the company. He has been assigned a very much younger female member of staff as his supervisor. Sheila has a doctorate and is a specialist in organisational analysis. Peter has never been employed by a woman and finds it very difficult to take direction from Sheila. Sheila finds it awkward to advise Peter, who clearly has a great deal of experience but in fact is taking a rather prosaic surface learning-oriented route through his research, documenting without asking questions or problematising, never being critical or evaluative, and never considering how and why decisions were made, instead recording events factually. Their supervisions always seem to end up with little movement forward and Peter as sure as ever that collecting and recording facts about the company he knows is the way to gain his master's dissertation.

Thoughts

Sheila needs to encourage Peter to problematise rather than accumulate. If eliciting interactions does not work she might have to seek support from a superior (not necessarily male) to let Peter know there are communication difficulties, or challenge these difficulties directly.

▶ **Further reading**

Cocks, J. (1985) 'Suspicious pleasures: On teaching feminist theory', in M. Culley and C. Portuges (eds), *Gendered Subjects: The Dynamics of Feminist Teaching* (London: Routledge & Kegan Paul).

Cryer, P. (1997) *Handling Common Dilemmas in Supervision* (London: SRHE and THES).

Culley, M. and Portuges, C. (eds) (1985) *Gendered Subjects: The Dynamics of Feminist Teaching* (London: Routledge & Kegan Paul).

Leonard, D. (2001) *A Woman's Guide to Doctoral Studies* (Philadelphia, PA: Open University Press).

Wisker, G. (1996) *Empowering Women in Higher Education* (London: Kogan Page).

15 A Little Too Close to Home: Supervising your Colleagues and/or Other Practice/ Professional-based Research

Many of us now supervise students who wish to engage with their own professional practice, perhaps including their clients, students, patients, colleagues, institutions, etc. as part of this research. Alternatively, we might supervise our own colleagues engaged in practice-based, professionally oriented and other research, some of which is action research.

> *This chapter considers:*
>
> * *untangling institutional politics*
> * *supervising practice- and professional-based research*
> * *action research supervision*
> * *supervising colleagues*

▶ Working with institutional politics

Students involved in encouraging change within their own practice and their own institutions are faced with a number of social, cultural and political issues. On the one hand, they may be asked to undertake postgraduate and undergraduate research into topics of importance for their own institution or practice context. Some trial new curricula or practices; others maintain and evaluate developments, for example of the uptake and appropriate learning use of IT, the acceptability of new policing strategies, the effectiveness of a newly-introduced personalised banking system, or the effectiveness of a training programme for fire officers. All of these could be areas encouraged by an institution, company or organisation to find out about itself – part of the experience of a 'learning organisation' in practice. There are benefits to working on semi-community, institutionally supported research. But for some students, this could also prove to be a problem. Perhaps they do not feel they 'own' the project themselves, or perhaps they could feel pressurised to carry it out and complete, and feel their jobs are at risk in relation to the conduct of the research. Another major issue for mid-career professionals researching elements of their professional practice is the form of the research and its product. Institutions might seek a report. Universities seek a dissertation or thesis. These two forms differ.

For some students, researching their own practice or the policy, practice and mechanisms of their own institution provides other delights and problems. They might meet barriers to their research from colleagues who resent the possible prying and intrusion into their own practices that it suggests. Others could feel threatened by what the research might reveal, and even jealous at the time investment or/and intellectual recognition related to the undertaking and achievement of, in particular, Master's or doctoral work. Students could face anything from over-intrusive and controlling to resentful and obstructive colleagues and bosses. More doors could be opened, or more could be shut to them. Of particular interest is the potential minefield of being actually supervised by one of your own colleagues, both for the supervisor, and the colleague. Because it is inevitably inflected by authority and power, being colleagues can enable or dangerously hamper the working relationship of supervisor and student, and the students' own research. It is a very uneasy relationship, but one increasing in new universities as colleagues seek higher degrees and can perhaps gain some element of fee waiver in undertaking them 'at home' rather than at a different institution.

Relationships are the key focus here. Maggi Savin Baden (at Coventry University) comments:

> For me the difficulty in supervising colleagues is complicated because the notion of 'being a colleague' can mean all sorts of different things. First it can mean supervising someone in the same department or school and that brings challenges about the power relationships. For example, I was supervising somebody in the same school whose line manager expected that doing a PhD was an extra and not part of academic life. The result was that if I encouraged that student to take study leave or time working at home the boss didn't approve, criticised the student and often gave them more teaching – which was tantamount to sabotage in my book.

There are also issues about when and where supervision happens at work and whether it is okay for them to pop their head around the door a few times a day when they are feeling stuck – which is okay for some of the time but not at others. Questions of boundaries seemed to become blurred in this relationship.

The other type of colleague is the person you got to know through conferences and through shared interests. These may be older than you, more experienced in their field, but not yours. Becoming a PhD student with you then changes the relationship and I find that there is often quite a bit of circling around one at the beginning (despite doing all the ground stuff) which is about sorting out the boundaries and power issues. Having said that, I feel I have done much better with this type of 'collegial' relationship so that after the PhD we have become friends and worked together as equal partners. (personal communication, March 2004)

There is a range of issues here. Practice-based or professionally oriented and located research is often felt to be decided by, controlled by and aimed at the benefit of the organisation which has commissioned it, allowed it to happen, and will use it. This could influence access, scope and the kind of research question, research processes, timing, outcomes, outputs and their use. Many students are happy to dovetail the requests and requirements of their profession and institution with their own practice and their research. Others choose to research their practice to improve it. Still others find the political, personal and structural issues this throws up extremely difficult and negative. As a supervisor, it is important to help, enable, support, and empower students in this. They *do* need to be involved in and to 'own' the research, even if it is to be used by and useful to others in their professional practice. They do need to produce a manageable, boundaried, achievable, sufficiently intellectually taxing, appropriately researched and written up piece of research for the award, even if (as is most probably the case) it is in rather a different shape to any *report* researched or commissioned by the institution or profession. You and they need to be sufficiently certain at the outset, during, and on completion that it is viable and valuable in itself as a piece of research.

These issues concern the research project. Others include the methodology and methods chosen and still others, the difficulties and worries that might arise should the practitioner-based researcher be a colleague of yours.

Many practice-based researchers in the social sciences or health choose to use action research as a methodology because it enables them to involve others, for example colleagues, patients, clients, and students as collaborators, sharing in and owning the research. Let us look at action research and its link to practice or practice-based research.

▶ Action research

Useful in practitioner research, action research resembles reflective practice and innovation plus reflection, but it is more rigorous. Often people reflect on practice and would like to try out innovations, address problems, and check on the effectiveness or otherwise of various elements of their practice. This we do on a daily basis, but action research enables a specifically focused, researched exploration, action and evaluation.

Action research involves partnership and collaboration – between the population and researcher, researcher and colleagues. All share in the research planning, processes and outcomes. In this way it becomes a shared development and evaluative process ensuring the research population are *subjects* not objects, and full partners in the research. Reflection is a key element of action research, enabling learning to be embedded.

Action Research is practical, participatory and emancipatory because it enables all to be aware of the research, and included as partners in it. It involves emotions and feelings, not merely actions, and is interpretative because after an intervention or research-underpinned innovation, results and responses are interpreted, analysed and agreed amongst subjects and researchers. Researchers take a critical attitude involving self-evaluation, development, professionalism and accountability. In action research, in order to ensure rigour and reliability, several research methods, or 'triangulation', are used to investigate the issues, matching the results of one method against those of at least one other. Action research encourages a sense of ownership and feeds into change. It is not scientific, in that it does not rely on experimental pre- and post-test models, and it is not 'done to' objects or a population but involves them in the construction and interpretation of the research.

Action research operates in cycles addressing problems, interventions, innovations and questions arising from practice. The different steps involved include:

- Focus on/define problem/intervention/innovation in context
- Involve participants and colleagues
- Produce general action plan
- Take action – try out an intervention
- Monitor the effect – using qualitative/quantitative methods
- Collect data
- Analyse and evaluate results
- Share and debate.

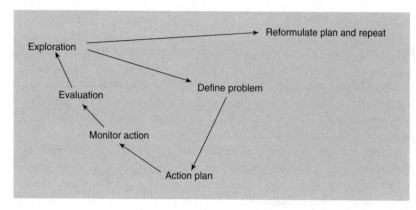

FIGURE 15.1   THE ACTION RESEARCH CYCLE

Much action research takes place in the theoretical framework of phenomenography, a methodology based on a philosophy of 'being in the world', recognising that all experiences are *interactions* in context (see Figure 15.1).

Whatever research students are involved in, they will need to ensure ethics and confidentiality. In action research, because participants are fully involved as subjects, this seems to be less of an issue – nothing 'is done to' them without consent. However, the research is likely to consider feelings, emotions, individual experiences and responses, so adhering to ethics and confidentiality processes are essential (see Chapter 7).

Why choose practitioner-based action research?

Practitioner-based and practice-based action research could provide insights into:

- the working practices and interactions of subjects
- the working practices ethos, faults, etc. of the organisation
- the students' own working practices
- your own practice and that of others in a beneficial manner – curriculum change, practice change and development, highlighting then avoiding bad practice.

However, it is useful to consider whether there are any problems, for example:

- confidentiality and access to participants as subjects
- are people being open about what they reveal?

- intrusiveness, position and power – the researcher's, 'the subject's'
- the very phenomenon that a student researches changes as they involve it/them in research
- there will need to be more than one cycle if it is action research – will it take too long?
- can they do anything about what they find out? or should they? should someone else? How can results and findings lead to action?

If your students look likely to select action research or practitioner-based research, then suggest they consider these questions:

- What kind of practitioner- or practice-based research would you like to undertake in the future or are you undertaking now?
- What kind of action research could you use? Which methods would you use within it and why?
- If this is action research, how will you go about its planning, ensuring confidentiality and collaboration, etc., and setting up cycles affected by each other?
- how will you share results?

Practice- and practitioner-related research

Researchers need to consider issues of research design, access, funding and the ability of the professional practice-based research to actually action changes, evaluate practices and make recommendations. Problems could arise at specific points: (1) during the research; or (2) while writing it up. At point (1), students need to consider whether their potentially transformational or change aims are achievable within the bounds of the research dissertation or thesis, or could lie beyond these bounds, that is whether others might be informed by their research and so develop changes, solve problems, or action new practices or programmes, but that trying them out and evaluating them might not be the *research itself.*

Consider the four-part model in Figure 15.2: which elements fits your student's research?

It is possible that a student's research could include all four parts, but it is more likely that it will:

(a) use history, experience and other evidence to identify a problem or need. **(1)**.
(b) use history etc. to identify a problem or need then suggest solutions **(1 and 4)**.

(c) use own experience of having developed a model/programme, produced, tested it out and evaluated it. Some background (1) would be included but this trial is the focus of the research. The research resembles an experimental model – scientific or social scientific **(mostly 2 and 4)**.

(d) describe a programme, model etc, evaluate its effectiveness and make recommendations for further action **(mostly 4)**.

(e) identify a problem and its history, evaluate theoretically or in terms of responses, feelings, others' solutions to these and draw up some guidelines **(1 leading to 2)**.

One successful colleague identified a problem (in health promotion), gave a brief history, built a programme, described it, tried it out, recorded the events, and evaluated its effectiveness, and participants' responses (1, 2, 3, 4). Attempting *all* of this is a popular first move amongst professional practitioners, but it is *usually to be avoided* as it is over-optimistic and extended.

So, combining all four stages is possible, but if not very tightly focused, a research project including all four could be too huge, and fail to really produce research outcomes. Professional bodies, however, tend to want exactly this shape for a report

In the course of scoping their research, students can be advised to look at the diagram and consider which sections of elements 1, 2, 3 or 4 are manageable for them. If pressured by work, students could decide that 3 and or 4 (model/programme and the evaluation plus recommendations) are outside the boundaries of their research for this award, but could lead to a report for their professional context.

This effectively splits the work, as it would also split the writing up process and a student might find they are then muddled or torn as a result. It could, however, help to solve problems of funding: a manageable piece of work should be completed even if funding runs out. If the programme or project fails, they can still write up the research, despite institutional politics, keeping confidential and crucial information away from management colleagues. The *report* can make recommendations while the research details methods and reasons for them, suggesting others take the work forward, so indicating further work, gaps and boundaries.

During the course of their postgraduate work, several APU students were involved in supervisory dialogues focusing on the experience of researching practice within their own institution in order to identify a need for change, maintain practices, evaluate processes and behaviours or changes. For all these students, subjectivity/objectivity is an issue. For some, using the self as a case study provides a rich opportunity to put their own experience legitimately into the research. For others, incorporating a log or journal offers the same without publicity. For some, the issues of identifying or evaluating practice *or* of causing change proves central, affecting their conceptual frameworks and choice of methods. Our research programme attempts to identify such issues and help/empower students towards the achievement of appropriate change/outcomes, if manageable, in their research project.

▶ Research methods: supervisory dialogues

Supervisory dialogues taped and transcribed using NUDIST (a computer package that analyses qualitative data thematically), are a major source of research data on our postgraduates' and supervisors' research projects at APU. Dialogues are conducted with the PhD students during the first, second and third stages of their research development programme. The extracts presented below represent some of the issues and experiences faced by students in relation to researching their practice.

Student: Ok? And I want to search specifically the Heads of the Departments in Seminaries who presented the middle level management, Ok? And I want to understand, I know because this is my job, the problem that in the same time I need to be simultaneously in contact with the high level management – there are very very wide level, higher than me – and with the subordinate. It's something like sandwich.

Supervisor: Yeah, a sandwich for the middle managers that are in the middle.

Student: Yes, yes. And I want to understand which characteristics help them to be simultaneously in contact with the two levels.

Supervisor: Ah, so how do middle managers go about their role which is a role that's upwards and downwards, a sandwich role?

This student has entered middle management and wants to look at the phenomenon of role conflict, demands made on *middle* managers and ways of overcoming problems *because* of being in the middle.

Student: . . . because I was one of them. So I try to, I start to understand that it's some point it's very very important, because that I came from this, the level of the subordinates.

She reflects on her own privileged position. Having been in the same situation as her (now) subordinates she feels she understands their needs, but now she is their manager and suddenly expected to solve all the problems. She mainly wants to look at role conflict solutions for *women* managers.

The student researches the role effectiveness of women in senior management positions in her own teacher training institution. One of the potential difficulties of researching your own practice in higher education emerges here as closeness to the subject matter. The student could be too involved to establish real perspectives about management. However, she could also be close enough to have unique insights, much enthusiasm, and then to use *herself* as a case study. The discussion goes on to suggest background reading and theories underpinning the research.

In research into ongoing practice, there is always a danger of the study turning into a personal reflection or a report. In order to ensure it is research, it is important that students conceptualise the work, develop conceptual frameworks, and identify informing theories and the arguments in the field, relating their own work to all of these.

Another student comments on difficulties of carrying out research into her own practice in the work context where colleagues find the research intrusive, resent it, or are confused by it. In this supervisory dialogue, the student identifies the moment when she realised her *practice* needed to be researched because it would be valuable to others, but that in order to conduct the research she needed to clarify theoretical background and inform her work with the concepts of experts. This is part of turning a practice development into a piece of action research from which can come generalisable as well as specific results, and which can be of use to other practitioners. Other difficulties, however, were produced by her position as teacher/facilitator and by her colleagues' views of the reasons for and usefulness of the action research.

Student: I think really, I am looking at the professional drama groups that are around. One of the things that I found out was that I talked about this business of insider and outsider and how your own university that was the XXX, can make you feel as an outsider because when you come up with something and you think well this needs to be developed and you need support, people think instinctively, well it's her work, it's her benefit you know and we want the students to concentrate and I am saying this is part of a development and I cannot do it alone, I need support hence the project had to go extra curricula because my own colleagues had blocked it. The students wanted to work with me because they were excited about working on some-

> thing new and we just went extra curricula and I think for me
> the most exciting part of it was actually going to look at some
> of these projects that have been implemented and you know
> getting together with the students at the end of an observation
> visit and say you know they would say oh well we wouldn't do
> that with our project, and we would do that and we'll take that.

This particular student has now successfully completed her PhD. A major problem along the way was the untangling of ongoing work. Teaching groups of students and staff development consultancies arose from the success of the programme she developed and from this actual *research* process, which lend to a thesis and thus to publication. As a piece of practice-based research, it was difficult to decide what element of the practice to formally research, which theories to use to scaffold and direct the research, and where to stop the research process for the PhD outcome, because action research by its nature is cyclical – each successive cycle fuelling the improvements in practice in the next. A practice-based piece of action research has to stop somewhere for the demands of the award, or transformational outcomes sought at the end of the programme whose processes are being researched will be endless. Students involved in practice-based and action research need to define, decide and defend their decisions about the scope and extent of their research project, their 'slice of the cake' in terms of ongoing work.

Management of a sufficient and coherent piece of practice-based action research allows a snapshot of the problem, issues, question, situation and innovation, which in itself could otherwise flow on without the kind of researched, evaluative shape to it that can be shared with others.

Students undertaking postgraduate work and undergraduates on work projects are involved in at least two projects : (1) the research that follows a proposal, related to a conceptual framework, meets peaks and troughs, risks, revelations and disasters and comes to some sort of conclusion; and (2) The writing of the dissertation/thesis that accompanies the research but also has a more coherent final shape; tracking plans, actions, reflection, findings and evaluations, but finally presenting the whole as a coherent, well-shaped thesis or dissertation, underpinned by a conceptual framework. While (1) is more of a journey with maps and some trips down variable byways, (2) is more like a piece of architecture, seeming, in retrospect, to be built logically on firm foundations and finally standing up coherently as a completed piece. For those undertaking practice- or work-related research there is a *third* process (see chapter 3). The project or the job, teaching practices, etc. in the case of higher education practice-based research, alongside the research, can interfere with it. Professional- and practice-related outcomes sought by research into one's work might lead a student into local political difficulties, or into the production of output without the speculative, theory-based, conceptual level of a dissertation or thesis.

EdD and professional doctorate

From a different perspective, Green and Lee (1995) call for a broader approach to theorising. In 1995 they edited a thematic edition of the *Australian Universities Review* on Postgraduate Studies/Postgraduate Pedagogy, and the theoretical nature of doctoral education. Green (1996) argues the importance of curriculum in discussions of the professional doctorate, seeing the professional doctorate, unlike discipline-based degrees, focusing on professional practice that leads to new relationships between the university, the profession and the workplace. In these writings and an ongoing ARC research project (1997) they take further the project in Evans and Green (1995), in which theorising is seen as a 'necessary first principle in meaningful and effective innovation in postgraduate research and training' (Pearson, 1999, p. 276).

In response to the need for professionally oriented research into practice, both the EdD and the PrD have been developed. They tend to focus on professional- and practice-based research. Their staged, accumulative nature, and for the PrD, the deliberate use of colleagues as supervisors, high-lights and helps to overcome issues amounting to conflicts of interest. In some instances, the PrD might lead to a thesis that resembles or serves the purpose of a report.

The Professional Doctorate differs from the PhD in that it:

- is interventionalist in its relationship to the topic being investigated;
- adopts a descriptive and/or developmental approach to research using an applied, problem-focused, or action-based approach;
- obliges candidates to become involved with implementing change in the organisations with which they are involved;
- recognises the importance of internal mentors, not only as hosts but also as sources of knowledge and expertise for, and the dissemination of, research findings;
- enhances the development of candidates through undertaking and use of their research.

These features may appear in any social science PhD, but they illustrate the uniqueness of the PrD because of its imperative to involve candidates in advancing professional learning in their own working situations. Its status and rigour, like the PhD, is reflected in the production of a research-based thesis (*PrD Handbook*, 2003, p. 1).

Within the PrD the relationships, where appropriate, between peers, client–worker, employer–employee and inter-organisational are the forum where research findings can be valued, and mutual expectations will exist regarding the achievement of organisational goals. The context has a central role in the development of the learner/researcher since it provides the source of research and it is where the findings from that research are disseminated and implemented (*PrD Handbook*, 2003, p. 2).

Aims and objectives of the professional doctorate programme (Health and Social Care)

The PrD (H&SC) will serve the needs of professionals in the field of health and social care who wish to undertake doctoral level study to:

- Advance knowledge and practice through the generation of original knowledge
- Provide apprenticeship in research methodology so that candidates are enabled to develop those research skills that have an impact on health and social care practice and education, which enables them to undertake research assignments
- Enable candidates to display a high level of academic rigour, and the capability to produce work that is acceptable for publication in refereed journals
- Prepare candidates to assume increasing responsibility for strategic planning, decision-making and leadership, and to fulfil a developmental role in their respective organisations
- Improve the quality of their services as practitioners and leaders
- Expand their theoretical understanding of educational, management and professional practice in health and social care
- Foster and develop inter-agency working and learning through the promotion of research in practice and services
- Evaluate the impact of interventions on internal mentors or services
- Work in partnership with service users
- Increase the esteem of their own organisation – raise the organisation's reputation, which in turn will aid recruitment and retention.

As a consequence of meeting these aims and objectives, candidates who are awarded the PrD will possess 'expert knowledge' in their chosen field of research through acknowledged scholarly achievement. They will also have made an original contribution to the understanding and application of contemporary education, training and management practice through solution-centred research. This will be demonstrated through having generated models, and other explanatory evidence, that display originality of ideas and independence of thought. Thus, the title will be an appropriate measure of their professional and academic achievement.

Structure of the PrD

The programme conforms to the University's Research Degrees Regulations for Professional Doctorates. Consisting of two stages, it involves workshops, working papers and a thesis (see *PrD Handbook*).

▶ Case studies

It may be useful to consider the following cases:

1 Student H is undertaking a Master's in Education considering the need for, structure of and effectiveness of continuing personal development provision. This felt fine at the beginning. He is a mid-career teacher in a school. This was his interest. Then management became aware simultaneously of government interest in CPD, and his project. Now he has been given the task, for the school, of identifying needs and evaluating the CPD to suggest further developments. His colleagues, previously happy to share their feelings and experiences, are unsure of 'who' they are talking to – which side he is on? (management stooge/researcher?)

2 Student C works to discover how and if nursing students are aware of the usefulness of their studies about and in research practices. She seeks curriculum change. She is a senior lecturer. In her lecturer role she sends out questionnaires but receives a 10 per cent response rate so decides to re-contact the respondents, this time owning up that it is for *her own* research. They are more willing to respond because it will support *her*.

3 The research group has been awarded funding to develop an acoustic-based engineering product to improve visually impaired people's ability to use their hearing to find their way around. As group member, your student seems confused about where his piece of work might fit in. If he succeeds and uses the funding, an affordable product could be produced. However, can he continue the research if funding dries up or if the product is faulty or rejected?

4 Your student is studying specific management relationships in a partner institution in another country. Half way through her data gathering, the

institution breaks off all relations with your own, leaving your student banned from gathering data and in a difficult legal position about publishing or writing up.

5 You and your student are colleagues and are working on an institutional development of which their research is a part. Work is coming in late, and of poor quality. Of course, the student is subject to the same work pressures as you and so you are sympathetic. But it is embarrassing to discuss (1) the work, which the institution needs completing and (2) the quality of the research so far.

These case studies focus on issues of:

- **funding**: the shape of research and professional practice-oriented activities; topic; usefulness, outputs and research quality; shape and kind of research output.
- **politics**: the role of research in organisations and in relation to post-graduate or undergraduate demands.
- **interpersonal relations** between colleagues.
- **rank**, power.

The case studies should produce some thoughts about professional practice-based research in practice.

▶ Further reading

Evans, T. and Green, W. (1995) 'Dancing at a distance? Postgraduate studies, "supervision", and distance education', *Australian Association for Research in Education Conference*, AARE, Hobart (Electronic), pp. 1–14.

Pearson, M. (1999) 'The changing environment for doctoral education in Australia: implications for quality management, improvement and innovation', *Higher Education Research and Development*, **18**(3), p. 276.

PrD (Professional Doctorate in Health and Social Care) Handbook (Cambridge: Anglia Polytechnic University, School of Health Care Practice, 2003).

16 New Ways: Supervising Creative Research Work and the PhD by Publication

Research and its outcomes are not merely presentable in standard formats of the dissertation, thesis or project reports. Indeed, historically, artists, musicians and others engaged in creative work have researched both the contextual background to their work and the ways of expressing the idea or argument they wish to explore, represented in their final work. In response to recognition that research and its outcomes may take many shapes for many ends, university systems are also changing not merely to accommodate but to encourage and help develop and recognise such creative work. This is particularly important for students undertaking dissertations and theses in the Arts, which include products.

In many universities, students are now undertaking research that leads to creative outcomes and outputs differing in both process and product from the more conventional dissertation or thesis. Often creative work is accompanied by an analytical account that more closely resembles the conventional format, linking the creative piece to the theories, concepts and arguments underpinning it, and which it expresses. Additionally, some research students, probably mid-career professionals, now seek to gain PhDs by recognition of their publications. In these cases, the shape of the PhD is different to that of the more conventional form, but the outcomes – original, well-argued, publishable research-based work – are the same.

This chapter considers:

- supervising students engaged in creative research-based projects
- supervising the PhD by publication.

At APU, undergraduates are able to produce dissertations in English involving the development of a sequence of short stories or poems, accompanied by analytical and critical discussion showing the development decisions made in the process of this work – and the ways in which it exemplifies and articulates creative, critical aims and outcomes. Students undertaking dissertations in women's or gender studies have traditionally been able to produce creative products for their dissertations, as have the MA Women's Studies students. On the MA, students can undertake a video dissertation for which they are co-supervised by someone in media production and their Women's Studies supervisor. The video dissertation includes three assessment products, based on research, creativity, and on conceptual, reflective and analytical work. They produce:

1 a log or journal of decisions made, methodological choices, their research journey;
2 an analytical, theorised, critical discussion/commentary;
3 the video or creative product itself.

The log is an ongoing exploration and reflection accompanying the stages of the student's research. Initially, it involves a record of brainstorming creative ideas, the argument or issue they wish to pursue through their work, and ways in which the creative format develops as an expression and exploration of ideas or issues. During the course of their research, they reflect on the development of skills and achievement or otherwise of elements of their research and creative production. They use the log rather like any other research log or journal to articulate questions they are asking and the choice of creative expression, the problems encountered, surprises, decisions made and changes in decisions made, as well as their own experience and emotional responses to their work. This in itself is part of the research process, because it engages with the thoughts, experiences, memories and feelings of the students, and so gets to the heart of the ways in which they generate, develop and finalise their research and both creative and analytical expressions of it.

The analytical commentary, or discussion, resembles a *theoretical perspectives* chapter. Here students enter into a dialogue with the critics and theorists whose work underlies and drives their own with similar or previous work, that is the context for their own work, and alternative possible theories or interpretation with which their own research and creative development are in dialogue.

For example, a Women's Studies student wished to explore her experience of relationship with the maternal and ways in which relationships with her mother and her own roles as a mother can be creatively expressed. She did this through the reproduction of a creative piece of stitchwork based on a gift, an apron from her own mother. She read widely in the French feminists – Julia Kristeva, Hélène Cixous, Luce Irigaray – on experts on mothering and motherhood – Gilligan and Chodorow – as well as in the work of artists whose products have been in stitchcraft of various sorts. She incorporated critical responses to the feminist critical theorists that she worked with, in the actual stitchwork around the apron, and also engaged in a dialogue critically in her accompanying piece. This explored and argued how mothering involves handing down conflicting ideas which women need to respond to both critically and in an empowering way; and how there are different notions of mothering and of women's work, women's expression, of relationships between mothers and daughters and tradition – and so on (it was extensive). She also explored and expressed how this piece of stitchcraft related her to her mother's versions of what she 'should' be like in the mother–daughter relationship, and how these expectations engaged with the theorists. This was a tripartite exploration of the personal, the creative and the analytical. The final product is fascinating – but alone without the log of developing arguments and the analysis it would just be an apron with writing and stitch work on it!

Another Women's Studies student produced a glamorous dress made out of pan scrubs and other domestic items, making a comment about conflicting representations of women and roles for women – from the glamorous to the domestic. Several students have been involved in the production of video dissertations. In each of these instances, they have produced a log of their questions, decisions and problems, etc.; and an analytical piece engaging with feminist critics, with methods of video production and ways in which video can engage with the issues and questions they have. These too are tripartite pieces. The video is a final product of theorised and personal research.

My examples are from women's studies. Discussion with colleagues from more practical arts reveal similar examples: children's book illustration projects, installations, sculptures, and photography sequences were each accompanied by logs of the creative process and reflections, and an analytical critical piece. While artists might argue their work needs no communication, since it stands alone and speaks for itself, I would suggest that if a student seeks an award for the work, it needs to be researched. The analysis and log serve as means of communicating its negotiation of meaning and expressions to others (not least to examiners and the academic community).

For students engaged in a variety of creative pieces at both undergraduate and postgraduate level, it is crucial that they are supervised in ways that help them bridge the gaps, as such, between the creative, the reflective and developmental and the analytically critical, so they can find a language with which to express their ideas and arguments that is both creatively sound, expressive, and at the level of the award. The supervisor then has a fascinating but difficult task working with the students' creativity. You could begin by helping and enabling them to brainstorm and explore their initial ideas and issues perhaps on one side of a page or a flipchart/whiteboard. Next they could explore what creative product might enable them to engage with these ideas and outcomes, and finally, which theories, concepts, theorists, areas of reading and argument can underpin and inform their work, and how much of the personal might appropriately be included. Supervisors would expect to encourage the creative expression into an appropriate form, to ensure the student reads and engages with the theorists and critics, expressing themselves analytically and critically in relation to the creative piece, and to produce really reflective pieces. These are three different kinds of expression and each needs development as part of the research as it is finally presented for assessment.

▶ Video dissertation example

'Anya' is a creative painter and installation artist who has worked in her adult life in the country of her birth, South Africa, mostly concentrating her work into productions of her own art and into teaching others to express their ideas through artistic production in workshops. Now living in the UK, she had a tremendous sense of homesickness for the South Africa of her past, but this was mixed with political tensions and confusions, and other ambivalences about memories of herself in relation to her family. What has this personal piece got to do with research? She wanted to explore and express:

Going home: the influence of home, family and memory on identity

This could of course take many forms in a dissertation or thesis, so let us consider how we might explore different readings and expressions of this idea. One student might decide to interview a number of people to explore in a semi-structured way their memories of family, home and the link between this and identity. Another might wish to pursue the question through statistical responses to questionnaires about identity, context, origin, background and family, and another might like to explore the expression and representations of these themes through the work of a novelist, poet or filmmaker. But

Anya wished to use her creative background and also to develop some further creative skills in the process. She decided with her supervisor that the production of a video dissertation was the best choice. Together they brainstormed the issues and questions with which she was concerned:

- family
- home
- context
- memory and its dependability, or not
- identity
- guilt
- longing
- feelings that relate to memory and family
- self and identity formed from the family and home and in spite of them or as a rejection or response to them – influenced overtly and covertly.

The creative element of Anya's work was, she hoped, going to enable her to not only explore and express what she was conscious of, but take her into new areas to explore and allow her to express unconscious contradictions, longing and guilt, good and bad memories, recognition of how she has been formed and what she misses, and things she needs to face up to. But this was an academic piece of work and the structure and rigour demanded of an MA dissertation were important. She and her supervisor were determined the dissertation structure was going to be exactly the enabling frame around which and upon which she could grow, nurture and express these ideas, arguments and explorations. The ideas and arguments form one part of the work. Brainstorming and decisions were recorded in a journal as the ideas took shape. Similarly, in part of each supervision, the supervisor and Anya discussed exactly what kind of creative work could help her explore, express and articulate her ideas and arguments. Anya decided she would make an art video since she had only basic video skills and many art skills. They worked out that this would mean using some of the strategies of art in the construction and texture, shape, content, images, etc. of the idea itself. Another brainstorm session followed – how might her idea enable her engagement with contradictory responses? She had a constant daily sense of travelling back home and feeling like a stranger there, but needing to go. She wished to be again part of her family, and felt she was an individual now, had moved on. They decided it would be necessary to re-visit South Africa for some of the footage but that other footage could be shot in the UK, since many of Anya's feelings about her origins and home constantly reasserted themselves here. Her sense of identity was formed in both places, reflected here and now. The supervisor offered to travel to South Africa, but such perks are hard to fund . . .

Anya's decisions about how to shoot and what to shoot are all recorded in her log. One of the important things she wanted to express was a contradictory set of memories, another of returning to clarify then test them, and another to record her sense of identity as made up of memories, thoughts now, fantasy about the past, and a desire to return and reflect on that return. She wrote of this and decided she would take footage of herself, her return, the home and family, a family gathering and herself, and her in the UK. It would be necessary to intersperse the two, to cut them together somehow. This was a matter for video technique but also for creative expression.

But what happened to the analytical elements? The third element of the work was constantly ongoing. In order to ask her questions about identity, family, homeland, memory and creative expressions of these, Anya carried out literature searches, did a great deal of reading and reflection on that reading critically, analytically and discursively, both establishing the critical framework of the theories, theorists, and the themes she was using, and establishing a personal engagement with the arguments and conflicting ideas they represented in terms of her own questions and creative explorations. As such she got into a typical research dialogue with her theorists – some critical and some creative – as any other research student would. Dealing with the decisions about the developing creative product, engaging in a skills development creative activity with the other supervisor in media production, and with the Women's Studies supervisor in terms of feminist film making and the arguments, caused her to move backwards and forwards between the three processes and products: log/journal; creative video work; and analytical, theoretical perspectives and engaged argument. Each moved on. One of the roles of the supervisor was traditional – ensuring that Anya developed time lines and was aware of how she reacted to them, changing them if necessary, enabling Anya to explore and express the right kind of shape for the outlet of her arguments and ideas; sending reading her way; putting her in touch with other students and others who have produced video projects, and creative projects; and meeting regularly for supervision to consider ongoing work and discuss any hitches or developments. Notes were kept of supervisions and Anya recorded decisions and thoughts, etc. in her log. As the elements of the video and the chapter on theoretical perspectives/engagement with the theorists and theories developed, the supervisor looked at and discussed these with the student. Both supervisors worked together with Anya over the video development.

In the event, the shape of her final product was even more creative than had been imagined, because of the desire to express a sense of return, yet the intrusion into the everyday of memories, a sense of the past lived in the present, and the integration into identity. Anya produced a video that was cut to replay returns to the South African home, and her in her home here. She used family stills and current family video taken specially on location. She talked over it, used sounds of family members and used expressive music. The written product was also creative. She and her supervisor decided there were two products but that they worked together and were not so easily separated. So they were interleaved, cut together and bound as a single piece. You could read the log/journal straight through on one colour-coded route through the product, followed by the analytical piece, or you could read the two in parallel since the pages were cut together and inter-leaved.

For assessment purposes, the video, log and analytical piece were appropriately produced and presented. With sensitive, informed supervisory dialogues throughout, Anya was also able to produce something unusual and creative, even in her log and analytical piece, as well as her video.

This extended case study serves as an example of the ways in which supervision can aid a student in producing an appropriate, creative dissertation or thesis at the right level, adhering to the university demands for assessment; shape; length; engagement with literature and defence of theory, theorists and methods; coherence; contribution to knowledge in the field; and so on, (but something which is *also* highly original and creative).

▶ How are creative research outputs examined?

As an external examiner, I have examined two creative PhDs that have clearly benefited from sensitive, creative, supervisory advice throughout in terms of the ways in which the actual innovative, creative expression can be engaged with by analytical response in a (relatively) conventional way. One performance PhD comprised a thesis which on the face of it, looked just like any other, and a CD ROM of the performance student's work. The thesis engaged with theories of performance art, the search for the self in performance, expression of the self through drama, expression of issues of identity and memory, and finally the part technology played in enabling or enhancing performance art. The student was a performance artist who used her own body in drama and performance, (thus engaging in the feminist and performance issues of the body in space, expression, and performance – self as subject). She also used technology, specifically video, which had been digitally re-worked. One of her comments is about engaging expressions of the self, identity, memory, gender and performance with ways of recording and re-writing it. The video medium enables this expression.

I was fascinated to also receive a standard PhD thesis linking arguments about drama, performance, self, technology, video, expression, identity, memory and all the theorists and theories, coherently worked through in an argument. This all operated with reference to the CD I was sent so that, in effect, I read the thesis as I watched the CD on the computer screen. CD excerpts of her performance and video performance interact as examples to illustrate arguments expressed in the text. The supervisor was able to advise this talented (profession of performance artist) student to both comply with the university regulations and to be able to explore and express her ideas creatively through a creative product engaged in dialogue with the thesis in a dialogue with the theories. There is argument in a conventional manner and a real, original creative outlet for her expression of her ideas. The whole entity felt as though it should have been worth more than one PhD! The examiner team needed to comprise performance artist theorists and academics. I was there because of the feminist nature of the work and also my own experience of working with creative research (video MAs and PhDs). It could be the case that a different team of examiners might question even the shape of the work itself. The supervisor had been involved in ongoing work with the student to explore ways in which the issues of identity, memory, gender and performance might be expressed through digital media, video and self-performance, and alongside these how she might, in a more conventional manner, engage in a dialogue with theorists, produce a standard abstract and a standard-looking thesis, and how the two could genuinely interlock, which they did. The performances on CD were the evidence of the theories in action, and part of the arguments and dialogues within the analytical piece. The CD was also a primary source – in this instance a creative product from the performer herself.

For the student, ensuring that she both engaged with the theories and practices of performing or expressing the self as subject *and* performed this in action was crucial. Indeed, it also would be crucial if the thesis had been based on using participant observation, or the self as a case in, for instance, education or business organisation research. One Australian colleague produced a cabaret as part of the thesis. He performed his research output (and passed).

Another PhD student's thesis contextualised the development, usefulness and contribution to the community of community theatres. Part of his thesis included his own community theatre-originated dramas, contextualised and explained in analytical and theoretical terms in relation to his arguments.

An MA student used her poetry as part of her research development and output based on a desire to explore theories and arguments about abuse and self-growth. She got stuck. The subject matter was too personal and painful. She felt detached when reading the theorists, but it was digging up too much excess personal material. She blocked and disappeared. She began to write poetry, got in touch, published the poetry and gained both an outlet for her complex feelings and a renewed sense of self-worth. 'You have here', I said, 'the core of your new version of your dissertation!' We brainstormed a shape enabling her to engage rigorously with those theorists and arguments that she said *now* helped her to focus on, contextualise and clarify what she was writing and why. Initially, there was a theoretical argument and the poems. Towards the end, now, we have just met again and decided to interleave fully the different kinds of writing. She is going to produce a separate log, but she will also:

1   introduce the dissertation with a poem
2   introduce the self and creative expression as subject
3   move into the theoretical perspectives and set them up
4   write analytically and critically alongside the personal, following each poem as evidence and exploration with a brief analytical discussion of how it works theoretically, why, and how this engages with arguments informed by theorists.

We have talked through instances and suggested using stuck-over additional critical pieces interleaved as notes, then rewriting and incorporating them. The poems are in a different colour to the rest of the text. We have a piece developing here which she owns, and which, in its interlocking shapes, can enable creative expression, reflection on that expression, creative discussion of how it engages with arguments underpinned by theories and the work of appropriate theorists.

The role of the supervisor in these cases expands from that of more standard research. There is a need to work alongside students to help them release their creative energies and develop creative engagement with ways of expressing the question they are asking, issues, theorists, and arguments they are making and putting forward. Some of this is done through brainstorming, trial, experiments, reflection and ongoing evaluation of the success of the developing creative expression in conveying the argument. We are all concerned with expression – but creative artists have two interlocked versions of expression, at least, to deal with.

Students in art and design and other creative disciplines should find a second communicative language other than their artwork to engage analytically, critically and in a dialogue with ideas and expressions in the field, with heorists and practitioners, as well as conveying ideas in creative forms, or hey might *not* communicate to others. Researchers must clarify methods or hey might not otherwise be able to bridge gaps between the internalised, personal, creative purpose and its expression – often clear to the producer – for the audience, in this case supervisor, examiners and hopefully other researchers and readers in their field (and other fields). It is an ongoing issue n art and design education, performance, creative writing, practical oriented architecture and other design or practice-related work. It is *crucial* to produce those two forms of expression and a bridge between them to enable others to engage with and evaluate expression and answering of research questions and the research-informed piece of practice that is the creative product as well as the dissertation or thesis.

As professionals, supervisors need to work with their students to find the appropriate creative output, and to help them articulate both what it communicates and how it engages with the theories underpinning it.

Figure 16.1 explores the tripartite process of the creative research product, indicating how the parts interlink, and what the supervisor stimulates with regard to reflection (log), *creativity* and analysis.

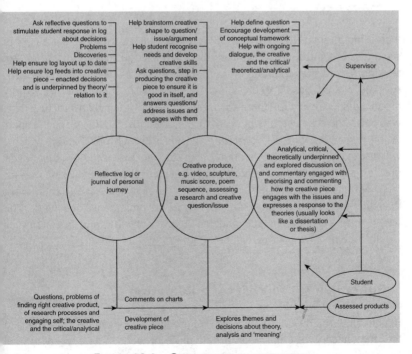

FIGURE 16.1   SUPERVISING CREATIVE WORK

Task

If you have students with a creative idea, proficiency in a creative process, or who would like to explore and express themselves creatively, consider how you can:

- stimulate and encourage them to brainstorm a creative response
- help them avoid a part-creative product itself
- engage them with appropriate theorists to underpin, inform and help analyse the importance of their creative response
- set up a commitment to producing a log of ideas and discussions
- check and support (1) the creative product; (2) the analytical and theoretical response; and (3) the reflective log
- advise your artistic and creative student who argues it is impossible to be analytical because the creative piece speaks for itself.

▶ Supervising creative work that has already been produced

Increasing numbers of students in professional or creative practice are seeking the opportunity to produce dissertations and theses, and some are seeking supervision enabling them to incorporate analysis and find a theoretically argued base for their own creative production, not necessarily produced specifically for the award, but as part of their own practice. This was partly the case with the performance artist, above. In this respect, supervision resembles that of supervising the PhD through publication, which I will discuss next. It involves working with students to select work that develops and expresses their argument, and to support them in their research for the theoretical underpinning – the critical and analytical base to their work that they then need to express as a way of understanding their work. The whole must be coherent and address central concerns and questions, as would a creative piece of research and its output.

▶ Supervising the PhD by publication

Historically, would-be students who had produced publications were advised that they needed to embark on a new piece of work in its entirety for the PhD. For many, this was fine – a chance to do something related to previous work perhaps but a completely new, coherent enterprise. For others, it represented an enormous hurdle – returning them to the beginning of their career. Now many UK and Australian universities are recognising and supervising the PhD by publication. In the most popular version, the candidate identifies a theme and question, issue, area or coherent focus underlying some of their work and selects elements of the work accordingly. This is similar to identifying a research question. They choose the published works, for instance, a book, four chapters, three other journal essays, and resources. These are part of the thesis; the other part of the thesis being a 'wrap' of normally about 10,000 words. This wrap resembles the introduction and theoretical perspectives chapter of a more conventional thesis, insofar as it draws together the theorised argument underpinning the exploration and expression in the published pieces. It involves elements of the published pieces in a dialogue with underpinning theorists, quoting but not extensively, from the pieces themselves to do so. To enable a coherent route to be seen through the rest of the thesis, there is a discussion of the published piece showing how arguments have developed over time, and how evidence-based pieces relate to theorised pieces, and books to essays in a developmental, complex sense, commenting on reasons behind the work, impact and so on.

In this way, the published work is brought together for the student as a personal, reflective and analytical journey. For many, this is a marvellous opportunity to track where, why and to what effect, and what links appear in the variety of publications they have produced to date throughout their career. For some others, it provides an opportunity at the outset of the PhD to identify existing work, and to research towards the production of further appropriate work that will complete the coherent case for a PhD, that is it acts as a route map with some of the route yet to be sketched in, planned and completed.

One colleague reflected on and selected his research educational development work, drawing out themes of the profession of educational development, with assessment as a special focus. Another recognised two items – the political and the gendered – in her published work on Spanish cinema and varied these with a theorised 'wrap'.

Supervisors have many standard supervisory tasks to perform in relation to students seeking a PhD by publication, with a few exceptions, such as that students are often advanced, even eminent, in their careers. It is important to establish a working relationship that begins with collegiality. Additionally, the supervisor is the link between the student, the PhD and university mechanisms. Power and authority relationships still operate that need to be respected in any learning contract and agenda, any response, or completion of agreed activities over time. The supervisor will probably, initially:

- Identify with the student the theories, issues, questions and themes that will form the backbone of the PhD by publication; identify the basics of a conceptual framework seen to inform the published pieces – the key themes, theorists, concepts and arguments running throughout the range of work.
- Identify which gaps in knowledge the work fills as a whole and particular pieces of it address or fill, encouraging the student to make a case for this early on in their 'wrap'.
- Identify their boundaries – this is certainly a difficult issue if there has been a great deal of disparate publication. For example, one student might have written poetry, essays about the teaching of literature, and essays about crime fiction, contemporary poets, and nineteenth-century novelists but must select a coherent route through this.
- Identify what this PhD is going to be about
  - One area might be "contemporary poetry". The student's own publication can be a case in point – so this would be a semi-creative PhD including publications (like those discussed above).
  - Another might be to suggest or think of taking a line of argument through the contemporary pieces, novels and poems, or a line of argument that is more historical and combines the nineteenth- and twentieth-century pieces and a rationale for that combination. Whatever the choice of underpinning argument and shape to the selection, there has to be a very clear rationale because this is the *main element* of the argument for the PhD itself – coherence. The PhD also has to have internal coherence and conform to the various descriptions produced by Winter *et al.* (2000) or others like them (see Chapter 5) to pass.

Brainstorming a variety of possible routes through the existing work, then identifying any further work that might need to be carried out is essential at this early stage. Identifying what needs to be left out and why, what put in and why, what developed and why, and what theorists, theoretical and conceptual framework underpin the whole is important. Equally important is the working relationship based on a learning contract – formal or informal – with clarity over who commits to what. Regularity of supervisions and realistic timeframes are important, as time is short.

As the work begins to come together, the supervisor will probably be involved in a series of supervisions focusing on the 'wrap' as if it were a dissertation in itself, for here lie the concepts, theorists and theories as well as the coherent argument, uniting the whole. This needs to be extremely clear and succinct, making reference to the publications in a dialogue throughout.

There will probably be moments when some favourite pieces of writing must be jettisoned because they just don't fit the emerging rationale and theoretical perspectives of the 'wrap', and where various holes are identified that need filling. It is preferable not to have too many new items, otherwise why not do a PhD from scratch rather than one by publication?

When the PhD by publication is complete, the student will have a viva like any other student. It is crucial here to ensure the internal and external examiners can understand the nature of a PhD by publication as having coherence along various themes and arguments, but not in itself being a completely coherent whole from the outset and throughout. Not absolutely everything that is written and already published as essays and books will in themselves contribute to the core themes – there will seem to be some extra tangents and excess elements, even in very coherent PhDs by publication, because the pieces were written separately, earlier, for other purposes and the published pieces as a whole are not chopped up to re-select only completely coherent elements. Instead, what the examiner (informed by the university) and the supervisors are looking for is a coherent *backbone* or 'wrap', with the published elements fitting this – and some other parts of those publications not fitting this.

One case for a doctorate is already answered and achieved by this form of PhD by publication, since all the work has in fact been published. It might well be different tones – some highly theoretical, some very specific and practical-oriented, and in some cases some in a different language (one colleague presented some of her work on developments in Spanish film in Spanish from Spanish journals).

The supervisor's work throughout is to help the student maintain momentum and to be able to see coherence in the choice of pieces to include or develop, making a case for these in the 'wrap', the introductory piece, and any final conclusion. At the end, the supervisor works with the student to review the coherence of the whole, ensuring theorists are mentioned; elements in the thesis are introduced in the wrap; ideas mentioned in the wrap appear somewhere else in the pieces comprising the thesis; and any introductory comments at the start and finish of different pieces are made to ensure that readers can see how they link together, one to the other.

Finally, the supervisor can work with the student in a mock viva where the student is ensuring he or she can:

- defend the contribution to knowledge made by elements of the work and as a whole
- argue for cohesion of the chosen pieces
- explain differences in kind and audience

- explore clearly the theoretical perspective underpinning various theories, themes and concepts throughout the different texts comprising the thesis
- make a case for a coherent contribution, emphasising development, and seeing variation as a plus.

Activity

What would you do?

1   A senior colleague retires and comes to you to supervise her PhD by publication. She has a series of internal reports and some publications in rather local documents or articles. A PhD, she says, will help her consolidate her career.
2   An eminent local writer decides to do a PhD by publication. The work contains: short magazine articles; creative pieces; a book on a related area; several jottings and ideas.
3   Your student has completed a PhD by publication. The examiner takes one look at it and says 'but this is a rag bag of disparate pieces and an essay about their links, not a PhD'.

For students undertaking creative-based research activities and products and PhDs by publication, there is the same supervisory duty of care during research and before the viva in conducting a supportive mock viva, and after the viva itself, supporting the student through any clarification and revisions necessary to achieve the award, in response to examiner expectations and university rules.

17 Maintaining Momentum

Research is exciting, demanding and rewarding but can also be a lonely and lengthy business compared, by one of our PhD students, to long-distance running. We have considered how students can make the most of research degree development programmes and peer group support as well as their supervisor (chapter 10) and we have looked at some of the interpersonal and research difficulties you and your student might face working together (Chapter 11).

This chapter considers:

- *supporting your student in their continuing research through to writing up*
- *dealing with potential difficulties*
- *involving personal, learning and institutional processes to maintain momentum*
- *significant development moments – transfer/confirmation of candidature, work-in-progress seminars, progress reports.*

The stages of the EdD, the PrD, and many Masters degrees are constructed partly with the maintenance of momentum in mind. Maintaining a staged process, requiring the production of work, and response to feedback on a regular basis helps minimize the chance of disappearance, lengthy periods of ill-defined work at a level of unnecessary or misdirected detail, repetition, lingering on with unsolvable problems, or working at an accumulative level summarising detail instead of problematising, analysing, conceptualising and writing critically in their own voice, *using* what they've read and discussed in a dialogue with the academic community.

Some students become bored, estranged, demotivated and isolated. Setting up and helping students to maintain peer group activities; supplying facilities; encouraging online discussion forums, work-in-progress seminars mini conferences; continuing to put students in touch with each other; maintaining regular supervisions whether face-to-face or by email or phone, following up on regular scheduled meetings; and feedback and response deadlines all help students to keep motivated and maintain momentum Some of these strategies rely mainly on the students, others on the supervisor and/or the university.

Several US and other universities, including the OU in the UK, use a series of staged examinations or progress reports, which serve to help students develop, action and reflect on the consequences of the processes of research; to carry out pilots; to evaluate their research in progress; to revisit the proposal; and to ensure the design of their study is monitored and changed if necessary to better ask and answer research questions. They ensure notes are kept of reasons for changes, even if the actual progress report does not ask for them. These personal, learning, developmental, institutional strategies and practices all help maintain momentum through to completion.

Activity

Consider:

- What effective strategies you use with research students to help them to maintain momentum
- What you do or could do to support doctoral students as they prepare for transfer, upgrade to PhD, confirmation of candidature
- What might go wrong and why?
- How could you help students deal with problems?

▶ Feedback and confidence

Part of what keeps students going is supervision feedback on their work. In Chapter 9 on encouraging good writing, we considered a range of supervisory responses building up critically, conceptually sophisticated and articulate engagement and expression – the kind of writing reflecting the research we hope students will produce, especially at postgraduate level. However, not all our comments can be quite as direct and honest as we might like, if we want students to keep going at different points in their work. This is particularly true when they are experiencing various degrees of a slump. Delamont, Atkinson and Parry (1997, p. 29) suggest that to build students' confidence, it is important occasionally to word feedback in a generalised or positive tone. There are, however, some students, particularly from different cultures, who take comments absolutely at face value and sometimes do more, wasted work than necessary as a result of misinterpreting our feedback. Perhaps *explaining* different kinds of feedback (Murray 2002) is important here.

Many institutions use transfer documents/confirmation of candidature and guidance reports/progress reports whether written, or written and orally defended to help student, supervisor and university identify progress. These are to ensure, with the supervisor, that:

- good progress has been made on the research
- the scope and range of the work has been appropriately shaped
- the work carried out to date is organised
- the work is liable to be of an appropriate level eventually
- it has achieved some of the planned stages
- it is sufficiently conceptualised
- it can be analysed, critiqued, summed up and the next research and writing steps planned
- if refocusing, extending or cutting back, reshaping, further developing the topic or methods are necessary, that the reasons for this are understood and explained in progress reports, research work-in-progress seminars, or in the student's log
- the candidate/research student now
  - focuses on the rest of the research
  - plans ahead to completion, writing up, presentation and
  - defence in the viva (if a PhD).

Working with your student, it might be useful to audit their work against the following range of characteristics of a good PhD developed by Richard Winter *et al.* (2000). Whatever the level of their award, they should be achieving these outcomes appropriately and be able to audit their own work to date, and with your help, evaluate it and re-plan. You could ask them to produce and discuss responses to the categories.

How far does your student's work achieve these qualities?

- originality
- organisation
- engagement with theories
- dialogue with the academic community

- publishability
- readable expression
- coherence of the text
- conceptual as well as factual findings.

Activity

This is an audit to conduct with your students. Have they:

- chosen an appropriate research topic of sufficient scope for the level of their award?
- gained satisfactory knowledge of background literature and work?
- chosen an appropriate research methodology and methods?
- produced original contributions to or filled a gap in knowledge?
- written eloquently at the right level, presenting well-expressed and backed up arguments throughout the work to date?
- discussed data/findings/analyses?
- met any surprises/blocks/problems? (there should have been!)
- developed a defence of a decision when meeting a surprise or a block?
- noted this in their research journal? Was it part of a supervision discussion?
- had to re-focus/cut/extend?
- changed their research methods or methodology? Why? Or why not?
- developed a defence of their choice to change or not?
- found new routes of thought?
- provided a potential doctorate/Master's/undergraduate dissertation?
- provided a justification for the award?
- developed sufficient skills in the metalanguage of research study to be able to describe, explain and defend what they have done and are doing?

As your students move on with their work, they need to think in a focused way about the qualities of a good thesis or dissertation; evaluate their work so far; pull their work together and see where it has been going; note what has or has not been achieved; note what has been or has not been successful; and identify what needs dropping, extending or refocusing.

Presentation issues

The dissertation or thesis must be students' own work and:

- presented in a satisfactory manner
- well argued and shaped
- readable – ensure quality of grammar, punctuation, spelling and expression.
- tell the story
- make explicit the architecture of the dissertation or thesis and links between ideas, methods and chapters
- display logic of argument
- use appropriate language.

Quality

In the middle of students' work, it is useful to consider how their work makes a significant contribution to knowledge. You could work with students to evaluate examples of other work, then look at their own to audit it. They can also focus on the shape and organisation of the developing thesis or dissertation, shaping their own work accordingly.

Organisation of a thesis

A good thesis requires the following elements, usually in this order:

- Abstract
- Preface and acknowledgements
- Introduction, setting context, aims, research questions, conceptual framework
- Theoretical perspectives – in a dialogue with experts and own work
- Methodology and methods, including design of the study
- Chapters (3–5) focusing on data, analysis and *discussion* of implications and meaning of data, findings, themes, continuing argument (NB a science thesis or dissertation is more likely to present data with less discussion than a social science thesis)
- Conclusion – conceptual and factual
- Bibliography
- Footnotes, references, appendices
- Statistical tables, diagrams, illustrations

In the middle of their research and writing up, it is important to look ahead and re-plan. Students can consider what they need to do in order to finalise their work and writing in these various categories.

Writing up and writing well

Wherever students turn for advice, they will hear that they need to start writing early, and to draft, re-draft, edit and edit until their writing says what they need it to say.

Not everyone is equally gifted at writing, even in their first language. Students can benefit from attending writing workshops run by research development teams, postgraduate students' associations, or writing groups. If your student's skills at academic writing are generally weak or they lack confidence, advise them to enrol in a course – earlier rather than later. It is hard to ask those who may already be balancing a job, family and research to fit this in, but they are essential skills, useful long after the research has been written up and the qualification gained. Advise your student to write something every day and to consult style guides that help with layout and presentation (see also Chapter 9).

Developing the shape and expression of the dissertation or thesis
For students beginning to hone their writing, advise that they read Chapters 9 and 18 and critique *several* dissertations or theses or *several* journal articles in their field, considering the:

- introduction
- expression
- link words
- organisation of arguments
- layout and presentation
- conclusions
- layout of appendices.

Many writers and researchers produce their introduction *last* but there is no harm in drafting parts of it early. Mine took six months to write. My dissertation supervisor was shocked it was taking so long. Each time she visited it seemed to have hardly moved on. In fact, I was honing it to ensure it:

- established a research question
- gave a sense of the current and established work in the field into which my own work was entering as part of an ongoing dialogue
- indicated that future chapters would expand on and clarify the theories and concepts, the theorists and the literature I was using as backbone and springboard to my own work
- indicated (effortlessly!!) how the argument was established and would be seen to proceed in the following chapters
- was *really* well expressed (examiners give the introduction a *very* serious reading)

- was well laid out and presented.

I learned a lot about myself as a writer through this process of rewriting the introduction: that I write fast and inaccurately then work obsessionally to try and get the expression and presentation right. Ask your students what they are learning about themselves as a writer and check with them how they are developing their:

- introduction
- theoretical perspectives chapter   ──▶ One chapter if a humanities or
- methodology and methods chapter   ──▶ literature dissertation/thesis.
- thematic chapters/results and discussion chapters

Have they decided:

- who to dedicate it to?
- who to acknowledge?
- what to put in the appendices?
- whether to use footnotes or not?
- any illustrations? tables? etc., etc.?

Final drafts

As students begin to produce second drafts of some, and third drafts of other chapters, they will need some help with both the quality of expression and presentation, and the quality of the argument. However, supervisors must not do the work for them. Ask your students to familiarise themselves with the rules for layout and presentation, and the conventions of a dissertation or thesis (see Chapter 18). For some thoughts on enabling guiding writing, see Chapter 9.

Theses and dissertations must be the candidate's own work and presented in a satisfactory manner. This involves students concentrating throughout on grammar, punctuation, spelling, clarity of expression, developing an argument, and appropriate language (subject specialist language, language that communicates to the readers).

In addition to the actual 'guts' – the research explored and discarded in the dissertation or thesis – students need to think carefully about their ongoing development, layout, organisation and expression and the quality product.

The student must set out the work according to the conventions of the field of study. There are, for example, different conventions of referencing between literature, science and social science work, which provide layout and referencing guidelines for fields of study, and for that particular university. With your student, look at past theses, considering organisation and layout.

▶ Progress reports

MA students are encouraged to deliver oral reports on their progress to peers. MPhil or PhD students will probably be expected to provide a report on progress, confirmation of candidature or a transfer document, usually after one year's study. Students on EdD or PrD provide a series of progress reports, each building upon the other, leading to transfer to the second stage of the EdD, the writing of the final thesis. The UK OU asks students to undertake an MA 'Educational research in action', enabling entry into the first stage of the EdD. They then build their progress reports upon each other, but the work is not merely cumulative; it needs to increase its complexity if students are to move through year 1, stage 1 and stage 2 of an EdD. Others might complete an MRes or MA with a research development element.

For PhD students desiring confirmation or those registered on MPhil wishing to transfer to PhD, transfer or confirmation of candidature documents crucially act as documentary evidence that students have been carrying out doctoral level research.

Progress, transfer, confirmation of candidature, upgrading reports

These documents all variously report on progress to date, noting how far the student has worked towards and achieved underlying aims, answered the questions, conducted the research, and met and dealt with problems. Some students need to produce an oral report, or a progress/transfer document, backed up by discussion with a supervisor or a peer session. Students will need to make full notes of the feedback given about developing work further (and possibly resubmitting if the appropriate committee or body decides they are not yet ready to proceed). Check with your university regulations as to what should be reported and explored, evidenced and planned in a transfer document, progress report, confirmation of candidature or upgrade document and find out about the process: how, where, when to submit; whether if your student will need to present their work orally; and the regulations about any resubmission if necessary.

The aim of transfer reports is to ensure students are on course to complete and write up a successful piece of research. It is an excellent opportunity for taking stock of work to date and for the future. The researcher can sum up the work to date, shape it, indicating what plans he or she has to complete the research and write up the thesis or dissertation. The student reflects on notes taken, supervisions, difficulties met, suspected achievements and decisions for the future.

When you are convinced that your student is working at PhD level, an application to transfer can be submitted to the appropriate research degrees committee. The arrangements for the transfer of a candidate's registration from MPhil to PhD will appear in the university's research degrees rules and regulations. If students do not have to write a transfer document, they will certainly have to produce progress reports. Below is a typical progress report outline for a PhD, although lengths differ in different universities.

Progress report for a transfer to PhD
With their supervisor's guidance, students should produce a progress report (of 3000–6000 words in length), consisting of:

- a critical review of the research so far *and*
- a statement of intended further work for the PhD, including details of the original contribution to knowledge. Once the progress report, *plus an ABSTRACT of not more than 500 words* are agreed by the supervisory team.
- the supervisory team must sign the form (giving reasons why you are ready to transfer to PhD); the *abstract* of the progress report must be included as part of the application.
- Details (name, address and telephone number) of an independent academic who is willing to complete a specialist report on the application must be provided with the application, which must be submitted *at least five weeks* before the appropriate committee meeting. The secretary of the research committee will send the external referee a copy of the application form, including the main progress report.

In several universities, including the London School of Hygiene and Tropical Medicine (LSHTM), students undertake an *upgrading* activity that acts as a transfer, or confirmation of candidature. Their work is then registered as a PhD. They both prepare documentation for this *and* present at an upgrading seminar in front of their peers. At the University of the West Indies also, this upgrading transfer moment is a public one, attended by peers as well as university staff, providing an opportunity to present work-in-progress for review and feedback, *and* to practice the defence skills necessary for the viva.

LSHTM also have a DrPH (Doctorate in Public Health) which, like the MPhil, includes a shorter thesis and an accordingly short literature review, study outline and further information about development plans required at this confirmation/upgrading stage.

The standard format for upgrading assessment for MPhil/PhD should include preparation of:

- an abstract of not more than 300 words
- a brief literature review on the background to the research work being presented for upgrading (2500 word maximum)
- a report (or protocol) of all or a section (to be agreed with the supervisor) of the research work already undertaken (or to be undertaken), to be written in a format appropriate to disciplines in the Faculty in which the student is registered (2500 word maximum in laboratory-based departments and *5000 word maximum* in non-laboratory-based departments); documents that are larger will not be accepted
- a two-page outline and timetable of the research proposed to complete the PhD programme
- a complete reference list for the report
- a confirmation that funding is available for field work, if field work is appropriate
- if registered part-time, confirmation from the employer that at least two days per week will be permitted for time to be spent on work for the research degree. (London School of Hygiene and Tropical Medicine: *Research Students' Handbook*, p. 30)
- whether this research is feasible, and will make a contribution to knowledge
- whether the student has shown an ability to undertake the research, analyse it and write it up.

The Committee will also want to know whether the student has strong expectations of funds being available to enable the fieldwork to be undertaken and to see a timeline of expected progress. (LSHTM, *Research Student's Handbook*, p. 32)

At several universities, the upgrading or review committee includes external as well as internal personnel and involves a presentation. Committee members normally confer for a short time after the seminar or presentation, ask the students to comment on this and then to hear the report. This is a valuable opportunity to get quality, objective feedback on the research and its progress, importance and viability. Some universities provide for an alternative way of indicating the scope and success of work to date, through submission of actual completed work, including chapters of the PhD, with accompanying discussions.

As an exception, you may submit a minimum of two completed chapters of your proposed thesis in lieu of a progress report. One chapter should deal with theoretical foundations upon which the research is based; the other may be a chapter on either the methodology or the fieldwork.   (adapted from APU documentation)

▶ Transfer criteria

Supervisors and students need to discuss criteria used in the discipline to determine whether research is of a doctoral standard. Some evidence of the following is normally required:

- originality and/or creativity
- the exercise of independent critical powers
- a significant contribution to the subject knowledge in the research field
- training in research techniques and methodology
- an appropriate doctoral research topic of sufficient scope
- satisfactory knowledge of the background literature and ability to relate the project to existing scholarship and research in the field
- started to work at a PhD level, especially in terms of theoretical insights and conceptual frameworks
- planned a suitable research programme to achieve successful doctoral conclusion.

In preparing an upgrading/confirmation/transfer document, report or activity, students could be asked to work towards the outcomes in the following activity.

Task

Suggest that your students consider:

- Looking back over the original proposal, how far have you achieved the overall aims and outcomes so far?
- What has been your research progress – what have you done in relation to the plans, design and timeline?
- What theories and theorists have you discovered to underpin your work and help you ask your research questions?
- What have you discovered so far from the literature in the subject

feeding into, underpinning and in a dialogue with your ideas and work?
- What theories are emerging from this that relate to your work?
- Summarise your literature review chapter and particularly indicate how this has fed into your research planning and activities and has helped you to contextualise your results to date.
- What methods have you used and why?
- What elements of the research activities, such as fieldwork, lab and bench work, and data collection have you carried out?
- How appropriate and successful (or otherwise) have they been in helping you to:
    (a) ask your research question
    (b) gather information and data
- What have been your findings so far?
- Have you conducted a pilot and if so, how did the results from the pilot feed into the reshaping or reconceptualising your main research?
- What avenues of thought and focus have you taken because of what you have found to date?
- Can you now provide a justification for the award? Look at the definitions of what constitutes a BA dissertation, Master's, MPhil, PhD, EdD etc. – how does your work fit the definitions to date?
- What areas of further work are needed for your research to fit these definitions?

▶ Planning and time

Students need to progress from their early pilot studies, if any, to ensure their work does look as though it will be at a significant *level*, that is, it will answering significantly important questions, fill in gaps in knowledge, and be complex enough for the level of the award. They can discuss all of this with you based on the audit undertaken with the questions and the production of a transfer, upgrading, confirmation or progress report document. They will need to re-plan their timeline for the rest of the research at this stage.

You could ask your student to provide a detailed plan for the next year/to completion. Discuss the stages of this plan in detail looking at:

- what you hope to find out about now/continue finding out about
- what you intend to do with your data and findings to analyse and draw conclusions

- the methods you will use – will you adapt or change them? Why? Why not?
- whether ther is any need for further extended study or any curtailing of the study
- whether there is any need to refocus because of any problems, contradictions, new lines of discovery or surprises.

Students should be asked to produce a time-plan (in the form of a critical path analysis) to help them to replan realistically and indicate their work plans to completion (see figure 17.1). They should:

- consider key dates
- plan key activities such as collecting data, analysing, writing up and giving presentations
- think also, as they replan, about what else is happening in their lives – what family, friends and work demands could affect their research and so which periods of time might be less useful for undisturbed work
- Consider some things that can't be planned for – the unforeseen activities. Allow some spare time just in case something goes wrong. Be realistic!

Students will probably be expected to submit time and progress plans along with any full transfer document or progress report, but if not, they should just keep them as a personal guide.

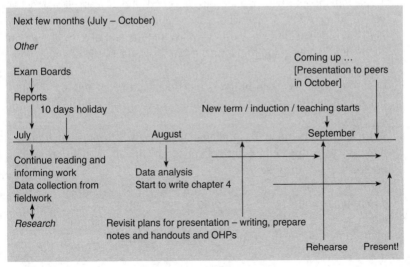

FIGURE 17.1   TIMELINE FOR A PRESENTATION OF WORK IN PROGRESS –
REPLANNED: AN EXAMPLE

▶ Strategies for keeping motivated

Other colleagues have also written about strategies for maintaining momentum so that the research and writing up keep moving along, and so does life. The following is adapted from Stevens and Asmar (1999).

- Revisit a paper that originally inspired you
- Read an eloquent account and enjoy the flow of ideas, the ease and elegance of it. Don't be daunted by this – see it as a challenge
- Realise that your own research and writing is improving all the time: you are enrolled in a training degree and it is alright to be learning
- Write an abstract for a conference that is being held in an appealing location – use the conference as a deadline for some work you need to complete and use the trip as an incentive
- Realise that working through the tough times will make you a more sympathetic and effective supervisor or team member later
- Watch others you admire: notice their ways of working, interacting and their generosity of spirit and ideas. Find your own strengths, know what you are good at and push those skills to their limit. Be aware, too, of your weaker aspects and work on them when you can
- Be aware you are the expert in your field – no one else knows as much about your research questions as you do. Be confident in this knowledge and use it to bolster your esteem when you need it
- Meet with people who make you feel good about yourself and what you're doing. Avoid people who make you feel bad about yourself
- Plan a positive event or reward for yourself at the end of a tough section – even if it is only going to the movies, or sharing a bottle of cheap wine with a friend
- Organise or join work-in-progress meetings with peers and ask them to act as critical friends to your presentation of your conceptual framework and work so far*
- Enrol a critical friend who is willing to read your nearly finished draft and make trustworthy, helpful but critical comments about style, argument and business of the research*
- Develop a routine that carries on alongside the research and has its own different ups and downs – this could be social, intellectual, physical*
- Draw up a list of things you like to do when you finish and set a few plans in motion but don't spend all your time on this!*

(*adapted from Stevens and Asmar, 1999)

These strategies all help to refresh reading and research, to help refocus on the topic, revive self-esteem, return the student to sharing with supportive colleagues, and let them see that *their* work *is* progressing but that life goes on too!

► Tackling problems

There could be a number of problems in the middle of the student's work. It might be useful to consider how you could handle these with your student. Think about how you would deal with these scenarios related to momentum:

1   Your student has lost their sample or population.
2   Your student has accumulated large amounts of data and seems unable to draw findings from them.
3   Your student has produced several chapters at a descriptive, not a conceptual level.
4   There seems to be little argument running through the work so far.
5   Little has been written/what is written is fragmented, not linked to other writing.
6   Midway into the research, the student has not made much progress and now wants to change the question or intended outcomes of the research.
7   The experiments have simply drawn a blank, their data set has fallen over.
8   So many personal and family/work/money crises and pressures have left the student unable to complete anything or develop work in a coherent fashion.

Transfer activities enable students to take stock and allow you to focus on any problems which they may need help overcoming.

Stage 4

Managing the Research Process to Completion and Beyond

18 Writing Up the Thesis or Dissertation

> *This chapter considers*
>
> - *definitions of a successful thesis or dissertation*
> - *writing up a thesis or dissertation*
> - *writing up a conclusions chapter and its relation to the research*
> - *factual and conceptual conclusions.*

The next chapter will extensively cover preparation for the viva, but this chapter considers what examiners are looking for and how to encourage and empower your student to produce a thesis or dissertation that examiners should want to pass.

The successful dissertation or thesis is structured along a continuum according to two main kinds of concerns: the journey and the structured argument. It gives a flavour of the research journey as a personal, somewhat impassioned experience, one with plans, hard work, commitment, personal context and interest, surprises, diversions, choices which can be defended, and explanations about activities, methods, interpretations of what was and what was not chosen and decided and why. It is also a well-constructed, clear, coherent piece of work resembling a building, a piece of architecture. These are metaphors – of personal exploration and the construction of an artefact that stands alone and will last – scaffolded by a conceptual framework; filled out by sound research and expression of that; and fuelled by hard work, decisions and the making of learning leaps.

As your students start to write up final drafts of their work, they need to be absolutely clear about:

- their research design and how it has been achieved in practice
- their conclusions and how to express them

- the quality of the writing
- the appropriateness of the structure of the written thesis or dissertation
- examinable quality and how their work will measure up against the expected characteristics of a successful dissertation or thesis
- what the examiners will be looking for:
  - research design (as a plan)
  - research design in action
  - what they found and how they interpreted it
  - their research journey – bumps, changes, problems, surprises, revelations, considerations, etc.
  - their conclusions
  - the worth of their work; why it all matters.

Elsewhere we look at developing and encouraging good writing (Chapter 9); the examination process, examiner expectations and behaviour (Chapter 19); the viva (Chapter 20) and at the architecture and journey of the thesis or dissertation. This enables supervisors to work with students to produce and be able to discuss a piece of written-up research with coherence organisationally so it argues and builds logically and reflects the intellectual journey undertaken – and the enthusiasm and excitement that suggests. We revisit the research design: initially for a social science or health-related thesis or dissertation, then a literature thesis or dissertation, since students of literature often find it difficult to conceptualise their work along lines seemingly more suited to social scientists and health practitioners. We consider inductive and deductive research designs and how they can be mapped out in practice through to conclusion.

▶ Inductive and deductive research designs in action

For inductive research we often, (but not always or exclusively) use qualitative methods and consider, finally, issues of *validity*, (that is how 'true' it all is given the evidence presented in terms of the question, research, the context, sample and methods).

Alternatively: For *deductive* research we often (but not always exclusively) use quantitative methods and consider, initially, issues of *reliability*, that is how far someone else could try out an experiment, use the same methods of data collection and come up with the same results. It is *dependable* as a design in action (see figure 18.1).

This might seem obvious, but some students use both inductive and deductive approaches at different times in their research. They need to be

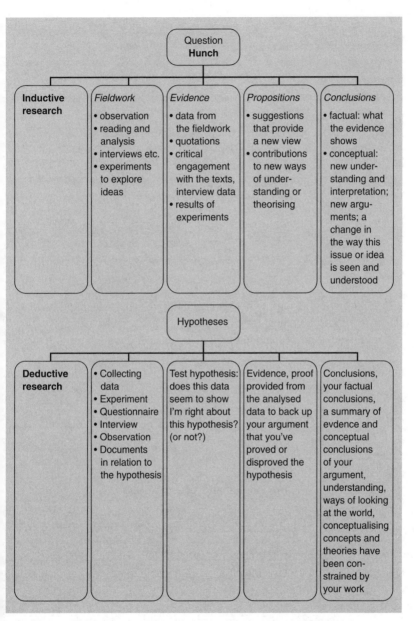

FIGURE 18.1   INDUCTIVE AND DEDUCTIVE RESEARCH DESIGNS

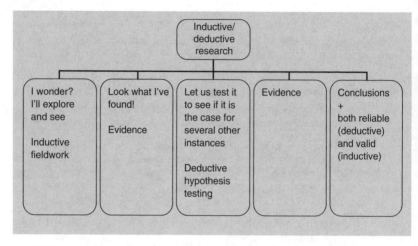

FIGURE 18.2   INDUCTIVE AND DEDUCTIVE RESEARCH – AN EXAMPLE

able to know and defend why they use them, to what ends, and how they articulate or lock together.

An example of the combined methodologies might be:

Inductive   I wonder what kinds of behaviour we would find if we put numbers of celebrities into a 'Big Brother' house?

↓

Fieldwork   Put them all in, observe, ask them – produce evidence from
and   this
evidence

↓

Interviews and observations

↓

Findings   It seem to me that some shine – they do so because they are actually pleasant people and team players. The really arrogant, self-absorbed propositions ones, on the other hand, find it very difficult and are horrible to everyone/break down etc.

↓

Proposition: the successful survival of celebrities in 'Big Brother' relates to their personal characteristics as all need to be team players

↓

Deductive   Test this out with three more rounds of 'Big Brother' celebrities who have undergone personality tests to identify team players etc, i.e. you are *operationalising* and *actioning* the different elements of your hypothesis

↓

Evidence: observation, interviews etc show that team players survive well (define survive!)

↓

Conclusions: are *factual* and *reliable* that is it should happen again this way, and *valid* – the evidence shows what truth is found. They are also *conceptual* – arguments about being a team player and survival are developed in this context

▶ The Masters' dissertation or thesis

Both taught Master's and Master's by research contain an element of a dissertation or a thesis. The differences lie in the length, breadth, depth and scope of the work being constructed and presented. For a taught Master's, coursework will comprise most assessment with possibly the equivalent of one 3000 – 5000-word essay, report or video and an analytical, critical write-up for each 30-credit module. Usually there is a dissertation or thesis of 30 or 60-credits, normally substantial in length – perhaps 20,000–25,000 words for a 60-credit dissertation. Every scheme has its own rules, so students are advised to consider rules on length, layout, and the house style in terms of presentation, references, diagrams, bibliographies and appendices. As they finally write up, many students find it useful to work with support from others, to proof read and act as a 'critical friend'. A research group can also help with this.

▶ The EdD and PrD

The EdD or doctorate in education is an increasingly popular route for education practitioners to gain a doctorate, while the PrD or professional doctorate is sought by others, for example health professionals. They are generally characterised by professional orientation, substantial taught elements, modular structure, and the production of a series of staged progress reports enabling students to gradually write up, focusing on the theoretical perspectives, revisiting research design and early findings, and producing drafts.

The Open University EdD, for instance, states that their MA is Part A, and

Part B is the doctoral level work (which lasts for two years, in two stages) – EdD/PrDs are often credit-rated and the shape will vary. In the Open University, the final report is 50,000 words and builds on a number of progress reports, each of differing amounts of between 3,000 and 15,000 words.

▶ Definitions of a good dissertation or thesis

PhD Thesis Structure and Content
A [perfect] PhD Thesis for London University
/Computer Science UCL

A thesis is:
. . . the acquisition and dissemination of new knowledge.

In order to demonstrate this, the author must demonstrate that they understand what the relevant state of the art is and what the strengths and weaknesses of the SoA are. For someone's work to be knowledge there must be a demonstration that suitable and systematic methods were used to evaluate the chosen hypothesis.

It is important that 'new' is not just new to the researcher, but also new to the community – PhDs were sometimes in the past failed because a paper was published by another researcher a few weeks previously dealing with the same work. I don't believe this is as common today, but novelty/originality/new understanding/ marshalling existing ideas in ways that provide new insights is what it is all about.

A PhD thesis must contain:
Knowledge, understanding, and appreciation of the field
This will show motivation, relevance to X, Y, & X, who is doing what, &c.
There must be critical analysis of related work: Person X is doing Y, this is important because . . ., this doesn't address these points . . . Link the failings of related work to your own work.
Importance (relevance) of own work.
State contributions: is this an incremental improvement on the state of the art, an evolution on existing work, &c. Beware of appearing to be too original, don't appear to have missed or ignored existing work.

A PhD thesis is:

Not 'a diary of work done'. In order to be awarded a PhD you must be able to present your work so that it is accessible to others and so that it demonstrates your mastery of a given subject. Although PhD theses may differ widely, you certainly won't be awarded a PhD just for doing three years' work and you won't be awarded a PhD for 'a diary of work done'. A common attitude is 'Well, I've done my PhD, now all I've got to do is write it up'. Beware! The thesis IS the PhD – it doesn't really matter how great your research has been during the three years – all that really matters is the thesis.

Not 'a big 3rd year project'. Though some 3rd yr projects are excellent, most do not contain sufficient *critical analysis* or *scientific method*.

Not 'a lone journey'. It is important to have other people involved, if for nothing else then for proof-reading. You need to have an experienced supervisor who can tell you when to stop! (this is often the biggest problem faced by students). As the person doing the PhD, you are too involved and therefore you have the worst judgement on what is good or bad – you *must* get external advice. Also remember that a thesis should be designed for the benefit of the reader, not the writer! So get lots of people to read your thesis and tell you which parts they could not understand.

University College London, online:
www.cs.ucl.ac.uk/staff/c.clack/phd.html

▶ **Level of work: Master's or doctorate**

Winter's definitions of doctorate-level work build developmentally upon Master's level, and undergraduate work (see Winter *et al.*, 2000). Critical reflectiveness is a key element in defining a Master's course outcome, but various elements of the dissertation are elided, and the originality of the contribution to knowledge is less than for a doctorate. So, with a Master's degree:

- a balance is maintained between original and secondary material
- methodology and data analysis are scarcely separated
- different investigative paradigms and their methodologies are understood
- there is critical self-appraisal of existing practices and beliefs
- work reaches a synthesis based on creative connections between different aspects of a problem or topic

- a commitment to and engagement with project/a discipline/a body of reading set alongside theoretical and ethical grounding.

All of these elements of quality will also be found in an MPhil or PhD thesis, but in Winter's accumulative model there are also some extra, deeper and more complex outcomes that help define higher level work.

Task

Consider with your students the different categories of achievement and quality necessary in a Master's or in an MPhil/PhD and scrutinise the developing dissertation or thesis.

- Does your students' work have these positive qualities? If so, where could they prove or show they exist?
- If not, could they write up to ensure that these qualities do exist within it?
- What further work needs to be done? And where?

(Winter et al., 2000, pp. 15–19)

A fuller version of questions and thoughts about these features and how to develop or support them appears in Wisker (2001).

Positive features of postgraduate (Mphil, PhD, EdD, PrD) research

Intellectual grasp
- grasps the scope and possibilities of the topic
- shows diligence and rigour in procedures – catholic and multi-factoral approaches to problems
- shows readiness to examine apparently tangential areas for possible relevance
- grasps the wider significance of the topic – how the analysis is related to its methodological and epistemological context
- shows iterative development, allowing exploration and rejection of alternatives
- possesses an internal dialogue – plurality of approach/method, to validate the one chosen

- a broad theoretical base is treated critically
- demonstrates a coherent and explicit theoretical approach fully thought through and critically applied – that is, noting its limitations
- gives a systematic account of the topic, including a review of all plausible possible interpretations
- demonstrates full mastery of the topic, that is, that the candidate is now an expert in the field
- indicates the future development of the work
- maintains clear and continuous links between theory, method and interpretation
- presents a reflexive, self-critical account of relationships involved in the inquiry and of the methodology
- connects theory and practice
- displays rigour.

Coherence
- displays coherence of structure (for example, the conclusions follow clearly from the data
- skilfully organises a number of different angles (required by the extended length of the work)
- is cogently organised and expressed
- possesses a definite agenda and an explicit structure
- presents a sense of the researcher's learning as a journey, as a structured, incremental progress through a process of both argument and discovery.

Engagement with the literature
- displays comprehensive coverage of the field and a secure command of the literature in the field
- shows breadth of contextual knowledge in the discipline
- successfully critiques established positions
- engages critically with other significant work in the field
- draws on literature with a focus different from the viewpoint pursued in the thesis
- maintains a balance between delineating an area of debate and advocating a particular approach
- includes scholarly notes, a comprehensive bibliography and accurately uses academic conventions in citations.

Grasp of methodology
- the methodology is clearly established and applied
- the methodological analysis indicates the advantages and the disadvantages of the approach adopted
- uses several methodologies for triangulation.

Presentation
- the thesis is clear, easy to read and is presented in an appropriate style
- it contains few errors of expression
- it displays flawless literacy.

▶ **Originality and publishability**

These two terms are often used as the fundamental 'criteria' for a PhD. This section attempts to give more guidance on how to interpret them. An MPhil might have less emphasis on these elements.

Summary of terms 'originality' and 'publishability'

'Originality'
- pushes the topic into new areas, beyond its obvious focus
- makes an original contribution to knowledge or understanding of the subject, in terms of topic area, method, experimental design, theoretical synthesis or engagement with conceptual issues
- solves some significant problem or gathers original data
- reframes issues
- is imaginative in its approach to problems
- is creative yet rigorous
- goes beyond its sources to create a new position that critiques existing theoretical positions
- uses the empirical study to enlarge the theoretical understanding of the subject
- contains innovation, speculation, imaginative reconstruction and cognitive excitement – the author has clearly wrestled with the method and tried to shape it to gain new insights
- is comprehensive in its theoretical linkages or makes novel connections between areas of knowledge

- opens up neglected areas or takes a new viewpoint on an old problem
- something new must have been learned and demonstrated, such that the reader is made to rethink a stance or opinion
- shows 'a spark of inspiration as well as perspiration'
- shows development towards independent research and innovation
- is innovative in content and adventurous in method, obviously at the leading edge in its particular field, with potential for yielding new knowledge
- makes a personal synthesis of an interpretative framework
- shows depth and breadth of scholarship, synthesising previous work and adding original insights/models/concepts
- argues against conventional views, presents new frameworks for interpreting the world
- applies established techniques to novel patterns, or devises new techniques that allow new questions to be addressed.

'Publishability'
- demonstrates publishable quality or potential for publication
- publishable in a refereed journal with a good scholarly reputation
- written with an awareness of the audience for the work
- stylishly and economically written.

(Winter, 1993, pp. 15–16)

For each section, your students could stop, review their work, judging how far it evidences these characteristics and where, and if it does not, what work needs to be done to enhance it. Questions examiners ask are based on expectations that the evidence of these characteristics will be clear in a successful thesis.

A thesis of merit will have all or most of these aspects, that is, publishability; coherence; sound methodology and a good grasp of the literature in a dialogue; originality; a sound intellectual grasp of the issues, reading and concepts; and an original contribution to fundamental and important arguments within the area.

It is never too early to start writing up drafts and you should encourage your students to start writing in the first month or so to try out ideas and arguments. This gives a sense of development and often helps clarify difficulties. It is also useful to help monitor their progress in relation to thought and expression (see Chapter 9 on encouraging good writing).

Once your students have produced a nearly complete first draft, ask them to audit their thesis or dissertation in the following ways:

1   By looking closely at a couple of paragraphs noting: presentation, argument, relationship to the research question, logic, clarity, referencing, grammar and punctuation. Ask them to mark these paragraphs and rewrite them to ensure coherence, sound argument, etc.

2   Rehearse the abstract with them orally, ask them to write down what they say, changing it to the third person and past or passive. Ask them what this research set out to argue, find, prove or test, and briefly how it did this. What factual and conceptual conclusions (contributions to knowledge and meaning) can it now offer, argue or prove?

3   Look through the dissertation or thesis as a whole considering:
    - How clearly is the research question stated?
    - How logically does the research design enable the student to ask the research question?
    - Is the evidence thorough and clear? Does it back up the research claim?
    - Are there interpretative conceptual as well as factual conclusions?

▶ Coherence and the structure of the thesis

The thesis needs to be coherent overall. Underpinning questions need to be explicit and to inform the exploration, investigation or examination that is the research. They need to be contextualised in terms of the field and the theories informing, underpinning and driving the set of questions and area of investigation. Research methodologies and methods need to flow obviously from the questions, the reading and the theories as the clearest (defined) ways of investigating and asking the questions. The findings need to be discussed and interpreted. Figures, graphs and tables should be selected and integrated into the discussion – explored, explained, and analysed, contributing to the overall argument. Finally, conclusions need not reiterate the introduction or produce the thesis in short but it should round off, finish off and clarify the effects and the importance of what has been found – what it means, why it matters and what might be done with it. At this stage in writing up, the level of the research should be clear. The justification for the award emerges from the coherence and importance of the questions, and the significance of the findings as finally tied together and made explicit in the conclusion.

Structurally there needs to be a logical flow of information and argument between the different sections of chapters and between the chapters themselves. Quotations, tables, figures and graphs, in extract, need to fit in with the text. They should be explored and explained in the text rather than left to stand alone or laboriously described.

Hierarchical headings and subheadings should indicate the significance and linking of different key parts of chapters, so a reader senses how they relate to each other, building and flowing between items or sections.

Use of the first person

Many readers fear writing as 'I' or 'we', although this is acceptable in feminist research practice and in using the self as a case. Certainly, if they are using themselves as a performative work, in relation to theory, it would be absurd to hide this with a third person record. Check the norms and conventions of your university and subject, and advise consistency. There is a great difference between using 'I' when just asserting an opinion and using 'I' when indicating that the writer themselves carried out the research, or had a personal experience, evidence-based claim to make. Students might feel more comfortable with third person passive ('interviews were transcribed'), or 'identifying roles' ('the researcher discovered'). Indicating the researcher's views can be achieved by the use of value-laden adjectives and adverbs: 'this sound argument', 'unnecessarily, it is argued that', 'Adams assesses more coherently than Bogs that . . .', rather than an opinionated 'I think that . . .'

Style of presentation

Examiners, like reviewers, tend to zoom in on presentation errors. Ensure:

- page numbers are in order,
- there is good visual layout of pages – so headings don't appear at the bottom,
- you have carefully checked all referencing,
- consistency!

As supervisors we can indicate good practice with feedback on some parts of the work, acting as a model. Suggest your student asks a trusted colleague or friend to proof the whole – we often do not see our own mistakes.

Thinking of your reader

A thesis ideally represents an interaction and communication between researcher, work, the field and reader(s). When your students have looked through the thesis and seen whether or not and where it does fulfil these expectations, they can prepare a defence of it ready for the viva. Suggest they scrutinise and evaluate other dissertations or theses for signs of the writer's criteria, coherence and readability, making notes about how to apply good practice to their own work accordingly.

The shape of the thesis

Title

This should appear on a separate title page, on one or two lines, and should be a clear statement suggesting the enquiry, and assertions made.

Abstract

Usually about 500 words. This answers the questions, 'What is this research/thesis about? What does it argue, prove, contend?', 'What has it achieved of importance?' Use the third person and passive, that is, 'It is argued that . . .', 'evidence is presented which suggests that . . .'.

The abstract is read *first* by a reader and so must state aims, outcomes and achievements of the dissertation or thesis clearly. The theories and arguments should be put in a clear and straightforward manner and be so interesting that the reader wishes to read on.

Preface and acknowledgements

Who do they want to acknowledge and to thank? Who helped? Leave no one out!

Introduction

This introduces the context for the research and how this piece of research fits into, grows out of, and extends other work in the field. It establishes the gap in knowledge, the boundaries to the research, the researcher's own position and why he or she undertook the research. It indicates how different elements of the research design have been carried out so they are seen to lead to the detailed, actioned, evaluated research, and the analysis data is then discussed in specific chapters. The design of the research and the dissertation or thesis are introduced and explained briefly here. Introductions also explain the researcher's passion and enthusiasm for the research journey.

Review of the literature/theoretical perspectives

This should contain carefully explored, referenced work with the underpinning *theories* and the work of essential *theorists* in a dialogue between the theorists, and the researcher's own work. It is crucial to ensure that the main underpinning concepts, themes and theories are explored here as are key terms. They will then be referred to and woven throughout the rest of the dissertation or thesis.

Methodology, design of the study and methods

All researchers need to explore, explain and defend their methodology, for example inductive, deductive, naturalistic; the methods, for example documentary analysis, interviews, case studies; and the design of the study, for example sample, population, which part of the research was undertaken in which order and why.

For scientists, the experimental method is relatively fixed, but still needs some explanation in terms of details. For health practitioners and those involved in an iterative process between theory and creative, critical, reflective, analytical work of any kind, this is where those stages and choices are explained.

Some literature and humanities students find this chapter difficult and relatively pointless because they are using critical practice, but this is the place to explore, define, explain and defend why they have, for instance, decided on a Marxist historicist reading practice involving interweaving historical and political debates and documents with their expression, reflection and symbolic representation in texts, and how they intend to work with the primary and secondary sources of several kinds – documents, novels, interviews and so on. Asking structural questions of the work really helps to focus students on what they have done – why, how, to what ends – so helping them to eventually draw conceptual conclusions and defend the shape of the work and its achievement in a viva.

Presentation of results

This is a clear, *annotated*, selected and discussed record of what has been discovered in science, social sciences, education and health.

Discussion of results

For science dissertations or theses there is sometimes a separate discussion chapter, whereas in social science, health or education dissertations the results and discussion are usually integrated. Tables, statistics, bar charts and so on, appear in extract, and are discussed fully in the main text, with narrative exploring and bringing in different results to develop arguments, presenting coherent points and findings. They might appear in full, or as examples in the appendices.

For a humanities- or literature-based thesis and also often for a social science-, health- or education-based thesis, there are often several chapters exploring different themes and issues in a linked discussion.

Conclusion

Dissertations and theses have a conclusions chapter that serves two purposes: (a) to briefly summarise what was researched and discovered, challenged, proved, disproved, how it was done and the main arguments; and (b) to indicate both factual conclusions (what new knowledge or information has been discovered) and conceptual conclusions (how arguments and reconceptualisations have been able to alter understanding, enabling us to see knowledge and interpretation of the world differently, and perceive new perspectives and meanings). The conclusion establishes the importance of the work, and, finally, indicates further work (recommendations perhaps, of other research, suggestions for change).

Appendices, statistical tables and illustrations
Tables, quotations and illustrations need to appear in extract with discussion and analysis in the main text, and usually as examples (e.g. an indicative questionnaire, a participant consent form), or in full if necessary in the appendices along with, for example, interview transcripts and products made in the process of the research.

References
Students are advised to reference footnotes systematically and carefully throughout the text at the foot of each page or in endnotes at the end of each chapter. Some writers leave all the endnotes to the end of the thesis, collected chapter by chapter at that point and integrated with the references. References can be signalled in the text by a number (1), which leads to the endnote and reference, or by a shortened form of the actual reference: for example 'Phillips, Estelle M. and Pugh, D.S. (1994), *How to Get a PhD: A Handbook for Students and their Supervisors* (Milton Keynes: Open University Press)' placed at the end in the references can be signalled in the actual text as: (Phillips and Pugh, 1994).

Bibliography
This is usually an alphabetical list of the books, journals, films and internet sites. It is a handy reference for any reader and if the student is *not* using endnotes or footnotes they will need to produce an alphabetical bibliography. Each university has its regulations and consistency is crucial.

Presentation of actual thesis
Ensure students have read university guidelines about layout, typeface, presentation format, binding (usually not until after the viva) and references, and that their work conforms to all of these. Many dissertations or theses meet difficulties in examination just because of presentation (see Chapter 19).

▶ Structures of research and the written text

Students undertaking postgraduate work are involved in at least two projects:

1   The research that follows a proposal, like a map, related to a conceptual framework, meets peaks and troughs, risks, revelations and disasters and comes to conclusions.
2   The writing of the thesis that accompanies the research but also has a more coherent final shape – tracking plans, actions, reflection, findings and evaluations – but finally presenting the whole as a coherent, well-shaped thesis underpinned by a conceptual framework.

While project (1) is more of a journey with maps and some trips down variable byways, project (2) is more a piece of architecture, seeming, in retrospect, to be built logically on firm foundations and finally standing up coherently as a completed piece. For those undertaking practice- or work-related research, there is a third process:

3   The project related to and influenced by the *job*, teaching practices, etc.

Figure 18.3 shows action- or practice-related research that is turned into a postgraduate thesis or dissertation. Each section starts from the bottom and moves on up. Work, the research and the writing of the thesis or dissertation proceed alongside each other over time. In the end, only the dissertation or thesis remains. Its architecture needs to be coherent and to stand on its own, but the thesis or dissertation also needs to give the reader a sense of the research journey, and in practitioner-based or action research, of the work context. The figure suits action- or practitioner-based research if all three sections are considered. Sections 2 and 3, however, are common to all research.

Problems of presentation
The greatest presentation problem is one of rigour, cohesion and originality. If a student has only gathered information – rather than moving the boundaries of the study onwards and having something original to add, contextualising the work – then this will show in the dissertation or thesis and lower its quality.

Conclusions
Your student might find that writing the conclusions chapter is a clear, logical exercise. However, many people find it as difficult as the abstract, and in the event, many conclusions to dissertations, theses, essays and books are:

• *rushed*: I've run out of time; there's nothing else to say

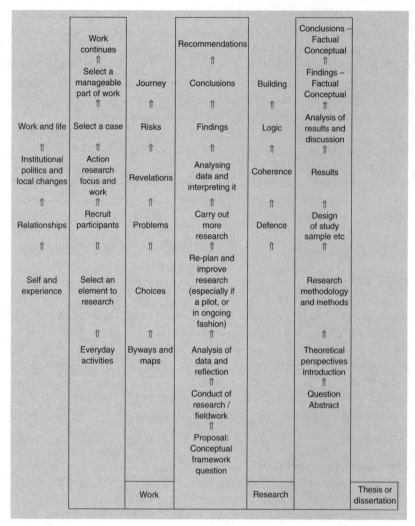

FIGURE 18.3 HOW PRACTICE-BASED RESEARCH LEADS TO A THESIS

- *dull and empty*: I said it all in the text
- *filled with ideas and things you haven't already said*: there must be space to put all of this somewhere, the conclusions will do
- *filled with recommendations*: I've done all of this work, now I must suggest what others should go and do as a result

In practice, examiners and readers often tend to read the abstract, contents page, conclusions and references and then get into the body of the text, rather like we might scan a book. As such then, the conclusions chapter, like the abstract, needs to be produced with very great care indeed. And of course, it is the key chapter to show what your students' contribution to knowledge really is in relation to their topic and question. After a brief reminder about the research topic and research designs, their findings, both factual and conceptual, should be the body of the conclusion.

A discussion or brainstorm followed by a writing exercise to draft a conclusion could usefully form part of a supervision activity or workshop in a research development programme, followed by a supervision. From discussion and feedback, the students can then proceed to writing a final version of their conclusion. To undertake the conclusion, students need to bear in mind the following points, which you could use as prompts:

1   Remind the reader of the research area and the questions or hypothesis which you have been exploring in your research (signpost).
2   Indicate and explain why it is important to ask the question or test the hypothesis now in relation to its topicality, context and why you wanted to undertake the work; and what your position contributed to that desire, to your enthusiasm. Reveal the gap in knowledge and your commitment.
3   Argue why the research design, approaches and activities were chosen as absolutely appropriate to enable you to ask your question/test your hypothesis.
4   Explain what the research journey was, how it revealed surprises and problems and how and why it was reshaped (if it was) from the initial plan.

These four points re-introduce and *position* the research as well as asserting its importance and topicality and how it fills a gap in knowledge. In addition, prompt your students to remember the following points:

5   Indicate in summary what your research has produced by way of *evidence* in terms of:

    - addressing your research question/hypothesis
    - relating in a dialogue with the work of others
    - how it has been/is informed, formed and interpreted by the underpinning and informing use of the theories and theorists and critics
    - how strong or weak it is and where and why

6   Develop factual conclusions, for example: 'in each of the 3 cohorts studied 1999, 2000, 2001 a number of students were found to exhibit

dissonance between their approaches to learning (largely accumulative) and their intended outcomes (largely transformational). There was a correlation between such dissonance and (i) the acceptance of the research proposal by the research degrees committee; (ii) students' ability to acquire and manage their data and to interpret the findings in relation to the outcomes sought as reflected in the research question itself and (iii) likelihood of successful completion.'

7   Develop conceptual conclusions, for example: 'It can be argued then, that there is an identifiable connection between students' research-as-learning approaches and their intended outcomes as expressed in the research question, which shows itself at each stage of the students' research. While this connection can for some be seen as a best fit, that is the right approach, design and methods for the question to be asked and outcomes achieved, for others, the mismatch or dissonance between research-as-learning approaches, research design, methods and research outcomes causes severe problems at each stage in the research.'

This conceptual conclusion (and there could be/are others from the research) provides a contribution to knowledge. Your student needs to ensure that the contribution is clear. It could be expressed as a major conceptual conclusion from *this* research in that it changes or firms up our *thinking* about the links between research-as-learning approaches, design and methods, and outcomes. What is a particularly original contribution to knowledge, here, is that it operates with research as a form of learning.

▶ Undertaking a literature dissertation

Let us consider some of the stages of work and interaction between student and supervisor as a literature student undertakes his or her dissertation or thesis. The literature dissertation or thesis involves the development of the question and conceptual framework – leading to the 'Theoretical Perspectives' chapter.

Student: 'I want to look at contemporary British and American writers who write rather like Virginia Woolf – I'm interested in the way they deal with the construction and representation of the self ('I') and how this self relates to the world (and I wonder whether writers have to be using *realism* to explore and express this engagement).

Supervisor: This is a bit vague!

Thinks: Must help her refine it into a question – but meanwhile discuss/suggest student reads widely in a range of critical and literary issues both to refine the question and find the areas in which to read.

The following questions help to direct students' reading and theorising:

1   Authors – who do you think you will use for this? Who fits into these ideas for you?
2   What are the *theories* or *concepts* that can help you structure your ideas and reading?

This will take you to theorists:

*   some on the *self* or '*I*' or *subjectivity* and its construction and representation (e.g. Erving Goffman)
*   some on *postmodernism* because this is the theoretical framework with which such questions are asked and answered now. Have a look too at philosophers, for example existentialists, phenomenologists (Sartre, Husserl, Merleau-Ponty)

This will also take you to critics:

*   Who else is looking at the self and at engagement with the world?
*   What are their critical views about the ways literary texts can ask and answer or deal with issues about the self in relation to the world and engagement – and why might we all be interested in this?

This is an early stage – setting students off to read, think about what (in social science terms) would be discussed as their *sample* from the field (authors and particular texts) and then the *theories* – self, being, engagement, etc. and the *critical* arguments using such theories on texts that they will find in different literary critics. They are asked to inform their reading with the kinds of theories and arguments emerging from the theorists and critics – so their own ideas and work starts to enter a dialogue with these critics and theorists.

Methodology

The methodology is inductive – they are doing fieldwork – they develop an active involvement with applying the theories to their sample – their chosen reading – as they start and continue to clarify the ways the theories and critical debates intersect with and help inform or interpret the texts. Some of these theories, critics and texts will be absolutely central as the argument thesis/dissertation develops. Others will turn out to be peripheral – not central to the emerging *argument*. This is a stage where *boundaries* begin to be further designed.

Methods

Methods will need to be clarified too. Literature students often state methods as reading and textual analysis, which is acceptable. They are also probably, and more specifically:

- determining how the formal elements of the text function to entertain, engage with issues and arguments in life and the world; engage with the times, culture, context, ideas of the time; and use *representational strategies* to do this, that is imagery, symbolism, metaphor at the level of expression and structural links (networks of these relate to meaning and arguments), character, event, action, setting, time, and so on, *who* stands for what kind of part of the author's argument, and exploration/articulation of ideas.

What events, actions, storyline, etc. act or try out some of these ideas?:

- how do the structural elements of, for example, time, narrative and point of view also enable texts to ask questions, suggest things could be otherwise and cause readers to reflect on and try out new perspectives and perceptions?
- students are developing elements of their critical text to represent, argue, engage and ask questions. This is at a different level to following and becoming immersed in a storyline or narrative (also necessary) and involves close reading with a constant oscillation between the literary text, theories and critics, to see how the theories and the critics can enlighten, inform, enhance and problematise our reading of the text.

Noting that:

- records of events, symbols, characters, etc. are some of the examples of *data* the student will take from the text to exemplify their argument developed, informed and guided by the theorists and critics;
- actual words and phrases are also data;
- Extracts from the theorists and critics are used to inform and engage

with the dialogue between student; interpretation; and argument, theories, critical views and the text.

There is a great deal of discussion, theory-building, interpretation and dialogue with critics and theorists to inform close reading and the developing argument.

Some textual analysis of other cultural and historical texts – historical documents, cultural artefacts, even images or music – might also form part of this carefully woven set of strands, that is student argument, theorists and theories, views from critics, and elements of primary texts and secondary texts.

If these are the methods, they or others need to be defined at some place in the dissertation or thesis. Seeing quotations as data helps students to realise they need to develop their argument. The data are the evidence for what they argue about, from the source, in this case authors' texts. Just like a social scientist or scientist, literature students will not need to include all their data, and their selection of a critical dialogue with it shows their awareness of how their question is being asked and answered, as opposed to just proving they can read and copy out large chunks. For scientists and social scientists, this equates to being able to process the data, select and argue with it as evidence, as opposed to just delivering it up in a totally raw lump for the reader to try and analyse, which would indicate difficulty on the part of the student in seeing *how*, then selecting and arguing *what* they have discovered (data), actually translates into something related to their question that is. findings.

Main body of the text
Chapters
Chapters in the literary dissertation or thesis are not likely to be sectioned into huge numbers of subsections, but instead to follow themes, historical or cultural differences and developments. Several of these are interlocked if the argument interlocks them, for example there is historically and culturally affected argument about how realism is a 'better' form for exploring issues to do with social problems and identity (e.g. culture, gender, class) than is fantasy. So, roughly speaking, the *engaged* writers up until, probably, the mid-twentieth century were expected to write some sort of realism (not that they did, but the critics expected them to and evaluated them accordingly). Now, in the early twenty-first century, there are discoveries that many engaged writers have 'always' used fantasy to explore this engagement. So here we have a set of arguments that the student would need to:

- express as arguments
- get involved with and find evidence to argue a case
- also get involved with in terms of historical and cultural change and thedevelopment of ideas.

Conclusions

By the time they have several chapters explaining and arguing their way through this, students reach their *conclusions*. Here their conceptual framework is evident, as are their theorists, critics and own ideas. Their *factual conclusions* will lead directly from the variety of ideas and forms of expression found in the chosen texts used as their *evidence* while their *conceptual conclusions* will provide a new contribution to understanding and arguments – in this latter case an argument or set of ideas that fantasy can also help explore and express engagement.

Literary research, as just explained is *inductive*; it builds theory. So too does much social science, health etc research. The shape of the thesis shows the research design.

Concluding comments on conclusions

Students should ensure that the conclusions chapter is neither too long (i.e. rambling – summarising the whole dissertation), nor too short (saying nothing). In addition to factual and conceptual conclusions arising clearly from and fitting into the plan of research question, hypothesis, research design and conceptual framework, the conclusions chapter should provide:

> The opportunity to leave your readers with a positive impression of the merit of your thesis as an exemplar of doctoral writing and doctoral reason.   (Trafford and Leshem, 2002)

Additionally, the student's commitment to and enthusiasm for the research should shine through.

Audit: How far does your students' work show

- Engagement with the theories and theorists' ideas in the field? Does the students' grasp and articulation of the context and theoretical perspectives show their work to be in a *dialogue* with theories and theorists, and that theories are clearly underpinning and driving or informing their work?
- Do they build on explanations of why they have chosen their methodology and how this articulates with their question, theories and chosen methods?

- Do results and findings spring logically from and start to answer research questions and address the research hunches, explanations and problems?
- Have both factual and conceptual conclusions been drawn and do they both develop logically and coherently from the question and research design; establish a contribution to knowledge; indicate further work?
- How are the chapters linked? – coherently with referencing back and forth between chapters; between the research questions in their introduction? Are themes developed and both theories and theorists referenced throughout?
- Does it read like a story, with gripping, readable expression, and like a journey? stage by stage?
- Is it clearly expressed without *excessive* long words or 'fog'?
- Does it avoid unnecessary repetitions and achieve clarity?
- Is it well and clearly punctuated, grammatical and devoid of typos?
- Is it well and accurately referenced in the text and in the bibliography?

▶ Further reading

Dunleavy, P. (2003) *Authoring a PhD* (Basingstoke: Palgrave Macmillan).

Winter, R. (1993) 'Continuity and progression: assessment vocabularies for higher education', unpublished research report data (Chelmsford: Anglia Polytechnic University Faculty of Health and Social Work).

19 The Examination Process and Examiners

This chapter considers the examination process from all perspectives: student, supervisor and examiner. While students producing dissertations, and those writing theses in Australia, are highly unlikely to be asked to take part in a viva, every dissertation or thesis is read by at least one or two examiners. The viva is discussed in Chapters 20 and 21.

> *This chapter considers:*
>
> - *supporting your student to produce a thesis or dissertation of sufficient quality to pass the examination*
> - *the examiner's expectations of what constitutes a passable or good dissertation or thesis*
> - *how examiners behave and respond*
> - *being an examiner yourself.*

Students are advised to consult chapter 9, which identifys the characteristics of good postgraduate work, and to consult all the internal documentation they can regarding examiner expectations (see Graves, 1997; Phillips, 1994; Trafford and Leshem, 2002).

Vernon Trafford and Shosh Leshem (2002) suggest that students should consider the expectations and behaviours of examiners as they *begin* their research. Additionally, as a supervisor, it might be useful to look at your *own* experience to help guide your student.

The discussions and suggestions are based on interviews with supervisors and successful doctoral candidates (2000–2003); my own experience of doctoral vivas and examination reports; the research of Trafford and Leshem (2002) and of the SORTI group; workshop discussions and responses with others including Margaret Kiley (September 2003); Margot Pearson (December 2002), HERDSA (Health Education Research Development Society of Australia) conferences in 2002 and 2003, and EARLI (European Association of Research into Learning and Instruction) conferences, 2003.

Dissertations and theses are examined by both internal and external examiners. For supervisors, the examination of students with whom we have had such a close developmental relationship resembles an examination of our own expertise and interactions.

▶ External examiners

The system for external examiners working with undergraduate and Master's research dissertations is similar to that for work with other undergraduate assessments – moderating internal marking, ensuring internal processes and procedures are fair and just, and ensuring standards are comparable internally and externally.

The role of the external examiner on a PhD, EdD or PrD is, however, different. Here, examiners are often first markers. There could be more than one external examiner working in a team with an internal examiner. In the USA there is a panel of internal examiners and no externals. The University of London, being federated, shares 'externals' with different University of London colleges.

The supervisor is the first to read through and deem as passable the thesis presented by the student but, after that, the supervisor's role in the assessment process ceases. The thesis has been produced in conjunction with the supervisor so for the supervisor to be part of the final assessment would be oddly like marking some of his or her own work. But, of course, this is one of the tensions. In the event that the supervisor reluctantly lets the student go forward for the examination and the student does so without supervisor support, the supervisor could be criticised for the production of a substandard or problematic thesis. Supervisors are prone to scrutiny as someone who has supervised, led, agreed with and nurtured the student to produce the work. It is a professional issue of some difficulty if the results are failure or a mass of revisions. A supervisor's work continues beyond any viva or examination result (see Chapters 20 and 21).

It is a very good idea to gain some practice in the role of an internal or external examiner yourself. This helps inform the supervising process, since you can then advise your student what to expect from the examination. As the role is notoriously underpaid given the hours of patient reading, commenting and processing required, undertaking an external examinership is usually done for several reasons: a mix of altruism; subject interest and academic development.

External examiners their history and role

The external examining system is central to the quality assurance systems and practices of Higher Education. External examiners, in their roles as subject specialists and experienced colleagues, are depended upon to help ensure the validity and reliability of (most specifically) assessment processes and awards, and the comparability of these processes and practices across the sector. They are a 'prisoner's friend', ensuring justice is done for students; a trusted colleague working alongside internal course managers and teachers, bridging the gap between internal assessment, quality assurance and external quality assurance; they are true outsider/insiders.

The role has come under a great deal of scrutiny in the UK. The National Enquiry into the Role of the External Examiner that began in 1985 and finally reported in 1989 (Warren Piper, Murray, Cox, Wisker and Weekes, 1989) was the first major project focusing on the work of the external examiner in a climate of gradual change towards modularity, prior to the increase in participation rates and incorporation. It sought to establish what were common practices in the external examiner system, in both old universities and the then polytechnic and colleges sectors, without being didactic as to good practice. It interfaced with the Lindop (1985) and Reynolds (1986) committee reports and the CNAA (1980) and CVCP (1984) guidance notes, all of which sought to lay down good practice guidelines for the extent of the role, norms of the provision of information and support, interrelationships between internal and external examiners and systems, and both the writing of and response to reports (Wisker, 1999, p. 1). It is an important role, which requires development, regulation and recognition.

> it is a bit of a 'Wizard of Oz' role i.e. that the external is supposed, more often than not without any kind of staff development and very little information, to operate effectively in relation to assessments and awards, ensuring all sorts of fairness and comparability almost by instinct; instinct shrouded in mystery and ritual. Lest the Wizard of Oz be unmasked as a rather vacuous personage and the quality assurance and credibility of HE be called into disrepute at the same time, the universities have themselves worked over the ten years since the inception of the Enquiry, to strengthen and clarify the system and to work to make it take its full role in a growing panoply of different quality assurance mechanisms and practices, including both refined and sharpened internal processes, and external audit.   (Wisker, 1999, p. 6)

Point (11) of the Silver report (Silver, 1995) urges that briefing and induction are essential: 'The adequate briefing and induction of external examiners by the institution should be a normal expectation and subject more than in the past to regular internal and external monitoring.'

In the early twenth-first century in the UK, the external examiner system is again coming under scrutiny and being revised by the Quality Assurance Agency, in relation to the work of the Higher Education Academy. The main drive (as expressed above) seems set to remain the same, although training, processes and consistency are to be enhanced so the system becomes more robust. For Master's and undergraduate research, externals are likely to moderate and confirm marks, sometimes to read only problematic dissertations, although in the case of Master's they usually read them all. They do not meet candidates. Their role is ensuring the quality and fairness of internal processes. For the PhD, EdD and PrD, the external examiner has a much closer relationship to the thesis and a clearer, very different role in terms both of the academic community and dialogue in the discipline. Examinations and vivas should be robust, collegial dialogues between academic equals with related specialisms who respect each other's research and publications and those of the supervisor, depending on aspects of the thesis to be examined. The examination and viva could be seen as presenting a protégé or new colleague to a broader (academic) community for acceptance following a rite of passage. However, such closeness *could* lead to an 'old boy's' network of mutual confirmation, barely relating to the thesis itself or, worse still for the candidate, infighting and the settlement of old scores.

Selecting external examiners

The Enquiry into the Role of the External Examiner (Warren Piper *et al.*, 1989) found that examiners for undergraduate courses were frequently chosen through the formal and informal networks of subject leaders, heads of department and academics, then formally approached by those responsible for academic standards in the university. Rules about numbers of external examinerships and about the proximity between examiners in networks using each other's services were laid down in the UK by the then CNAA, which accredited new university and polytechnic courses, and among older universities less formally. There are similarities in the ways external examiners are chosen for PhD, PrD and EdDs, but no body legislating nationally or internationally to ensure any parity in the process as yet in either the UK or Australasia. Traditionally, ex-colonial countries such as Australia, South Africa, New Zealand and the Caribbean seek some external assessors from overseas (Australia 50 per cent – see Kiley, 2003). Historically this derives from their international origins, and the gradual growth of research cultures and research capacity-building, and numbers of universities and colleagues established – experienced and practised in supervising then examining research degrees. Australia does not have vivas, yet, and one reason for this could be the cost of flying international external examiners in, set against the difficulty of attracting a diverse and large enough body of external examiners from among what was once quite a small number of universities. Locally, examiners tend to be chosen for a number of reasons. Some are chosen for their subject expertise, others for their expertise with the theoretical under- pinning of the thesis (e.g. feminist research, Marxist historical, a particular version of therapy or methods). Not all will have PhDs themselves, necessar- ily, particularly if the student is working in a practice- or commercially related area, or performance. A practising doctor of medicine, architect or artist might be an appropriate external examiner because of their back- ground in theorised practice as up-to-date subject experts. Other externals could be chosen for their expertise in methodology or methods.

Choosing examiners for your own student's thesis is a politically sensitive matter. Questions have been raised about examiner quality, with reasons given for choice of examiners and their 'independence' (Hansford and Maxwell, 1993; Johnston, 1997; Tinkler and Jackson, 2000). Selecting or agreeing to the selection of someone whose conceptualisation of the subject area is at odds with those of yourself and your student could lead to unnec- essarily damaging results, so it is important to ensure the examiner is in alignment with the *version* of the subject within which your student has been working, and the methodology or methods that they have used. This is not the same as collusion, nepotism or dumbing down. It's about ensuring the right match between external, philosophy, epistemology and thesis. Whether examiners are involved in vivas or not, all produce reports. Research has concentrated on the kind and quality of reports, and on the viva. Advice from both research areas can feed into your work with your students, preparing them as they write up, and, if necessary, as they prepare for a viva.

It is important that all examiners are well briefed about what is expected from them. For colleagues who have not themselves been through the PhD process, it is absolutely essential they have guidance about what to expect from a good, passable piece of research or thesis and a standard against which to measure them. Rowena Murray warns us to beware of arrogance:

> Does the potential examiner suffer from the 'drawbridge' mentality? This is a common disease. The examiner, having achieved a higher degree, believes that he or she should be the last person to enter the ivory tower before the drawbridge is raised, and unworthy unwashed multitudes lay siege to the castle. In practice, that means that all attempts by higher degree candidates to join the elite are repulsed as below standard. The second issue relates to broadmindedness or matching. The good examiner

needs either to be a user of the same broad theory and methods of data collection and analysis as the candidate, and have an interest in the empirical subject matter, or to be broadminded enough to appreciate the merits of approaches other than his or her own. It is reasonable to expect students to have a reasoned defence of their theories, methods and topic choices, both in the thesis and orally in the viva. However, it is not reasonable to ask the student to defend a school of thought against blind prejudice, if the external examiner is implacable and irrationally hostile to a position, she or he will in all likelihood not prove a fair examiner. (Murray, 2001, p. 146)

Murray also comments on the importance of choosing the right external in relation to the student's future so:

It is important to have an external who is not just about to retire but will be active for a decade or so, so that he or she can write references, open opportunities and make recommendations for the candidate for years to come. (Murray, 2001 p. 144)

In their work on the relative location and significance of questions in the doctoral viva, Trafford and Leshem (2002) found examiners asked questions about the student's research design and scholarship, tending to ask more questions about content and structure when less sure of the significance of the scholarship. Examiners asked questions about the research question, conceptual framework and implications of the findings.

▶ Writing up a successful thesis and working towards the examination

A template of assessment criteria used by examiners may assist candidates in the design of research proposals and the presentation of their doctoral theses. It can also provide a framework in which candidates and their supervisors can discuss research issues 'in which both have a common interest' (Delamont, Parry and Atkinson, 1998). Such a template should not be seen as a 'do-it-yourself' kit, but rather a contribution to 'demystifying the doctoral process' (Burnham, 1994; Trafford and Leshem, 2002, pp. 31–49).

Australian universities rely on written reports rather than vivas, seek international external examiners, typically assessing against a rating scale at one end of which is an unconditional pass, at the other a terminal fail. 'In between are several levels of suggested amendment ranging from minor amendments to a requirement to revise and resubmit the thesis for further examination' (Holbrook and Bourke, 2002, p. 1). Examiner reports are usually three and a half pages long in Australia. In the UK and elsewhere there are often draft reports produced prior to a viva, final reports according to a proforma of varied lengths:

> the production of this report has been shown to be the culmination of intensive and extended engagement with a thesis (Kiley and Mullins 2002). After examining 51 examiner reports and noting the depth of much of the comment, Johnston (1997) was moved to ask, is the resource intensiveness of this unique form of reporting necessary? Is it used? Equally pertinent questions are whether the assessments of a thesis are consistent and credible.   (Holbrook and Bourke, 2002, p. 8)

Supervisors and students might find it useful to pull together advice from Trafford and Leshem (2002), Holbrook and Bourke (2002) and Winter et al's (2000) definitions of a good thesis, in order to guide students in designing, beginning to write, rewriting and finalising a successful thesis that should pass the examination. However, research conducted by Holbrook and Bourke (2002), Trafford and Leshem (2002) and Hartley and Jory (2000), indicated a series of issues to do with examiner quality, consistency and transparency of criteria, hidden examiner agendas, variation in areas covered and in some cases a tendency to focus on presentation to the detriment of the substantive dissertation or thesis, or on the contribution it makes to knowledge.

Research on examinations and examiners of PhD theses to date suggest opaqueness and huge diversity, hardly very helpful for the preparing candidate:

> On the whole we know very little about what examiners expect and in what ways expectations affect the process of examination. There are tantalising glimpses that beg further investigation, such as findings by Johnston (1997) and Pitkethly and Prosser (1995) that examiners treat the thesis as an end in itself. In addition, research indicates that examiners are inherently interested in examining a thesis and they approach the task in a positive light (Johnston, 1997, Kiley and Mullins, 2002; Tinkler and Jackson, 2001). Kiley and Mullins also noted a positive predisposition among experienced examiners to pass a thesis. However, a poorly written thesis generally had a negative effect on the examiner suggesting disengagement.   (Kiley and Mullins, 2002, cited in Holbrook, 2002, p. 3)

Part of the deviation is probably the fault of the institutions. Perhaps, to date, there has just been too little exchange of information about expectations, in the sector internationally, and each examiner or institution tends to re-invent criteria and practice.

Kiley and Mullins (2002) and Becher (1993) report examiner reluctance to fail a thesis. However, little is yet known about the relationship between what an examiner says and the criteria against which they are examining a thesis (Pitkethly and Prosser, 1995) and while some research indicates a similarity between Australia and international examiner comments, Kouptsov (1994) reveals international diversity.

Asked how they approach thesis examination (Kiley and Mullins, 2002), Australian examiners saw their role as important, particularly with respect to upholding standards – a position echoed in the findings of research under-taken by Tinkler and Jackson (2001). A small number of (non-replicable) Australian studies subjected PhD examiner reports to content analysis (Johnston, 1997; Nightingale, 1984; Pitkethly and Prosser, 1995). Reported shortcomings included limited disciplinary coverage, unexplicated analysis, and partial or narrow investigation of content (Holbrook and Bourke, 2002, pp. 3–4).

Hansford and Maxwell (1993) and Johnston (1997) draw attention to a possible lack of consistency in examination standards (i.e. between exam-iner ratings and comments on the same thesis) and between an examiner's rating and specific comments. They identified common types of comment and emphasis in examiner reports, including a disproportionate amount focusing on 'presentation'. Other studies have explored to what extent insti-tutional guidelines or disciplinary standards documents determine the struc-ture of comments, and how final results decided upon in a committee reflect examiner rating and/or comment (Kiley and Mullins, 2002; Tinkler and Jackson, 2000). Some researchers have explored how examiners differentiate between pass and fail theses, the threshold of an acceptable thesis, and outstanding theses (Kiley and Mullins, 2002; Winter, Griffiths and Green, 2000; Holbrook and Bourke, 2002, p. 4).

Holbrook and Bourke (2002) asked specific questions about ratings between examiners marking the same theses; types of evaluative comment; differences between discipline, functions and the roles examiners projected through comments in their reports; and patterns of comments about students and theses between institutions, asking:

> What skills and knowledge have to be present for a candidate to pass outright, and how consistently are such criteria applied? How do examin-ers translate the concepts of 'originality, significance and contribution' into practice?   (Holbrook and Bourke, 2002, p. 6)

Examiners tend to engage with a thesis as part of that dialogue in the academic community in which students themselves are engaged.

Johnston's (1997) research suggests examiners might take an editorial role, operating rather like a supervisor in providing formative feedback. Some examiners 'use' the reporting process to achieve more than merely assessing the thesis – instead they enter into a dialogue with the student's work, acting like a colleague or mentor, so they open a dialogue with more than one audience, adopting multiple roles, mediated by institutional frames and personal history (i.e. what the examiner expects to be able to find and change in the thesis by virtue of their rating and comments (Holbrook, 2002, p. 7).

▶ What decisions do examiners make about doctoral theses and why?

Kiley and Mullins (2002) indicated that examiners were very clear in their differentiation between poor, acceptable and outstanding theses and undertook the examination expecting students to pass. We could argue that this effect is because of the sense that supervisors have already 'passed' the thesis or dissertation (in most cases) by the time it reaches examiners. Johnston (1997) suggests the effort expended in writing the report is inconsistent with its use or importance. Tinkler and Jackson (2001) reiterate this in respect of the viva. What does a pass represent if an examiner writes a report seemingly contradicting it, or if the report contains requirements for a wealth of alterations? Some reports are clearly political:

> In their reports examiners are consciously 'positioning' themselves in relation to 'knowledge' – what it is to know, how they 'know', what it is important to know and why. It is to be anticipated that examiners, as members of a particular group, will share a familiar set of 'common sense' understandings about examination process and outcomes. Moreover, that such understandings (or at least the interpretative repertoire they draw on to express them) will be captured in what they say about examination and what they write in their reports.   (Holbrook and Bourke, 2002b, p. 2)

Examiners react badly to a poorly written or presented thesis, which could overwhelm their judgement, blinding them to the quality of the argument and persuading them to spend their time suggesting a wealth of corrections to expression. This could be of particular concern to students for whom English is a second or third language. Kiley and Mullins (2002) also comment on the tendency of examiners to want to work with a thesis of great promise, not just passing it, but making suggestions for improvement prior to the award. So, the *good enough* thesis might pass with minimal amendments, while the potentially *excellent* one has more work to be done to make it excellent. This information is very important for students who are used to quite a different kind of more summative marking. Advice for significant improvement of an excellent thesis is formative, at odds with much assessment. Students need to realise that it represents a recognition of and support for the quality of their work.

Institutions tend to differ markedly in the guidelines they provide for examiners. On the basis of content analysis of reports, Johnston (1997) found examiners tended to follow university guidelines or recommendations about how to report on a thesis, whereas Kiley and Mullins (2002) reported the opposite on the basis of interview data. Most researchers in the field have discovered that editorial errors and presentation issues attract a substantial proportion of examiner comment. Hansford and Maxwell (1993), Holbrook and Bourke, 2002, pp. 2–3; and Johnston (1997) note that examiners comment on changing labels, sentences and words and could have a whole section of a report on typographical errors, which Holbrook and Bourke (2002, p. 7) call negative 'fix-it' comments.

Recently, to my knowledge, a student with a perfectly sound argument and good supervision did not follow the final 'tidying up' suggestions of her supervisor. She was presented with a *book* of typos, etc. comments to alter from the examiner who, disturbed by the presentational issues, found it impossible to see the quality of the work. The student was *not* happy. We need to ensure our students produce *perfectly* presented work so that this is not a hostage to fortune in the examination process. However, examiners also look for positive elements to comment on and sometimes pick out specific parts of a thesis, such as the literature review or analysis, for comment.

Holbrook and Bourke (2002) found a variety of categories of evaluative comment, some of which relate to 'communicative inaccuracies' or 'significance and contribution'. Some are summative or judgemental. Others have an instructive focus: 'formative instruction', 'instructive commentary' and 'prescription' (Holbrook and Bourke, 2002, p. 8). Some examiners sum up their feelings holistically with 'this is a fine thesis'.

Examiners instruct candidates on improvement using instructions ranging from the philosophical to the presentational. Some are slippery and vague, some potentially useful, some generalised, some specific. Students need to consider the range of such responses as indications of what examiners seek in successful theses deciding, before submission, how to ensure findings and existing literature are integrated, and the whole well expressed. After the examination they will need to view examiner response both holistically and at the level of particular comments suggesting improvements (see Chapter 22). Holbrook and Bourke (2002) warn us about vagueness in examiner reports, so, supervisors will need to check out *exact* demands and help translate them for students to act on.

Most usefully, Holbrook and Bourke (2002) distinguish between 'formative instructional comment', where examiners are engaged with issues and embed suggestions about how to deal with developments, writing 'instructive commentary' that often tends to be non-contextual, rather general advice; and very specific requirements about substantive or presentational issues. Some advice is explicit, other advice needs interpretation. So, problematically, examiners might provide a kernel of potentially useful knowledge insufficiently extended for clear understanding, or a statement of such breathtaking scope that it cannot be interpreted other than that the thesis or elements of it should have been different. Such comments may include rhetorical or broad questions, and be wide-ranging (suggesting or showcasing the examiner's expertise). The examples below leave the reader grasping for direction and puzzling about implied action.

> the candidate did not integrate his findings into the existing literature, and did not provide much of his own analysis. Linking the findings into the literature situates them in their scholarly traditions, and demonstrates their wider applicability.   (Holbrook and Bourke, 2002, p. 10)

However, a specific, useful 'instructional comment' could look like this:

> Your arguments suggest fundamental differences in leadership behaviour between male and female managers. However, results from your interviews show some similarities at least in the sense of role and conflict . . . What are your views on the specific areas where their authority, responsibility or role conflicts do differ?

'Instructive commentary' could read 'the Candidate did not fully relate her findings into her (conflicting) arguments about leadership roles' – and a 'fix-it' comment, rather like a quick trip to the garage, would say 'p. 64 – just focus on the women managers or it's confusing'; 'leave out para 6 on p. 10'. These suggest the thesis can be closed down quickly in order to get through – avoiding ongoing debate.

There are other comments relating the student's work to that of the examiner and the research group, engaging students in a research community.

Considering academic community and negotiating with the candidate's construction of knowledge and perception of the world, Terry Lovat uses Habermas's theories to explore the critical or self-reflective kind of comments that are actually quite rare.

> When dealing with knowing of the critical/self-reflective type, the traditional roles of teacher/supervisor/examiner and learner are potentially reversed, with the learner being acknowledged as the one who is in control of their own knowing, and the role of the former being as listener. If the listener wishes to know what the learner has learned, and even more so if the listener wants to 'know' what the learner now knows, then she/he will be dependent upon the learner sharing what is known. (Lovat, 2002, p. 4)

The knowing of the learner could go beyond that of the teacher or examiner. This resembles true collegial exchange.

Education is seen as ethical, related to justice and self-actualisation – something you might expect to find in the PhD thesis. But Lovat found this surprisingly rare:

> There was only one report that offered a text that I found convincingly expressed something of the self-reflective dimension. . . . The difference in tone from the norm would likely catch the eye of even the casual reader. This report began: 'There are those pleasant occasions when one is asked to review a paper or examine a thesis and you wish that you had written it. I believe that this is one of those experiences.' (Lovat, 2002, p. 6)

Few reports recognise self-actualisation and contribution to knowledge offered by a thesis. Lovat suggests examiners need *training* in giving the kind of feedback that *does* represent collegiality and appraisal rather than issues of typos, vague phatic suggestions, or 'fix-it' solutions.

This leads us to consider not so much how to prepare our students, but how to act as examiners ourselves, and to ensure in our own systems that examiners are encouraged to move beyond the level of local, specific comment to engagement with the ways research and a thesis contribute new knowledge.

► Being an examiner for a viva

External examiners are expected to read the work thoroughly for a report and in advance of a viva, advised by the university's guidelines in their response. In some instances, they produce a draft report on the thesis, shared with another external examiner (if there is one) and the internal examiner, so there are issues which the team can take up on the day, approved in advance. However, some institutions keep the draft report confidential so the examiners have not shared their responses. Discussion about the quality of the thesis is decided at the meeting preceding, and following any viva.

On the day of the viva, examiners usually meet to discuss differing responses to the thesis. This is a relatively informal discussion, most usually between the examiners themselves, excluding the chair, although some institutions involve all three. The supervisor is rarely, if ever, involved, as he or she might pass clues about questions to the candidate. However, in some institutions, there could be only one external examiner who might discuss with the supervisor, enabling them to brief the candidate. Before you set up your examination, you need to be absolutely certain what the procedures are. The internal chair is tasked with ensuring that everyone decides on the order and kind of questions to be asked; that no one acts unfairly; and that meetings are conducted in accordance with university policy. Outcomes need reporting back with agreement from all concerned. Usually, the chair and externals/internal decide who will ask which kinds of questions. Subject specialists will probably ask subject-related questions, and methodology or methods specialists would ask those questions. Questions related to conceptual frameworks, reasons for choosing the topic, why the research matters, and what kind of conceptual conclusions have been discovered might be the province of one examiner or shared between them.

Questions resemble areas discussed in mock vivas, with the addition of subject-related questions. There will probably also be questions about the perspective taken on the subject; the use of specific texts, theories, and any theorists, and what is considered important reading. Trafford and Leshem, (2002) and Holbrook and Bourke (2002) found examiners asked those two kinds of questions with the addition of some social warm up or of later relaxation questions about the candidate's journey, the weather, and some other more general but subject-related collegial questions about issues or other reading in the field.

If this is a developmental activity to recognise work by a collegial equal, rather than a final summative test for pass or fail, why are examiners not involved in discussions with supervisors who relay questions to candidates readying them for vivas and future work?

▶ Examinations and vivas

The aim is not to fail the candidate. It is not an interview for which there are several others in competition for a job, and it is not meant to be 'The Inquisition'. It is not an opportunity to settle old scores with supervisors or the institution at the expense of the candidate, or to deliver a presentation on your own work in the field, arguing heatedly about the conceptualisation or construction of the subject. This latter is more appropriately something you might do in a seminar, conference or conversation with colleagues. The former, the settling of scores, can be done in private. The thesis has been presented because it is considered of passable quality and the viva is there to examine it and to question and problematise elements of the thesis to make absolutely clear the candidate's sense of the importance of the contribution, and why the candidate conducted this research in this way, using this conceptual framework, these theorists, and these methodologies and methods, and that the candidate understands the significance of the results and findings, is fascinated by the work and has ownership of it, not just in terms of 'not cheating', but understanding why and how the candidate asked what was asked, what was found and why it is expressed the way it is in that shape and order in the thesis. This is a defence, but among colleagues. Collegial discussing and colleague friendliness are part of expected behaviours.

Questioning

All the characteristics of good questioning practice apply to vivas. Questions should be clearly phrased and not leading. Several questions should not be asked simultaneously. Instead, they should be divided up and staged so that they build on each other rather than pulling several threads together into one question.

Do not run questions about choices, structure, findings and commitment all together – that is separate out metaquestions, questions about the justification or contribution of the research, and on details about content or expression. These are all important areas, but conflated they can confuse the candidate. It is up to examiners to be at least as clear in questions as they expect the candidates to be in their answers. If the candidate becomes upset or confused, the examiners need to ask themselves whether they have asked questions in a clear manner or have confounded several areas together. Body language is also very important, as in any interaction. If the candidate seems to dry up or become confused, the examiner needs to ask whether their body language is sceptical, hostile, bored, unfocused or misleading in some way. There is nothing to be gained by negative body language. It only switches people off and when a positive developmental discussion is needed this is inappropriate. Candidates who appear confident can be reduced to relative incoherence by body language or verbal responses that suggest that the thesis is not considered worthy of the discussion and the examiner's time. If a candidate does seem to be confused, go back to séparating out the questions and asking them one by one, building them up as the responses emerge. While the viva is certainly an opportunity for defence and articulation of arguments on the part of the candidate, it is not a hostile verbal sparring match in public and it is not meant to be an opportunity to belittle someone. If candidate appears a little confused, rephrase the question and pause until the answer becomes clearer, and if he or she really does not seem to know what has been written or talked about, probe further without being hostile. The candidate could be too nervous to be totally in control of the material and a gentle building up of questions could calm the candidate down and free up his or her articulacy. Candidates who have had appropriate opportunities to take part in mock vivas might, we hope, be less likely to freeze, gabble, become incoherent or silent (all interview experiences), but it could also be that, like the written examination candidate, they over rehearse and so become worried if they hear questions they have not thought of in advance or whose wording is challenging. If they seem to need a few moments to look through the thesis or collect their thoughts, this is appropriate. You might well find after they have gathered themselves together that an explanation you feel was missing in the thesis can be discovered. This would then make you more confident about their ownership of a piece of work, which makes a sound contribution to knowledge at the doctoral level.

▶ Further reading

Delamont, S., Parry, O. and Atkinson, P. (1998) 'Creating a delicate balance: the doctoral supervisor's dilemmas', *Teaching in Higher Education*, **3**(2), pp. 157–72.

Holbrook, A. (2002) 'How do examiners of doctoral theses utilise the written report?', paper presented at 'Examining the Quality of Doctoral Research' AERA Symposium, New Orleans, 1–5 April.

Holbrook, A. and Bourke, S. (2002) 'PhD assessment: design of the study, qualities of examiner reports and candidature information', paper presented at 'Examining the Quality of Doctoral Reaserch' AERA Conference New Orleans, 1–5 April.

Johnston, S. (1997) 'Examining the examiners: an analysis of examiners' reports on doctoral theses', *Studies in Higher Education*, **22**(3), pp. 333–47.

Kiley, M. and Mullins, G. (2002) 'It's a PhD, not a Nobel Prize: how experienced examiners assess research theses', *Studies in Higher Education*, **27**(4), (2002).

Tinkler, P. and Jackson, C. (2001a) 'Back to basics: a consideration of the purposes of the PhD viva', *Assessment & Evaluation in Higher Education*, **26**(4), pp. 355–66.

Tinkler, P. and Jackson, C. (2001b) 'Examining the doctorate: institutional policy and the PhD examination process in Britain', *Studies in Higher Education*, **25**(2), pp. 167–80.

Trafford, V. and Leshem, S. (2002) 'Starting at the end to undertake doctoral research: predictable questions as stepping stones', *Higher Education Review*, **35**(1), pp. 31–49.

Winter, R., Griffiths, M. and Green, K. (2000) 'The "academic" qualities of practice: what are the criteria for a practice-based PhD?' *Studies in Higher Education*, **25**(1), 25–37.

20 Supporting Students towards a Successful PhD Viva

> *This chapter considers:*
>
> - *how to support students working towards a successful viva*
> - *mock viva preparation*
> - *the actual viva and what is expected*
> - *managing stress*
> - *research into preparing for the viva*

Not every country has a PhD viva but the UK, New Zealand and those with European-based PhD systems expect postgraduate students to undertake a viva – a defence of their written thesis. Unlike the kind of viva that is conducted with students whose work might be borderline, the PhD viva itself is neither a test of cheating or plagiarism, nor an activity conducted to see which side of a grade border a student's work lies. Instead, it aims to evaluate and assess to what extent the doctoral candidate has full ownership of his or her written thesis. It aims to engage students in a defence of the arguments and cohesion of their research as expressed in the thesis, and to engage them in a dialogue about ways in which *their* work engages in a dialogue with experts in the field. As such, then, it is interestingly both an examination and a collegial discussion. The further it moves towards the latter, and the earlier it gets to this stage and remains there, the better the likelihood for the candidate that there will be no or few corrections to make to their thesis. However, only 12 per cent of UK PhD candidates actually succeed in achieving their doctorates without any revisions following the viva. In other words, 12 per cent actually succeed in getting through the viva completely successfully, first time. The viva is a defence of the written thesis and it is the thesis that is being examined. So, a good thesis should not be adversely affected by a bad viva. However, performance in the viva either confirms the quality of the written work or indicates that there are confusions, ideas and decisions which, because they cannot be clarified orally, need to be further explained and expressed in writing. Not every PhD candidate knows this, and some are still surprisingly naïve and unprepared for the rigour of the viva, assuming that their work will stand alone, speak for them, and that the viva is a mere formality.

Building on work by Hartley and Fox (2003) and Winter, Griffiths and Green (2000), Trafford and Leshem (2002) base their findings on attending 25 doctoral vivas. Questions asked by examiners were collected and textually analysed, identifying clusters of themes which can be used as templates or stepping stones to help prospective researchers defend a doctoral thesis. Their findings are helpful for doctoral candidates not least because they identify the typical range of questions and the commentary found in vivas.

There are very definite, clear oral skills that students need to develop in order to present their ideas, the coherence and value of their research in the viva, in the best possible light. This discussion will draw on research into oral skills, and their assessment (Hartley and Wisker, 2004), into the quality of a successful PhD, and PhD examinations, of which the viva is a special case, exploring particular ongoing research and development work with which I and colleagues have been involved since 1997, working with our cohorts of PhD students.

The third stage of our research development and support programme focuses on the production of a thesis of a quality that is sound evidence of good research, and on the successful defence of this thesis and research in the viva. To this end, we conduct viva training and mock vivas as well as supervisory dialogues encouraging students to develop the kind of clarity, coherence and skills of exploration and defence needed in the PhD viva. Some experiences of mock vivas inform discussion and suggestions in this chapter, as does experience of being the supervisor or the examiner in several PhD vivas.

Ongoing work producing a CD ROM to support students in preparing for the viva feeds into some suggested activities (Hartley and Wisker, 2004).

▶ Research into the viva and suggestions

Little has been published on the problems and experiences of vivas, either real or mock. Most of the literature on undertaking the viva is anecdotal (Denicolo, *et al.*, 2000; Morley, Leonard and David, 2002). Other work is in the form of advice to students (Leonard, 2001; Murray, 2003; Tinkler and

Jackson, 2002). Data-based studies are beginning to emerge (Delamont and Egglestone, 1983; Hartley and Jory, 2000; Jackson and Tinkler, 2001; Tinkler and Jackson, 2000; Trafford and Leshem, 2002). There is scant advice on the mock viva (e.g. Delamont *et al.*, 1997; Murray, 2003; Tinkler and Jackson, 2000) except for recent work by Hartley and Fox (2003).

Hartley and Jory (2000) have produced one of the few studies on the viva that in some countries is a public defence, and in the UK tends to be privately conducted. Their work largely depends upon a questionnaire, based (in its pilot phase), on responses received in semi-structured interviews with five academics and one recent postgraduate at the University of Keele. Subsequently (in January 1997) an email was sent to 100 heads of psychology departments in the UK, identifying a sample of those who had recently undertaken vivas. A questionnaire was followed by letters to non- respondents, achieving a total of 100 replies, a 75 per cent response rate. Respondents were 60 women, 40 men; 71 full-time, 29 part-time. Most had experienced positive viva outcomes.

This study suggests that greater preparation with mock vivas should help candidates, and that examiners need training to standardise the experience of the viva more thoroughly, so resolving unfairness, and making it more straightforward to prepare for the viva. Indeed, if the aim of the viva is to clarify and defend the thesis rather than trip anyone up, both these suggestions make clear sense.

► Mock vivas

Hartley and Fox (2003) argue that mock vivas are much more complex than many postgraduates and supervisors think. Tinkler and Jackson (2002) usefully distinguish between five kinds of formal arrangements for mock vivas, providing examples and discussing advantages and disadvantages:

1 where the student takes part in a 'practice run' organised by the supervisor(s);
2 where the students take part in giving each other mock vivas as part of a training course;
3 where students observe staff members simulating a real viva as part of a training course;
4 where the student undergoes a viva as part of the procedure for upgrading from a Master's to a doctorate;
5 where the student observes an actual doctoral viva taking place;

Two other kinds of mock vivas are:

6   where the students read a 'mock thesis' and suggest questions for a subsequent viva role-play;
7   where students observe a video of a real or simulated viva as part of a training course.   (adapted from Tinkler and Jackson, in Hartley and Fox, 2003, pp. 2–3).

Only 23 of the 100 psychology PhD students studied by Hartley and Jory (2000) had experienced any kind of mock viva (Hartley and Fox, 2003, pp. 2–3).

Hartley and Fox (2003) talked initially with three PhD students about the differences between the mock and real viva. They then sent out questionnaires, of which 31 were returned. Three respondents described mock vivas used as part of an upgrading exercise, up to a year before the real viva, noting that advice was often vague.

> questions were designed to see if experiencing a mock viva would reduce any anxieties that the students might hold . . . the majority of the candidates were apprehensive to some degree and the women full-time respondents felt more anxious than did the men before their mock vivas. (Hartley and Fox, 2003, p. 11)

Another issue they examined was whether, following quite a rigorous mock viva, the viva itself was a 'let down', since earlier studies indicated such disappointment for 20 per cent of students (Hartley and Jory, 2000; Jackson and Tinkler, 2001). They discovered approximately 30 per cent of students did feel let down to some extent after the real viva:

> Yes, this was a real problem. I expected to be beaten up and was seriously nonplussed when I realised that I didn't need to fight every point. I felt I hadn't quite earned the award.   (Hartley and Fox, 2003, p. 10)

But two respondents reported that these kinds of feelings had nothing to do with the mock viva. Either the real viva was 'a nightmare' or 'a lot easier'. Several suggestions arise from Hartley and Fox's research:

> if mock vivas are to be held, they need to be treated seriously, and that common ground rules need to be established, at least within departments. It would seem sensible to try to arrange mock vivas at a specified time before the real one for all candidates. It would be realistic for the student

if there were at least two examiners, and the viva to run for at least one hour. It would be helpful if all candidates were given advice on preparation for both the mock and the real viva, and were given feedback on their performance in the mock viva.   (Hartley and Fox, 2003, p. 12)

Students themselves will probably benefit from undertaking mock vivas and also finding out more about typical questions and behaviours in the real viva. Trafford and Leshem (2002) and Murray (2003) and provide such insights.

It is possible that if students are made more aware of the nature of the real viva via their experiences with the mock one, then some of the feelings of disappointment with the real viva may be reduced. These feelings seem to result from (i) the examination being insufficiently searching, (ii) the negative behaviour of some examiners, and (iii) the fact that what has been built up for some time as a huge 'life-event' is now over.   (Hartley and Fox, 2003, pp. 15–16).

► Preparing for the viva

The Institute of Education, London University, contains academic advice on its website, aimed at students. This is reproduced in the box.

How to prepare for a viva

You should prepare for the oral examination (the viva voce). There are many ways to prepare and there will be different views expressed on how you should do so. Here are some possible ways:

- if possible practise presenting and discussing your work at conferences, and dealing with questions;
- find colleagues/staff who are willing to read parts of the thesis and then ask you questions;
- Phillips and Pugh suggest that you make a systematic summary of your thesis so that you know the contents of every page;
- talk to colleagues who have gone through their oral examination successfully and ask for their advice;
- make sure that you have read through your thesis and are thoroughly familiar with it, particularly the whole argument, the main findings and the major contribution of your work;

- one suggestion is to write a book proposal based on your thesis, thus requiring you to present your work and to justify to a prospective publisher why it should be published, what is original, what are the competitors in the market;
- read any new relevant material as it is published.

Source: http://www.ioe.ac.uk/doctoralschool/info-viva.htm

It is important, as postgraduate students prepare for the viva, that they know their thesis well and have had some experience in explaining, exploring and defending it. Offer students these few tips on being prepared for the viva:

- know the thesis very well in order to defend it;
- develop a brief outline of the main argument, conceptual conclusions, key points you would like to make, responses to common questions;
- know the abstract and conclusions well;
- find out about your examiners;
- rehearse with friends and supervisor;
- manage stress before and during the viva.

Students need to prepare to explain the conceptual framework, and how it underpins and drives everything in the research. Generally, they will be expected to be clear about the main issues, and answer questions about interesting or strange problems. They need to be ready to defend and define the importance of factual and conceptual findings, why the research matters and what it contributes to knowledge and understanding in the subject.

Students should prepare some very brief notes handy for the viva (if they write answers to the postgraduate viva CD questions below, they could use these at this stage as tips) and to be sure to know where answers could be found in the thesis:

- make reference points in notes/answers
- place post-its in the thesis where questions could arise or where specific points should be made.

Some practice in using the metalanguage of viva defence is very useful. It is not every day that someone asks about gaps in knowledge (what did this research set out to explore/address?); boundaries (why did the student choose these issues, this methodology and methods and not all the other related issues, larger sample, different methods?); what is the conceptual framework?; what are the theoretical perspectives?; why these theories and theorists?; why not others?; what are the main factual and conceptual conclusions?; and what makes this a doctorate? Yet such questions about the research conceptualisation and the shape, contribution and importance of the research are common in vivas.

Suggestions about stress and time management should help your student. Wisker (2001) suggests managing stress in a number of ways, including confidence in the thesis, ensuring the student is well rested, fed, relaxed, wearing loose clothes, on time, manages their breathing, controls stress immediately beforehand, prepares adequately and has post-its in key points in readiness for reference (Wisker, 2001, pp. 301–2).

Vivas usually:

- take about 1½ to 2 hours (in some European countries up to 6 hours)
- include one or two externals and an internal, a chair from the university. Supervisors can be invited but are expected to be *silent and passive*. In Europe vivas are conducted with large audiences, held on a stage.
- candidates who *require* and *request* it can have a translator present.

The aim of the viva is

- To explore and defend the thesis and the research of which it is a record.

Examiners want to discover the student's ability to clarify and defend his or her research and contribution to knowledge in the field. They ask *generic* questions about how students go about their research, methods, questions, processes and then questions considering local arguments and issues in the text. In so doing, they could refer to particular pages and sections. They are likely also to ask questions about:

- reason for the research
- context of research
- choice of question/topic
- gaps and boundaries
- conceptual framework
- theories and theorists
- methodology and methods
- sampling
- handling and analysing data

- problems and surprises
- conclusions, both factual and conceptual
- contribution to knowledge
- why this is a doctorate
- further work.

They seek passion, excitement, enthusiasm and ownership. They also sometimes wish to insist on additive or different theories underpinning the work, and on different interpretations of data and findings.

▶ During the viva

Your student might find these ideas and tips useful:

- Sit down and place the thesis at hand but don't open it. Feel secure about it being there.
- Thank the examiners for the opportunity to talk with them about your work. These people are key figures in your field/methods and they have spent time on your work.
- Answer questions clearly and concisely throughout, but ask them to clarify questions you are unsure of – buying time.
- Use the arguments, ideas and examples from your thesis in answering the questions. You will need to feel secure with them (so rehearse beforehand).
- Back up your cohesive and coherent piece of research by making it clear how the conceptual framework links questions, themes, methodology, methods, fieldwork, findings and conclusions.
- Be able to refer to key texts you have used and agree or disagree with and explain your position (reference the authors and dates, etc.).
- Use eye contact throughout – appear confident and positive.
- Do not fumble through your thesis – use book markers or post-its to allow you easy access to pages you feel might be useful (but not all pages). Mark key chapters, problem points and any original points you would like to discuss.
- If the examiners do not seem to mention what you think are key issues, new findings or important contributions, mention them and ask what they think about these issues. Engage them in conversation. If you finish the viva and they have not asked about your key points, introduce them unless you feel it would upset the viva.
- If they point out problems, think on the spot and let them know if you do

not know/agree/disagree/or indicate that these issues can lead to further work beyond the scope of this thesis.

- Don't try to answer questions that you don't understand. Ask them to clarify them (and use the time to think).
- Don't introduce new information and new ideas that are not in the thesis (this could lead to suggestions that you go off and do more work now) but do recognise (and say) that other people might be interested in pursuing these ideas and areas, or that you might do so at postdoctoral level (and think then – this is ongoing research).
- Be prepared to talk for a couple of minutes in an argued way about the main contribution your work makes – rehearse this.
- Make sure you relate to and answer the questions of each examiner.
- Thank the examiners at the end of the session.
- It is rather like a job interview – but you are not in competition with other people. It is all about your work.
- It's also like an examination but you will know more about what's being examined – your work - than the examiners do!
- If everyone relaxes and talks as intellectual equals about your work, you will probably have very little else to do to it.
- Good luck!

(adapted from Wisker, 2001)

Remember: many candidates have revisions to make (some large, some small), so prepare students not to be dismayed if this happens to them and they are asked to revise. They will need to clarify it, schedule it in and get on with it.

Colleagues in other universities produce advice sheets or websites. One such lively example is that of Joe Wolfe at UNSW, reproduced in the box.

Wolfe has some wise suggestions for handling examiners and their questions by somewhat flattering them, but not entering into a *real* argument as distinct from a discussion, unless there's nothing to lose. There *are* awkward examiners – this is a human interaction, but a respectful exchange is what you hope for and usually get. Wolfe notes:

- The phrase 'That's a good question' is exceedingly useful. It flatters the asker and may get him/her onside, or less offside; it gives you time to think; it implies that you have understood the question and assessed it already and that you have probably thought about it before. If necessary, it can be followed by the stalwart 'Now the answer to that is not obvious/straightforward . . . ,' which has the same advantages.
- If the nightmare ever did come true, and some questioner found a ques-

---

How to survive a thesis defence

This document is an appendix to 'How to Write a Thesis'

- The thesis defence or viva is like an examination in some ways. It is different in many ways, however. The chief difference is that the candidate usually knows more about the syllabus than do the examiners.
- Some questions will be genuine questions: the asker asks because s/he doesn't know and expects that the candidate will be able to rectify this. Students often expect questions to be difficult and attacking, and answer them accordingly. Often the questions will be much simpler than expected.

Source: Joe Wolfe, School of Physics, University of New South Wales, Sydney

---

tion that put something in the work in doubt ... mind you this is thankfully very rare ... then what? Well the first thing would be to concede that the question imposes a serious limitation on the applicability of the work, 'Well, you have identified a serious limitation in this technique, and the results have to be interpreted in the light of that observation'. The questioner is then more likely to back off and even help answer it, whereas a straight denial may encourage him/her to pursue more ardently. Then go through the argument in detail – showing listeners how serious it is while giving yourself time to find flaws in it or to limit the damage that will ensue. In the worst case, one would then think of what can be saved. But all this is hypothetical because this won't happen.

- What usually happens is that the examiners have read the work perhaps twice, and looked closely at some parts that interested them most. These are usually the good bits. They are not out to fail you. *It is a lot more complicated to fail you than to pass you.* In general, they feel good about the idea of a new, fresh researcher coming into their area. You are no immediate threat to them. They have to show that they have read it and they have to give you the opportunity to show that you understand it (you do, of course). And they usually have a genuine interest in the work. Some of them may feel it is necessary to maintain their image as senior scholars and founts of wisdom. Judicious use of the 'Good question',

'Yes, you're right of course', 'Good idea . . . ' and 'Thanks for that' will allow that with a minimum of fuss and a maximum of time for champagne drinking.

Joe Wolfe/J.Wolfe@unsw.edu.au/ 61-2-9385 4954 (UT + 10, +11 Oct–Mar)

Source: http://www.phys.unsw.edu.au/%7Ejw/viva.html

▶ **Workshops**

Such strategies are really useful if trying to manage a result that requires a few minimal as opposed to very full thorough revisions (i.e., on resubmission).

In the third stage of the research development and support programme at APU, we discuss the role of the viva in the final stages of the student's work, providing activities to help students focus on its demands, their oral skills in defending their work, and development needs to address before entering the viva itself.

One activity involves revisiting the qualities of a good PhD thesis, asking students to match their own developing thesis against identified qualities (Winter et al., 2000). Students are asked to consider in what ways their own thesis (under production or complete at this stage) matches the qualities identified.

They share evaluations of their own work with colleagues in small groups identifying what work they feel they need to do in order to further or finalise their thesis so it is indeed a thesis of quality, likely to pass. To some extent, this reflective and evaluative exercise is a focus on the written text, of course it is, because that has to be perfected (as near as possible) before the candidate can defend it. But it also has to be owned. Some students are so immersed in their work that they cannot stand back from it and see it whole. The architecture of the thesis needs to become central to them. Those who might have been completing it piecemeal alongside a demanding set of domestic responsibilities or a job could often have difficulty in envisaging the whole 'building' of the thesis, the whole knowledge object which it represents. This is necessary so they can identify its aims and achievements, its conceptual framework, the decisions made, the successes and challenges, what they have achieved, and ways forward, all of these are areas which they are likely to be asked about in the opening questions of any viva. So, finalising, exploring, developing and explaining the research and its expression in the thesis to their colleagues is a necessary first step towards a successful thesis and an equally successful viva.

Students who can explain their thesis structure, and can answer questions about conceptual framework, the coherence between questions, aims, theories, methodology and methods, data collection and interpretation of findings, and conclusions are those who are also more likely to be able to see the holes or the gaps in their work and to identify weak points. We ask them to compare a thesis to a piece of architecture – firmly built and easy to get around with a clear structure. I compare themes and theories to a piece of weaving. If the threads of the question, theories and themes established at the beginning are appropriately taken through and woven into the fabric of the whole throughout – occasionally some emerge as clearer than others, but always underlying, always holding the whole together – then this extensive piece of work is more likely to be coherent and defined, clearly conceived and described, and explored and expressed. The examiners can be seen as taking perhaps a single thread at a time through it, or focusing on a whole area of complex patterning, and the student can show they know how these elements fit into the overall pattern of the whole, how they serve the purpose originally intended (or others which have emerged as equally important). But even at the point of submission, *some* theses still appear as 'patchwork quilts' or 'jumpers with holes' in them rather than a piece of weaving. You can see the gaps and the dropped stitches of the patterns of the argument and findings as a whole, the bits at the edges where arguments are frayed, not followed up in research collection or analysis, left hanging, untied. The researcher, later, can take further work forward, continue with these threads, but *the thesis as a whole* must be seen to be coherent, finished off.

▶ Mock vivas at APU

On the research and development Programme at the Anglia Polytechnic University (APU), workshop, brainstorm and groundwork are followed by a mock viva that is staged, analysed and discussed, and then individual mock vivas, which are observed by others in the group so that each can identify the patterns of questioning and response, the kinds of language used and the thought processes expected of the candidate. This is not merely a routine recognition of a quality thesis in itself, it is also an on-the-spot activity where candidates are expected to conceptualise, indicate coherence and achievement of the whole of their research and thesis, and to be able to frame and explore this with their examiners, orally. This involves not only the ownership of the project itself, but the development of a certain facility with the metalanguage of postgraduate research and the postgraduate thesis. It really is not an ordinary question to ask or answer 'what is the conceptual framework?' In my own experience, most students faced with this question, unprepared, will find it difficult to conceptualise their work and frame an answer operating both at the metacognitive level at which it is pitched, and at the particular level of the thesis in front of them, reflective of and encapsulating a representation of their work.

In preparing students for mock vivas at APU, we are careful to concentrate on 'telling the story' and 'mapping the journey'; ensuring a clear conceptual framework running throughout. Students are encouraged, first of all, to focus on answering questions about their research question and aims; how their conceptual framework springs from this; how their research methods have enabled them to action and direct their investigations towards these aims; how their findings, analyses and results grow from the question; and their methods. Second, they are encouraged to describe the stages as a journey; the pitfalls and the creative leaps, moments when the research fell into place. They indicate any problems experienced (many of these turn out to be related to methods). Some include: observations that failed to enable them to pinpoint specific change moments; questionnaires asking the wrong questions, generating heaps of information, missing issues investigated; and the moments when they learned to jettison information and focus tightly down onto what mattered, adding further methods and vehicles if necessary.

▶ The usefulness of mock vivas

Mock viva preparation exercise

Tutor: So I just want to ask about the shape of the viva. So, what sort of preparation did you do beforehand?

Student H: Anyway, she ran a few questions at me and we had a practice of dialogue, backwards and forwards and the kind of thing I might get, and then she said what you need to do is to prepare about 12 or 13 or so various angles on your writing and that should cover you if it's, say, 4 hours or something like that, but try not to be too wooden about it. You know, don't learn a set answer, but to have areas that you've prepared.

You might like to run a mock viva with your student *initially* at the upgrading/confirmation of candidature moment (for PhD) then at the end for viva preparation. Here are some questions frequently asked in a PhD viva. These are extracts adapted from the text of the CD ROM *Interviewer: Viva* (Hartley and Wisker, 2004). It is useful to ask the questions – let the student answer and then fill in with hints and tips; following this with the examiners' views. Several of these exercises are useful for Australian PhDs, MA/MSc and BA/BSc students, too, to enable *clear thinking* as students begin to write up, rather than just as preparation for a viva. You could ask these questions, or give them to your student to consider and respond to; initially make notes, perhaps (if at a distance) sending written responses; or questioning on their own, with you, or in a student support situation with others.

▶ Postgraduate Viva Questions

Choosing your topic
1 Tell me how your research area and topic/career has developed?
2 What made you choose this research?
3 What was your research question?
4 What attracted you to work in this context?
5 If you were starting again today, would you change your research question in any way?

Concepts and theories
6 Could you explain briefly your conceptual framework?
7 What are the main theories you have chosen to underpin your work?
8 Why did you choose these main theories?
9 Did you consider other theories or approaches?
10 In retrospect, are there any other theories or approaches you could have considered?

Your research methodology
11 What methodologies and research methods did you select and why?
12 Why did you not select other methodologies/methods?
13 How did you gain access to your sample(s)?
14 In retrospect, are there any other theories, approaches or research methods you could have considered?
15 What is the most important thing you have learned about research methodology from doing this work?

How the research progressed
16 What stages did your research go through?

17 Were there any particularly problematic moments that caused difficulties? How did you overcome these?

18 Did you need to make any changes to your methods when you were designing or carrying out your research? Why and how?

19 Did you have any particularly revelatory or surprise moments? What did you do?

20 If you were given the opportunity to start again, would you do anything differently?

Your research results

21 How did you analyse your data?

22 Why did you choose this form of analysis?

23 What were your main findings?

24 How do these findings relate to your previous work in this field?

25 What is the most important implication of these findings?

The importance of your work

26 How would you justify your work as being at the level of a PhD?

27 How do you feel your work fills a gap in knowledge?

28 Why does your work matter?

29 Are you going to take this work any further?

30 Would you suggest any further work for other future researchers?

There now follows extracts from the *Interviewer: Viva* CD ROM (Hartley and Wisker, 2004) as examples of questions, tips and what is expected. These could provide extended activities for a mock viva or insights for a student working alone. You could:

- ask the question
- the student answers
- you run through the hints, tips and examiners' views together and *reflect* on the quality of the student's response and how he or she can improve the response.

Choosing your topic

1 How has your research career developed?

Hints and tips:
- Did you explain what choices you have made to reach this point?

- Did you look at what kind of research you have been doing? Why this interested you?
- Did you demonstrate your enthusiasm for research?
- Did you show how your interest in the present topic/area developed?

Examiner's view:
I am asking this general question to give the candidate a chance to relax and become less nervous before the really important questions start.

2   *What made you choose this topic/area?*

Hints and tips:
- Did you explain what inspired or interested you to pick the topic/ area?
- Did you demonstrate that you are in a particularly appropriate context to look at the topic/area?
- Is it so topical that you felt researching it would be fascinating or useful or interesting or important?
- Did you show how your interest in the topic/area developed? For example, did it come out of any particular professional or personal experience or long-established interest or sudden life change?

Examiner's view:
I am looking to gain an insight into what inspired the candidate to begin the research in the first place. I want to know if he or she has had a lifelong or relatively recent interest, and in what way this area or topic of enquiry enables the student to ask questions, to research something which fascinates him or her. Is it a professional interest? Is it a personal one or both? Is the area of research and the research question really topical *now*? Would others be interested in it? Why is it an important question to be addressed or answered? Why does it matter? What prompted this work now? I'm looking for passion, commitment, engagement and enthusiasm here. This prompts the student to start to suggest that it is topical and then to define how the work makes a sound contribution to debates in the field.

3   *What was your research question?*

Hints and tips:
- Did you explain your main research *question* and mention any sub-questions?
- Did you indicate how you developed a question from a broad area of

interest? How wanting to cast a perspective on an area, to ask questions about it, led to the question and sub-questions?

Examiner's view:
Here I need to find out how the broad area of interest in which you are working [has] developed into a specific question that can be asked and in some ways answered (sometimes asking reveals so much that the question can only be addressed and those complexities revealed). I need to know that a question has been developed because otherwise the work might well be merely descriptive. I want to know how you have problematised the area or field, what elements of a broader area you are going to focus on here. There might well be many questions and issues in the broad area, so I am looking for the specific question and sub-questions that enable the candidate to interrogate and problematise the area.

Often we know the broad area of interest we are working in, but it is important to be clear about a major question that interrogates this area, that problematises it, and that engages in debates and arguments around it. For instance an *area* might be: 'Cultural difference and learning approaches', but the question could be: 'How does cultural difference affect learning approaches?' and the sub-question could then be: 'In what ways do culturally affected learning approaches (e.g. Western and Confucian learning) show themselves in the way students preconceive and approach their learning, their motivation and their outcomes?'

I am looking, also, for the boundaries to all of this, for the recognition that other people or the candidate themselves at another time might wish to explore other elements of the area of research, other questions around it or developing from it.

Boundaries are important because the candidate might try and cover too many issues and accumulate too much information and confuse the clarity of their question and discussion if they don't have boundaries and a clear focus to the question. Having a clear question provides a focus, a way in to the area of work.

Concepts and theories

4   *Could you explore for me your conceptual framework?*

Hints and tips:
• Did you explain how the research question(s) relate to or involved some key concepts?

- Did you explain how the research question(s) relate to or involved some key ideas?
- Did you explain how you selected theorists and reading that informed your understanding of the concept and helped you to ask the question(s)? How did they provide theoretical perspectives, and helped you to engage with debates in the field?
- Did you explain how the methodologies and methods you have used arose from the question and how the theoretical perspectives you have read about developed the question and helped you ask it?

Examiner's view:
I am looking to see if you have a thorough sense of the structure and design of your work, and of the concepts underlying it. You need to be able to show how the key concepts or ideas in your work are underpinned by reading in the appropriate theorists and experts, and that the questions you are asking can be asked using the vehicles, the methodologies and methods selected. I am looking for overall coherence throughout the research and an expression of it in the thesis, which you can explore here in discussion.

5 *Can you explore any particularly problematic moments that caused difficulties? How did you address and overcome these?*

Hints and tips:
- Did you explain any stages that caused problems for you and how you overcame or addressed these?
- Did you explore any moments when the research met difficulties, such as inability to discover appropriate theories and theorists, to work at a conceptual level, and to draw conceptual conclusions; or other kinds of difficult moments when the sample disappeared or you were refused access, when a specific methodology or method did not yield the information and ideas needed and so you had to redesign the research approach differently and to express it differently?
- Did you explain how you identified problems and what problem-solving strategies you used to overcome them and proceed with the research?

Examiner's view:
This question wishes to discover how you deal with problems such as scientific experiments not working, the sample disappearing, difficulties with analysis and so on. It shows me that you can spot, deal with and solve prob-

lems and so can take a creative, responsive, developmental questioning and problem-solving attitude to your work.

These are fleshed out versions of some of the questions asked and tips towards answers on the CD ROM *Interviewer: Viva* (Hartley and Wisker, 2004). You might like to develop your own further, and/or ask these of your student, exploring the expected kinds of response. Students at a distance can be asked to send written responses to the mock viva questions and to rehearse them with a friend or a colleague, and with you in a last minute mock viva before they go into the real thing. However, although these questions have been put together based on research and experience – my own, and that of Peter Hartley, Trafford and Leshem (2002), and John Hartley (Hartley and Fox, 2003), students need to be made aware that there is no guarantee these will be asked, though some almost certainly will.

Specialised questions

Note that these are generic, that is they are *not* the subject- and thesis-specific questions that will very probably also be asked. It is useful to work with your student over these latter kinds of questions based on the following thoughts:

- Is there a particular 'take', interpretation, approach, conceptual interpretation of knowledge or key issues in the subject underpinning this thesis, which will need clarifying and defending? What are the competing conceptualisations or versions?
- Is there a particular reading of a key theory, belief, ideology, text that needs clarifying and defending?
- Are there any relatively controversial choices, interpretations and arguments about the subject matter that need defending?
- Are there any relatively controversial choices about the use of specific methodology or methods?

There will also be some absolutely specific questions you and your student will need to rehearse, and these you will have to determine for yourself. Some which have related to my own students which have appeared in vivas include:

Student A (writing on access to higher education via regional colleges in Israel):

Can you clarify and show me where you explore the underlying ideals of *democracy* and democratic education?

Student B (writing on gay male writing in a historical period):

Your argument about the development of two different approaches in gay male writing, which you label 'radical' or 'assimilationist', seems to be related to different *forms* of novels ranging from self-disclosure to fantasy – why did you not decide to focus on *form* alongside the argument?

Student C (writing on Heads of Department in a teacher training college as middle managers):

Your theories about middle management and role conflict are applied here to both men and women, but you express them as deriving from feminist theory. Why did you not concentrate on women managers? Is there some argument here about a feminised approach? How would it apply to men?

▶ Conclusion

Students and their supervisors should find it useful to undertake mock vivas because they help prepare and rehearse the student, particularly in terms of conceptualising and clarifying their work, showing they are passionate about it, making it clear why they made the developmental choices they made, and how they *know* it contributes to knowledge and understanding in a major way. It is important for us to debrief and provide formative feedback so students can improve their readiness for the viva.

A viva is a real opportunity for students to articulate, explore and discuss their work with experts who have read it thoroughly.

▶ Further reading

Jackson, C. and Tinkler, P. (2001) 'Back to basics: a consideration of the purposes of the PhD viva', *Assessment and Evaluation in Higher Education*, **26**(4), pp. 351–62.
Hartley, J. and Jory, S. (2000) 'Lifting the veil on the viva: The experiences of PhD candidates in the UK', *Psychology Teaching Review*, **9**, pp. 76–90.

Murray, R. (2003) *How to Survive Your Viva: Defending your Thesis in an Oral Examination* (Buckingham: Open University Press.

Trafford, V. and Leshem, S. (2002) 'Starting at the end to undertake doctoral research: Predictable questions as stepping stones', *Higher Education Review*, **35**, pp. 31–49.

21 Supporting your Student post Viva/Exam

The supervision process is often thought to end when students submit the dissertation, or at PhD level, when they submit the thesis and undertake the viva. In actuality, this only seems to be the end of the supervision project, because submission appears as such a cathartic and final process. In this chapter we will look at ways in which our supervision extends to support students *after* submission and examination including (for PhD) the viva process, should there be revisions and resubmission.

This chapter considers:

- *the effects of and next steps following examiner response to the thesis and/or conducting a PhD viva*
- *the supervisor's role in interpreting examiner responses and their implications*
- *supervisor support, working in a partnership towards the student carrying out further work and re-submission where necessary*

Undergraduate and Master's student dissertations are normally summatively assessed, subject to grades. This summative assessment is not a developmental process as such. When your student finishes, that is the end of the supervisory process. Should they fail, however, students are asked to re-submit, or to undertake a new dissertation. In these instances, supportive supervision for re-submission is as important at undergraduate and Master's level as it is for the PhD, where revision or work to do and re-submission are actually many times more common than passing or failing outright.

Sometimes, mistakenly, for PhD students, the viva feels as though it might just be a discussion among near equals, nothing too taxing because the main work is the thesis. How surprising it is then for both student and supervisor if there are revisions to be undertaken following a viva and the examination process. Students who need to revise will need supervision and support through what could otherwise be a painful and isolated process. If, however, revision for improvement is seen as a natural step in the production of a PhD, and we can be constructive and supportive, revision can be viewed rather like responding to referees or reviewers after submitting an essay to a journal – a natural part of the development process.

The 'discussion among equals' view of a viva is only partially true because a viva is an examination, a defence. Corrections required of a thesis, following a viva, relate to improving something, which might just be 'good enough' or nearly so, so far, and could be really excellent. So, comments and changes required to a PhD thesis are often developmental. Some could be interpreted by negotiation and the result should be a *good* or *excellent* PhD. Passing outright is rare with a PhD/EdD/PrD and examiner responses usually include a sliding scale of different modifications insisted on so the thesis can pass and be of *quality*. This chapter, then, will concentrate mostly on the PhD re-writing for resubmission, although it can inform supervision for supporting undergraduate and Master's students' re-writing.

The viva in itself is an examination. The link between performance in the thesis and performance in the viva is crucial, has to be clear and well-articulated, for the PhD to be awarded. But let's look at the reality. The thesis is rather like a journal article, or a book sent to the publishers. Although the author and his or her editor (you, the supervisor) may feel it is well thought through and well enough expressed, nonetheless others are now in judgement on it, others who are not close to the project and who bring a more objective scrutiny. Like a journal article or book, a thesis usually requires revisions in order to be acceptable to its audience, here, the examiners and potential other readers in the wider academic community. It is important that it is sound in processes, conceptualisation and final presentation, in its structure and arguments, sound in its use of data and analysis, in theory, choice of methodology and methods, in its conclusions, in its overall coherence and its referencing, in its elegance of expression (see Chapter 7). The viva also needs to be a clear, authoritative defence of the thesis and the research.

Very few students pass a PhD outright first time with absolutely no corrections (in the UK around 12 per cent). So it is likely that post-viva revisions will need to be supported by supervisory dialogues and guidance. There are 4–5 versions of results following the examination of a thesis, either standing alone as in some countries, including Australia, or followed by a viva as in the UK, New Zealand, Europe and elsewhere.

It is useful to ensure very careful note-taking at the viva – your own as supervisor if you are allowed to be there, or perhaps the chair's if you can't be there, or the administrative officer's – someone's dependable notes of the areas to address.

These notes inform an initial basis of a 'recipe' of work to be done before any improvements or resubmission. They will be augmented by full reports and detailed requirements, but act as useful broad areas to consider preceding a full report, just to get the process restarted.

What do the examiners suggest or insist on at the viva? Or if there is no viva, following their reading of the thesis? Consider the following areas for work: you could audit these with your student after their examination and viva and, matching the audit against the examiners' requirements, word for word, draw up a 'to do' list to action the points, a timeline for the work – for interim supervisions – and scrutiny of work produced.

▶ Different results of a PhD viva and examination, and some suggested supportive responses

1 **Passing without any alterations at all**: wonderful! The supervisor and student celebrate, and start to discuss future publishing, conferences and jobs.

2 **Passing except for a few minor revisions**: same kind of response as above followed by, perhaps a few meetings to clarify these revisions if they need it, based on the careful notes taken by the supervisor and student at the end of the viva, and the official examiner's reports. After the revisions have been completed and the thesis sent to and confirmed as acceptable by the examiner(s), chair or whoever is designated to make that decision in this instance, then the celebrations and discussions about publication can begin in earnest.

3 **Passing except for a few, quite substantial revisions**: responses as above, but with much more considered scrutiny.

Consider: what do the examiners suggest or insist on at the viva? (or from the examination if no viva is conducted). Have they indicated a further area of reading, of theorising; further work to be done on the organisation of the thesis to make it more coherent; further clarification or re-casting of sections; further analysis and interpretation of findings; the clarification of conceptual findings; or cutting stray areas of discussion that distract from the main work for example too much historical background and too much of a theory or a line of argument that in the end does not really underpin the work?

Base further sensitive, focused work, supported by sensitive, focused supervision on notes taken at the viva (to start the process), and formal requirements post viva. It is important to get agreements post viva about exactly what the examiners require, and to arrange a session clarifying the exact implications of the workload (students are often in shock!). I prefer to do this as soon as possible after the viva. In the perfect situation, *initial* discussions would take place *immediately* following the viva, sitting with notes and a cup of coffee, just to keep the process going. The student will need further clarification, and will hand in work to the *formal* advice or demands, but can start to identify with you an agenda for further work on expression and alteration. The student is less likely to feel this is a moment of loss and absence, but instead one that is a natural process leading to refining work for success. Over the days, weeks or maybe even months using this initial reflection and planning as an agenda for improvement, you and your student will need to work carefully to the advice and demands from the examiners to produce a thesis that can pass. Involvement of a critical friend is helpful. Support re-writing and then, hopefully, the results outlined in 1 or 2 will follow.

Note that many universities move straight from option 2 to option 4, so substantial changes require formal resubmission and the option to undertake a second viva.

4   **Resubmit**: This is a much more substantial task involving all of the above (2 and 3) activities but probably also some new work, further analysis, restructuring, fundamental re-working, and re-directing the work in relation to the viewpoints and interpretation provided by other theorists and so on.

Collate all the examiners' advice and requirements into a list. Students could be asked to draw up on one side of an A4 sheet of paper the preferred new shape to the thesis, and/or a 'to do' list of any minor or extensive new work and any changes. It is important to have a realistic timescale and to build in sessions together to review the developing work before it 'goes cold' and students could develop a distance, fear, writing block about it; or in some cases, lose their sample, their place to live, their time, and the topicality of the project.

There are particular potential problems here for some international students who might find their funding, their fees, their visa and their rights to library and other university facilities timed out. You will need to check the regulations about student rights for the period following the thesis submission and before resubmission so that your student is not left feeling unsupported, as though they have overstayed their welcome, just at this most sensitive moment. For some international students, continuing work, your comments and support of this work might have to be at a distance, using email. If this is the case, then ground rules for submission of changes and responses need to be established, emails seen to work, a further meeting set up if possible, and several friendly supportive nudging email exchanges added to the ones dealing with actual work so that the student does not lose momentum upon return to the complexities of homeland and work, family and so on (especially since the students are returning having *not* yet achieved what they set out to achieve – or so it appears).

With an on-campus student, or one who lives at an accessible distance, you could set up regular work review meetings, establish work to be completed in advance, measure the work against examiner demands – interpreted together – and advise the student to re-submit when ready, and when you have read the work, matching it against the examiners' requirements.

As with 5 below, it is sometimes useful to have some fresh support if there are major reinterpretations to be conducted and major revisions to be carried out. Perhaps another colleague might talk with and support the student, particularly if the area that needs re-writing is their specialism. Maybe the colleague can help with areas in which you feel the need for support, or some fresh reiteration of your advice (that was ignored or overlooked?) from someone else will help. Maybe the college can help with recasting the work, with statistical interpretation, specific focus on, for example, areas of content or context, further insights into theoretical and critical approaches now realised to be necessary in interpreting the findings – whatever the work is that needs refining, including and reinterpreting. But beware that the colleague does not lead your student off the point at this stage. The intention is to re-write *this* thesis and follow the examiners' comments strictly, rather than going off at a tangent.

Keep progress checks of developments so you can both identify progress towards achieving the examiners' demands. Some students might be tempted to race at the changes, carrying them out rather superficially. If they have been asked to re-submit, there is probably some substantial re-writing and re-casting to be done. If they race, under-theorise and under-conceptualise at this stage, or hand in something that is unclear and fragmented, they stand the chance of not having their work accepted and passed, which would be a very bad outcome. Proceed carefully and slowly, allowing time for any re-thinking so that the re-written thesis is both theoretically sound and coherent in expression.

At the moment of resubmission, it is essential that your student includes a detailed checklist and discussion, indicating the examiner demands matched against the new work, chapters and cuts, indicating changes in the text with, for example, post-its and a cover note. In this way, examiners can find their way around changes to their satisfaction, rather than re-reading almost from scratch (in which instance, heaven forbid, they *could* find something else).

5   **Fail**. In the most logical circumstances, if *you* have done your job properly, students are unlikely to have your agreement to *submit if* they are likely to fail. However, this is an 'I wouldn't start from here' statement. Things go wrong. The anecdotes and horror stories are legion, as they are whenever there are human interactions and differences of opinion. It is important that your student does not get caught up in this if possible. Examiners dispute, there could be different politics, values and interpretations of the subject and of work produced. Perhaps your student does not clearly defend the work, although the thesis itself is relatively strong. Perhaps examiners are seriously doubtful about the sample and the validity, even though you and the student thought it might be adequate.

While you comfort your student, you also need to find out any rules for potential resubmission and begin the process of re-conceptualising, and re-writing (as above, in 2, 3, 4) if this is an option, and if you both feel it can be done in the light of the examiners' comments.

If it does not look like this project can be rescued at all, or if your university refuses further attempts following a fail (unusual), it might be better to:

- accept defeat – and ensure your student does too, and/or
- devise together a more suitable and manageable project, perhaps with the best elements of the one that has failed in it, and start again. You will know more about how they go about research, learning and work, now, and it is possible that this *second* project might be much more realisable as a successful piece of research. Perhaps bringing in a third party or another colleague to support some of the new work or to provide a different perspective and different kinds of guidance on the re-conceptualising and re-writing would be beneficial at this stage, both psychologically, and, given the changing nature of the new work, logically.

▶ Possible areas to address following examiner demand for rewriting

Theoretical perspectives
Has the student included a fully developed, engaged, referenced discussion of the appropriate themes and theories? Some examiners suggest other theoretical approaches and background arguments. These need to be read, processed, analysed and fed into the thesis. Maybe suggested developments will have to be undertaken with supportive supervision throughout the work and could involve methods, analysis and conclusions. Certainly, theoretical perspectives and reference to theorists would need to be threaded all through the thesis.

Gaps
There may be gaps in the student's reading, in methods, in the expression, in interpretation of data and in the arguments arising from analysis and findings. The student will need to revisit the data and its analysis, then discuss it in an argument related to this. The student could be enabled by prompting questions, for example what else could be suggested here? Are there contradictions in our reading of *this* . . . in relation to *that* . . .? What else could you say here? How much more analysis and discussion could you produce here?

Claims are unsupported by evidence
This could be a problem in any subject area where a student omits the link between research claims made and the evidence indicating they are well-founded. The student might not have the data, quotations, statistics or references to back up a claim, or might need to revisit this evidence, selecting from it more precisely in a careful, focused manner, accompanying evidence by signposting and reflection so it substantiates its claims.

Sample, methods, data
If the sample, methods, data set and findings are a problem, the student might have to revisit the design of the study and even redesign as well as gather new data. If such large-scale revisions are necessary, they will need your support to undertake them, to re-question, re-design and re-write in line with new analysis of new data.

Looking at research (Holbrook and Bourke, 2002; Trafford and Leshem, 2002) that considers examiner reports, we see that often examiners might disagree with something simple, or substantial, such as conceptions of the subject, epistemology, research design, and still pass the thesis, but that they could be tipped over into failing it or demanding major revisions rather than accepting this is a perfectly creditable albeit a *different* 'take' on the subject research, if the thesis is poorly presented and written. Analyses of examiner responses and evidence from vivas indicate both a mixture of examiner responses that would lead to specific revisions, and that holistic viva experience in which personalities, interaction, the dynamic of the moment (lack of control by the chair? examiner rivalry or narcissism? candidate seems to be unable to articulate what's asked for at that moment?) tip the result into a fail. For the read-only, no-viva thesis, the Master's or undergraduate dissertation, personalities in the room are not an issue, but presentation is.

If students 'fail' or have to resubmit, whether the result is 2, 3, 4, or 5 above, they would benefit from a meeting in which a new agenda, timeline and tasks are decided in order that they can visualise that it is *possible* to rewrite, resubmit or start again. An upbeat, organised supervisory approach might help at this stage. Remember these three final points:

- Make sure that advice and decisions, details of changes, due dates, etc. are all clear and are understood by the student.
- Make sure regulations are clear and advise the student to produce a clear cover note explaining how and where they have fulfilled examiner requirements in any resubmission.
- With sensitive support in place, this can be a developmental moment, rather than a disaster.

▶ Further reading

Holbrook, A. (2001) 'PhD Examination – Assessment's Least-Mapped Frontier', paper presented at AARE Conference Fremantle, December.

Trafford, V. and Leshem, S. (2002) 'Questions in a doctoral viva', in *UK Council for Graduate Education Research Degree Examining Symposium* (London, April).

22 Life after Research

This chapter considers our roles with students after they have effectively and successfully completed their research project, and how students can be encouraged to utilise their research and experience. Many will, of course, want to share their work in conferences and publications long before they have finally handed in the thesis or dissertation and will need support in deciding when, where, how and what to present or publish. Similarly, students should be thinking throughout their research about the kinds of skills and learning outcomes that they are likely to achieve, both through undertaking successful research (and some unsuccessful research) and taking an active part in research development programmes.

This chapter considers:

- *sharing research*
- *developing the work (or parts of it) for presentations at work-in-progress sessions and major conferences*
- *developing the work (or parts of it) for publication in journals and books*
- *identifying and reflecting on research skills, values and research-as-learning outcomes for employability and life*
- *developing further research*
- *being recognised as an expert – seeking a place in the academic community.*

The completion of the research project is an exciting moment, but it can also leave a student feeling somewhat adrift – this is what they have been working towards for such a long time, and it may have taken over their life – what next?

The supervisory process does not end with the successful dissertation or thesis. Indeed, what you might have established now is an ongoing academic working relationship. Certainly, students often expect some hints, tips, suggestions and invitations to carry out further work, further research, publications, information about conferences and suggestions for furthering their academic careers. One of the major gains from a successful piece of research is the student's entrance into the academic community. For undergraduates, this might be the last piece of research they undertake, or the first, depending on their choices of future study, career and the kinds of work they are called upon to do in the future. For some, job-related research will involve them in report writing, consultancies, and summarising and synthesising the work of others to advise on decisions. For others, academic research will be a major feature of their future, whether in terms of continuing professional development, work-related or more theoretical research towards qualifications, or as part of their formal research activity in research projects. Judy Newman (2001) identifies our ongoing responsibilities:

> I don't underestimate the many miseries of postgraduate studies or the need for first-rate supervision, primarily in intellectual terms but also as part of a mentoring process. Like every other supervisor I know, I spend a lot of time writing references, helping with funding applications, making sure postgraduates get to the right conferences, and responding to tales of woe. But there is a big difference between smoothing the path to knowledge, and managing students' ideas; between giving professional advice, and seeing the doctorate as merely part of the training of a professional group. (Newman, 2001, pp. 16–17)

Cryer (1997) suggests doctoral students should recognise that generic, postgraduate skills developed during study could equip them for employment in a variety of contexts, while Francis (1997) and Leonard (2002) indicate that personal expectations are more likely to be achieved than are career expectations.

> Surveys suggest students' personal expectations are more likely to be fulfilled by doing a doctorate than career aspects. Few regret doing a doctorate, or what it has cost to them. Of course, the most disgruntled may get left out of samples; there are certainly horror stories of bad supervision, wasted time, too heavy teaching requirements on low pay, and exploitation in labs; and initial hopes may have been changed and modified along the way. Nonetheless, 'a self forged through tackling the difficulties of research, especially when stress from other sources is high, is a new self. So is the self that overcomes the doubts about ability to do the work'. (Francis, 1997, p. 18, in Leonard, 2002, p. 59)

Contribution to developing knowledge in disciplines is a very important product of research. Students should be encouraged to continue with research if this has been something they both enjoy and for which they seem to be developing/have developed the skills. They also need the opportunities to identify such skills developed during the course of their research, since many of these are directly transferable into paid work. The achievement of some suggests to employers an ability to undertake a whole variety of projects and roles. Identification of transferable graduate and postgraduate research-related skills enhances self-esteem as well as opportunities on the job market. One of the first things students need to ensure they do is to share their research in presentations and via publications.

▶ Sharing the research – presentations

Research students need to be encouraged to develop their work for presentation whether for their own peer group or for major international conferences. For undergraduates and postgraduates alike, the opportunity to present in front of peers while working on their dissertation or thesis provides a rich opportunity for sharing decisions, ideas and questions and gaining support in solving various problems in appropriateness of methods, data and findings, emerging or maintaining momentum, and managing one's supervisor. Following peer-supported, work-in-progress sessions, students should be encouraged to work together to produce short research conference presentations enabling them to experience preparing work for presentation at more demanding, national and international conferences, when they complete. The supervisor plays a key role in helping students select appropriate parts of their research and in guiding them through preparation for all kinds of presentation. This support involves encouraging them through the preparatory work up to and through a presentation: from choice of an appropriate element of the research to present; through to managing time so the audio visual aids and handouts, etc. are ready; organising ideas and the presentation itself; then managing nerves, time, questions, and adding elements that entertain as well as inform their audience.

There are many opportunities for students to share their work in mini-presentations before completion (see Chapter 10), forming a key part both of development of ongoing work, and a contribution to the academic community, in turn supporting students. They might seek to present at:

• work-in-progress seminars

- in-house seminars and presentations with colleagues
- conferences.

Research is a contribution to knowledge and ideas in the subject(s). Sharing work in progress and, after completion, helps researchers to clarify, control and evaluate the continuation and significance of their research. It also contributes to the academic community, and shares and builds knowledge. Specifically for the student, presentations enable them to seek analytical responses from others and develop work after highlighting faults and achievements.

Students might be apprehensive about public evaluation but with support can be advised, respond to, seek, reflect on and use all kinds of feedback. Students will also find that attending the presentations of others enables them to stand back from their own work, to advise, reflect and develop. Sharing their work in a research community should be seen not as 'giving it away' but about supportive, analytical critique for constructive purposes.

Conference presentations
There are several opportunities to present at conferences and students might think of starting with a poster and leading up to a whole paper in a symposium.

Kinds of presentation

- whole paper presentation
- paper in a symposium – synergy
- round table
- running a seminar/workshop consisting of an open paper, followed by questions and prompts
- poster presentation.

Advise students of the need to:

- define the area of research they wish to share and explore
- clarify the questions this addresses
- contextualise research in other work in the field, topical developments, their previous work
- clarify research strategies and methods used in structuring and directing this research
- define and clarify investigations, questions and findings
- organise information and arguments into a presentation format

- consider time management: for planning and writing, and for the actual presentation – avoid overrunning.

Consider the four Ps:

- **plan** – who do they want to present to, when, why, what are their interests?
- **prepare** – decide on a title, a coherent part of the work to present for this audience/conference, carry out any other necessary research (limit this), involve necessary colleagues, organise and write the paper, put headings on cards/OHTS/PowerPoint slides, produce handouts, organise AVA; start with an interesting opening
- **practise** – with a friend or family member – avoid irritating habits, use eye contact, manage the time, memorise opening and closing, manage stress
- **present**.

This should help students identify elements of their work to present and to decide the scope of the research work to date ready for presentation. Then they need to think of organising the actual paper or presentation itself. Extensive advice appears in Wisker (2001).

Preparing papers for presentation and organising the talk

- There are two main ways to organise:
  - (a) produce an outline and headings, then fill in with information
  - (b) produce a full paper, with headings, then extract headings
- you need a more or less full (but not necessarily finished) text
- some elegant phrasing (for the introduction and conclusion – memorise these)
- a shorter form you can talk to – because you will probably be unable to read the whole paper out (and this is usually inadvisable because it would be written, not spoken language and could be dense and wooden!)
- a written text is not in presentation format
- you can ensure more complex parts of your presentation are delivered through handouts
- spoken language is much simpler and more accessible than written

language; audiences find it difficult to follow the complexity of written prose when read out rapidly in a presentation

- organise points under headings, starting with an introduction and selecting main points
- decide how to structure your presentation: what will come first, what follows, arguments and ideas, where to place OHTs, charts and handouts, where to show slides, video clips or music; etc.
- organise charts, slides, video clips, handouts and OHTs as necessary
- separate points on index cards/bold in a large font on paper, collate main parts (not too many!) separately on OHTs.
- Produce materials carefully

Remember six OHTs are adequate for a 20–30-minute presentation and *one* might do.

- don't overwhelm the audience with information and OHTs!
- don't put vast amounts of unrelated data up on an OHT – keep it straightforward, selected and focused.

You could discuss with your students which elements of their work would be suitable for which local, national or international presentation. Help them to decide what is topical, what can be extracted and shaped from their work, and how to organise it in terms of a talk backed up and aided by OHTs and handouts to aid audience accessibility. Students need to produce handouts for summaries and any extended information, so an exercise developing a visible handout for some of the work could be useful preparation.

Increasingly in presentations many people use PowerPoint. The same rules about appropriateness, keeping paper copies, amount of text, etc. suit PowerPoint. With PowerPoint students can add *relevant* rather than excessive images. It is crucial they neither over-clutter nor over-simplify.

PowerPoint *can* really create excellent visuals – but can also be boring and mechanical. OHT backups are essential in case of technology failing. Students also need to ensure they have carefully prepared what they are going to say and how they are going to say it. They need a good, clear script for presentations. You should discuss this with them and if possible help them rehearse or advise them to rehearse with a friend or colleague, and to time themselves. To be absolutely on top of their work they probably need to memorise the opening and closing paragraphs and to commit to memory the key points of the talk. I advise students (and myself) to develop a 14-point bold annotated version of a talk highlighting key points, noting in the margins where the OHT or handouts appear. Some prefer to put this on index cards, others to keep it on A4 sheets. They will, additionally, need large copies of all OHTs and handouts, placed in the order they appear in the presentation. Students should practise to avoid irritating habits and to keep good eye contact, pace, time, and if possible, to be interactive.

▶ Supporting students in getting their work published

For PhD students, publishing should be part of their *ongoing* research process, even before they complete. An important element of being part of the research community is getting the research actually out there in dialogue with others in the field. To this end, students should be encouraged to publish. For undergraduates this might be too daunting. However, they can be encouraged to write up their work jointly with others working in similar areas, or to write up for internal dissemination among the student group. Some undergraduate dissertations are worthy of publication because of their contribution to knowledge and originality, while others form the basis for later postgraduate work and publications in a variety of outlets ranging from students' union newspapers to academic journals and books.

Postgraduates should be encouraged to begin to write for publication as soon as they have completed substantial work that can make a contribution to the field. They will need guidance in the selection of appropriate work from their research area as a whole. They also need to learn to balance the demands of writing for specific publications that have their own agendas and formats, with the actual research process and writing up, so they do not become sidetracked in an unhelpful manner. An expanded version of these short tips appears in Wisker (2001). You might find it useful to go through the tips with your students; identify suitable work to publish; seek publication outlets; encourage them to write, edit and submit; and take some of their work through to publication.

Stages of getting published
Students need to be clear about what they want published and where.

- **Identify**. Their favourite subject might not be topical/interesting to others. They could, refocus for specific publication outlets, find another topic, respond to calls for papers or identify a journal. Once a journal is identified they need to read the journal guidelines and previous essays, then organise the overall essay, title, tone, presentation, and focus to suit this journal. Many journals now put their publication guidelines and sample text online.

- **Write and send**. Students should contact editors to discuss proposals, send in abstracts, and negotiate the likelihood of publication. Next, they send the perfectly presented paper to the journal – probably two hard copies, on disk, and then email, and await: (i) the editor's response; (ii) the referees' response, (iii) requests to rewrite. They then rewrite where indicated and resubmit (there may be a couple of iterations of this), then copy-edit and proof before publication.

Publishing is not like handing in work. Students can be totally rejected, and have to deal with upsetting or obscure, conflicting comments. To get published, they need to develop a thick skin, an eye for how and where to pitch an essay, how to turn critical comments into helpful feedback, and remarkable stubborn tenacity – in order to *finally* get the essay published – perhaps in a different form, perhaps in a different journal, but out there. Then they can tell people to look out for their publications, and let future editors know of their publication record.

Task

Together with your student:

- identify useful ideas about working toward publication
- how can your student make the best of sharing information, skills, peer support and networking – editing, refereeing?
- which elements of their work could they usefully develop now to publication?
- what would they need to do to their current work in order to carry out the writing?
- where might they send it? Why?
- could you publish together and why might that be a good idea?
- together consider an example of a journal they might write for and discuss its format, layout, tone and preferences for kinds of essays.

Draft outline and elements of a book proposal

You might find it useful to talk with your students about turning their research, particularly postgraduate PhD work, into a book, although PhDs theses usually need a lot of work *before* they become books. They will need to consider:

1   the shape of the proposal
2   the right kind of publisher
3   preparing work for publication
4   coping with responses.

Typical proposal shape

- **Introduction** – outlining main area of argument and interest in the book
    - accessible in style
    - containing main arguments, conceptual points and discourse

- **Rationale and audience** (can be separate)
    - Explain why this is topical and interesting. What kinds of readers might it expect? (be as full as possible and relevant)
    - Why is it worth doing right now? What will it contribute to the field of knowledge and ideas?

- **Market** – Carry out market research:
    - What other books and articles? are these on this topic? Identify, list and evaluate
    - Detail why your work is different, how it adds to theirs or improves on it
    - Who might read it?

- **Draft chapters and contents**
    - Include draft contents page, outlining chapters
    - Information on chapter topics and arguments, some of the work referred to
    - Include a draft chapter. This can be the introduction, more usually a later chapter

- **Timing and length**
    - Give a realistic date for its completion and a realistic length.
    - Ensure it all looks marvellous!
    - Add a short letter, mention previous work, contacts where appropriate

The next step

If students hear nothing they should chase, refine outlines in response to publishers' suggestions *or* resubmit elsewhere. It is rarely a good idea to write a whole book before getting a contract or the work could be wasted. However, publishers' readers often want to see a chapter, which, can for the student, be seen as an investment towards the book, or a future journal essay if the book fails to be commissioned. Reasons for turning proposals down differ, including the quality of conceptualisation or presentation, competing books, or simply that it is inappropriate for this publisher's list. Students need to do market research, be honest about the competition and state why *their* book contributes something new, topical, is bound to sell and is necessary to the field (rather like research!).

If and when they find a publisher, they are advised to read all the small print and check on advances and obligations (will they have to pay if it goes over-length, or is pulped after a few months?) They need to enquire about how it will be marketed (no point spending a year of your life perfecting a great contribution to knowledge if it sits in a warehouse, no one knows of it and shops don't stock it).

Writing

Your student could usefully follow the good writing guidelines earlier in this book and advice in the suggested further reading. A book is a wonderful achievement, and a real millstone. Authors need to be perfectionist completer-finishers to get a good enough book out. They will need to:

- rearrange time, seek support, develop a critical eye for their own writing
- edit, edit, edit
- ensure layout and presentation are visually attractive, appropriate, consistent
- proofread fastidiously (obsessively) and ask others to do so too
- ask a critical friend to check the 'final' text
- learn to respond well and constructively to criticism, refining the book until it is ready to send off
- keep in touch with the editor
- send off hard copy, disk, email copies and keep backups
- be prepared to rewrite until *their* critical processes are complete
- when it has gone to the publisher it will return for copy editing, proofing and indexing as well as agreements about blurbs, jackets, who to send copies to, and where to publicise. This part is fun and it is crucial to get it right.

► Skills, and transfer into the job market

Patterson (2001) looks at the problems of drowning the market with post-graduates:

> a kind of gradual academic drift meaning more and more people have to have undergraduate and then postgraduate qualifications (whether relevant or not) in order to gain any kind of employment. In contrast to this, graduates of all levels need to recognise the value of the skills they have developed and how they can transfer these directly into work. (Patterson, 2001, p. 12)

However, there are many transferable skills developed through undertaking research, while other achievements are a greater sense of confidence and self-worth. Nerad and Cerny (1999) asked open-ended questions about the perceived value of doctoral programmes to those who emerge from them. Graduates identify skills:

> By professionalization, these ex-graduate students referred not only to being taught how to publish and acquire professional visibility, but to learning teamwork, collaboration and organizational and managerial skills, all of which they subsequently needed, whether inside or outside the teaching profession.   (Patterson, 2001, pp. 12–13)

Students sum up their feeling about the English PhD being a preparation for work:

> Do not enter this field unless you feel you would never be happy doing anything else. You should have as strong a sense of vocation as one entering the ministry because the sacrifices required for teaching in this field are as great as those required of a pastor. You will have no time to call your own and you will never be paid what you are worth.   (Patterson, 2001, pp. 12–13)

Judy Newman (2001) argues most philosophically about the real need for research and higher learning not just for the market place, nor for a job. Studies, she says, need to be seen as of value in themselves, not merely as an investment for a future career or a tool of sponsors and employers. Newman and Patterson deal realistically, perhaps cynically, certainly philosophically with issues about the focus, usefulness and outcomes of the research process. Students should be enabled to reflect on the skills they have developed as results of research, to recognise these, use them in future employment and also to enhance their quality of life. Publications, a good CV and a personal or professional portfolio can all help students explore and evidence other achievements than the postgraduate qualification in itself, and as supervisors, we should play a part in this recognition and evidencing.

Students themselves are aware of what they have gained, and how the research achievement has helped develop them as learners. One postdoctoral colleague comments:

> I really think that I have developed as a learner from this PhD process in the sense that I think things through and in the sense I think that I have developed ways of how to think and how to write and how to be a good researcher. The most important thing for this intellectual experience, it's really a trigger to continue, and every time I have this dream that when I finish my PhD I'm going to carry out more significant research. I feel even more motivated to go on and research things and I am more critical about things and when I attend a lecture or when I read something I read it with a deeper understanding of its contribution to knowledge, its structure and its significance. I now have a conclusive desire to research the issue more and publish and to write more and this PhD has been a stepping stone for me in this way.
>
> (Interview with postdoctoral colleague, 2003)

Another says:

> It was a very hard slog, but while I was studying I had an imaginative life, and a kind of focus on providing something worthwhile which ran for me alongside all I did at work, at home, crises and sickness. It was like becoming another person, working towards something useful. I really changed as a learner, now I always question the conceptual and theoretical bases of all I hear and read and do – and I am more confident as a person. I *know* I can come up with a good idea, systematically discover, test and then analyse and draw conclusions – I can manage my time too. And I *know* I can finish off something, a project of worth.
>
> (Interview with postdoctoral colleague, 2003)

Skills

Increasingly, research and postgraduate study as well as undergraduate study, are being undertaken with a very direct view to skills development and employability. If you and your student completed the earlier skills audit, you might like to return to it at this stage to review development; and reflect on skills and attitudes learned and what else has been character-building, could lead to employability, and can go on the CV or in a personal development portfolio (PDP), should PDPs be brought in for postgraduates as they are in the UK for undergraduates (by 2006).

Australian colleagues identify ways in which research development programmes can encourage and enable postgraduate students to develop and be aware of their research related skills:

> The move to more explicit skills formation in 'research training' has come from a number of stakeholders. Industry and employer groups have been calling for a broader skill set for research and related employment in industry. Some students are looking for career preparation in an increasingly fluid job market. Within academia, there is concern that research education has become too narrow and concerned with producing research results at the risk of limiting the educational function. This is seen to be more likely where students are being used to carry out funded research work on grants of various kinds, including commercial projects. (Cullen *et al.*, 1994; LaPidus, 1997)

Recognising research-related graduate and postgraduate skills
The list of possible skills developed during research includes:

- Questioning givens, formulating questions to ask of situations, problems, innovations
- Searching and finding varieties of information and concepts
- Documenting, cataloguing, storing and managing varieties of information and concepts
- Managing people, time, space, completing and finishing, dealing with and overcoming difficulties
- Developing an enquiring, problem-solving, problematising, investigative mind set – and the strategies that enable this to be actioned
- Identifying problems, needs, issues and questions that interest you in areas in need of research – identifying gaps in knowledge and significant subjects for study
- Forming a broad 'nosiness' or fascination into succinct and focused, manageable questions that have boundaries to them – not asking everything and becoming confused as a result
- Finding out whom to ask questions, where to find information, how to go about discovering who and what to contact, where to look
- How to forage; pursue questions and leads; find information against odds; access library and journal internet information; sample people;

access discussion lists; acquire, sift, engage, store and then begin to use information and arguments

- How to analyse; synthesise; summarise; problematise; argue and, get in a dialogue with experts, using their work in a dialogue with your own, contributing to debates furthering or deepening the field
- Working tirelessly against a variety of odds from poor pay to bad light; lack of heat; intrusions; difficulties with data acquisition and management; disasters; difficult supervisory relationships; the absence of supervisor support; isolation from friends, family, peers; pressure; being considered self-indulgent because you are pursuing something esoteric (or so it seems to others) irritating colleagues who feel a bit guilty that they aren't researching themselves
- ICT skills – computing data analysis of all sorts
- Communication – with others, for example supervisors, examiners, the public, information source owners, your sample, the field
- Method-specific skills such as:
  - interviewing, managing tape recorders and transcribing
  - devising, distributing, analysing and drawing conclusions from questionnaires
  - documentary analysis, close reading and selection
  - experimental techniques
  - the ability to make and present a case to others, both written and, for postgraduate PhD, orally.

All of these and more are graduate and postgraduate skills specifically developed as a result of being involved in research. Probably the most important one is the lifelong learning skills of having an enquiring mind, a problematising and problem-solving, innovative approach and an ability to devise, manage and carry out a research project to completion.

Students will certainly expect their supervisor to be supportive of their endeavours to enter the job market and to write references for many years.

An Australian industry-oriented view on postgraduate skills, presented in Mullins and Kiley (1998, p. 4), identifies:

- good communication/presentation skills
- good work practices and collaborative skills
- information technology/computer literacy
- the ability to use fundamental and technical knowledge to applied systems
- occupational health and safety, and hazard analysis
- good manufacturing practice

- intellectual property management skills
- highly developed skills to adapt to new areas of activity
- a reasonably broad practical knowledge
- familiarity and knowledge of broader literature
- skills in the scientific method and linkage to the broad context
- experimental design, modelling, statistics
- good laboratory practice.

Lists of postgraduate research-related skills are becoming more popular as a way of describing what else other than the thesis is achieved. The broad areas can also be mapped into undergraduate achievements to differing degrees and tend to range from the general to the particular. Pearson and Brew (2002) comment on what other colleagues produce:

> a list of attributes drawn up by the Committee on Science, Engineering and Public Policy (COSEPUP), which is based on views of academics and industry representatives in science and technology fields in the USA. They prize individuals who:
>
> - are educated to think and to solve problems inventively
> - are broadly based, rather than narrowly oriented to a specific technology
> - can communicate effectively to non-experts as well as peers, both orally and in writing
> - understand technology transfer and can develop as well as initiate ideas
> - are able to work comfortably in a collaborative group environment, and have respect for the employment milieu and their place within it
>
> These attributes include those that are important for professional lifelong learning, and for adaptability as part of being professional. The COSEPUP attributes also foreground social capabilities such as the ability to communicate, work with others and perform in different work roles. Acceptance of such attributes as desirable outcomes demands a holistic approach to defining the curriculum of research training, one that makes the full range of desired outcomes explicit, and integrates the acquisition of the relevant skills and capabilities with the research process itself. (Pearson and Brew, 2002, p. 138)

Using references and advice from the Careers Advisory Board, surveys of employers, graduate recruitment brochures, application forms and the skills module of PROSPECT (HE) – the computer-assisted guide and system for higher education students – Ralph Coates (2002) lists several key postgraduate skills:

- communication – written, interpersonal, oral
- teamwork
- planning and organising
- problem-solving
- initiative
- adaptability

and other skills – numeracy, computer literacy and languages skills.

> Finally, each person has a *unique profile of skill and knowledge*. (Coates, 2002, p. 363.

A crucial part of our work with postgraduate students is to encourage them to develop and achieve, recognise, build on and evidence these skills. The Arts and Humanities Board (AHRB) has several pages of postgraduate skills and learning outcomes on their website, (headings reproduced in the box). With our students, we could usefully conduct an audit during and at the end of their postgraduate study to build on that conducted early on, for them to become aware of skills and learning outcomes achieved. We could also encourage them to put together a personal development programme file or portfolio to evidence these skills and learning outcomes, which will both embed them in their *own* consciousness, aiding meta-learning, and helping them to indicate achievements and abilities to future employers.

AHRB skills and learning outcomes

A Research skills and techniques
B Research environment
C Research management
D Personal effectiveness
E Communication skills
F Networking and team-working
G Career management

Source: http://www.grad.ac.uk/3_2_1.jsp

In terms of research at both undergraduate and postgraduate levels, students could have developed skills and attitudes related to:

- critical and conceptual thinking
- scoping – identifying a problem/issue/need and the project-planning to approach it
- project-planning
- carrying out a project or mini-projects through to completion
- time management
- knowledge identification, searching, retrieval, transfer, management
- knowledge creation
- presentation skills
- writing for different audiences and different outcomes
- negotiating and managing funding
- coping with disasters, for example, experiments failing.

Skills identification, reflection, evidencing and transfer could be carried out at any depth or scope.

Newman (2001) usefully generalises about the importance of research and learning for individuals and society:

> Two facts need to be kept in view. Firstly, society can never have too many people who have learned the importance of the search and the respect for truth. As James Armstrong recently argued, society needs people who have learned to take part in critical discourse and to make appropriate judgments, who have developed a sense of the ethics of inquiry and the responsibilities involved, who can see possibilities beyond the immediate status quo, who know that they will go on learning throughout their lifetimes, and who have learned to cope with failure. (In any successful doctorate there are many lines of inquiry which fail to produce results.) Society needs more people trained at the highest levels of critical thinking, not less.   (Newman, 2001, pp. 16–17)

Funding education and research might be seen as a kind of social gift to other people's children and intellectually based 'work' as entertainment, a privilege. Of course education is a privilege – and a *right*, if used as a key to more than a pay packet. Educational research can enhance social health, the development of knowledge, the ability to recognise the questionable, the relative nature of values, decisions and knowledge *and* the importance of informed decision making. Research and education should help us move beyond blinkered stubborn ignorance – it is not for selfish self-development, but for both individual growth and human good.

Activity

Skills identification evidence and transfer exercise

This is *one* example of *one* skill students could usefully identify and reflect on from all the skills listed above. In this example, reflection and evidencing could be aided by prompts from supervisors, reflected on and evidenced.

Skill	Elements	Developed where	Evidence – examples and reflection	Could be transferred to/used in situations …
Knowledge retrieval and management	• searching databases, information sources • taking selected and focused notes and other information to use in own work • referencing • dialoguing with information and arguments	• listing and cataloguing research interviews, etc. of people • note-taking • summarising, labelling and cataloguing notes and information • writing up using processed research information • drafts, for thesis/ dissertation	• files and folders of notes on information catalogued and thematically stored • referenced and selected notes, quotes, information cited in thesis/ dissertation • comments on the patterns or identification, statistical or thematic analysis, collection, storage, referenced and used in written work	• any situation where information needs to be identified and searched for, e.g. books, internet, people • any situation where information and knowledge needs to be processed, catalogued, categorised, analysed, managed and then selectively used • for example for a project, for selection, collection and analysis of evidence for reports, projects etc.

▶ Further reading

Mullins, M. and Kiley, M. (1998) 'Quality in postgraduate education: the changing agenda', in M. Kiley and G. Mullins (eds), *Quality in Postgraduate Education: Managing the New Agenda* (Adelaide: Advisory Centre for University Education, pp. 1–14).

Nerad, M. and Cerny, J. (1999) 'From rumors to facts: career outcomes of English PhDs results from the PhDs – ten years later study', *Communicator*, **XXXII** (7), pp. 1–11.

Newman, J. (2001) 'The shape of graduate studies in English', *Issues in English: Doctor! Doctor! Doctoral Studies in English in Twenty-first Century Britain*, **1**, pp. 15–24.

Patterson, A. (2001) 'Overproduction', *Issues in English: Doctor! Doctor! Doctoral Studies in English in Twenty-first Century Britain*, **1**, pp. 5–13.

Pearson, M. and Brew, A. (2002) 'Research training and supervision development', *Studies in Higher Education*, **27**(2), pp. 135–50.

References

Acker, S., Hills, T. and Black, E. (1994) 'Thesis supervision in the social sciences: managed or negotiated?' *Higher Education*, **28**, pp. 483–98.

Adam, T. (1995) 'Internationalizing the university: an Australian case study', *Higher Education Policy*, **8**(2), pp. 40–3.

Adams, A. (1986) *Bullying at Work* (London: Virago).

Anderson, G., Boud, D. and Sampson, J. (1996) *Learning Contracts: A Practical Guide* (London: Kogan Page).

Anderson, L. W. (1997) *Highways to Postgraduate Supervision* (Sydney: University of Western Sydney Press).

Asmar, C. and Peseta, T. (2001) 'Figuring things out from my friends: encouraging collaboration among first-year students at undergraduate and postgraduate level', Institute for Teaching and Learning, University of Sydney, Australian Association for Research in Education conference, Fremantle, 2–6 December 2001.

Aspland, T. and O'Donoghue, T. (1994) 'Quality in supervising overseas students', in Zuber-Skerritt, O. and Ryan, Y. (eds), *Quality in Postgraduate Education* (London: Kogan Page).

Aspland, T., Hill, G. and Chapman, H. (2002) *Journeying Postgraduate Supervision*, a website production for Queensland University of Technology.

Ballard, B. (1991) 'Helping students from non-English speaking backgrounds to learn effectively', occasional paper, Educational Research and Development Unit (Australia: Royal Melbourne Institute of Technology).

Ballard, B. and Clanchy, J. (1984) *Study Abroad: Manual for Asian Students* (Kuala Lumpur: Longman).

Bargar, R. and Duncan, J. (1982) 'Cultivating creative endeavour', *Doctoral Journal of Higher Education*, **53**(1), pp. 1–31.

Barnett, J. (2002) 'Writing to research: a supervisor's perspective', in M. Kiley and G. Mullins (eds), *Quality in Postgraduate Research: Integrating Perspectives* (Canberra: University of Canberra).

Bartlett, A., May, M. and Holzknecht, S. (1994) 'Discipline-specific academic skills at postgraduate level: a model', in K. Chanock (ed.), *Integrating the Teaching of Academic Discourse into Courses in the Disciplines* (Melbourne: Language and Academic Skills Units of La Trobe University), pp. 284–7.

Basch, R. and Bates, M. E. (2000) *Researching Online for Dummies* (Foster City, CA: IDG Books).

Beasley, C. J. (1990) 'Content-based language instruction: helping ESL/ELF students with foreign language and study skills at tertiary level', *TESOL in Context*, **1**, 10–14.

Becher, T. (1993) 'Graduate education in Britain: the view from the ground', in B. R. Clark (ed.), *The Research Foundations of Graduate Education: Germany, Britain, France, United States, Japan* (Berkeley, CA: University of California Press), pp. 115–53.

Becher, T. (1994) 'The significance of disciplinary differences', *Studies in Higher Education*, **19**(2), pp. 151–61.

Becher, T., Henkel, M. and Kogan, M. (1994) *Graduate Education in Britain* (London: Jessica Kingsley).

Becker, H. (1970) *Sociological Work* (New Brunswick, NJ: Transaction Books).

Biggs, J. B. (1978) 'Individual and group differences in study processes and the quality of learning outcomes', *Higher Education*, **48**, 266–79.

Biggs, J. B. (ed.) (1991) T*eaching for Learning: The View from Cognitive Psychology* (Hawthorn, Vic: ACER).

Biggs, J. and Collis, K. (1991) 'Multimodal learning and the quality of intelligent behaviour', in H. Rowe (ed.), *Intelligence, Reconceptualization and Measurement* (New Jersey: Laurence Erlbaum).

Blanton, J. (1983) 'Midwifing the Dissertation', *Teaching of Psychology*, **10**(2)

Bloor, M. and Bloor, T. (1991) 'Cultural expectations and socio-pragmatic failure in academic writing', in P. Adams, B. Heaton and P. Howarth (eds), *Socio-cultural Issues in English for Academic Purposes* (Basingstoke: Macmillan), pp. 1–12.

Blume, S. (1986) 'The development of current dilemmas of postgraduate education', *European Journal of Education*, **21**(3), pp. 217–22.

Bochner, D., Gibbs, G. and Wisker, G. (1995) *Supporting More Students, Teaching More Students*, 6 (Oxford: Oxford Centre for Staff Development, Oxford Brookes University).

Boehmer, E. (1995) *Colonial and Postcolonial Literature: Migrant Metaphors* (Oxford: Oxford University Press).

Boice, R. (1990) *Professors as Writers: A Self-Help Guide to Productive Writing* (Stillwater, OK: New Forums).

Boud, D. (1995) *Enhancing Learning Through Self-Assessment* (London: Kogan Page).

Boud, D., Cohen, R. and Walker, D. (1993) 'Using experience for learning', *Issues of Teaching and Learning*, **3**(2).

Boud, D., Keogh, R. and Walker, D. (1985) 'What is reflection in learning?' in *Reflection: Turning Experience into Learning* (London: Kogan Page), pp. 7–17.

Boud, D., Keogh, R. and Walker, D. (eds) (1985) *Reflection: Turning Experience into Learning* (London: Kogan Page).

Brew, A. (2001) *The Nature of Research: Inquiry in Academic Contexts* (London: Routledge Falmer).

Brew, A. (2000a) 'Bringing research and teaching together strategically'. Poster presented at the 8th International Symposium on Improving Student Learning.

Brew, A. (2000b) 'Taking research seriously: the role of inquiry in staff and educational development'. Keynote presentation to the SEDA conference, November.

Brew, A. and Peseta, T. (2002) *Improving Research Higher Degree Supervision through Recognising and Rewarding Supervision Development* (Australia: University of Sydney).

Brew, A. and Peseta, T. (2004) 'Changing postgraduate supervision practice', *Innovations in Education and Teaching International*, **41**(1), pp. 5–22.

Brookfield, S. D. (1986) *Understanding and Facilitating Adult Learning: Comprehensive Analysis of Principles and Effective Practices* (Milton Keynes: Open University Press).

Brown, G. and Atkins, M. (1988) *Effective Teaching in Higher Education* (London: Methuen).

Bruce, C. (1994) 'Research students' early experiences of the dissertation literature review', *Studies in Higher Education*, **19**(2), pp. 217–29.

Bruner, J. (1986) *Actual Minds, Possible Worlds* (Cambridge, MA: Harvard University Press).

Bryman, A. (1988) *Quantity and Quality in Social Research* (London: Unwin Hyman).

Bryman, A. (ed.) (1988) *Doing Research in Organisations* (London: Routledge).

Buchanan, D., Boddy, D. and McCalman, J. (1988) 'Getting in, getting on, getting out and getting back', in Bryman, A. (ed.), *Doing Research in Organisations* (London: Routledge).

Bulmer, M. (1988) 'Some reflections upon research in organisations', in A. Bryman (ed.), *Doing Research in Organisations* (London: Routledge).

Burgess, R. G. (ed.) (1994) *Postgraduate Education and Training in the Social Sciences: Processes and Products* (London: Jessica Kingsley).

Burgess, R., Pole, C. and Hockey, J. (1994) 'Strategies for managing and supervising the social science PhD', in R. Burgess (ed.), *Postgraduate Education and Training in the Social Sciences: Processes and Products* (London: Jessica Kingsley).

Burnham, P. (1994) 'Surviving the viva; unravelling the mysteries of the PhD oral', *Journal of Graduate Education*, **1**(1), pp. 30–4.

Caffarella, R. S. and Barnett, B. G. (2000) 'Teaching doctoral students to become scholarly writers: the importance of giving and receiving feedback', *Studies in Higher Education*, **25**(1), pp. 3–52.

Cargill, M. (1996). 'An integrated bridging program for international postgraduate students', *Higher Education Research and Development*, **15**(2), pp. 177–88.

Chen, J. R. (2001) 'The cross cultural adjustment of Taiwanese postgraduate students in England' (unpublished PhD thesis, University of Warwick).

Clark, B. R. (ed.) (1993) *The Research Foundations of Graduate Education: Germany, Britain, France, United States, Japan* (Berkeley, CA: University of California Press).

CNNA (1980) *Notes on Guidance for External Examiners for Courses* (London: CNNA).

Coates, R. (20002) 'Career opportunities', in T. Greenfield (ed.) *Research Methods for Postgraduates* (London: Hodder & Stoughton Educational).

Cocks, J. (1985) 'Suspicious pleasures: on teaching feminist theory', in M. Culley and C. Portuges (eds), *Gendered Subjects: The Dynamics of Feminist Teaching* (London: Routledge & Kegan Paul).

Conrad, L. (1998) 'Enhancing research through academic staff development', *International Journal for Academic Development*, **3**(2), pp. 115–23.

Conrad. L. (1999) 'Contextualising postgraduate supervision to improve quality', in G. Wisker and N. Sutcliffe (eds), *Effectiveness in Postgraduate Supervision* (Birmingham: Staff and Educational Development Association), pp. 13–24.

Cooke, A. (1999) *A Guide to Finding Quality Information on the Internet: Selection of Evaluation Strategies* (London: Library Association Publishing).

Cooper, H. M. (1985) *The Integrative Research Review: A Systematic Approach* (London: Sage).

Cryer, P. (1996) *The Research Students Guide to Success* (Buckingham: Open University Press).

Cryer, P. and Okarocha, J. (1997) *Handling Common Dilemmas in Supervision: Issues in Postgraduate Supervision, Teaching and Management*, Guide no. 2 (London: Society for Research into Higher Education and the *Times Higher Education Supplement*).

Cullen, D., Pearson, M., Saha, L. and Spear, R. (1994) *Establishing Effective PhD Supervision* (Canberra: Australian Government Publishing Service).

Culley, M. and Portuges, C. (eds) (1985) *Gendered Subjects: The Dynamics of Feminist Teaching* (London: Routlege and Kegan Paul).

CVCP (1984) *The External Examiner System for First Degree and Taught Courses* (London: CVCP).

Dearing, R. (1997) *Higher Education in the Learning Society, National Committee of Inquiry into Higher Education* (London: HMSO).

Delamont, S. (1997) 'Peons or colleagues? Everyday life in graduate school', United Kingdom Council for Graduate Education Summer Conference, Southampton, 16–17 July.

Delamont, S., Atkinson, P. and Parry, O. (1997) *Supervising the PhD: A Guide to Success* (Buckingham: Open University Press).

Delamont, S., Parry, O. and Atkinson, P. (1998) 'Creating a delicate balance: the doctoral supervisor's dilemmas', *Teaching in Higher Education*, **3**(2), pp. 157–72.

Delamont, S. and Eggleston, J. (1983) *Supervision of Students for Research Degrees* (London: British Educational Research Association).

Denicolo, P., Boulter, C., Fuller, M., Fisher, J. and Savage, D. (2000) *The Higher Degree Viva: A Case of Constructive Alternativism – Beyond Experimentation into Meaning* (Farnborough: EPCA Publications).

Dewey, J. (1969) *Moral Principles in Education* (New York: Greenwood Press).

Dingwall, R. (1980a) 'Ethics and ethnography', *Sociological Review*, **28**(4), pp. 871–91.

Dingwall, R. (1980b) 'Orchestrated encounters', *Sociology of Health and Illness*, **2**(2), pp. 151–73.

Dunleavy, P. (2003) *Authoring a PhD* (Basingstoke: Palgrave Macmillan).

Eagleton, T. (2000) *The Idea of Culture* (Oxford: Blackwell Publishers).

Easterby Smith, M., Thorpe, R. and Lowe, A. (1991) *Management Research: An Introduction* (London: Sage).

Elbow, P. (1973) *Writing without Teachers* (Oxford: Oxford University Press).

Entwistle, N. (1998) 'Improving teaching through research on student learning', in J. J. F. Forest (ed.), *University Teaching: International Perspectives* (New York: Garland Publishing).

Entwistle, N. J. and Ramsden, P. (1983) *Understanding Student Learning* (London: Croom Helm).

Evans, T. and Green, W. (1995) 'Dancing at a distance? Postgraduate studies, "Supervision", and distance education', Australian Association for Research in Education Conference, AARE, Hobart (Electronic), pp. 1–14.

Felix, U. (1993) 'Support strategies for international postgraduate students', *HERDSA News*, **15**, pp. 6–8.

Flavell, J. H. (1977) *Cognitive Development* (Englewood Cliffs, NJ: Prentice-Hall).

Fowler, H. W. (1994) *A Dictionary of Modern English Usage* (Ware: Wordsworth Editions).

Francis, H. (1997) 'The research process', in N. Graves and V. Verma (eds), *Working for a Doctorate: A Guide for the Humanities and Social Services* (London: Routledge).

Freckleton, L., Creighton, E. and Wisker, G. (2003) 'Internationalisation of the curriculum and employability', *World Views: The Magazine for UKCOSA Members*, **11**, pp. 10–12.

Gelsthorpe, L. (1990) 'Feminist methodologies in criminology: a new approach or old wine in new bottles?' in L. Gelsthorpe and A. Morris (eds), *Feminist Perspectives in Criminology* (Buckingham: Open University Press).

Gergen, M. M. and Gergen, K. J. (1993) 'Narratives of the gendered body in popular autobiography', in R. Josselson and A. Lieblich (eds), *The Narrative Study of Lives*, vol. 1 (Newbury Park, CA: Sage), pp. 191–218.

Gibbons, M., Limoges, C., Nowotny, H., Schwartzman, S., Scott, P. and Trow, M. (1994) *The New Production of Knowledge: The Dynamics of Science and Research* (London: Sage).

Gibbs, G. (1981) *Teaching Students to Learn* (Buckingham: Open University Press).

Gibbs, G. (1991) *Lecturing to More Students* (Oxford: OCDS).

Ginsberg, E. (1992) 'Not just a matter of English', *HERDSA*, **14**(1), pp. 6–8.

Goffman, E. (1959) *The Presentation of Self in Everyday Life* (Garden City, NY: Doubleday).

Gordon, William, J. J. (1961) *Synectics: The Development of Creative Capacity* (New York: Harper & Harper).

Gower, E. (1986) *The Complete Plain Words*, rev. edn prepared by S. Greenbaum and J. Whitcut (London: HMSO).

Graves, N. (1997) *Working for a Doctorate: A Guide for the Humanities and Social Sciences* (London: Routledge).

Gray, B. (1994) 'Women in higher education: What are we doing to ourselves?', in S. Davies, C. Lubelska and J. Quinn (eds), *Changing the Subject* (London: Taylor & Francis).

Green, B. (1996) 'E-quality, postgraduate supervision and the education doctorate: the Deakin experience', paper presented at the 'Quality in Postgraduate Education – Is it happening?' Conference, Adelaide, April.

Green, B. and Lee, A. (1995) 'Theorising postgraduate pedagogy', *Australian Universities Review*, 2, pp. 40–5.

Greenfield, T. (ed.) (2002) *Research Methods for Postgraduates* (London: Edward Arnold).

Guile, D. and Young, M. (1998) 'Apprenticeship as a conceptual basis for a social theory of learning', *Journal of Vocational Education and Training*, **50** (2), pp. 173–92.

Gumport, P. (1993) 'Graduate education and research imperatives: views from American campuses', in B. Clark (ed.), *The Research Foundations of Graduation Education* (Berkeley, CA: University of California Press).

Gumport, P. J. (1999) 'Graduate education and research: interdependence and strain', in P. G. Altbach, R. O. Berdahl and P. J. Gumport (eds), *American Higher Education in the 21st Century: Social, Political and Economic Challenges* (Baltimore, MD: Johns Hopkins University Press).

Halpin, D. (2003) *Hope and Education: The Role of the Utopian Imagination* (London: Routledge Falmer).

Hansford, B. C., and Maxwell, T. W. (1993) 'A Master's degree program: structural components and examiners' comments', *Higher Education Research and Development*, **12**(2).

Harris, R. (1995) 'Overseas students in the UK university system', *Higher Education*, **29**, pp. 77–92.

Hartley, J. and Fox, C. (2003) *Assessing the Mock Viva: The Experience of British Doctoral Students* (Keele: Keele University Press).

Hartley, J. and Jory, S. (2000) 'Lifting the veil on the viva: the experiences of PhD candidates in the UK', *Psychology Teaching Review*, 9, pp. 76–90.

Hartley, P. and Wisker, G. (2004) *Interviewer Postgraduate Viva*, CD Rom (Sheffield Hallam University).

Hartnett, R. T. and Katz, J. (1977) 'The education of graduate students', *Journal of Higher Education*, **48**(6), pp. 646–64.

Haug, F. (1987) *Female Sexualisation* (London: Verso).

Hensel, N. (1991) 'Realizing gender equality in higher education: the need to integrate work/family issues', ASHE-ERIC Higher Education Report 2 (Washington, DC: George Washington University Press).

Heron, J. (1975) *Six Category Intervention Analysis* (London: Tavistock Institute).

Hodge, B. (1995) 'Monstrous knowledge: doing PhDs in the new humanities', *Australian Universities Review*, **38**(2), pp. 35–9.

Holbrook, A. and Bourke, S. (2002) 'PhD assessment: design of the study, qualities of examiner reports and candidature information', paper presented at AERA Conference, New Orleans, 1–5 April.

Holbrook, A. (2001) 'PhD examination – assessment's least-mapped frontier', paper presented at AARE Conference Fremantle, December.

Holbrook, A. (2002) 'How do examiners of doctoral theses utilise the written report?', paper presented at 'Examining the Quality of Doctoral Research', AERA Symposium, New Orleans, 1–5 April.

Holdaway, E. (1996) 'Current issues in graduate education', *Journal of Higher Education Policy and Management*, **18**(1), pp. 59–74.

Honey, P. and Mumford, A. (1986) *Using Your Manual of Learning Styles* (London: Peter Honey Publications).

Horn, R. (1996) 'Negotiating research access to organisations', *The Psychologist*, December.

Hughes, S. and Wisker, G. (1998) 'Improving the teaching and learning experiences of overseas students', in C. Rust (ed.), *Improving Student Learning: Curriculum Development* (Oxford: Oxford Brookes University).

Hunt, J. (1984) 'The development of rapport through the negotiation of gender in field work among the police', *Human Organisation*, **43**(4), pp. 283–96.

Hutchings, P. (1991) 'The teaching portfolio', *The Department Chair*, **2**(1), pp. 33–5.

Hutchings, P. (1999) *Using Cases to Improve College Teaching: A Guide to More Reflective Practice*, 2nd edn (Washington, DC: American Association for Higher Education).

Jackson, C. and Tinkler, P. (2000) 'Examining the doctorate: institutional policy and the PhD examination process in the UK', *Studies in Higher Education*, **25** pp. 167–80.

Jackson, C. and Tinkler, P. (2001) 'Back to basics: a consideration of the purposes of the PhD viva', *Assessment and Evaluation in Higher Education*, **26**, pp. 351–62.

Jalongo, M. R. and Isenberg, J. P. with Gerbracht, G. (1995) *Teachers' Stories: From Personal Narrative to Professional Insight* (San Francisco, CA: Jossey-Bass).

Johnson, L., Lee, A. and Green, B. (2000) 'The PhD and the autonomous self: gender, rationality and postgraduate pedagogy', *Studies in Higher Education*, **25**(2), pp. 135–47.

Johnson, N. B. (1986) 'Ethnographic research and rites of incorporation: a sex- and gender-based comparison', in T. L. Whitehead and M. E. Conaway (eds), *Self, Sex and Gender in Cross-cultural Fieldwork* (Urbana: University of Illinois Press).

Johnston, S. (1997) 'Examining the examiners: an analysis of examiners' report on doctoral thesis', *Studies in Higher Education: Journal of Higher Education:* **22**(3), pp. 333–47.

Kandlbinder, P. and Peseta, T. (2000a) 'Online professional development for postgraduate supervisors', in A. Herrmann and M. M. Kulski (eds), *Flexible Futures in Tertiary Teaching: Proceedings of the 9th Annual Teaching Learning Forum, 2–4 February 2000.* Perth: Curtin University of Technology. http://lsn.curtin.edu.au/tlf/tlf2000/kandlbinder2.html.

Kandlbinder, P. and Peseta, T. (2000b) *In Supervisors' Words: An Insider's View of Postgraduate Supervision* (Sydney: Institute for Teaching and Learning).

Kerby, A. (1991) *Narrative and the Self* (Bloomington: Indiana University Press).

Kiely, M. (1982) 'Creative sensitivity in doctoral research: the supervisor's contribution', paper presented at the Annual Meeting of the American Psychological Association, Washington, DC.

Kiley, M. (2003) 'What examiners' comments can tell us about the postgraduate learning environment', 11th Improving Student Learning conference, Hanover International Hotel, Hinckley, Leicestershire.

Kiley, M. and Mullins, G. (eds) (1998) *Quality in Postgraduate Research: Managing the New Agenda* (University of Adelaide: Advisory Centre for University Education).

Kiley, M. and Mullins, G. (2002) '"It's a PhD, not a Nobel Prize": how experienced examiners assess research theses', *Studies in Higher Education*, **27**(4).

Kirkpatrick, A. and Mulligan, D. (1996) 'Cultures of learning in Australian universities: reading expectations and practice in the Social and Applied Sciences', paper presented at the Applied Linguistics Association of Australia, 21st Annual Conference, Worlds of Discourse, Sydney, New South Wales.

Kitzinger, C. (1990) 'Resisting the discipline', in E. Burman (ed.), *Feminists and Psychological Practice* (London: Sage).

Klein, R. D. (1987) 'The dynamics of the women's studies classroom: a review essay of the teaching practice of women's studies in higher education', *Women's Studies International Forum*, **10**(2), pp. 187–206.

Koestler, A. (1964, 1979) *The Act of Creation* (Basingstoke: Pan Books).

Kolb, David A. (1984) *Experimental Learning: Experience as the Source of Learning and Development.* (Englewood Cliffs, NJ: Prentice Hall).

Kouptsov, O. (1994) *The Doctorate in the Europe Region* (CEPES UNESCO).

La Pidus, J.B. (1997) 'Doctoral education: preparing for the future', a report presented to the Council of Graduate Schools. Available Internet: http://www.cgsnet.org/publicationpolicynes/index-htm/

Landbeck, R. and Mugler, F. (1994) *Approaches to Study and Conceptions of Learning of Students at the University of the South Pacific* (University of the South Pacific: CELT).

Lankshear, C. and McLaren, P. (1995) 'Critical literacy and the postmodern turn', in L. A. McLaren, (ed.), *Critical Literacy: Politics, Praxis and the Postmodern, (*New York: State University of New York Press).

Lankshear, C. and McLaren, P. (eds) (1994) *Politics of Liberation: Paths from Freire.* (London: Routledge).

Lave, J. and Wenger, E. (1991) *Situated Learning: Legitimate Peripheral Participation* (Cambridge: Cambridge University Press).

Lee, R. M. (1993) *Doing Research on Sensitive Topics* (London: Sage).

Lee, A., and Williams, C. (1999) 'Forged in fire: narratives of trauma in PhD supervision pedagogy', *Southern Review*, **32**(1), pp. 6–26.

Leonard, D. (2001) *A Women's Guide to Doctoral Studies* (Buckingham: Open University Press).

Leonard, D. (2002) *The Politics of Gender and Education*, Conference Proceedings (London: Institute of Education).

Linden, J. (1999) 'The contribution of narrative to the process of supervising PhD students', *Studies in Higher Education*, **24**(3), 351–69.

Lindop, N. (1985) *Academic Validation in the Public Sector of Higher Education*, Report of the Committee of Enquiry (London: HMSO).

Loomba, A. (ed.) (1998) *Colonialism/Post Colonialism* (London: Routledge).

Lovat, T. (2002) *What is This Thing Called RE: A Decade on?*, 2nd edn (Sydney: Social Science Press).

Love, A., and Street, A. (1998) in M. Kiley, and G. Mullins (eds), *Quality in Postgraduate Research: Managing the New Agenda* (University of Adelaide: Advisory Centre for University Education).

Lowenthal, D. and Wason, P. C. (1977) 'Academics and their writing', *The Times Literary Supplement*, 24 June, p. 781.

Malcolm, I. (1996) 'Literary events across cultures in higher education'. Faculty of Arts, Edith Cowan University.

Marton, F. and Saljo, R. (1976) 'On qualitative differences in learning – 1 outcome and process', *British Journal of Educational Technology*, **46**, pp. 4–11.

McCormack, C. (1998) 'Memories bridge the gap between theory and practice in women's leisure research', *Annals of Leisure Research*, **1**, pp. 37–49.

McCormack, C. and Pamphilon, B. (1998, revised 2002) *The Balancing Act: Exploring Women's Experiences of Postgraduate Study, Supervision and Workload. A Workshop Manual* (Canberra: Centre for the Enhancement of Learning, Teaching and Scholarship, University of Canberra).

McCormack, C. and Pamphilon, B. (2004) 'More than a confessional: post-modern groupwork to support postgraduate supervisors' professional development', *Innovations in Education and Teaching International,* **41**(1), January–February.

McNamara, D. (ed.) (1997) *Overseas Students in Higher Education* (London: Routledge).

Melamed, L. (1987) 'The role of play in adult learning'. in D. Boud, and, V. Griffin (eds), *Appreciating Adults Learning: From the Learner's Perspective.* (London: Kogan Page).

Metcalfe J., Thompson, Q. and Green, H. (2002) *Improving Standards in Postgraduate Research Degree Programmes,* October (Bristol: HEFCE).

Meyer, J. H. F. and Boulton-Lewis, G. M. (1997) 'Reflections on Learning Inventory (ROLI)', questionnaire (available from J. H. F. Meyer, Department of Education, University of Durham).

Meyer, J. H. F. and Kiley, M. (1998) 'An exploration of Indonesian postgraduate students' conceptions of learning', *Journal of Further and Higher Education,* **22**(3), pp. 287–98.

Meyer, J. H. F. and Shanahan, M. P. (2002) 'On variation in conception of "price" in economics', *Higher Education,* **43**, pp. 4–11.

Miles, M. B. and Huberman, A. M. (1984) *Qualitative Data Analysis: A Sourcebook for New Methods* (London: Sage).

Mirza, H. S. (1995) 'Black women in higher education: defining a space/finding a place', in L. Morley, and V. Walsh (eds), *Feminist Academics: Creative Agents for Change* (London: Taylor and Francis).

Morley, L., Leonard D. and David M. (2002) 'Variations in vivas: quality and equality in British PhD assessments', *Studies in Higher Education,* **27**(3).

Morris, J. and Meyer, J. H. F. (2003) 'Variation in the conceptions of learning of physiotherapy students in England and Wales: a longitudinal multicentre study', in C. Rust (ed.), *Improving Student Learning Theory and Practice – 10 Years on* (Oxford: OSCLD).

Moses, I. (1984) 'Supervision of higher degree students – problem areas and possible solutions', *Higher Education Research and Development,* **3**, pp. 153–65.

Moses, I. (1985) *Supervising Postgraduates,* HERDSA, Green Guide no. 3 (University of New South Wales, Kensington: Higher Education Research and Development Society of Australasia).

Moses, I. (1990) *Barriers to Women's Participation in Postgraduate Study* (Canberra: Australian Government Publishing Service).

Moses, I. (1993) 'Issues in women's participation', in D. Cullen (ed.), *Proceedings from the Symposium: Quality in PhD Education* (Canberra: Centre for Educational Development and Academic Methods (CEDAM) and The Graduate School, Australian National University).

Mullins, G. and Kiley, M. (1998) 'Quality in postgraduate education: the changing agenda', in M. Kiley and G. Mullins (eds) *Quality in Postgraduate Education: Managing the New Agenda* (Adelaide: Advisory Centre for University Education), pp. 1–14.

Murray, R. (July 2001) 'Integrating teaching and research through writing development for students and staff', *Active Learning in Higher Education*, **2**(1), pp. 31–45.

Murray, R. (2002) *How to Write a Thesis* (Buckingham: Open University Press).

Murray, R. (2003) *How to Survive Your Viva: Defending your Thesis in an Oral Examination* (Buckingham: Open University Press.)

Nerad, M. and Cerny, J. (1999) 'From rumors to facts: career outcomes of English PhDs results from the PhDs – ten years later study', *Communicator*, **XXXII**(7), pp. 1–11.

Newman, J. (2001) 'The shape of graduate studies in English', *Issues in English: Doctor! Doctor! Doctoral Studies in English in Twenty-First Century Britain*, **1**, pp. 15–24.

Nightingale. P. (1984) 'Examination of research theses'. *Higher Education Research and Development Journal*, **3**(2), 13–150.

Nishio, A. (2001) 'The experience of Japanese postgraduate students at the University of London, with special reference to gender', PhD thesis, University of London.

Okorocha, E. (1997) 'Supervising international research student', *Issues in Postgraduate Supervision, Teaching and Management* (London: SRHE).

Oleson, V. and Whittaker, E. (1968) *The Silent Dialogue* (San Francisco, CA: Jossey Bass).

Ottewill, R., Shephard, K. and Fill, K. (2002) 'Assessing the contribution of collections of case studies to academic development in higher education', *International Journal for Academic Development*, **7**(1), pp. 51–62.

Ozga, J. (1998) 'The entrepreneurial researcher: re-formations of identity in the research marketplace', *International Studies in Sociology of Education*, **8**(2), pp. 143–53.

Parker, L., Kirkpatrick, A. and Slaney, K. (1996) 'Communication skills, in the context of postgraduate supervision of students from language backgrounds other than English'. Report from Curtin University of Technology, Perth.

Parry, O., Atkinson, P. and Delamont, S. (1992) 'Free range or battery laid: doing a PhD in the social sciences'. Paper presented at the September conference, 'Research Training in the Social Sciences', St John's College, Cambridge.

Patterson, A. (2001) 'Overproduction', in *Issues in English: Doctor! Doctor! Doctoral Studies in English in Twenty-First Century Britain,* **1**, pp. 5–13 [8].

Pearson, M. (1999) 'The changing environment for doctoral education in Australia: implications for quality management, improvement and innovation', *Higher Education Research and Development,* **18**(3).

Pearson, M. and Brew, A. (2002) 'Research training and supervision development, in *Studies in Higher Education,* **27**(2), pp. 135–150.

Phillips, E. (1994) 'Appendix 1a: Some suggestions for staff development concerning the supervision of research and research students', in L. Elton and USDU's Task Force Three (1994), *Staff Development in Relation to Research,* occasional Green Paper No. 6 (Sheffield: Universities' Staff Development Unit).

Phillips, E. (1998) *Postgraduate Supervision, Teaching and Management* (London: SRHE).

Phillips, E. and Pugh, D. S. (1994) *How to Get a PhD: A Handbook for Students and Their Supervisors,* 2nd edn (Buckingham: Open University Press).

Pitkethly, A. and Prosser, M. (1995) 'Examiners' comments on the international context of PhD theses, in C. McNaught and K. Beattie (eds), *Research into Higher Education: Dilemmas, Directions and Diversions* (Melbourne: HERDSA, pp. 129–36).

Power, M. (1997) *The Audit Society: Rituals of Verification* (Oxford: Oxford University Press).

PrD (Professional Doctorate in Health and Social Care) Handbook (Cambridge: Anglia Polytechnic University, School of Health Care Practice, 2003).

Purkiss, D. (1994) 'The lecherous professor revisited: Plato, pedagogy and the scene of Harassment', in C. Brant and Y. Lee Too (eds), *Rethinking Sexual Harassment* (London: Pluto).

Ramazanoglu, C. (1987) 'Sex and violence in academic life or you can keep a good woman down, in J. Hanmer, and M. Maynard (eds), *Women, Violence and Social Control.* (Basingstoke: Macmillan).

Ramsden, P. (1979) 'Student learning and perceptions of the academic environment'. *Higher Education,* **8**, pp. 411–27.

Reeve, F., Cartwright, M. and Edwards, R. (2002) *Supporting Lifelong Learning: Organising Learning* (London: Falmer Press).

Reeves, P. and Robins, J. L. (1995) *Postgraduate Supervision Project: Report* (Bentley: Curtin TLG).

Reid, I. (1996) *Higher Education or Education for Hire? Language and Values in Australian Universities* (Rockhampton: Central Queensland University Press).

Rendel, M. (1996) 'How many women academics in 1912–1977?', in R. Deem (ed.), *Schooling for Women's Work* (London: Routledge, pp. 142 –61).

Reynolds, P. (1986) *Academic Standards in Universities* (London: CVCP).

Rich, A. (1985), 'Taking women students seriously', in M. Culley and C.

Portuges (eds), *Gendered Subjects: The Dynamics of Feminist Teaching* (London: Routledge & Kegan Paul).

Richardson, L. (1990) *Writing Strategies: Reaching Diverse Audiences* (Newbury Park, CA: Sage).

Richardson, L. (1997) *Fields of Play: Constructing an Academic Life* (New Brunswick, NJ: Rutgers University Press).

Richardson, V. and Robinson, D. (eds) (1993) *Introducing Women's Studies: Feminist Theory and Practice,* 1st edn. (London: Macmillan).

Robinson, K. (1992) 'R4 : The real world of research', in *Nursing Times*, **88**.

Rudd, E. (1985) *A New Look at Postgraduate Failure* (Guildford: SRHE).

Samuelowicz, K. (1987) 'Learning problems of overseas students: Two sides to a story', *Higher Education Research and Development*, **6**(2), pp. 121–33.

Sandler, B. (1993) 'The campus climate revisited: chilly for women faculty, administrators, and graduate students', in J. S. Glazer, E. M. Benisimon and B. K. Townsend (eds), *Women in Higher Education: A Feminist Perspective* (Needham Heights, MA: Ginn Press).

Schmeck, R. R. (1986) *Learning Styles and Learning Strategies* (New York: Plenum).

Schön, D. A. (1983) *The Reflective Practitioner* (New York: Basic Books).

Schön, D. A. (1987) *Educating the Reflective Practitioner* (San Francisco, CA: Jossey-Bass).

Silver, H. (1995) *The External Examiner System: Possible Futures*, a report of a project commissioned by the Higher Education Quality Council (London: Open University Quality Support Centre).

Slaney, K. (1996) 'Models of supervision for enhancing the English language communication skills of postgraduate students', in G. Wisker and N. Sutcliffe (eds), *Good Practice in Postgraduate Supervision* (SEDA Publications).

Slaney, K. (1999) in M. Kiley and G. Mullins (eds) (2000) *Quality in Postgraduate Research: Making Ends Meet* (Adelaide: Advisory Centre for University Education, University of Adelaide).

Squires, G. (1994) *A New World of Teaching and Training* (Hull: University of Hull).

Stanley, J. (1995) 'Pain(t) for healing: the academic conference and the class/embodied self', in L. Morley and V. Walsh (eds), *Feminist Academics: Creative Agents for Change* (London: Taylor and Francis).

Stevens, K. and Asmar, C. (1999) *Doing Postgraduate Research in Australia* (Carlton: Melbourne University Press).

Stoltenberg, C. D., McNeill, B. W. and Crethar, H. C. (1994) 'Changes in supervision as counsellors and therapists gain experience: a review', in *Professional Psychology: Research and Practice*, **25**(4), pp. 416–49.

Strauss, A. and Corbin, J. (1990) *Basics of Qualitative Research: Grounded Theory Procedures and Techniques* (Newbury Park, CA: Sage).

Svensson, L. (1978) 'Some notes on a methodological problem in the study of the relationship between thought and language: describing the thought content in terms of different conceptions of the same phenomenon', *Reports from the Institute of Education*, no. 69 (Gothenburg: Gothenburg University, Department of Education and Educational Research).

Tanner, T. (1971) *City of Words* (London: Jonathan Cape).

Thomas, P. and Bain, J. D. (1982) 'Consistency in learning strategies', *Higher Education*, **11**, pp. 249–59.

Thompson, J. (1983) *Learning Liberation: Women's Response to Men's Education* (London: Croom Helm).

Tiffin, H. (1987) 'Comparative literature and post-colonial counter discourse', *Kunapipi*, **9**, p. 3.

Tinkler, P. and Jackson, C. (2000) 'Examining the doctorate: institutional policy and the PhD examination process in Britain', *Studies in Higher Education*, **25**(2), pp. 167–80.

Todd, L. (1996) 'Supervising post-graduate students: problem or opportunity?' in D. McNamara and R. Harris (eds), *Quality Teaching in Higher Education for Overseas Students* (London: Routledge).

Todd, S. (1997) 'Supervising overseas students: problem or opportunity', in D. McNamara (ed.), *Overseas Students in Higher Education* (London: Routledge).

Trafford, V. and Leshem, S. (2002) 'Questions in a doctoral viva', in *UK Council for Graduate Education Research Degree Examining Symposium* (London, April).

Trafford, V. N. and Leshem, S. (2002) 'Starting at the end to undertake doctoral research: Predictable questions as stepping stones', *Higher Education Review*, **35**, pp. 31–49.

Traweek, S. (1988) *Beamtimes and Lifetimes* (Cambridge, MA: Harvard University Press).

Warren Piper, D., Murray, R., Cox., P., Wisker, G. and Weekes, J. (1989) *Enquiry into the Role of the External Examiner* (London: HMSO).

Warren, C. A. B. (1988) *Gender Issues in Field Research* (London: Sage).

Wason, P.C. (1974) 'Notes on the supervision of PhDs', *Bulletin of the British Psychological Society*, **27**, pp. 25–39.

Watkins, D. and Hattie, J. (1981) 'The learning processes of Australian university students: investigations of contextual and personological factors', *British Journal of Education Psychology*, **15**, pp. 384–93.

Wenger, E. (1998) *Communities of Practice: Learning, Meaning, and Identity* (Cambridge: Cambridge University Press).

White, M. (1997) *Narratives of Therapists' Lives* (Adelaide: Dulwich Centre Publications).

White, M. and Epston, D. (1990) *Narrative Means to Therapeutic Ends* (New York: W. W. Norton).

Williams, S. (2003) 'Postgraduate training in research methods: current practice and future needs in English', English subject centre report, no. 3 (February), Lancaster.

Winter, R. (1993) 'Continuity and progression: assessment vocabularies for higher education', unpublished research report data (Chelmsford: Anglia Polytechnic University, Faculty of Health and Social Work).

Winter, R., Griffiths, M. and Green, K. (2000) 'The "academic" qualities of practice: what are the criteria for a practice-based PhD?', *Studies in Higher Education*, **25**(1), pp. 25–37.

Wisker, G. (1996) *Empowering Women in Higher Education* (London: Kogan Page).

Wisker, G. (1998) *The Research as Learning Questionnaire* (Cambridge: Anglia Polytechnic University).

Wisker, G. (1999) 'Learning conceptions and strategies of postgraduate students (Israeli PhD students) and some steps towards encouraging and enabling their learning', Paper presented to the 2nd Postgraduate Experience Conference: Developing Research Capacity in the New South Africa, conference proceedings, Cape Town, South Africa.

Wisker, G. (2000) 'Postgraduate learning styles and enabling practices: a multi-cultural action research study', in M. Kiley and G. Mullins (eds) (2000) *Quality in Postgraduate Research: Making Ends Meet* (Advisory Centre for University Education, University of Adelaide).

Wisker, G. (2001) *The Postgraduate Research Handbook: Succeed with your MA, MPhil, EdD and PhD* (Basingstoke: Palgrave Macmillan).

Wisker, G. and Hartley, P. (2004) *The Interviewer Viva* (CD-ROM) (Sheffield: Sheffield Hallam University).

Wisker, G., Robinson, G., Trafford, V., Creighton, E. and Warnes, M. (2003) 'Recognising and overcoming dissonance in postgraduate student research', *Studies in Higher Education*, **28**(1).

Wisker, G. and Sutcliffe, N. (eds) (1999) *Good Practice in Research Supervision.* (Birmingham: SEDA).

Wisker, G., Waller, S., Richter, U., Robinson, G., Trafford, V., Wicks, K. and Warnes, M. (2003) 'On nurturing hedghogs: Development online for distance and offshore supervision'. HERDSA Conference, Christchurch, New Zealand.

Wolfe, J. (2003) *How to Write a Thesis*, http://www.phys.unsw.edu.au/~jw/thesis.html (Sydney: University of New South Wales).

Woods, P. (1990) *Teacher Skills and Strategies* (London: Falmer Press).

Wright, J. and Lodwick, R. (1989) 'The process of the PhD: A study of the first year of a doctoral study', *Research Papers in Education*, 4, pp. 22–56.

Zuber-Skerritt, O. (2002) *Supervising Postgraduate Students from Non-English-Speaking Backgrounds* (Buckingham: Open University Press).

Zuber-Skerrit, O. and Ryan, Y. (1994) *Quality in Postgraduate Education* (London: Kogan Page).

Website addresses
www.apu.ac.uk/research/gradsch/gshome.shtml
www.bubl..ac.uk/link
www.cryer.freeserve.co.uk/supervisors.htm
www.cs.ucl.ac.uk/staff/c.clack/phd.html
www.grad.ac.uk/3_2_1.jsp
www.grad.ac.uk/downloads/rdp_report/rdp_framework_report.pdf
www.ilthe.ac.uk
www.ioe.ac.uk/doctoralschool/info-viva.htm
www.phys.unsw.edu.au/%7Ejw/viva.html
www.sosig.ac.uk
www.uq.edu.au

Index